D1278059

EDUCATORS GUIDE TO FREE
Elementary/Middle School

*

Edited by
Kathleen Suttles Nehmer

*

Educational Consultant
Michael Belongie, B. S.
Curriculum Manager, Randolph Public Schools

*

TWELFTH ANNUAL EDITION
2011-2012

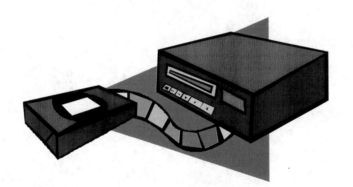

EDUCATORS PROGRESS SERVICE, INC.
214 Center Street
Randolph, Wisconsin 53956

Published by

Educators Progress Service, Inc.

Randolph, Wisconsin 53956

Copyright Educators Guide to FREE Videotapes, Elementary/Middle School 2000, 2001, 2002, 2003, 2004, 2005, 2006, 2007, 2008

Copyright Educators Guide to Free Videos, Elementary/Middle School 2009, 2010, 2011 by Educators Progress Service, Inc.

All rights reserved.

Reproduction of this work, in whole or in part, without written permission of the publisher is prohibited.

Printed and Bound in the United States of America

International Standard Book Number 978-0-87708-531-7

TABLE OF CONTENTS

FROM THE PUBLISHER'S DESK

Welcome to the Twelfth Annual EDUCATORS GUIDE TO FREE VIDEOS–Elementary/Middle School edition. When we first began compiling information about FREE videos appropriate for, and applicable to, the field of education, the technology was brand new–after all, it was more than 50 years ago. Hence, few such videos were in existence. Well, the availability as well as quality of FREE videos has literally mushroomed. Today, more than 1,000 FREE videos are targeted specifically to the preK-8 student. Well over 900 hours of video are available for viewing. In fact, you will find that a number of videos can be viewed INSTANTLY right over your Internet connection. Please note, that while You-tube videos and similar sites can be educational and definitely entertaining, these are not the types of streaming videos we have included. We've listed purely educational videos produced by known sources.

Now we know teachers are very busy people. We wanted to make it easier for elementary and middle school teachers everywhere to find out about FREE videos applicable to their classes, without having to weed through videos that are at a level too advanced for their students. Therefore, we introduced this grade specific edition a few years ago–and it was very well received.

While being a fairly new publication, it still utilizes our 77 years of experience at producing quality EDUCATORS GUIDES TO FREE MATERIALS, on an annual basis. As you might imagine, the process of revising the annual editions of the EDUCATORS GUIDES is a time consuming process (there are now seventeen titles in the series). In our efforts to find new materials every year, we write thousands of letters to companies inquiring about materials they are willing to offer free to educators and others. Each and every year these letters are written. If no response is received, no materials from that source are included. All addresses are verified as well. Your requests for FREE educational aids WILL BE ANSWERED.

It's a lot of work but it is very rewarding. It really is a pleasure to be able to point educators to teaching aids that not only **save tight budgets** but **add to the educational environment**. We like to find materials that "help teachers teach," not only to make their jobs easier but to help students learn more. Any comments you may have regarding this GUIDE are welcomed–we like to learn from you, too.

Kathy

Kathy Nehmer

P. S. **Be sure to use only the 2011-2012 GUIDE for the current school year**, as hundreds of titles available last year are no longer available!

HOW TO USE THE EDUCATORS GUIDE TO FREE VIDEOS--
Elementary/Middle School

The 2011-2012 EDUCATORS GUIDE TO FREE VIDEOS–Elementary/Middle School edition provides busy teachers with information about more than 1,010 free videotapes, DVDs, and streaming videos to help save money and enrich the classroom. Finding the materials you desire, and requesting them, is easy.

The **BODY** of the GUIDE (white pages) gives you full information on each of the 1,011 titles, **ALL of which are new in this edition**. These 1,011 new titles dramatically illustrate one reason that it is so important to use only the most current edtion of the GUIDE.

The **TITLE INDEX** (blue pages) is an alphabetical listing of all items appearing in the body of the GUIDE, with page references. This enables readers to locate any item whose title is known. The TITLE INDEX guides you directly to any specific item in the GUIDE, where you can read the description of the material and find all ordering information.

In the **SUBJECT INDEX** (yellow pages) all materials relating to topics of a more specific nature than the general subject headings in the body of the GUIDE are categorized. These "yellow pages" work like the familiar "yellow pages" of a telephone directory.

The **SOURCE INDEX** (green pages) provides an alphabetical list of the names of the organizations from which materials can be obtained. Also included in each entry are page numbers which indicate where the materials from that particular source appear in the body of the GUIDE. Use of this feature facilitates the ordering, with one letter, of more than one selection if a source offers several.

ANALYSIS OF EDUCATORS GUIDE TO FREE VIDEOS–
Elementary/Middle School Edition–2011

	TOTAL ITEMS
Agriculture and Pets	20
Business and Economics	19
Career Education	13
Entertainment	28
Famous People	34
Fine Arts	
Art and Handwork	96
Music and Drama	55
Guidance	26
Health	29
Home Economics	73
Language Arts	28
Mathematics	24
Physical Education and Recreation	32
Religion and Philosophy	57
Science	
Environmental Education	55
General Science	36
Nature Study	30
Social Studies	
Geography–US	40
Geography–World	164
History	72
World Affairs	42
Special Education	14
Teacher Reference	<u>24</u>
TOTALS	**1,011**

YOUR LETTERS OF REQUEST

When requesting materials, please make your letter of request clear. Identify yourself and your organization. Be sure to use any identifying numbers provided and **observe any restrictions** on distribution as indicated in the GUIDE.

Do not be alarmed if everything you request does not come. The list of materials changes; materials go out of date and are replaced by new items. We cannot tell at the time of printing how long each item will last. Sponsors are asked to assure us, with reasonable certainty, that their materials will be available for approximately one year. It is to meet this need that the GUIDE is revised annually.

There are more than 40 sources of free materials listed in the **2011-2012 EDUCATORS GUIDE TO FREE VIDEOS–Elementary/Middle School Edition.** Please make certain that the request you are making is to the proper company.

In writing for materials, the following form is suggested. The listing used as an example is selected from page 191.

REGIONAL SCHOOL #7
Central Avenue
Winstead, Connecticut 06098

June 10, 2011

Appomattox Court House National Historical Park
Education Coordinator
P. O. Box 218
Appomattox, VA 24522

Dear Sponsor:

We would like to borrow one copy of the following DVD as listed in the 2011 EDUCATORS GUIDE TO FREE VIDEOS–Elementary/Middle School Edition:

The Appomattox Campaign

We would like to view the video on July 28, if that date is not available August 7 would be acceptable. Thank you for your cooperation in assisting us to enrich the curriculum of our school.

Sincerely,

Gina Sabel
7th Grade Teacher

HOW TO COOPERATE WITH THE SPONSORS

.Subscribers to EPS services have frequently asked us for guidelines to follow in requesting sponsored materials. The following 14 questions are quoted from an address given by Thomas J. Sinclair, Ph.D., formerly Manager of Educational and Group Relations for the Association of American Railroads, at a convention of the National Science Teachers Association.

1. Poor handwriting, which you strive to correct in your pupils, often makes coupons and other requests useless. Is your handwriting distinct on requests?

2. Neither industry nor the U. S. Postal Service is omniscient. Do you include complete and accurate details of your address, including zip number?

3. Postcards, small social stationery, or slips of paper present filing problems and can easily be lost. Do you use standard sized stationery?

4. Remember that in big companies thousands of pieces of mail go in and out every day. Do you allow sufficient time for handling your request.

5. Most students advise businesses that they are studing a topic. Do you check your spelling?

6. If you were on the receiving end, you'd have a different view of mass classroom letter-writing projects to the same business organization. Do you make certain that only one request goes to a particular source from your classroom?

7. Instructions on a coupon, in a guide, or on an order form are there for a purpose. Do you read and follow these instructions?

8. Some organizations have dozens—sometimes hundreds—of different teaching aids. Specific needs should be outlined. Do you say "Send me everything you've got" or its equivalent?

9. Source lists and guides get out of date. Do you check to see if the list you are consulting is a recent one?

10. Sometimes aids are in limited supply or available only to teachers in single copies. Do you keep requests reasonable and show some respect for the costs of materials?

11. Sample copies are for examination, with the privilege of ordering quantities subsequently. Do you order classroom quantities blind—without first examining an item for suitability for your purpose?

12. Companies keep records and files. They frequently like to know precisely where their materials are going. Are you careful to mention your school connection?

13. Do you make a real effort to make certain the organization you are writing to is the correct one, and that it could reasonably have the material you are seeking?

14. Duplications and unnecessary correspondence only slow good service to the teaching profession. Do you consult your associates to see whether needed materials have already been supplied to your school?

These questions provide specific suggestions that should, in the long run, make for happier sponsors and better service to educators.

EVALUATION OF INDUSTRY-SPONSORED EDUCATIONAL MATERIALS

The business community has long recognized its obligation to support the agencies of the community that contribute to its security and well-being. In partial fulfillment of this obligation, industry trade associations and non-profit organizations have been producing supplementary materials for use in our nation's schools for some time. Properly planned, sponsored educational resources serve a valuable role and are particularly effective in giving information to students in an area where the sponsoring organization has achieved a high degree of specialization. When properly designed, sponsored materials can be used to motivate students and direct their energies into productive channels of growth.

Educational systems can respond more effectively to changes in technology, job structure, income, population, and manpower requirements with close support and involvement of industry. Both sectors have a common goal of strengthening the institutional programs at all levels in our schools. Operationally, this requires a strong industry-education alliance, particularly at the local level in preparing people for a productive role in the marketplace.

The National Association for Industry-Education Cooperation (NAIEC) was established in 1964 as a logical development out of the Business Industry Section of the National Science Teachers Association. Its purposes were (and still are) to bring about a better understanding between Education and the Business community and to mobilize the resources of education and industry to improve the relevance and quality of educational programs at all levels.

NAIEC members represent a variety of private and public organizations. Major trade associations, corporations, schools, and school districts are members. School superintendents, college presidents, curriculum and other education coordinators, business executives, industry-education coordinators, deans, department chairpersons, career education and job placement specialists, and faculty participate in the Association's programs.

The membership works together to identify problems of mutual interest, formulate plans and procedures, develop acceptable business-sponsored instructional materials, and communicate the advantages of industry-education cooperation.

The NAIEC membership has determined that the set of guiding principles (see below) for the preparation of materials for distribution to schools established by a study financed by American Iron and Steel Institute and carried out by the George Peabody Teachers College are valid and has found that materials embracing these criteria have usually found acceptance and use in the nation's schools and classrooms.

1. Work with a representative group of teachers and administrators to ensure meeting a curricular need.

2. Provide factual material desired by the schools. Include only that information which is significant to the study of particular problems or topics of concern to the teacher and student.

3. Exclude all advertising. A credit line naming the sponsor is enough; indeed schools need to know the publisher and the date of the material.

4. Materials must be written to the particular age level, reading level, interests, and maturity of the group for whom they are intended.

5. Keep the materials free of persuasion; avoid special pleading of the interests of any one point of view or group.

6. Make the materials available to educators only upon request.

X

In 1976 members of the NAIEC developed "A Guide for Evaluating Industry-Sponsored Educational Materials" which embodies the above listed criteria from the educator's viewpoint. This guide is an effort by the National Association for Industry-Education Cooperation (NAIEC) to present teachers with an instrument for evaluating sponsored education resources. These supplemental materials may take the form of teacher guides, filmstrips, games actually designed for the classroom, or pamphlets, reprinted articles, annual reports which may provide valuable background information but are not developed specifically for the teacher's use. (It is suggested that the Guide is more effective with the items actually designed for the classroom.)

If, after completing your evaluation of those items designed for the classroom, you have no further use for the instrument, the sponsoring organization providing the item would appreciate your evaluation with any comments you might have for guidance in the development of future materials. Hopefully this will foster closer industry-education cooperation.

A GUIDE FOR EVALUATING INDUSTRY-SPONSORED EDUCATIONAL MATERIALS

Title of material _____ Date produced, if available _____

Sponsor (name of organization)_____

Type of material: Audio _____ Audiovisual _____ Printed _____ Other _____

Type of instruction suitable for this material: Individual _____ Group _____

This evaluation is based on usage in _____ (grade level)

Evaluator _____ Date _____

Subject area/School _____

Address _____

_____

INSTRUCTIONS FOR USE:

Use the following scale by evaluating the material as it relates to your situation. Each of the descriptive statements is followed by a scale of (1), (2), (3), (4), (5). Indicate your assessment of the material by circling the appropriate number in the scale:

(1) Definitely yes   (4) Definitely no
(2) Yes   (5) Material cannot be evaluated on this concept
(3) No

OBJECTIVES

Identified outcomes may be obtained through use of the material.   1 2 3 4 5

The materials are representative of the curriculum involved; that is, they help further the objectives of the curriculum.   1 2 3 4 5

ABILITY RANGE

The materials provide for the range of abilities and aptitudes of all pupils.   1 2 3 4 5

CONTENT

The material is contemporary.   1 2 3 4 5

The material is controversial.   1 2 3 4 5

The material presents alternative views.   1 2 3 4 5

The material does not present a bias for a product, organization, or social cause.   1 2 3 4 5

The material does present a bias for a product, organization, or social cause.   1 2 3 4 5

If such a bias exists, it does not invalidate the material for my purposes.   1 2 3 4 5

The nature and scope of the material content is adequate to meet curriculum objectives.   1 2 3 4 5

The material is supplementary to the curriculum.   1 2 3 4 5

The material offers opportunity for integration of the subject within the existing curriculum.   1 2 3 4 5

The material correlates with a specific discipline area.   1 2 3 4 5

The material introduces experiences that would not otherwise be available in the classroom.   1 2 3 4 5

The material suggests other resources, supplementary and/or instructional.   1 2 3 4 5

XII

UTILIZATION CHARACTERISTICS   SCALE

The anticipated time utilization is commensurate with
anticipated value of outcome.   1 2 3 4 5

The material demands special conditions for use.   1 2 3 4 5

The material is appropriate for student's reading level.   1 2 3 4 5

The material is appropriate for student's interest level.   1 2 3 4 5

The material is attractive to students.   1 2 3 4 5

The material provides motivation for students.   1 2 3 4 5

PRESENTATION OF MATERIALS

Provisions are made for evaluating the material as it is
used within the educational program.   1 2 3 4 5

Instructional procedures are outlined.   1 2 3 4 5

The style of the presentation is likely to lead students
toward accomplishing basic goals.   1 2 3 4 5

Sample student activities and questions are included.   1 2 3 4 5

The instructions to teachers are clearly stated.   1 2 3 4 5

The intended use is easily understood.   1 2 3 4 5

The production quality of the materials is acceptable.   1 2 3 4 5

EVALUATION

The material provides for feedback to the user.   1 2 3 4 5

The material provides for self-evaluation.   1 2 3 4 5

Agricultural Treasures

Tells about agriculture in Japan.

Availability: Schools, libraries, homeschoolers, and nursing homes in OREGON AND SOUTHERN IDAHO ONLY. Please make requests via the web site.

Suggested Grade: 4-12
Order Number: 410
Production Date: 1996
Format: VHS videotape

Terms: Borrower pays return postage. Return within three weeks after scheduled showing date. Book one month in advance if possible. Rewind the video and wrap securely for return. Be certain to indicate video number, date needed, name of your organization, and address to which video should be sent, along with phone number. Audience report enclosed with the video must be completed and returned.

Source: Consulate General of Japan, Oregon
Attn: Tamara, Video Library
1300 S. W. Fifth Avenue, Suite 2700
Portland, OR 97201
Phone: 1-503-221-1811, ext. 17
World Wide Web URL:
http://www.portland.us.emb-japan.go.jp/en/index.html
Email Address: tamara@cgjpdx.org

Agricultural Treasures of Japan

Shows some of the agricultural products that Japan exports. These include shiitake mushrooms, fuji apples, and 20th century pears.

Availability: Schools, libraries and homeschoolers in Alabama, Georgia, North Carolina, South Carolina, and Virginia.

Suggested Grade: 7-12
Order Number: 215
Production Date: 1991
Format: VHS videotape

Terms: Borrower pays return postage. Two tapes may be borrowed at a time. Return within 7 days after receipt. Reservations may be made by filling the application found on the web site.

Source: Consulate General of Japan, Atlanta
Japan Information Center
One Alliance Center
3500 Lenox Road, Suite 1600
Atlanta, GA 30326
Phone: 1-404-365-9240
Fax: 1-404-240-4311
World Wide Web URL:
http://www.atlanta.us.emb-japan.go.jp
Email Address: info@cgjapanatlanta.org

Agricultural Treasures of Japan

Shows some of the agricultural products that Japan exports. These include shiitake mushrooms, fuji apples, and 20th century pears.

Availability: Staff at schools with NET, WIC, CSFP, FDPIR, CACFP, UMD or Child Nutrition Program food programs in the United States. Those not having such an affiliation should contact their library to place an interlibrary loan request.

Suggested Grade: 7-12
Order Number: NAL Video 2504
Production Date: 1991
Format: VHS videotape

Terms: Borrower pays return postage. RETURN the day after scheduled use. Book at least 4 weeks in advance. Requests must include your name, phone, mail address, eligibility program, title, NAL number, show date, and a statement, "I have read the warning on copyright restrictions and accept full responsibility for compliance." One title per request.

Source: National Agricultural Library
Document Delivery Services Branch
4th Floor, Photo Lab
10301 Baltimore Avenue
Beltsville, MD 20705-2351
Phone: 1-301-504-5994
Fax: 1-301-504-5675
World Wide Web URL: http://www.nal.usda.gov/fnic
Email Address: lending@nal.usda.gov

Alabama, the Place for Aquaculture!

Profiles the size of the Alabama aquaculture industry and its infrastructure.

Availability: Staff at schools with NET, WIC, CSFP, FDPIR, CACFP, UMD or Child Nutrition Program food programs in the United States. Those not having such an affiliation should contact their library to place an interlibrary loan request.

Suggested Grade: 7-12
Order Number: NAL Video 2118
Production Date: 1991
Format: VHS videotape

Terms: Borrower pays return postage. RETURN the day after scheduled use. Book at least 4 weeks in advance. Requests must include your name, phone, mail address, eligibility program, title, NAL number, show date, and a statement, "I have read the warning on copyright restrictions and accept full responsibility for compliance." One title per request.

Source: National Agricultural Library
Document Delivery Services Branch
4th Floor, Photo Lab
10301 Baltimore Avenue
Beltsville, MD 20705-2351
Phone: 1-301-504-5994
Fax: 1-301-504-5675
World Wide Web URL: http://www.nal.usda.gov/fnic
Email Address: lending@nal.usda.gov

Animal Hospital

High-tech health care comes to veterinary medicine-radiology to surgery, intensive care to sports medicine.

Availability: All requesters
Suggested Grade: 7-Adult

Order Number: not applicable
Production Date: 1998
Format: Streaming Video

Source: NOVA
World Wide Web URL:
http://www.pbs.org/wgbh/nova/programs/index.html

Beekeeping in Northern Climates

Dr. Marla Spivak discusses basic principles of beekeeping.

Availability: Staff at schools with NET, WIC, CSFP, FDPIR, CACFP, UMD or Child Nutrition Program food programs in the United States. Those not having such an affiliation should contact their library to place an interlibrary loan request.
Suggested Grade: 7-12
Order Number: NAL Video 2509
Production Date: 1996
Format: VHS videotape
Special Notes: Includes a 68-page manual.
Terms: Borrower pays return postage. RETURN the day after scheduled use. Book at least 4 weeks in advance. Requests must include your name, phone, mail address, eligibility program, title, NAL number, show date, and a statement, "I have read the warning on copyright restrictions and accept full responsibility for compliance." One title per request.

Source: National Agricultural Library
Document Delivery Services Branch
4th Floor, Photo Lab, 10301 Baltimore Avenue
Beltsville, MD   20705-2351
Phone: 1-301-504-5994
Fax: 1-301-504-5675
World Wide Web URL: http://www.nal.usda.gov/fnic
Email Address: lending@nal.usda.gov

Biodiversity for Forests and Farms

Presents concepts of ecosystem management: conservation of biodiversity, specific management for forests and farms.

Availability: Staff at schools with NET, WIC, CSFP, FDPIR, CACFP, UMD or Child Nutrition Program food programs in the United States. Those not having such an affiliation should contact their library to place an interlibrary loan request.
Suggested Grade: 7-12
Order Number: NAL Video 2427
Production Date: 1996
Format: VHS videotape
Terms: Borrower pays return postage. RETURN the day after scheduled use. Book at least 4 weeks in advance. Requests must include your name, phone, mail address, eligibility program, title, NAL number, show date, and a statement, "I have read the warning on copyright restrictions and accept full responsibility for compliance." One title per request.

Source: National Agricultural Library
Document Delivery Services Branch
4th Floor, Photo Lab, 10301 Baltimore Avenue
Beltsville, MD   20705-2351

Phone: 1-301-504-5994
Fax: 1-301-504-5675
World Wide Web URL: http://www.nal.usda.gov/fnic
Email Address: lending@nal.usda.gov

Dairy Farm

Kate visits a dairy farm when a new calf is born. While there, she learns how cows are fed, milked, and cared for. Demonstrates how they are milked twice a day, and how the milk is stored. Also shows how it is collected, processed, and readied for the consumer.

Availability: Schools, libraries, and homeschoolers in the United States who serve the hearing impaired.
Suggested Grade: 2-6
Order Number: 13073
Production Date: 1994
Format: DVD
Special Notes: Produced by Films for the Humanities & Sciences.
Terms: Sponsor pays all transportation costs. Return one week after receipt. Participation is limited to deaf or hard of hearing Americans, their parents, families, teachers, counselors, or others whose use would benefit a deaf or hard of hearing person. Only one person in the audience needs to be hearing impaired. You must register--which is free. These videos are all open-captioned--no special equipment is required for viewing.

Source: Described and Captioned Media Program
National Association of the Deaf
4211 Church Street Ext.
Roebuck, SC   29376
Phone: 1-800-237-6213
Fax: 1-800-538-5636
World Wide Web URL: http://www.dcmp.org

Japanese and Rice Cultivation, The

Explains how rice is cultivated in this country.

Availability: Schools, libraries, and nursing homes in Illinois, Indiana, Iowa, Kansas, Minnesota, Missouri, Nebraska, North Dakota, South Dakota, and Wisconsin.
Suggested Grade: 4-Adult
Order Number: 01006
Production Date: 1992
Format: VHS videotape
Terms: Borrower pays return postage by U. S. Mail, UPS, or Federal Express, including insurance for "original" videos. Write, call, fax, or e-mail to request an application. An application form MUST be sent in one month in advance but not more than six months in advance. Include alternate titles and dates if provider can substitute titles. Send a SASE with request if you require confirmation. Return immediately after scheduled showing date. Videos may not be copied or broadcast without permission from the producer of the video. Borrower is responsible if video is lost or damaged.

Source: Consulate General of Japan at Chicago
Japan Information Center
Library
737 North Michigan Avenue, Suite 1000
Chicago, IL 60611
Phone: 1-312-280-0430
Fax: 1-312-280-6883
World Wide Web URL:
http://www.chicago.us.emb-japan.go.jp/jic.html
Email Address: jicchicago@webkddi.com

Japanese and Rice Cultivation, The

Explains how rice is cultivated in this country.

Availability: Schools, libraries, homeschoolers, and nursing homes in OREGON AND SOUTHERN IDAHO ONLY. Please make requests via the web site.
Suggested Grade: 4-12
Order Number: 413
Production Date: 1996
Format: VHS videotape
Terms: Borrower pays return postage. Return within three weeks after scheduled showing date. Book one month in advance if possible. Rewind the video and wrap securely for return. Be certain to indicate video number, date needed, name of your organization, and address to which video should be sent, along with phone number. Audience report enclosed with the video must be completed and returned.
Source: Consulate General of Japan, Oregon
Attn: Tamara, Video Library
1300 S. W. Fifth Avenue, Suite 2700
Portland, OR 97201
Phone: 1-503-221-1811, ext. 17
World Wide Web URL:
http://www.portland.us.emb-japan.go.jp/en/index.html
Email Address: tamara@cgjpdx.org

Japan's Leading Edge Agricultural Technology at Work in Biotechnology

Explains how biotechnology has benefitted agriculture in Japan.

Availability: Schools, libraries and homeschoolers in Alabama, Georgia, North Carolina, South Carolina, and Virginia.
Suggested Grade: 6-12
Order Number: 223
Production Date: 1996
Format: VHS videotape
Terms: Borrower pays return postage. Two tapes may be borrowed at a time. Return within 7 days after receipt. Reservations may be made by filling the application found on the web site.
Source: Consulate General of Japan, Atlanta
Japan Information Center
One Alliance Center
3500 Lenox Road, Suite 1600
Atlanta, GA 30326
Phone: 1-404-365-9240
Fax: 1-404-240-4311

World Wide Web URL:
http://www.atlanta.us.emb-japan.go.jp
Email Address: info@cgjapanatlanta.org

Japan's Leading Edge Agricultural Technology at Work in Biotechnology

Explains how biotechnology has benefitted agriculture in Japan.

Availability: Schools, libraries, homeschoolers, and nursing homes in OREGON AND SOUTHERN IDAHO ONLY. Please make requests via the web site.
Suggested Grade: 6-12
Order Number: 411
Production Date: 1996
Format: VHS videotape
Terms: Borrower pays return postage. Return within three weeks after scheduled showing date. Book one month in advance if possible. Rewind the video and wrap securely for return. Be certain to indicate video number, date needed, name of your organization, and address to which video should be sent, along with phone number. Audience report enclosed with the video must be completed and returned.
Source: Consulate General of Japan, Oregon
Attn: Tamara, Video Library
1300 S. W. Fifth Avenue, Suite 2700
Portland, OR 97201
Phone: 1-503-221-1811, ext. 17
World Wide Web URL:
http://www.portland.us.emb-japan.go.jp/en/index.html
Email Address: tamara@cgjpdx.org

Large DVD Pack

Contains several programs that discuss animals and animal abuse.

Availability: Schools and libraries in the United States and Canada.
Suggested Grade: 8-Adult
Order Number: order by title
Format: VHS videotape
Special Notes: May be retained permanently. Also available as live streaming video over the Internet.
Source: TeachKind.org
501 Front Street
Norfolk, VA 23510
Phone: 1-757-962-8242
World Wide Web URL: http://www.teachkind.org
Email Address: info@teachkind.org

Oranges: From Farm to Table

Where do oranges and orange juice come from? How do they get to the supermarket? Shows how orange trees grow, how the fruit is harvested, how it is sorted into two groups, and how it becomes either fruit to eat or orange juice. Shows fruit-packing and juice-processing procedures.

Availability: Schools, libraries, and homeschoolers in the United States who serve the hearing impaired.
Suggested Grade: 3-6

*All materials listed in this 2011-2012 edition are **BRAND NEW**!*

Order Number: 13055
Production Date: 1994
Format: DVD
Special Notes: Produced by Aims Multimedia.
Terms: Sponsor pays all transportation costs. Return one week after receipt. Participation is limited to deaf or hard of hearing Americans, their parents, families, teachers, counselors, or others whose use would benefit a deaf or hard of hearing person. Only one person in the audience needs to be hearing impaired. You must register--which is free. These videos are all open-captioned--no special equipment is required for viewing.
    Source: Described and Captioned Media Program
    National Association of the Deaf
    4211 Church Street Ext.
    Roebuck, SC 29376
    Phone: 1-800-237-6213
    Fax: 1-800-538-5636
    World Wide Web URL: http://www.dcmp.org

Pigs!

Spend the day with pigs on a farm, from the time they wake until their afternoon nap. See sows feed their piglets, pigs eat at a trough, and others use their snouts to find bugs. Learn some of the behaviors, characteristics, and differences of pigs.

Availability: Schools, libraries, and homeschoolers in the United States who serve the hearing impaired.
Suggested Grade: K-3
Order Number: 13059
Production Date: 1995
Format: DVD
Special Notes: Produced by Churchill Media.
Terms: Sponsor pays all transportation costs. Return one week after receipt. Participation is limited to deaf or hard of hearing Americans, their parents, families, teachers, counselors, or others whose use would benefit a deaf or hard of hearing person. Only one person in the audience needs to be hearing impaired. You must register--which is free. These videos are all open-captioned--no special equipment is required for viewing.
    Source: Described and Captioned Media Program
    National Association of the Deaf
    4211 Church Street Ext.
    Roebuck, SC 29376
    Phone: 1-800-237-6213
    Fax: 1-800-538-5636
    World Wide Web URL: http://www.dcmp.org

Primary School Small DVD Pack

Uses fascinating animal facts and footage to introduce students to the many similarities between people and other animals.

Availability: Schools and libraries in the United States and Canada.
Suggested Grade: 2-5
Order Number: order by title
Format: Set of 2 DVDs

Special Notes: May be retained permanently. Also available as live streaming video over the Internet.
    Source: TeachKind.org
    501 Front Street
    Norfolk, VA 23510
    Phone: 1-757-962-8242
    World Wide Web URL: http://www.teachkind.org
    Email Address: info@teachkind.org

Pumpkin Circle

Pumpkins! Every fall we carve them for jack-o'-lanterns, munch their seeds, and cook delicious things with them. But where do they come from? How do they grow? Close-up and time-lapse photography chart the growth of the pumpkin plant from sprouting seed to maturity. Danny Glover narrates in verse accompanied by George Winston's music.

Availability: Schools, libraries, and homeschoolers in the United States who serve the hearing impaired.
Suggested Grade: preK-6
Order Number: 12844
Production Date: 1997
Format: DVD
Special Notes: Also available as live streaming video over the Internet.
Terms: Sponsor pays all transportation costs. Return one week after receipt. Participation is limited to deaf or hard of hearing Americans, their parents, families, teachers, counselors, or others whose use would benefit a deaf or hard of hearing person. Only one person in the audience needs to be hearing impaired. You must register--which is free. These videos are all open-captioned--no special equipment is required for viewing.
    Source: Described and Captioned Media Program
    National Association of the Deaf
    4211 Church Street Ext.
    Roebuck, SC 29376
    Phone: 1-800-237-6213
    Fax: 1-800-538-5636
    World Wide Web URL: http://www.dcmp.org

Sacred Land, The

The Japanese have always had a very special bond with the land. But as young people are increasingly lured to the big city and other jobs, what does the future hold for the Japanese farmer?

Availability: Schools, libraries and homeschoolers in Alabama, Georgia, North Carolina, South Carolina, and Virginia.
Suggested Grade: 6-12
Order Number: 407
Production Date: 1988
Format: VHS videotape
Special Notes: Part of the "Faces of Japan" series.
Terms: Borrower pays return postage. Two tapes may be borrowed at a time. Return within 7 days after receipt. Reservations may be made by filling the application found on the web site.

Source: Consulate General of Japan, Atlanta
Japan Information Center
One Alliance Center
3500 Lenox Road, Suite 1600
Atlanta, GA 30326
Phone: 1-404-365-9240
Fax: 1-404-240-4311
World Wide Web URL:
http://www.atlanta.us.emb-japan.go.jp
Email Address: info@cgjapanatlanta.org

Sacred Land, The
The Japanese have always had a very special bond with the land. But as young people are increasingly lured to the big city and other jobs, what does the future hold for the Japanese farmer?

Availability: Schools, libraries, homeschoolers, and nursing homes in OREGON AND SOUTHERN IDAHO ONLY. Please make requests via the web site.

Suggested Grade: 6-12
Order Number: 520
Production Date: 1988
Format: VHS videotape
Part of the "Faces of Japan" series.

Terms: Borrower pays return postage. Return within three weeks after scheduled showing date. Book one month in advance if possible. Rewind the video and wrap securely for return. Be certain to indicate video number, date needed, name of your organization, and address to which video should be sent, along with phone number. Audience report enclosed with the video must be completed and returned.

Source: Consulate General of Japan, Oregon
Attn: Tamara, Video Library
1300 S. W. Fifth Avenue, Suite 2700
Portland, OR 97201
Phone: 1-503-221-1811, ext. 17
World Wide Web URL:
http://www.portland.us.emb-japan.go.jp/en/index.html
Email Address: tamara@cgjpdx.org

BUSINESS AND ECONOMICS

Borderline Cases

Describes problems created by the maquiladoras, factories on the US-Mexico border, and promises for the future.

Availability: Schools, libraries, and nursing homes in the United States.
Suggested Grade: 6-12
Order Number: GEMEX12-video
Production Date: 1997
Format: VHS videotape
Terms: Borrowers must have a User's Agreement on file with this source--available by mail or via the Internet. Return postage is paid by borrower; return 12 days after showing. Book at least three weeks in advance. All borrowers are limited to a total of ten items per semester.
Source: Latin American Resource Center
Stone Center for Latin American Studies
Tulane University
100 Jones Hall
New Orleans, LA 70118
Phone: 1-504-862-3143
Fax: 1-504-865-6719
World Wide Web URL:
http://stonecenter.tulane.edu/pages/detail/48/
Lending-Library
Email Address: crcrts@tulane.edu

Brazilian Connection, The

Traces roots of Brazil's current economic crisis, over the last five decades.

Availability: Schools, libraries, and nursing homes in the United States.
Suggested Grade: 6-12
Order Number: HCBRA2-video
Production Date: 1982
Format: VHS videotape
Terms: Borrowers must have a User's Agreement on file with this source--available by mail or via the Internet. Return postage is paid by borrower; return 12 days after showing. Book at least three weeks in advance. All borrowers are limited to a total of ten items per semester.
Source: Latin American Resource Center
Stone Center for Latin American Studies
Tulane University, 100 Jones Hall
New Orleans, LA 70118
Phone: 1-504-862-3143
Fax: 1-504-865-6719
World Wide Web URL:
http://stonecenter.tulane.edu/pages/detail/48/
Lending-Library
Email Address: crcrts@tulane.edu

Business of Hunger, The

By focusing on the Philippines, Senegal, Brazil, and the Dominican Republic, this program shows how multinational corporations acquire land and grow cash crops for export, while local people go hungry. Small farmers lose their land and become migrant workers on plantations or slum dwellers in the cities. Alternatives are offered in this program.

Availability: Schools, libraries, homeschoolers, and nursing homes in the United States.
Suggested Grade: 5-Adult
Order Number: order by title
Format: VHS videotape
Terms: Borrower pays return postage. Return the day after scheduled showing, via UPS or Priority Mail, insured for $100.00. Book 4 weeks in advance and include an alternate date. Order should include name of person responsible for handling the video, and complete mailing address. Please mention this Guide when ordering. Tapes may not be duplicated, edited or exhibited for a fee.
Source: Church World Service
Film & Video Library
28606 Phillips Street, P. O. Box 968
Elkhart, IN 46515
Phone: 1-800-297-1516, ext. 338
Fax: 1-574-262-0966
World Wide Web URL: http://www.churchworldservice.org
Email Address: videos@churchworldservice.org

Commodities: Black Market

This video looks at the ways banks, corporations, governments, workers, and consumers are affected by such ordinary items as coffee, tea, and sugar.

Availability: Schools, libraries, and nursing homes in the United States and Canada.
Suggested Grade: 6-12
Order Number: CV003
Format: VHS videotape
Terms: Borrower pays return postage. Return with 14 days after scheduled showing, via UPS or U. S. Mail. All requests must included an educational institution affiliation, a current address, and phone number. Order through web site only.
Source: Cornell University East Asia Program
World Wide Web URL:
http://www.einaudi.cornell.edu/eastasia/outreach/video.asp
Email Address: east_asia1@cornell.edu

Cuba: Waters of Destiny

Discusses waters and fish of Cuba, and the lobster industry and farms. Also brief interview with Fidel Castro.

Availability: Schools, libraries, and nursing homes in the United States.
Suggested Grade: 6-12
Order Number: GECUB1-video
Production Date: 1986
Format: VHS videotape
Terms: Borrowers must have a User's Agreement on file with this source--available by mail or via the Internet. Return postage is paid by borrower; return 12 days after showing. Book at least three weeks in advance. All borrowers are limited to a total of ten items per semester.
Source: Latin American Resource Center
Stone Center for Latin American Studies
Tulane University, 100 Jones Hall
New Orleans, LA 70118

*All materials listed in this 2011-2012 edition are **BRAND NEW!***

Phone: 1-504-862-3143
Fax: 1-504-865-6719
World Wide Web URL:
http://stonecenter.tulane.edu/pages/detail/48/
Lending-Library
Email Address: crcrts@tulane.edu

Deadly Embrace: Nicaragua, The World Bank and The International Monetary Fund.

Tells what has happened to the Nicaraguan people and the economy since linking to the policies of the International Monetary Fund.

Availability: Schools, libraries, and nursing homes in the United States.
Suggested Grade: 6-12
Order Number: DEVNIC5-video
Production Date: 1996
Format: VHS videotape
Terms: Borrowers must have a User's Agreement on file with this source--available by mail or via the Internet. Return postage is paid by borrower; return 12 days after showing. Book at least three weeks in advance. All borrowers are limited to a total of ten items per semester.
Source: Latin American Resource Center
Stone Center for Latin American Studies
Tulane University
100 Jones Hall
New Orleans, LA 70118
Phone: 1-504-862-3143
Fax: 1-504-865-6719
World Wide Web URL:
http://stonecenter.tulane.edu/pages/detail/48/
Lending-Library
Email Address: crcrts@tulane.edu

Debt Crisis, The - New Perspectives

Causes, effects, and possible solutions for the Latin American debt crisis.

Availability: Schools, libraries, and nursing homes in the United States.
Suggested Grade: 6-12
Order Number: DEVLA16-video
Production Date: 1990
Format: VHS videotape
Terms: Borrowers must have a User's Agreement on file with this source--available by mail or via the Internet. Return postage is paid by borrower; return 12 days after showing. Book at least three weeks in advance. All borrowers are limited to a total of ten items per semester.
Source: Latin American Resource Center
Stone Center for Latin American Studies
Tulane University, 100 Jones Hall
New Orleans, LA 70118
Phone: 1-504-862-3143
Fax: 1-504-865-6719
World Wide Web URL:
http://stonecenter.tulane.edu/pages/detail/48/
Lending-Library
Email Address: crcrts@tulane.edu

Food from Farm to City

This video shows the path that food takes as it moves from farmlands to the dinner table. It focuses on a few commodities such as milk, showing their complete production and distribution process. It shows how city and suburban dwellers depend upon farmers for the food products they buy in the supermarkets.

Availability: Staff at schools with NET, WIC, CSFP, FDPIR, CACFP, UMD or Child Nutrition Program food programs in the United States. Those not having such an affiliation should contact their library to place an interlibrary loan request.
Suggested Grade: K-8
Order Number: NAL Video 980
Production Date: 1987
Format: VHS videotape
Special Notes: This program includes a teacher's guide.
Terms: Borrower pays return postage. RETURN the day after scheduled use. Book at least 4 weeks in advance. Requests must include your name, phone, mail address, eligibility program, title, NAL number, show date, and a statement, "I have read the warning on copyright restrictions and accept full responsibility for compliance." One title per request.
Source: National Agricultural Library
Document Delivery Services Branch
4th Floor, Photo Lab
10301 Baltimore Avenue
Beltsville, MD 20705-2351
Phone: 1-301-504-5994
Fax: 1-301-504-5675
World Wide Web URL: http://www.nal.usda.gov/fnic
Email Address: lending@nal.usda.gov

Global Assembly Line, The

Focusing on lives of women in manufacturing, from Tennessee to Mexico's Northern border, from Silicon Valley to the Philippines.

Availability: Schools, libraries, and nursing homes in the United States.
Suggested Grade: 5-Adult
Order Number: DEVMEX10-video
Format: VHS videotape
Terms: Borrowers must have a User's Agreement on file with this source--available by mail or via the Internet. Return postage is paid by borrower; return 12 days after showing. Book at least three weeks in advance. All borrowers are limited to a total of ten items per semester.
Source: Latin American Resource Center
Stone Center for Latin American Studies
Tulane University, 100 Jones Hall
New Orleans, LA 70118
Phone: 1-504-862-3143
Fax: 1-504-865-6719
World Wide Web URL:
http://stonecenter.tulane.edu/pages/detail/48/
Lending-Library
Email Address: crcrts@tulane.edu

BUSINESS AND ECONOMICS

Human Relations in Japan

The clever use of animation and a well-directed presentation explain how relationships are formed among the Japanese. The two important concepts of "uchi" and "soto" are discussed, as viewers are shown how an American businessman can enter into an "uchi" relationship with his Japanese business associates.

Availability: Schools, libraries, homeschoolers, and nursing homes in OREGON AND SOUTHERN IDAHO ONLY. Please make requests via the web site.
Suggested Grade: 7-12
Order Number: 160
Production Date: 1978
Format: VHS videotape
Terms: Borrower pays return postage. Return within three weeks after scheduled showing date. Book one month in advance if possible. Rewind the video and wrap securely for return. Be certain to indicate video number, date needed, name of your organization, and address to which video should be sent, along with phone number. Audience report enclosed with the video must be completed and returned.

Source: Consulate General of Japan, Oregon
Attn: Tamara, Video Library
1300 S. W. Fifth Avenue, Suite 2700
Portland, OR 97201
Phone: 1-503-221-1811, ext. 17
World Wide Web URL:
http://www.portland.us.emb-japan.go.jp/en/index.html
Email Address: tamara@cgjpdx.org

Math: Kids & Cash: Money and You

Looks at various aspects of banking, finance, and money management.

Availability: Schools, libraries, and homeschoolers in the United States who serve the hearing impaired.
Suggested Grade: 4-9
Order Number: 12252
Format: DVD
Terms: Sponsor pays all transportation costs. Return one week after receipt. Participation is limited to deaf or hard of hearing Americans, their parents, families, teachers, counselors, or others whose use would benefit a deaf or hard of hearing person. Only one person in the audience needs to be hearing impaired. You must register--which is free. These videos are all open-captioned--no special equipment is required for viewing.

Source: Described and Captioned Media Program
National Association of the Deaf
4211 Church Street Ext.
Roebuck, SC 29376
Phone: 1-800-237-6213
Fax: 1-800-538-5636
World Wide Web URL: http://www.dcmp.org

Mexico: For Sale

Interviews discuss both sides of the Mexican viewpoint on the North American Free Trade Agreement.

Availability: Schools, libraries, and nursing homes in the United States.
Suggested Grade: 6-12
Order Number: DEVMEX8-video
Production Date: 1993
Format: VHS videotape
Terms: Borrowers must have a User's Agreement on file with this source--available by mail or via the Internet. Return postage is paid by borrower; return 12 days after showing. Book at least three weeks in advance. All borrowers are limited to a total of ten items per semester.

Source: Latin American Resource Center
Stone Center for Latin American Studies
Tulane University
100 Jones Hall
New Orleans, LA 70118
Phone: 1-504-862-3143
Fax: 1-504-865-6719
World Wide Web URL:
http://stonecenter.tulane.edu/pages/detail/48/
Lending-Library
Email Address: crcrts@tulane.edu

Money People, The

How is money used? How is it made? Why is it important? Presents a general overview of money and the people who work with it. Gives the basic banking information, such as savings, withdrawals, loans, interest, and checking. Shows money being made.

Availability: Schools, libraries, and homeschoolers in the United States who serve the hearing impaired.
Suggested Grade: 3-7
Order Number: 13054
Production Date: 1994
Format: DVD
Special Notes: Produced by Barr Media Group.
Terms: Sponsor pays all transportation costs. Return one week after receipt. Participation is limited to deaf or hard of hearing Americans, their parents, families, teachers, counselors, or others whose use would benefit a deaf or hard of hearing person. Only one person in the audience needs to be hearing impaired. You must register--which is free. These videos are all open-captioned--no special equipment is required for viewing.

Source: Described and Captioned Media Program
National Association of the Deaf
4211 Church Street Ext.
Roebuck, SC 29376
Phone: 1-800-237-6213
Fax: 1-800-538-5636
World Wide Web URL: http://www.dcmp.org

One World, One Economy

Four-part video examining the economies of Mexico, Poland, Ghana, and the role of the IMF.

Availability: Schools, libraries, and nursing homes in the United States.
Suggested Grade: 6-12
Order Number: DEV21-video

Production Date: 1990
Format: VHS videotape
Special Notes: Includes 23-page instructor's guide.
Terms: Borrowers must have a User's Agreement on file with this source--available by mail or via the Internet. Return postage is paid by borrower; return 12 days after showing. Book at least three weeks in advance. All borrowers are limited to a total of ten items per semester.

Source: Latin American Resource Center
Stone Center for Latin American Studies
Tulane University
100 Jones Hall
New Orleans, LA 70118
Phone: 1-504-862-3143
Fax: 1-504-865-6719
World Wide Web URL:
http://stonecenter.tulane.edu/pages/detail/48/
Lending-Library
Email Address: crcrts@tulane.edu

Secret History of the Credit Card

Explains how the credit card industry operates.
Availability: All requesters
Suggested Grade: 7-Adult
Order Number: not applicable
Format: Streaming Video
Special Notes: Supported by online teaching materials.
Source: PBS
World Wide Web URL:
http://www.pbs.org/wgbh/pages/frontline/shows/credit/view/

Small Business, A

Though many Americans view Japan as a country dominated by big business, smaller firms play a vital role in the economy, producing a large share of Japan's exports. Here is more information.
Availability: Schools, libraries and homeschoolers in Alabama, Georgia, North Carolina, South Carolina, and Virginia.
Suggested Grade: 6-12
Order Number: 410
Production Date: 1988
Format: VHS videotape
Special Notes: Part of the "Faces of Japan" series.
Terms: Borrower pays return postage. Two tapes may be borrowed at a time. Return within 7 days after receipt. Reservations may be made by filling the application found on the web site.

Source: Consulate General of Japan, Atlanta
Japan Information Center
One Alliance Center
3500 Lenox Road, Suite 1600
Atlanta, GA 30326
Phone: 1-404-365-9240
Fax: 1-404-240-4311
World Wide Web URL:
http://www.atlanta.us.emb-japan.go.jp
Email Address: info@cgjapanatlanta.org

Small Business, A

Though many Americans view Japan as a country dominated by big business, smaller firms play a vital role in the economy, producing a large share of Japan's exports. Here is more information.
Availability: Schools, libraries, homeschoolers, and nursing homes in OREGON AND SOUTHERN IDAHO ONLY. Please make requests via the web site.
Suggested Grade: 6-12
Order Number: 523
Production Date: 1988
Format: VHS videotape
Special Notes: Part of the "Faces of Japan" series.
Terms: Borrower pays return postage. Return within three weeks after scheduled showing date. Book one month in advance if possible. Rewind the video and wrap securely for return. Be certain to indicate video number, date needed, name of your organization, and address to which video should be sent, along with phone number. Audience report enclosed with the video must be completed and returned.

Source: Consulate General of Japan, Oregon
Attn: Tamara, Video Library
1300 S. W. Fifth Avenue, Suite 2700
Portland, OR 97201
Phone: 1-503-221-1811, ext. 17
World Wide Web URL:
http://www.portland.us.emb-japan.go.jp/en/index.html
Email Address: tamara@cgjpdx.org

South America: The Southern Plains

Examines the methods of transportation of the region, from the Rio de la Plata to the major highways of today, and how this has made it possible for production centers and trade to develop.
Availability: Schools in the United States.
Suggested Grade: 6-12
Order Number: order by title
Production Date: 1992
Format: VHS videotape
Terms: Borrower pays return postage. Return 14 days after receipt, via USPS including insurance. All borrowers must have a current lending agreement on file with the Outreach program. This agreement is available via the web site or may be requested via phone or fax.

Source: Center for Latin American Studies
University of Florida
319 Grinter Hall
P. O. Box 115530
Gainesville, FL 32611-5530
Phone: 1-352-392-0375
Fax: 1-352-392-7682
World Wide Web URL: http://www.latam.ufl.edu/outreach
Email Address: maryr@ufl.edu

U. S., Mexico, and NAFTA

Explores the economic and human rights ramifications of the implementation of NAFTA.

Availability: Schools in the United States.
Suggested Grade: 7-Adult
Order Number: order by title
Production Date: 1996
Format: VHS videotape
Terms: Borrower pays return postage. Return 14 days after receipt, via USPS including insurance. All borrowers must have a current lending agreement on file with the Outreach program. This agreement is available via the web site or may be requested via phone or fax.

Source: Center for Latin American Studies
University of Florida
319 Grinter Hall
P. O. Box 115530
Gainesville, FL 32611-5530
Phone: 1-352-392-0375
Fax: 1-352-392-7682
World Wide Web URL: http://www.latam.ufl.edu/outreach
Email Address: maryr@ufl.edu

Career Videos

An incredible number of videos depicting the duties of people in many different career fields.

Availability:	All requesters
Suggested Grade:	7-12
Languages:	English; Spanish
Order Number:	not applicable
Format:	Online Streaming Video

Source: America's Career InfoNet
**World Wide Web URL: http://www.acinet.org/acinet/
videos_by_occupation.asp?id=27&nodeid=28**

Heavy Equipment Operator

Three young boys learn about the duties of heavy equipment operators.

Availability:	Schools, libraries, and homeschoolers in the United States who serve the hearing impaired.
Suggested Grade:	2-5
Order Number:	10858
Production Date:	1993
Format:	DVD
Special Notes:	Also available as live streaming video over the Internet.
Terms:	Sponsor pays all transportation costs. Return one week after receipt. Participation is limited to deaf or hard of hearing Americans, their parents, families, teachers, counselors, or others whose use would benefit a deaf or hard of hearing person. Only one person in the audience needs to be hearing impaired. You must register--which is free. These videos are all open-captioned--no special equipment is required for viewing.

Source: Described and Captioned Media Program
National Association of the Deaf
4211 Church Street Ext.
Roebuck, SC 29376
Phone: 1-800-237-6213
Fax: 1-800-538-5636
World Wide Web URL: http://www.dcmp.org

Mastery of the Chef's Blade

Shows the life of an aspiring chef working at a restaurant in a major Japanese hotel. On the surface, the restaurant seems as modern as the hotel itself, but a look behind the scenes reveals the unchanging, traditional world of the Japanese chef.

Availability:	Schools, libraries, and nursing homes in Illinois, Indiana, Iowa, Kansas, Minnesota, Missouri, Nebraska, North Dakota, South Dakota, and Wisconsin.
Suggested Grade:	6-12
Order Number:	14003
Format:	VHS videotape
Special Notes:	Part of the "Japan: Life and Nature" series.
Terms:	Borrower pays return postage by U. S. Mail, UPS, or Federal Express, including insurance for "original" videos. Write, call, fax, or e-mail to request an application. An application form MUST be sent in one month in advance but not more than six months in advance. Include alternate titles and dates if provider

can substitute titles. Send a SASE with request if you require confirmation. Return immediately after scheduled showing date. Videos may not be copied or broadcast without permission from the producer of the video. Borrower is responsible if video is lost or damaged.

Source: Consulate General of Japan at Chicago
Japan Information Center
Library
737 North Michigan Avenue, Suite 1000
Chicago, IL 60611
Phone: 1-312-280-0430
Fax: 1-312-280-6883
World Wide Web URL:
http://www.chicago.us.emb-japan.go.jp/jic.html
Email Address: jicchicago@webkddi.com

Natural Resources: A Career Choice that Matters

An upbeat production showing a variety of opportunities available in the field of natural resources.

Availability:	Schools, libraries, and homeschoolers in Connecticut, Maine, Massachusetts, New Hampshire, Rhode Island, and Vermont.
Suggested Grade:	6-12
Order Number:	VID 067
Format:	VHS videotape
Terms:	Borrower pays return postage. Return within three weeks of receipt. If the tape you request is available, it will be mailed within 5 business days. If not, you will be notified that this video is already out on loan. No more than three titles may be borrowed by one requestor at a time. No reservations for a specific date will be accepted. It is most efficient to order via the web site.

Source: U. S. Environmental Protection Agency, Region 1
Customer Service Center
One Congress Street, Suite 1100
Boston, MA 02214
World Wide Web URL:
http://yosemite.epa.gov/r1/videolen.nsf/

Postal Station, The

Where does a letter go after it's mailed? After briefly tracing the history of postal service, viewers visit a postal station where mail from all over Canada is processed. Watch fast machines and people sort letters and packages and send them to the correct location.

Availability:	Schools, libraries, and homeschoolers in the United States who serve the hearing impaired.
Suggested Grade:	3-5
Order Number:	12366
Production Date:	1994
Format:	DVD
Special Notes:	Produced by Films for the Humanities & Sciences.
Terms:	Sponsor pays all transportation costs. Return one week after receipt. Participation is limited to deaf or hard of hearing Americans, their parents, families, teachers, counselors, or others whose use would benefit a deaf or hard of hearing person. Only one person in the audience

needs to be hearing impaired. You must register--which is free. These videos are all open-captioned--no special equipment is required for viewing.

Source: Described and Captioned Media Program
National Association of the Deaf
4211 Church Street Ext.
Roebuck, SC 29376
Phone: 1-800-237-6213
Fax: 1-800-538-5636
World Wide Web URL: http://www.dcmp.org

Skill and Ability Videos
A number of videos about skills and abilities people use to do certain types of work.

Availability:	All requesters
Suggested Grade:	7-12
Order Number:	not applicable
Format:	Online Streaming Video

Source: America's Career InfoNet
World Wide Web URL: http://www.acinet.org/acinet/
videos_by_ability.asp?id=27&nodeid=31

To Celebrate the Harvest
Presents the account of a day in the life of a priest in the tiny village of Kangin, in South Korea.

Availability:	Schools, libraries, homeschoolers, church groups, nursing homes, and service clubs in the United States.
Suggested Grade:	7-Adult
Order Number:	order by title
Format:	VHS videotape
Special Notes:	A study guide is also sent.
Terms:	Borrower pays return postage. Return within 21 days after receipt. Book at least 3 weeks in advance. You will be notified as soon as possible, if your order cannot be filled. All videos are cleared for television broadcast use.

Source: Columban Fathers Mission Society
Mission Education Department
Attn: Connie Wacha
P. O. Box 10
St. Columbans, NE 68056
Phone: 1-402-291-1920
Fax: 1-402-715-5575
World Wide Web URL: http://columban.org/missioned

Veterinary Medicine: More Than You Think
Gives students an excellent overview of the diversity of opportunities available to them in veterinary medicine today.

Availability:	Single copies to schools, libraries, and homeschoolers in the United States and Canada.
Suggested Grade:	6-Adult
Order Number:	order by title
Production Date:	2007
Format:	DVD
Special Notes:	May be retained permanently. Cleared for broadcast.

Source: American Veterinary Medical Association
Attn: Order Dept.
1931 North Meacham Road, Suite 100
Schaumburg, IL 60173-4360
Phone: 1-847-285-6655
Fax: 1-847-925-1329
World Wide Web URL: http://www.avma.org
Email Address: productorders@avma.org

Veterinary Medicine: More Than You Think
Gives students an excellent overview of the diversity of opportunities available to them in veterinary medicine today.

Availability:	Teachers, librarians and group leaders in the United States.
Suggested Grade:	6-Adult
Order Number:	order by title
Format:	DVD
Terms:	It is asked that you complete a brief survey included with each program. Videos may not be duplicated--copies will be provided if you need them. Mail and FAX requests must be on school letterhead and contain a statement of total school enrollment, estimated number of student viewers, classes/subjects in which video is used and audience grade level (must match audience specified in description). Allow at least four weeks for delivery.

Source: American Veterinary Medical Association
Please forward all requests on official letterhead to:
Video Placement Worldwide
25 Second Street North
St. Petersburg, FL 33701
Fax: 1-813-823-2955
World Wide Web URL: http://www.vpw.com

Way of Life in Japan, The: Mastery of the Chef's Blade
Shows the life of an aspiring chef working at a restaurant in a major Japanese hotel. On the surface, the restaurant seems as modern as the hotel itself, but a look behind the scenes reveals the unchanging, traditional world of the Japanese chef.

Availability:	Schools, libraries and homeschoolers in Alabama, Georgia, North Carolina, South Carolina, and Virginia.
Suggested Grade:	6-12
Order Number:	217
Format:	VHS videotape
Special Notes:	Part of the "Japan: Life and Nature" series.
Terms:	Borrower pays return postage. Two tapes may be borrowed at a time. Return within 7 days after receipt. Reservations may be made by filling the application found on the web site.

Source: Consulate General of Japan, Atlanta
Japan Information Center
One Alliance Center
3500 Lenox Road, Suite 1600
Atlanta, GA 30326
Phone: 1-404-365-9240
Fax: 1-404-240-4311

World Wide Web URL:
http://www.atlanta.us.emb-japan.go.jp
Email Address: info@cgjapanatlanta.org

Way of Life in Japan, The: Mastery of the Chef's Blade
Shows the life of an aspiring chef working at a restaurant in a major Japanese hotel. On the surface, the restaurant seems as modern as the hotel itself, but a look behind the scenes reveals the unchanging, traditional world of the Japanese chef.

Availability: Schools, libraries, and nursing homes in Hawaii.
Suggested Grade: 6-12
Order Number: CU-131
Format: VHS videotape
Special Notes: Part of the "Japan: Life and Nature" series.
Terms: Borrower pays return postage. A maximum of 3 videos may be borrowed per person. Return within one week of date borrowed.

Source: Consulate General of Japan, Honolulu
1742 Nuuanu Avenue
Honolulu, HI 96817-3294
Phone: 1-808-543-3111
Fax: 1-808-543-3170
World Wide Web URL:
http://www.honolulu.us.emb-japan.go.jp

Way of Life in Japan, The: Mastery of the Chef's Blade
Shows the life of an aspiring chef working at a restaurant in a major Japanese hotel. On the surface, the restaurant seems as modern as the hotel itself, but a look behind the scenes reveals the unchanging, traditional world of the Japanese chef.

Availability: Schools, libraries, homeschoolers, and nursing homes in OREGON AND SOUTHERN IDAHO ONLY. Please make requests via the web site.
Suggested Grade: 6-12
Order Number: 500
Production Date: 1994
Format: VHS videotape
Special Notes: Part of the "Japan: Life and Nature" series.
Terms: Borrower pays return postage. Return within three weeks after scheduled showing date. Book one month in advance if possible. Rewind the video and wrap securely for return. Be certain to indicate video number, date needed, name of your organization, and address to which video should be sent, along with phone number. Audience report enclosed with the video must be completed and returned.

Source: Consulate General of Japan, Oregon
Attn: Tamara, Video Library
1300 S. W. Fifth Avenue, Suite 2700
Portland, OR 97201
Phone: 1-503-221-1811, ext. 17
World Wide Web URL:
http://www.portland.us.emb-japan.go.jp/en/index.html
Email Address: tamara@cgjpdx.org

Work Option Videos
Videos about specific types of work like apprenticeship, on-the-job training, and non-traditional work

Availability: All requesters
Suggested Grade: 7-Adult
Order Number: not applicable
Format: Online Streaming Video

Source: America's Career InfoNet
World Wide Web URL: http://www.acinet.org/acinet/videos_by_summary.asp?id=27&nodeid=30

Beauty and the Beast

A handsome but vain prince falls under a spell that turns him into a horrible Beast who can only be saved by Beauty's love. Does not follow the traditional fairy tale, but retains its essence.

Availability: Schools, libraries, and homeschoolers in the United States who serve the hearing impaired.
Suggested Grade: 3-8
Order Number: 13622
Production Date: 1979
Format: DVD
Special Notes: Produced by Gibbe Productions.
Terms: Sponsor pays all transportation costs. Return one week after receipt. Participation is limited to deaf or hard of hearing Americans, their parents, families, teachers, counselors, or others whose use would benefit a deaf or hard of hearing person. Only one person in the audience needs to be hearing impaired. You must register--which is free. These videos are all open-captioned--no special equipment is required for viewing.
Source: Described and Captioned Media Program
National Association of the Deaf
4211 Church Street Ext.
Roebuck, SC 29376
Phone: 1-800-237-6213
Fax: 1-800-538-5636
World Wide Web URL: http://www.dcmp.org

Boots and Her Kittens

Boots, a mother cat, cares for her three newborn kittens during their first year of life as they learn the necessary skills for survival.

Availability: Schools, libraries, and homeschoolers in the United States who serve the hearing impaired.
Suggested Grade: K-6
Order Number: 2041
Production Date: 1986
Format: DVD
Special Notes: Produced by Encyclopedia Britannica Educational Corporation.
Terms: Sponsor pays all transportation costs. Return one week after receipt. Participation is limited to deaf or hard of hearing Americans, their parents, families, teachers, counselors, or others whose use would benefit a deaf or hard of hearing person. Only one person in the audience needs to be hearing impaired. You must register--which is free. These videos are all open-captioned--no special equipment is required for viewing.
Source: Described and Captioned Media Program
National Association of the Deaf
4211 Church Street Ext.
Roebuck, SC 29376
Phone: 1-800-237-6213
Fax: 1-800-538-5636
World Wide Web URL: http://www.dcmp.org

Brave One, The

Won the Academy Award for bet original story in 1956--a very enjoyable film.

Availability: Schools in the United States.
Suggested Grade: All ages
Order Number: order by title
Production Date: 1956
Format: VHS videotape
Terms: Borrower pays return postage. Return 14 days after receipt, via USPS including insurance. All borrowers must have a current lending agreement on file with the Outreach program. This agreement is available via the web site or may be requested via phone or fax.
Source: Center for Latin American Studies
University of Florida
319 Grinter Hall
P. O. Box 115530
Gainesville, FL 32611-5530
Phone: 1-352-392-0375
Fax: 1-352-392-7682
World Wide Web URL: http://www.latam.ufl.edu/outreach
Email Address: maryr@ufl.edu

Cat & Canary

Their owner assumes they do nothing all day, but Cat and Canary have an adventure with a kite over the rooftops and buildings of New York City. Cat enjoys his flight until a storm approaches. Rescued by Canary and safely home, Cat dreams of flying again. Based on the book by Michael Foreman.

Availability: Schools, libraries, and homeschoolers in the United States who serve the hearing impaired.
Suggested Grade: preK-4
Order Number: 12336
Production Date: 1994
Format: DVD
Special Notes: Produced by Weston Woods Studios.
Terms: Sponsor pays all transportation costs. Return one week after receipt. Participation is limited to deaf or hard of hearing Americans, their parents, families, teachers, counselors, or others whose use would benefit a deaf or hard of hearing person. Only one person in the audience needs to be hearing impaired. You must register--which is free. These videos are all open-captioned--no special equipment is required for viewing.
Source: Described and Captioned Media Program
National Association of the Deaf
4211 Church Street Ext.
Roebuck, SC 29376
Phone: 1-800-237-6213
Fax: 1-800-538-5636
World Wide Web URL: http://www.dcmp.org

Children's Stories

Four delightful children's tales from Japan are told using animation and real life actors.

Availability: Schools, libraries, and nursing homes in Hawaii.
Suggested Grade: 2-12
Order Number: CU-20
Format: VHS videotape

Terms: Borrower pays return postage. A maximum of 3 videos may be borrowed per person. Return within one week of date borrowed.
Source: Consulate General of Japan, Honolulu
1742 Nuuanu Avenue
Honolulu, HI 96817-3294
Phone: 1-808-543-3111
Fax: 1-808-543-3170
World Wide Web URL:
http://www.honolulu.us.emb-japan.go.jp

Dust to Dust
A gentle comedy about family and friendship.
Availability: Schools, libraries, and nursing homes in the United States.
Suggested Grade: 6-12
Languages: Spanish with subtitles
Order Number: FFMEX75-videoc02
Production Date: 2000
Format: DVD
Special Notes: Winner of the 2001 Chicago Latino Film Festival's Audience Award.
Terms: Borrowers must have a User's Agreement on file with this source--available by mail or via the Internet. Return postage is paid by borrower; return 12 days after showing. Book at least three weeks in advance. All borrowers are limited to a total of ten items per semester.
Source: Latin American Resource Center
Stone Center for Latin American Studies
Tulane University
100 Jones Hall
New Orleans, LA 70118
Phone: 1-504-862-3143
Fax: 1-504-865-6719
World Wide Web URL:
http://stonecenter.tulane.edu/pages/detail/48/
Lending-Library
Email Address: crcrts@tulane.edu

El Peregrinaje de las Flores
Flower vendors retell ancient legends while traveling to market in brightly-decorated barges.
Availability: Schools, libraries, and nursing homes in the United States.
Suggested Grade: 6-12
Language: Spanish
Order Number: DFMEX14-video
Production Date: 1974
Format: VHS videotape
Terms: Borrowers must have a User's Agreement on file with this source--available by mail or via the Internet. Return postage is paid by borrower; return 12 days after showing. Book at least three weeks in advance. All borrowers are limited to a total of ten items per semester.
Source: Latin American Resource Center
Stone Center for Latin American Studies
Tulane University
100 Jones Hall
New Orleans, LA 70118
Phone: 1-504-862-3143

Fax: 1-504-865-6719
World Wide Web URL:
http://stonecenter.tulane.edu/pages/detail/48/
Lending-Library
Email Address: crcrts@tulane.edu

Emperor's New Clothes, The
An animated Japanese version of the story by Hans Christian Andersen. Two dishonest tailors dupe a vain emperor into believing their imaginary "fabric of dreams" really exists. Because the tailors have said only the wise can see the cloth, no one will tell the truth. Just one child innocently blurts out the fact that the emperor isn't wearing any clothes. Narrated by Robert Guillaume.
Availability: Schools, libraries, and homeschoolers in the United States who serve the hearing impaired.
Suggested Grade: 4-6
Order Number: 12407
Production Date: 1995
Format: DVD
Special Notes: Produced by Ambrose Video Publishing, Inc..
Terms: Sponsor pays all transportation costs. Return one week after receipt. Participation is limited to deaf or hard of hearing Americans, their parents, families, teachers, counselors, or others whose use would benefit a deaf or hard of hearing person. Only one person in the audience needs to be hearing impaired. You must register--which is free. These videos are all open-captioned--no special equipment is required for viewing.
Source: Described and Captioned Media Program
National Association of the Deaf
4211 Church Street Ext.
Roebuck, SC 29376
Phone: 1-800-237-6213
Fax: 1-800-538-5636
World Wide Web URL: http://www.dcmp.org

Goldilocks and the Three Bears
Portrays, in animated form, the classic story of a little girl who wanders through the woods, disturbs the house of the three bears, and learns that she should obey her mother and never wander through the woods alone.
Availability: Schools, libraries, and homeschoolers in the United States who serve the hearing impaired.
Suggested Grade: K-3
Order Number: 11621
Production Date: 1993
Format: DVD
Special Notes: Also available as live streaming video.
Terms: Sponsor pays all transportation costs. Return one week after receipt. Participation is limited to deaf or hard of hearing Americans, their parents, families, teachers, counselors, or others whose use would benefit a deaf or hard of hearing person. Only one person in the audience needs to be hearing impaired. You must register--which is free. These videos are all open-captioned--no special equipment is required for viewing.

Source: Described and Captioned Media Program
National Association of the Deaf
4211 Church Street Ext.
Roebuck, SC 29376
Phone: 1-800-237-6213
Fax: 1-800-538-5636
World Wide Web URL: http://www.dcmp.org

Good Morning

A comedy that makes a genuine statement about family relationships.

Availability:	Schools, libraries, and nursing homes in the United States and Canada.
Suggested Grade:	All ages
Languages:	Japanese; subtitled in English
Order Number:	JV087
Format:	VHS videotape
Terms:	Borrower pays return postage. Return with 14 days after scheduled showing, via UPS or U. S. Mail. All requests must included an educational institution affiliation, a current address, and phone number. Order through web site only.

Source: Cornell University East Asia Program
World Wide Web URL:
http://www.einaudi.cornell.edu/eastasia/outreach/video.asp
Email Address: east_asia1@cornell.edu

Harold and the Purple Crayon

Through animation, Harold creates his own little world with the help of a magical purple crayon. Harold takes a midnight walk and draws himself into and out of a variety of situations. Based on the book by Crockett Johnson.

Availability:	Schools, libraries, and homeschoolers in the United States who serve the hearing impaired.
Suggested Grade:	preK-3
Order Number:	1870
Production Date:	1989
Format:	DVD
Special Notes:	Produced by Weston Woods Studios.
Terms:	Sponsor pays all transportation costs. Return one week after receipt. Participation is limited to deaf or hard of hearing Americans, their parents, families, teachers, counselors, or others whose use would benefit a deaf or hard of hearing person. Only one person in the audience needs to be hearing impaired. You must register--which is free. These videos are all open-captioned--no special equipment is required for viewing.

Source: Described and Captioned Media Program
National Association of the Deaf
4211 Church Street Ext.
Roebuck, SC 29376
Phone: 1-800-237-6213
Fax: 1-800-538-5636
World Wide Web URL: http://www.dcmp.org

Instrucciones para John Howell

Cortazar at his absurdist height in this story about the misadventure of a museum tour guide.

Availability:	Schools, libraries, and nursing homes in the United States.
Suggested Grade:	6-12
Languages:	Spanish with English subtitles
Order Number:	LMARG12-video
Production Date:	1988
Format:	VHS videotape
Terms:	Borrowers must have a User's Agreement on file with this source--available by mail or via the Internet. Return postage is paid by borrower; return 12 days after showing. Book at least three weeks in advance. All borrowers are limited to a total of ten items per semester.

Source: Latin American Resource Center
Stone Center for Latin American Studies
Tulane University
100 Jones Hall
New Orleans, LA 70118
Phone: 1-504-862-3143
Fax: 1-504-865-6719
World Wide Web URL:
http://stonecenter.tulane.edu/pages/detail/48/
Lending-Library
Email Address: crcrts@tulane.edu

In the Jungle There Is Lots to Do

Charming animated film based on a children's story, encourages cooperation, not competition.

Availability:	Schools and libraries in Iowa, Illinois, Michigan, Minnesota, and Wisconsin.
Suggested Grade:	2-8
Order Number:	ENVURUIN1VHS
Format:	VHS videotape
Terms:	Borrower pays return postage. Return 8 days after showing. Book 2 weeks in advance. Order may also be picked up for those near the Center.

Source: Center for Latin American and Caribbean Studies
UW-Milwaukee
P. O. Box 413
Milwaukee, WI 53201
Phone: 1-414-229-5987
World Wide Web URL: http://www.uwm.edu/Dept/CLACS
Email Address: audvis@usm.edu

Journey to the West: Legends of the Monkey King

Tells the story of Monkey, a most unlikely hero, on a most extraordinary journey as he and his friends travel together on incredible adventures.

Availability:	Schools, libraries, and nursing homes in the United States and Canada.
Suggested Grade:	K-8
Order Number:	CV056
Format:	VHS videotape
Terms:	Borrower pays return postage. Return with 14 days after scheduled showing, via UPS or U. S. Mail. All requests must included an educational institution affiliation, a current address, and phone number. Order through web site only.

Source: Cornell University East Asia Program
World Wide Web URL:
http://www.einaudi.cornell.edu/eastasia/outreach/video.asp
Email Address: east_asia1@cornell.edu

Lejania

A middle-aged woman who 10 years earlier left her teenager son and Cuba for Miami, returns to a world she cannot accept or forget.

Availability: Schools, libraries, and nursing homes in the United States.
Suggested Grade: 6-12
Languages: Spanish with English subtitles
Order Number: FFCUB2-video
Production Date: 1985
Format: VHS videotape
Terms: Borrowers must have a User's Agreement on file with this source--available by mail or via the Internet. Return postage is paid by borrower; return 12 days after showing. Book at least three weeks in advance. All borrowers are limited to a total of ten items per semester.

> **Source: Latin American Resource Center**
> **Stone Center for Latin American Studies**
> **Tulane University**
> **100 Jones Hall**
> **New Orleans, LA 70118**
> **Phone: 1-504-862-3143**
> **Fax: 1-504-865-6719**
> **World Wide Web URL:**
> **http://stonecenter.tulane.edu/pages/detail/48/**
> **Lending-Library**
> **Email Address: crcrts@tulane.edu**

Macario

A fable about a peasant who despairs at his inability to feed his family.

Availability: Schools, libraries, and nursing homes in the United States.
Suggested Grade: 6-12
Languages: Spanish with English subtitles
Order Number: DFMEX19-video
Production Date: 1989
Format: VHS videotape
Terms: Borrowers must have a User's Agreement on file with this source--available by mail or via the Internet. Return postage is paid by borrower; return 12 days after showing. Book at least three weeks in advance. All borrowers are limited to a total of ten items per semester.

> **Source: Latin American Resource Center**
> **Stone Center for Latin American Studies**
> **Tulane University**
> **100 Jones Hall**
> **New Orleans, LA 70118**
> **Phone: 1-504-862-3143**
> **Fax: 1-504-865-6719**
> **World Wide Web URL:**
> **http://stonecenter.tulane.edu/pages/detail/48/**
> **Lending-Library**
> **Email Address: crcrts@tulane.edu**

Mahabharata, The

Peter Brook's innovative contemporary adaptation of the Indian epic, with an international cast. In three parts: "The Game of Dice," "Excile in the Forest," and "The War."

Availability: Schools, libraries, homeschoolers, and nursing homes in the southeastern United States.
Suggested Grade: 7-12
Order Number: order by title
Format: Set of 3 VHS videotapes
Terms: Borrower pays return postage. Return 2 days after showing via United Parcel Service, insured. Book 2 weeks in advance.

> **Source: Center for South Asian Studies**
> **University of Virginia**
> **Video Library Coordinator**
> **P. O. Box 400169, 110 Minor Hall**
> **Charlottesville, VA 22904-4169**
> **Phone: 1-434-924-8815**
> **Email Address: southasia@virginia.edu**

Mulan

This animated cartoon film is based on an ancient Chinese folk tale.

Availability: Schools, libraries, homeschoolers, and nursing homes in the United States and Canada.
Suggested Grade: K-6
Order Number: order by title
Production Date: 1998
Format: VHS videotape
Terms: Postage is paid by borrower both ways--send $3.00 per tape to cover initial shipping to you--MONEY MUST BE SENT WITH REQUEST. Return 10 days after showing via U. S. Postal Service, library rate. Shipping is $5.00 to Canadian addresses.

> **Source: Center for Teaching About China**
> **Kathleen Trescott**
> **1214 West Schwartz**
> **Carbondale, IL 62901**
> **Phone: 1-618-549-1555**
> **Email Address: trescott@midwest.net**

Panda and the Magic Serpent

Set in the magic land of China, a young boy and his panda friend travel through a series of adventures with a magic serpent and a sorcerer.

Availability: Schools, libraries, homeschoolers, and nursing homes in the United States and Canada.
Suggested Grade: K-4
Order Number: order by title
Production Date: 1961
Format: VHS videotape
Terms: Postage is paid by borrower both ways--send $3.00 per tape to cover initial shipping to you--MONEY MUST BE SENT WITH REQUEST. Return 10 days after showing via U. S. Postal Service, library rate. Shipping is $5.00 to Canadian addresses.

Source: Center for Teaching About China
Kathleen Trescott
1214 West Schwartz
Carbondale, IL 62901
Phone: 1-618-549-1555
Email Address: trescott@midwest.net

Querido Diario

Animated story of a young girl who visits the ruins of Teotihuacan on a school trip, where she meets a pre-Columbian boy who shows her what life was like.

Availability: Schools, libraries, and nursing homes in the United States.
Suggested Grade: K-12
Language: Spanish
Order Number: APMEX40-video
Production Date: 1992
Format: VHS videotape
Special Notes: Recommended for language classes.
Terms: Borrowers must have a User's Agreement on file with this source--available by mail or via the Internet. Return postage is paid by borrower; return 12 days after showing. Book at least three weeks in advance. All borrowers are limited to a total of ten items per semester.
**Source: Latin American Resource Center
Stone Center for Latin American Studies
Tulane University
100 Jones Hall
New Orleans, LA 70118
Phone: 1-504-862-3143
Fax: 1-504-865-6719
World Wide Web URL:
http://stonecenter.tulane.edu/pages/detail/48/
Lending-Library
Email Address: crcrts@tulane.edu**

Snowman, The

Illustrates the perils and joys of winter through the thoughts of a young boy who dreams that his snowman has come to life. Based on the books by Raymond Briggs.

Availability: Schools, libraries, and homeschoolers in the United States who serve the hearing impaired.
Suggested Grade: preK-3
Order Number: 12807
Production Date: 1982
Format: DVD
Special Notes: Produced by Weston Woods Studios. Also available as live streaming video via the Internet.
Terms: Sponsor pays all transportation costs. Return one week after receipt. Participation is limited to deaf or hard of hearing Americans, their parents, families, teachers, counselors, or others whose use would benefit a deaf or hard of hearing person. Only one person in the audience needs to be hearing impaired. You must register--which is free. These videos are all open-captioned--no special equipment is required for viewing.

Source: Described and Captioned Media Program
National Association of the Deaf
4211 Church Street Ext.
Roebuck, SC 29376
Phone: 1-800-237-6213
Fax: 1-800-538-5636
World Wide Web URL: http://www.dcmp.org

Tales from Exotic Lands

Animated versions of four legends from Latin America.

Availability: Schools, libraries, and nursing homes in the United States.
Suggested Grade: 4-8
Order Number: LPLA3-video
Production Date: 1986
Format: VHS videotape
Special Notes: Includes comprehension questions.
Terms: Borrowers must have a User's Agreement on file with this source--available by mail or via the Internet. Return postage is paid by borrower; return 12 days after showing. Book at least three weeks in advance. All borrowers are limited to a total of ten items per semester.
**Source: Latin American Resource Center
Stone Center for Latin American Studies
Tulane University
100 Jones Hall
New Orleans, LA 70118
Phone: 1-504-862-3143
Fax: 1-504-865-6719
World Wide Web URL:
http://stonecenter.tulane.edu/pages/detail/48/
Lending-Library
Email Address: crcrts@tulane.edu**

Valiant Little Tailor, The

A Nigerian version of the Grimm's fairy tale. Bongo, a short tailor in a land of tall people, kills seven flies with one blow. He is so pleased with himself, he sets out to seek his fortune. Using his wits, honesty, and confidence, he defeats a giant, outsmarts the king, and wins the hand of the princess. Narrated by Robert Guillaume.

Availability: Schools, libraries, and homeschoolers in the United States who serve the hearing impaired.
Suggested Grade: 4-8
Order Number: 12431
Production Date: 1995
Format: DVD
Special Notes: Produced by Ambrose Video Publishing, Inc..
Terms: Sponsor pays all transportation costs. Return one week after receipt. Participation is limited to deaf or hard of hearing Americans, their parents, families, teachers, counselors, or others whose use would benefit a deaf or hard of hearing person. Only one person in the audience needs to be hearing impaired. You must register--which is free. These videos are all open-captioned--no special equipment is required for viewing.

*All materials listed in this 2011-2012 edition are **BRAND NEW**!*

Source: Described and Captioned Media Program
National Association of the Deaf
4211 Church Street Ext.
Roebuck, SC 29376
Phone: 1-800-237-6213
Fax: 1-800-538-5636
World Wide Web URL: http://www.dcmp.org

Viva Zapata

Marlon Brando stars as the peasant who fights his way to power and glory during the Mexican Revolution.

Availability: Schools, libraries, and nursing homes in the United States.
Suggested Grade: 6-12
Order Number: FFMEX31-video
Production Date: 1939
Format: VHS videotape
Special Notes: Stars Marlon Brando.
Terms: Borrowers must have a User's Agreement on file with this source--available by mail or via the Internet. Return postage is paid by borrower; return 12 days after showing. Book at least three weeks in advance. All borrowers are limited to a total of ten items per semester.
Source: Latin American Resource Center
Stone Center for Latin American Studies
Tulane University
100 Jones Hall
New Orleans, LA 70118
Phone: 1-504-862-3143
Fax: 1-504-865-6719
World Wide Web URL:
http://stonecenter.tulane.edu/pages/detail/48/
Lending-Library
Email Address: crcrts@tulane.edu

West Side Story

The Academy Award winning film for best picture of 1961.
Availability: Schools in the United States.
Suggested Grade: 7-Adult
Order Number: order by title
Production Date: 1961
Format: VHS videotape
Terms: Borrower pays return postage. Return 14 days after receipt, via USPS including insurance. All borrowers must have a current lending agreement on file with the Outreach program. This agreement is available via the web site or may be requested via phone or fax.
Source: Center for Latin American Studies
University of Florida
319 Grinter Hall
P. O. Box 115530
Gainesville, FL 32611-5530
Phone: 1-352-392-0375
Fax: 1-352-392-7682
World Wide Web URL: http://www.latam.ufl.edu/outreach
Email Address: maryr@ufl.edu

Where the Wild Things Are

In Maurice Sendak's story, mischievous Max "acted wild" and was sent to bed without supper. His room turned into a jungle where wild animals lived. Max tamed them and became their king, but soon tired of the wild things. So he returned to reality where his still-warm supper was waiting.
Availability: Schools, libraries, and homeschoolers in the United States who serve the hearing impaired.
Suggested Grade: 2-3
Order Number: 12976
Production Date: 1973
Format: DVD
Special Notes: Produced by Weston Woods Studios.
Terms: Sponsor pays all transportation costs. Return one week after receipt. Participation is limited to deaf or hard of hearing Americans, their parents, families, teachers, counselors, or others whose use would benefit a deaf or hard of hearing person. Only one person in the audience needs to be hearing impaired. You must register--which is free. These videos are all open-captioned--no special equipment is required for viewing.
Source: Described and Captioned Media Program
National Association of the Deaf
4211 Church Street Ext.
Roebuck, SC 29376
Phone: 1-800-237-6213
Fax: 1-800-538-5636
World Wide Web URL: http://www.dcmp.org

FAMOUS PEOPLE

Arruza

Greatest matador, Carlos Arruza, whose style and courage changed the art of bullfighting forever.

Availability: Schools, libraries, and nursing homes in the United States.
Suggested Grade: 6-12
Order Number: DFMEX6-video
Production Date: 1967
Format: VHS videotape
Terms: Borrowers must have a User's Agreement on file with this source--available by mail or via the Internet. Return postage is paid by borrower; return 12 days after showing. Book at least three weeks in advance. All borrowers are limited to a total of ten items per semester.
Source: Latin American Resource Center
Stone Center for Latin American Studies
Tulane University
100 Jones Hall
New Orleans, LA 70118
Phone: 1-504-862-3143
Fax: 1-504-865-6719
World Wide Web URL:
http://stonecenter.tulane.edu/pages/detail/48/
Lending-Library
Email Address: crcrts@tulane.edu

Benedita da Silva

The life of Benedita da Silva, the first Black woman to be elected to the Brazilian national congress, touching on racism, feminism, ageism, politics and poverty.

Availability: Schools, libraries, and nursing homes in the United States.
Suggested Grade: 8-Adult
Languages: Portuguese with English subtitles
Order Number: SIBRA3-video
Production Date: 1991
Format: VHS videotape
Terms: Borrowers must have a User's Agreement on file with this source--available by mail or via the Internet. Return postage is paid by borrower; return 12 days after showing. Book at least three weeks in advance. All borrowers are limited to a total of ten items per semester.
Source: Latin American Resource Center
Stone Center for Latin American Studies
Tulane University
100 Jones Hall
New Orleans, LA 70118
Phone: 1-504-862-3143
Fax: 1-504-865-6719
World Wide Web URL:
http://stonecenter.tulane.edu/pages/detail/48/
Lending-Library
Email Address: crcrts@tulane.edu

Carlos Fuentes

Author, teacher, and diplomat offers perspective on current Latin American economics and prospects for political independence.

Availability: Schools and libraries in the United States and Canada.
Suggested Grade: 6-12
Order Number: order by title
Production Date: 1988
Format: VHS videotape
Terms: Videos will typically be lent for seven days if mailed out--due date will be indicated. Films not returned within the time limit will be subject to overdue fines of $2 per video, per day. All borrowed must have a lending agreement on file. Form can be downloaded from http://isa.unc.edu/film/borrow.asplaform. Borrowers are responsible for the cost of return shipping. Materials must be returned via a shipping method that has tracking information.
Source: Latin American Film Collection
3219 Fed Ex Global Education Center
301 Pittsboro Street, CB 3205
Chapel Hill, NC 27599-3205
Email Address: LA_Films@email.unc.edu

Carlos Fuentes

Author, teacher, and diplomat offers perspective on current Latin American economics and prospects for political independence.

Availability: Schools, libraries, and nursing homes in the United States.
Suggested Grade: 6-12
Order Number: HCLA14-video
Production Date: 1988
Format: VHS videotape
Terms: Borrowers must have a User's Agreement on file with this source--available by mail or via the Internet. Return postage is paid by borrower; return 12 days after showing. Book at least three weeks in advance. All borrowers are limited to a total of ten items per semester.
Source: Latin American Resource Center
Stone Center for Latin American Studies
Tulane University
100 Jones Hall
New Orleans, LA 70118
Phone: 1-504-862-3143
Fax: 1-504-865-6719
World Wide Web URL:
http://stonecenter.tulane.edu/pages/detail/48/
Lending-Library
Email Address: crcrts@tulane.edu

Carmen Miranda: Bananas Is My Business

Traces Carmen Miranda's life from her birth in Portugal, to her childhood in Rio de Janeiro, and as a performer in the United States.

Availability: Schools and libraries in Iowa, Illinois, Michigan, Minnesota, and Wisconsin.
Suggested Grade: 6-12
Languages: English and Portuguese with English subtitles
Order Number: order by title
Production Date: 1994
Format: VHS videotape

*All materials listed in this 2011-2012 edition are **BRAND NEW!***

Terms: Borrower pays return postage. Return 8 days after showing. Book 2 weeks in advance. Order may also be picked up for those near the Center.

Source: **Center for Latin American and Caribbean Studies**
UW-Milwaukee
P. O. Box 413
Milwaukee, WI 53201
Phone: 1-414-229-5987
World Wide Web URL: http://www.uwm.edu/Dept/CLACS
Email Address: audvis@usm.edu

Carmen Miranda: Bananas Is My Business

Traces Carmen Miranda's life from her birth in Portugal, to her childhood in Rio de Janeiro, and as a performer in the United States.

Availability: Schools and libraries in the United States and Canada.
Suggested Grade: 6-12
Order Number: order by title
Production Date: 1994
Format: VHS videotape
Terms: Videos will typically be lent for seven days if mailed out--due date will be indicated. Films not returned within the time limit will be subject to overdue fines of $2 per video, per day. All borrowed must have a lending agreement on file. Form can be downloaded from http://isa.unc.edu/film/borrow.asplaform. Borrowers are responsible for the cost of return shipping. Materials must be returned via a shipping method that has tracking information.

Source: **Latin American Film Collection**
3219 Fed Ex Global Education Center
301 Pittsboro Street, CB 3205
Chapel Hill, NC 27599-3205
Email Address: LA_Films@email.unc.edu

Carmen Miranda: Bananas Is My Business

Traces Carmen Miranda's life from her birth in Portugal, to her childhood in Rio de Janeiro, and as a performer in the United States.

Availability: Schools, libraries, and nursing homes in the United States.
Suggested Grade: 6-12
Languages: English and Portuguese with English subtitles
Order Number: MUBRA10-video
Production Date: 1994
Format: VHS videotape
Terms: Borrowers must have a User's Agreement on file with this source--available by mail or via the Internet. Return postage is paid by borrower; return 12 days after showing. Book at least three weeks in advance. All borrowers are limited to a total of ten items per semester.

Source: **Latin American Resource Center**
Stone Center for Latin American Studies
Tulane University
100 Jones Hall
New Orleans, LA 70118
Phone: 1-504-862-3143
Fax: 1-504-865-6719

World Wide Web URL:
http://stonecenter.tulane.edu/pages/detail/48/
Lending-Library
Email Address: crcrts@tulane.edu

Compassion in Exile

A portrait of the 14th Dalai Lama, now living in exile in India that documents his nonviolent struggle to preserve his people and their culture from destruction under Chinese occupation, as well as his upbringing and important moments in his life.

Availability: Schools, libraries, homeschoolers, and nursing homes in the southeastern United States.
Suggested Grade: 7-12
Order Number: order by title
Production Date: 1992
Format: VHS videotape
Terms: Borrower pays return postage. Return 2 days after showing via United Parcel Service, insured. Book 2 weeks in advance.

Source: **Center for South Asian Studies**
University of Virginia
Video Library Coordinator
P. O. Box 400169, 110 Minor Hall
Charlottesville, VA 22904-4169
Phone: 1-434-924-8815
Email Address: southasia@virginia.edu

David Alfara Siqueiros: Uno de Tres Grandes

Traces Siqueiros' emergence as an artist dedicated to social change.

Availability: Schools and libraries in Iowa, Illinois, Michigan, Minnesota, and Wisconsin.
Suggested Grade: 6-12
Language: Spanish
Order Number: ART/FOLMEXD28VHS
Production Date: 1999
Format: VHS videotape
Terms: Borrower pays return postage. Return 8 days after showing. Book 2 weeks in advance. Order may also be picked up for those near the Center.

Source: **Center for Latin American and Caribbean Studies**
UW-Milwaukee
P. O. Box 413
Milwaukee, WI 53201
Phone: 1-414-229-5987
World Wide Web URL: http://www.uwm.edu/Dept/CLACS
Email Address: audvis@usm.edu

Dialogo Entre Augusto Roa Bastos y Fernando Alegria

Interview of Paraguayan poet laureate, Augusto Roa Bastos.

Availability: Schools, libraries, and nursing homes in the United States.
Suggested Grade: 6-12
Language: Spanish
Order Number: LMPAR1-video
Production Date: 1985
Format: VHS videotape

Terms: Borrowers must have a User's Agreement on file with this source--available by mail or via the Internet. Return postage is paid by borrower; return 12 days after showing. Book at least three weeks in advance. All borrowers are limited to a total of ten items per semester.

Source: Latin American Resource Center
Stone Center for Latin American Studies
Tulane University, 100 Jones Hall
New Orleans, LA 70118
Phone: 1-504-862-3143
Fax: 1-504-865-6719
World Wide Web URL:
http://stonecenter.tulane.edu/pages/detail/48/
Lending-Library
Email Address: crcrts@tulane.edu

Dream Across Time and Place, A--The Legacy of Tsuda Umeko

Umeko traveled to the United States in 1871. At age six, she was the youngest of five young women sent to study there by the Japanese Government as part of its effort to modernize Japan. She spent a total of 14 years in two stays in America, returning home determined to create a school of higher learning for women so that other Japanese women benefit from education as she has done.

Availability: Schools, libraries, and nursing homes in the United States and Canada.
Suggested Grade: 6-Adult
Language: Japanese
Order Number: JV104
Format: VHS videotape
Special Notes: An English text accompanies the production.
Terms: Borrower pays return postage. Return with 14 days after scheduled showing, via UPS or U. S. Mail. All requests must included an educational institution affiliation, a current address, and phone number. Order through web site only.

Source: Cornell University East Asia Program
World Wide Web URL:
http://www.einaudi.cornell.edu/eastasia/outreach/video.asp
Email Address: east_asia1@cornell.edu

Ernesto Che Guevara: The Bolivian Diary

Che Guevara's personal diary account of his 11-month attempt to foment revolution in Bolivia, before his execution in 1967.

Availability: Schools and libraries in Iowa, Illinois, Michigan, Minnesota, and Wisconsin.
Suggested Grade: 6-12
Order Number: order by title
Production Date: 1998
Format: VHS videotape
Terms: Borrower pays return postage. Return 8 days after showing. Book 2 weeks in advance. Order may also be picked up for those near the Center.

Source: Center for Latin American and Caribbean Studies
UW-Milwaukee
P. O. Box 413
Milwaukee, WI 53201

Phone: 1-414-229-5987
World Wide Web URL: http://www.uwm.edu/Dept/CLACS
Email Address: audvis@usm.edu

Ernesto Che Guevara: The Bolivian Diary

Che Guevara's personal diary account of his 11-month attempt to foment revolution in Bolivia, before his execution in 1967.

Availability: Schools, libraries, and nursing homes in the United States.
Suggested Grade: 6-12
Order Number: HCBOL1-video
Production Date: 1998
Format: VHS videotape
Terms: Borrowers must have a User's Agreement on file with this source--available by mail or via the Internet. Return postage is paid by borrower; return 12 days after showing. Book at least three weeks in advance. All borrowers are limited to a total of ten items per semester.

Source: Latin American Resource Center
Stone Center for Latin American Studies
Tulane University
100 Jones Hall
New Orleans, LA 70118
Phone: 1-504-862-3143
Fax: 1-504-865-6719
World Wide Web URL:
http://stonecenter.tulane.edu/pages/detail/48/
Lending-Library
Email Address: crcrts@tulane.edu

Evita: The Woman Behind the Myth

Explores the life of Eva Duarte de Peron, from her origins to her marriage to Juan Peron and her tragic death from cancer at age 33.

Availability: Schools, libraries, and nursing homes in the United States.
Suggested Grade: 6-12
Order Number: HCARG2-video
Production Date: 1996
Format: VHS videotape
Terms: Borrowers must have a User's Agreement on file with this source--available by mail or via the Internet. Return postage is paid by borrower; return 12 days after showing. Book at least three weeks in advance. All borrowers are limited to a total of ten items per semester.

Source: Latin American Resource Center
Stone Center for Latin American Studies
Tulane University
100 Jones Hall
New Orleans, LA 70118
Phone: 1-504-862-3143
Fax: 1-504-865-6719
World Wide Web URL:
http://stonecenter.tulane.edu/pages/detail/48/
Lending-Library
Email Address: crcrts@tulane.edu

All materials listed in this 2011-2012 edition are **BRAND NEW!**

Forgotten Genius

Against all odds, African-American chemist Percy Julian became one of the great scientists of the 20th century.

Availability:	All requesters
Suggested Grade:	7-Adult
Order Number:	not applicable
Production Date:	2007
Format:	Streaming Video

Source: NOVA
World Wide Web URL:
http://www.pbs.org/wgbh/nova/programs/index.html

Frida Kahlo

Depicts the life and paintings of this artist who was ravaged with pain from the age of 16.

Availability:	Schools and libraries in Iowa, Illinois, Michigan, Minnesota, and Wisconsin.
Suggested Grade:	7-12
Order Number:	ART/FOLMEXK12.1VHS
Production Date:	1988
Format:	VHS videotape
Terms:	Borrower pays return postage. Return 8 days after showing. Book 2 weeks in advance. Order may also be picked up for those near the Center.

Source: Center for Latin American and Caribbean Studies
UW-Milwaukee
P. O. Box 413
Milwaukee, WI 53201
Phone: 1-414-229-5987
World Wide Web URL: http://www.uwm.edu/Dept/CLACS
Email Address: audvis@usm.edu

Gabriel Garcia Marquez: Magic and Reality

Rare archival footage and appearances by the author and characters of "One Hundred Years of Solitude" and "The Autumn of the Patriarch."

Availability:	Schools, libraries, and nursing homes in the United States.
Suggested Grade:	6-12
Order Number:	LMCOL1-video
Production Date:	1981
Format:	VHS videotape
Terms:	Borrowers must have a User's Agreement on file with this source--available by mail or via the Internet. Return postage is paid by borrower; return 12 days after showing. Book at least three weeks in advance. All borrowers are limited to a total of ten items per semester.

Source: Latin American Resource Center
Stone Center for Latin American Studies
Tulane University
100 Jones Hall
New Orleans, LA 70118
Phone: 1-504-862-3143
Fax: 1-504-865-6719
World Wide Web URL:
http://stonecenter.tulane.edu/pages/detail/48/
Lending-Library
Email Address: crcrts@tulane.edu

Genghis Khan

This biography takes the viewers to the ancient lands of China, Mongoli, and Persia to trace the life and conquests of Khan.

Availability:	Schools, libraries, homeschoolers, and nursing homes in the United States and Canada.
Suggested Grade:	6-12
Order Number:	order by title
Production Date:	1995
Format:	VHS videotape
Terms:	Postage is paid by borrower both ways--send $3.00 per tape to cover initial shipping to you--MONEY MUST BE SENT WITH REQUEST. Return 10 days after showing via U. S. Postal Service, library rate. Shipping is $5.00 to Canadian addresses.

Source: Center for Teaching About China
Kathleen Trescott
1214 West Schwartz
Carbondale, IL 62901
Phone: 1-618-549-1555
Email Address: trescott@midwest.net

George Washington Carver: Man of Vision

Presents the biography of this man.

Availability:	Schools, libraries, homeschoolers, and nursing homes in the United States.
Suggested Grade:	All ages
Order Number:	order by title
Format:	VHS videotape
Terms:	Borrower pays return postage. Return within 21 days after scheduled showing date via US Postal Service. Book 2-3 weeks in advance.

Source: George Washington Carver National Monument
5646 Carver Road
Diamond, MO 64840
Phone: 1-417-325-4151
Fax: 1-417-325-4231

George Washington Carver's Life

Learn more about this man.

Availability:	Schools, libraries, homeschoolers, and nursing homes in the United States.
Suggested Grade:	2-Adult
Order Number:	order by title
Production Date:	1984
Format:	VHS videotape
Terms:	Borrower pays return postage. Return within 21 days after scheduled showing date via US Postal Service. Book 2-3 weeks in advance.

Source: George Washington Carver National Monument
5646 Carver Road
Diamond, MO 64840
Phone: 1-417-325-4151
Fax: 1-417-325-4231

George Washington Carver Traveling Trunk

A complete trunk of videos, biographies, lesson plans, an audiotape of Dr. Carver, and much more.

FAMOUS PEOPLE

Availability: Schools, libraries, homeschoolers, and nursing homes in the United States.
Suggested Grade: 3-6
Order Number: order by title
Format: VHS videotape
Special Notes: Includes much more than a videotape! This special item should be booked up to one year in advance.
Terms: Borrower pays return postage. Return within 21 days after scheduled showing date via US Postal Service. Book 2-3 weeks in advance.
Source: George Washington Carver National Monument
5646 Carver Road
Diamond, MO 64840
Phone: 1-417-325-4151
Fax: 1-417-325-4231

Hernan Cortes
Conflict when Cortes' army clashed with the forces of Montezuma, resulting in the birth of modern Mexico.
Availability: Schools, libraries, and nursing homes in the United States.
Suggested Grade: 6-12
Order Number: HMEX8-video
Production Date: 1970
Format: VHS videotape
Terms: Borrowers must have a User's Agreement on file with this source--available by mail or via the Internet. Return postage is paid by borrower; return 12 days after showing. Book at least three weeks in advance. All borrowers are limited to a total of ten items per semester.
Source: Latin American Resource Center
Stone Center for Latin American Studies
Tulane University, 100 Jones Hall
New Orleans, LA 70118
Phone: 1-504-862-3143
Fax: 1-504-865-6719
World Wide Web URL:
http://stonecenter.tulane.edu/pages/detail/48/
Lending-Library
Email Address: crcrts@tulane.edu

Hugo Chavez Show, The
Traces the life and accomplishments of this Venezuelan leader.
Availability: All requesters
Suggested Grade: 7-Adult
Languages: English; Spanish
Order Number: not applicable
Format: Streaming Video
Source: PBS
World Wide Web URL:
http://www.pbs.org/wgbh/pages/frontline/hugochavez/view/

I. M. Pei
Narrated by this famous architect, he leads the viewers through the Louvre, National Gallery of Art, Rock and Roll Hall of Fame and more places that show his work. He talks about his life, his studies, his clients, and his philosophy.

Availability: Schools, libraries, homeschoolers, and nursing homes in the United States and Canada.
Suggested Grade: 7-12
Order Number: order by title
Production Date: 1997
Format: VHS videotape
Terms: Postage is paid by borrower both ways--send $3.00 per tape to cover initial shipping to you--MONEY MUST BE SENT WITH REQUEST. Return 10 days after showing via U. S. Postal Service, library rate. Shipping is $5.00 to Canadian addresses.
Source: Center for Teaching About China
Kathleen Trescott
1214 West Schwartz
Carbondale, IL 62901
Phone: 1-618-549-1555
Email Address: trescott@midwest.net

Looking for Chano Pozo
1930's musical genius Chano Pozo, who is credited with introducing Latin rhythms and instruments into Jazz.
Availability: Schools, libraries, and nursing homes in the United States.
Suggested Grade: 6-12
Languages: Spanish with English subtitles
Order Number: MUCUB10-video
Production Date: 1987
Format: VHS videotape
Terms: Borrowers must have a User's Agreement on file with this source--available by mail or via the Internet. Return postage is paid by borrower; return 12 days after showing. Book at least three weeks in advance. All borrowers are limited to a total of ten items per semester.
Source: Latin American Resource Center
Stone Center for Latin American Studies
Tulane University, 100 Jones Hall
New Orleans, LA 70118
Phone: 1-504-862-3143
Fax: 1-504-865-6719
World Wide Web URL:
http://stonecenter.tulane.edu/pages/detail/48/
Lending-Library
Email Address: crcrts@tulane.edu

Machito: A Latin Jazz Legacy
In a career spanning 50 years, Cuban band leader Frank "Machito" Grillo embodied Latin Jazz. Vintage clips and recordings.
Availability: Schools, libraries, and nursing homes in the United States.
Suggested Grade: 6-12
Order Number: MUCUB9-video
Format: VHS videotape
Terms: Borrowers must have a User's Agreement on file with this source--available by mail or via the Internet. Return postage is paid by borrower; return 12 days after showing. Book at least three weeks in advance. All borrowers are limited to a total of ten items per semester.

*All materials listed in this 2011-2012 edition are **BRAND NEW!***

Source: Latin American Resource Center
Stone Center for Latin American Studies
Tulane University
100 Jones Hall
New Orleans, LA 70118
Phone: 1-504-862-3143
Fax: 1-504-865-6719
World Wide Web URL:
http://stonecenter.tulane.edu/pages/detail/48/
Lending-Library
Email Address: crcrts@tulane.edu

Marco Polo: Journey to the East

This biography traces the explorer's life. It begins with his trek through Asia, to the courts of Kublai Khan, and to other Asian cities.

Availability:	Schools, libraries, homeschoolers, and nursing homes in the United States and Canada.
Suggested Grade:	4-12
Order Number:	order by title
Production Date:	1995
Format:	VHS videotape
Terms:	Postage is paid by borrower both ways--send $3.00 per tape to cover initial shipping to you--MONEY MUST BE SENT WITH REQUEST. Return 10 days after showing via U. S. Postal Service, library rate. Shipping is $5.00 to Canadian addresses.

Source: Center for Teaching About China
Kathleen Trescott
1214 West Schwartz
Carbondale, IL 62901
Phone: 1-618-549-1555
Email Address: trescott@midwest.net

Maysa Matarazzo

Documentary about a Brazilian popular singer/composer of the '50s and '60s, Maysa Matarazzo.

Availability:	Schools, libraries, and nursing homes in the United States.
Suggested Grade:	6-12
Language:	Portuguese
Order Number:	MUBRA3-video
Format:	VHS videotape
Terms:	Borrowers must have a User's Agreement on file with this source--available by mail or via the Internet. Return postage is paid by borrower; return 12 days after showing. Book at least three weeks in advance. All borrowers are limited to a total of ten items per semester.

Source: Latin American Resource Center
Stone Center for Latin American Studies
Tulane University, 100 Jones Hall
New Orleans, LA 70118
Phone: 1-504-862-3143
Fax: 1-504-865-6719
World Wide Web URL:
http://stonecenter.tulane.edu/pages/detail/48/
Lending-Library
Email Address: crcrts@tulane.edu

Pablo Milanes: Nueva Trova Cubana

Biographical documentary of the performer and composer with interviews and clips of him performing.

Availability:	Schools, libraries, and nursing homes in the United States.
Suggested Grade:	6-12
Language:	Spanish
Order Number:	MUCUB3-video
Production Date:	1985
Format:	VHS videotape
Terms:	Borrowers must have a User's Agreement on file with this source--available by mail or via the Internet. Return postage is paid by borrower; return 12 days after showing. Book at least three weeks in advance. All borrowers are limited to a total of ten items per semester.

Source: Latin American Resource Center
Stone Center for Latin American Studies
Tulane University
100 Jones Hall
New Orleans, LA 70118
Phone: 1-504-862-3143
Fax: 1-504-865-6719
World Wide Web URL:
http://stonecenter.tulane.edu/pages/detail/48/
Lending-Library
Email Address: crcrts@tulane.edu

Pancho Villa

Francisco Villa began as a cattle thief and bandit and ended his life as a champion of Mexico's peasants.

Availability:	Schools, libraries, and nursing homes in the United States.
Suggested Grade:	6-12
Order Number:	HCMEX7-video
Production Date:	1982
Format:	VHS videotape
Terms:	Borrowers must have a User's Agreement on file with this source--available by mail or via the Internet. Return postage is paid by borrower; return 12 days after showing. Book at least three weeks in advance. All borrowers are limited to a total of ten items per semester.

Source: Latin American Resource Center
Stone Center for Latin American Studies
Tulane University
100 Jones Hall
New Orleans, LA 70118
Phone: 1-504-862-3143
Fax: 1-504-865-6719
World Wide Web URL:
http://stonecenter.tulane.edu/pages/detail/48/
Lending-Library
Email Address: crcrts@tulane.edu

Rigoberta Menchu: Broken Silence

This extraordinary woman, a human rights activist, has become a symbol of the sufferings of the indigenous people of the Americas.

Availability:	Schools, libraries, and nursing homes in the United States.

Suggested Grade: 6-12
Order Number: INDGUA3-video
Production Date: 1993
Format: VHS videotape
Terms: Borrowers must have a User's Agreement on file with this source--available by mail or via the Internet. Return postage is paid by borrower; return 12 days after showing. Book at least three weeks in advance. All borrowers are limited to a total of ten items per semester.

Source: Latin American Resource Center
Stone Center for Latin American Studies
Tulane University
100 Jones Hall
New Orleans, LA 70118
Phone: 1-504-862-3143
Fax: 1-504-865-6719
World Wide Web URL:
http://stonecenter.tulane.edu/pages/detail/48/
Lending-Library
Email Address: crcrts@tulane.edu

Sokui-no-Rei, The
Shows the history of Emperor Akihito, his leisure activities, and his love of the environment. The full accession ceremony is shown with glimpses of the parade and court banquet.
Availability: Schools, libraries and homeschoolers in Alabama, Georgia, North Carolina, South Carolina, and Virginia.
Suggested Grade: 4-12
Order Number: 013
Production Date: 1992
Format: VHS videotape

Terms: Borrower pays return postage. Two tapes may be borrowed at a time. Return within 7 days after receipt. Reservations may be made by filling the application found on the web site.

Source: Consulate General of Japan, Atlanta
Japan Information Center
One Alliance Center
3500 Lenox Road, Suite 1600
Atlanta, GA 30326
Phone: 1-404-365-9240
Fax: 1-404-240-4311
World Wide Web URL:
http://www.atlanta.us.emb-japan.go.jp
Email Address: info@cgjapanatlanta.org

Sokui-no-Rei, The
Shows the history of Emperor Akihito, his leisure activities, and his love of the environment. The full accession ceremony is shown with glimpses of the parade and court banquet.
Availability: Schools, libraries, and nursing homes in Hawaii.
Suggested Grade: 4-12
Order Number: CU-1
Format: VHS videotape
Terms: Borrower pays return postage. A maximum of 3 videos may be borrowed per person. Return within one week of date borrowed.

Source: Consulate General of Japan, Honolulu
1742 Nuuanu Avenue
Honolulu, HI 96817-3294
Phone: 1-808-543-3111
Fax: 1-808-543-3170
World Wide Web URL:
http://www.honolulu.us.emb-japan.go.jp

Sokui-no-Rei, The
Shows the history of Emperor Akihito, his leisure activities, and his love of the environment. The full accession ceremony is shown with glimpses of the parade and court banquet.
Availability: Schools, libraries, homeschoolers, and nursing homes in OREGON AND SOUTHERN IDAHO ONLY. Please make requests via the web site.
Suggested Grade: 4-12
Order Number: 402
Production Date: 1992
Format: VHS videotape
Terms: Borrower pays return postage. Return within three weeks after scheduled showing date. Book one month in advance if possible. Rewind the video and wrap securely for return. Be certain to indicate video number, date needed, name of your organization, and address to which video should be sent, along with phone number. Audience report enclosed with the video must be completed and returned.

Source: Consulate General of Japan, Oregon
Attn: Tamara, Video Library
1300 S. W. Fifth Avenue, Suite 2700
Portland, OR 97201
Phone: 1-503-221-1811, ext. 17
World Wide Web URL:
http://www.portland.us.emb-japan.go.jp/en/index.html
Email Address: tamara@cgjpdx.org

Academy of San Carlos, The

The role of the Academy in Mexican art form from the late 18th century to early 20th century.

Availability: Schools, libraries, and nursing homes in the United States.
Suggested Grade: 6-12
Order Number: AMEX2-video
Production Date: 1994
Format: VHS videotape
Terms: Borrowers must have a User's Agreement on file with this source--available by mail or via the Internet. Return postage is paid by borrower; return 12 days after showing. Book at least three weeks in advance. All borrowers are limited to a total of ten items per semester.

Source: Latin American Resource Center
Stone Center for Latin American Studies
Tulane University
100 Jones Hall
New Orleans, LA 70118
Phone: 1-504-862-3143
Fax: 1-504-865-6719
World Wide Web URL:
http://stonecenter.tulane.edu/pages/detail/48/
Lending-Library
Email Address: crcrts@tulane.edu

Adoration of the Magi

Close-ups of the Florentine painting of the Adoration by Fra Angelico and Fra Filippo Lippi are accompanied by verses from the Coventry cycle miracle plays and medieval and Renaissance music.

Availability: Schools, community groups, homeschoolers and individuals in the United States.
Suggested Grade: 7-12
Order Number: VC 114
Format: VHS videotape
Special Notes: Programs may not be broadcast, reproduced, or transferred to another medium or format without special license from the National Gallery of Art. Closed captioned version also available as CC 114.
Terms: Borrower pays return postage. Return within 5 days of scheduled use. Book at least one month in advance, and provide alternate date. You will receive a confirmation noting our Shipping Date and your Return Date for each program. Large organizations that can provide programs to extensive audiences--such as school systems, instructional resource centers, museums, libraries, and public and instructional television stations--can arrange an Affiliate Loan for three years, with subsequent renewal to provide their audiences more immediate access to these free-loan extension programs.

Source: National Gallery of Art
Department of Education Resources
2000B South Club Drive
Landover, MD 20785
Phone: 1-202-842-6280
Fax: 1-202-842-6937

World Wide Web URL:
http://www.nga.gov/education/classroom/loanfinder/
Email Address: EdResources@nga.gov

Alejandro Obregon Paints a Fresco

The Colombian painter demonstrates fresco techniques.

Availability: Schools, libraries, and nursing homes in the United States.
Suggested Grade: 6-12
Order Number: AMCOL3-video
Production Date: 1970
Format: VHS videotape
Terms: Borrowers must have a User's Agreement on file with this source--available by mail or via the Internet. Return postage is paid by borrower; return 12 days after showing. Book at least three weeks in advance. All borrowers are limited to a total of ten items per semester.

Source: Latin American Resource Center
Stone Center for Latin American Studies
Tulane University
100 Jones Hall
New Orleans, LA 70118
Phone: 1-504-862-3143
Fax: 1-504-865-6719
World Wide Web URL:
http://stonecenter.tulane.edu/pages/detail/48/
Lending-Library
Email Address: crcrts@tulane.edu

American Impressionist, An: William Merritt Chase at Shinnecock

Highlights Chase's years at Shinnecock, on Long Island, New York, where in 1891 the artist established the first important outdoor summer school of art in America.

Availability: Schools, community groups, homeschoolers and individuals in the United States.
Suggested Grade: 7-12
Order Number: VC 150
Format: VHS videotape
Special Notes: Programs may not be broadcast, reproduced, or transferred to another medium or format without special license from the National Gallery of Art. Closed captioned version also available as CC 150.
Terms: Borrower pays return postage. Return within 5 days of scheduled use. Book at least one month in advance, and provide alternate date. You will receive a confirmation noting our Shipping Date and your Return Date for each program. Large organizations that can provide programs to extensive audiences--such as school systems, instructional resource centers, museums, libraries, and public and instructional television stations--can arrange an Affiliate Loan for three years, with subsequent renewal to provide their audiences more immediate access to these free-loan extension programs.

Source: National Gallery of Art
Department of Education Resources
2000B South Club Drive
Landover, MD 20785

Phone: 1-202-842-6280
Fax: 1-202-842-6937
World Wide Web URL:
http://www.nga.gov/education/classroom/loanfinder/
Email Address: EdResources@nga.gov

Art and Meaning of Ikebana, The

The significance of Ikebana and the underlying thought and emotion of this unique art are shown through explanations of its historical development, theory, practice, and its relationship to modern daily life.

Availability: Schools, libraries, and nursing homes in Illinois, Indiana, Iowa, Kansas, Minnesota, Missouri, Nebraska, North Dakota, South Dakota, and Wisconsin.
Suggested Grade: 4-Adult
Order Number: 04002
Production Date: 1972
Format: VHS videotape
Terms: Borrower pays return postage by U. S. Mail, UPS, or Federal Express, including insurance for "original" videos. Write, call, fax, or e-mail to request an application. An application form MUST be sent in one month in advance but not more than six months in advance. Include alternate titles and dates if provider can substitute titles. Send a SASE with request if you require confirmation. Return immediately after scheduled showing date. Videos may not be copied or broadcast without permission from the producer of the video. Borrower is responsible if video is lost or damaged.
Source: Consulate General of Japan at Chicago
Japan Information Center
Library
737 North Michigan Avenue, Suite 1000
Chicago, IL 60611
Phone: 1-312-280-0430
Fax: 1-312-280-6883
World Wide Web URL:
http://www.chicago.us.emb-japan.go.jp/jic.html
Email Address: jicchicago@webkddi.com

Art and Revolution in Mexico

Abstract documentary deals with the art of the Mexican Revolution.

Availability: Schools and libraries in the United States and Canada.
Suggested Grade: 6-12
Order Number: order by title
Format: DVD
Terms: Videos will typically be lent for seven days if mailed out--due date will be indicated. Films not returned within the time limit will be subject to overdue fines of $2 per video, per day. All borrowed must have a lending agreement on file. Form can be downloaded from http://isa.unc.edu/film/borrow.asp|aform. Borrowers are responsible for the cost of return shipping. Materials must be returned via a shipping method that has tracking information.

Source: Latin American Film Collection
3219 Fed Ex Global Education Center
301 Pittsboro Street, CB 3205
Chapel Hill, NC 27599-3205
Email Address: LA_Films@email.unc.edu

Art Nouveau 1890-1914

Explores the development of Art Nouveau in Europe and North America, focusing on works of art and architectural landmarks.

Availability: Schools, community groups, homeschoolers and individuals in the United States.
Suggested Grade: 7-12
Order Number: VC 163
Format: VHS videotape
Special Notes: Programs may not be broadcast, reproduced, or transferred to another medium or format without special license from the National Gallery of Art. Closed captioned version also available as CC 163.
Terms: Borrower pays return postage. Return within 5 days of scheduled use. Book at least one month in advance, and provide alternate date. You will receive a confirmation noting our Shipping Date and your Return Date for each program. Large organizations that can provide programs to extensive audiences--such as school systems, instructional resource centers, museums, libraries, and public and instructional television stations--can arrange an Affiliate Loan for three years, with subsequent renewal to provide their audiences more immediate access to these free-loan extension programs.
Source: National Gallery of Art
Department of Education Resources
2000B South Club Drive
Landover, MD 20785
Phone: 1-202-842-6280
Fax: 1-202-842-6937
World Wide Web URL:
http://www.nga.gov/education/classroom/loanfinder/
Email Address: EdResources@nga.gov

Art of Haiti, The

Juxtaposes shots of contemporary Haiti with radiance of Haitian art. Examines the co-existence of Christian and voodoo beliefs.

Availability: Schools, libraries, and nursing homes in the United States.
Suggested Grade: 6-12
Order Number: AMHAI2-video
Format: VHS videotape
Terms: Borrowers must have a User's Agreement on file with this source--available by mail or via the Internet. Return postage is paid by borrower; return 12 days after showing. Book at least three weeks in advance. All borrowers are limited to a total of ten items per semester.
Source: Latin American Resource Center
Stone Center for Latin American Studies
Tulane University, 100 Jones Hall
New Orleans, LA 70118

Phone: 1-504-862-3143
Fax: 1-504-865-6719
World Wide Web URL:
http://stonecenter.tulane.edu/pages/detail/48/
Lending-Library
Email Address: crcrts@tulane.edu

Art of Indonesia

This documentary explores Indonesia's ancient treasures and its "shadow world," the rituals, myths, and performances by which the harmony of the universe is maintained. Weaving together old Javanese poetry, sculpture, stunning landscapes, music, and performances by traditional artists, this visually and acoustically splendid video introduces viewers to the myths and symbols that have permeated Indonesian culture for more than a thousand years. Shot on location in Java and Bali, this videotape presents beautiful images of the artistry and history of Indonesia.

Availability: Schools, community groups, homeschoolers and individuals in the United States.
Suggested Grade: 7-12
Order Number: VC 209
Format: VHS videotape
Special Notes: Programs may not be broadcast, reproduced, or transferred to another medium or format without special license from the National Gallery of Art. Closed captioned version also available as CC 209.
Terms: Borrower pays return postage. Return within 5 days of scheduled use. Book at least one month in advance, and provide alternate date. You will receive a confirmation noting our Shipping Date and your Return Date for each program. Large organizations that can provide programs to extensive audiences--such as school systems, instructional resource centers, museums, libraries, and public and instructional television stations--can arrange an Affiliate Loan for three years, with subsequent renewal to provide their audiences more immediate access to these free-loan extension programs.

Source: National Gallery of Art
Department of Education Resources
2000B South Club Drive
Landover, MD 20785
Phone: 1-202-842-6280
Fax: 1-202-842-6937
World Wide Web URL:
http://www.nga.gov/education/classroom/loanfinder/
Email Address: EdResources@nga.gov

Art of Mexico, Central America, & South America, The

Narration and photos provide overview of Latin American art.

Availability: Schools, libraries, and nursing homes in the United States.
Suggested Grade: 6-12
Order Number: ALA2-video
Production Date: 1993
Format: VHS videotape

Special Notes: Accompanying guide with additional information.
Terms: Borrowers must have a User's Agreement on file with this source--available by mail or via the Internet. Return postage is paid by borrower; return 12 days after showing. Book at least three weeks in advance. All borrowers are limited to a total of ten items per semester.

Source: Latin American Resource Center
Stone Center for Latin American Studies
Tulane University
100 Jones Hall
New Orleans, LA 70118
Phone: 1-504-862-3143
Fax: 1-504-865-6719
World Wide Web URL:
http://stonecenter.tulane.edu/pages/detail/48/
Lending-Library
Email Address: crcrts@tulane.edu

Art of Romare Bearden, The

Narrated by Morgan Freeman with readings by Danny Glover, this film traces Bearden's career using new and archival footage to demonstrate the artistic impact of his memories and art historical models.

Availability: Schools, community groups, homeschoolers and individuals in the United States.
Suggested Grade: 7-12
Order Number: VC 170
Format: VHS videotape
Special Notes: Programs may not be broadcast, reproduced, or transferred to another medium or format without special license from the National Gallery of Art. Closed captioned version also available as CC 170.
Terms: Borrower pays return postage. Return within 5 days of scheduled use. Book at least one month in advance, and provide alternate date. You will receive a confirmation noting our Shipping Date and your Return Date for each program. Large organizations that can provide programs to extensive audiences--such as school systems, instructional resource centers, museums, libraries, and public and instructional television stations--can arrange an Affiliate Loan for three years, with subsequent renewal to provide their audiences more immediate access to these free-loan extension programs.

Source: National Gallery of Art
Department of Education Resources
2000B South Club Drive
Landover, MD 20785
Phone: 1-202-842-6280
Fax: 1-202-842-6937
World Wide Web URL:
http://www.nga.gov/education/classroom/loanfinder/
Email Address: EdResources@nga.gov

Art of the Fantastic, The

Review of exhibition of Latin American contemporary art at the Indianapolis Museum of Art.

Availability: Schools, libraries, and nursing homes in the United States.
Suggested Grade: 6-12
Order Number: AMLA10-video
Production Date: 1987
Format: VHS videotape
Terms: Borrowers must have a User's Agreement on file with this source--available by mail or via the Internet. Return postage is paid by borrower; return 12 days after showing. Book at least three weeks in advance. All borrowers are limited to a total of ten items per semester.

Source: Latin American Resource Center
Stone Center for Latin American Studies
Tulane University
100 Jones Hall
New Orleans, LA 70118
Phone: 1-504-862-3143
Fax: 1-504-865-6719
World Wide Web URL:
http://stonecenter.tulane.edu/pages/detail/48/
Lending-Library
Email Address: crcrts@tulane.edu

Art + Science = Conservation

Introduces the concepts of art and science in museum conservation. Takes viewers behind the scenes to a conservation lab and discusses conservation issues related to art objects. Discussion is focused on the effects of light on works of paper, environmental conditions on outdoor sculpture, and the use of varnish on oil painting.

Availability: Schools, community groups, homeschoolers and individuals in the United States.
Suggested Grade: 7-12
Order Number: VC 166
Format: VHS videotape
Special Notes: Programs may not be broadcast, reproduced, or transferred to another medium or format without special license from the National Gallery of Art. Closed captioned version also available as CC 166.
Terms: Borrower pays return postage. Return within 5 days of scheduled use. Book at least one month in advance, and provide alternate date. You will receive a confirmation noting our Shipping Date and your Return Date for each program. Large organizations that can provide programs to extensive audiences--such as school systems, instructional resource centers, museums, libraries, and public and instructional television stations--can arrange an Affiliate Loan for three years, with subsequent renewal to provide their audiences more immediate access to these free-loan extension programs.

Source: National Gallery of Art
Department of Education Resources
2000B South Club Drive
Landover, MD 20785
Phone: 1-202-842-6280
Fax: 1-202-842-6937
World Wide Web URL:
http://www.nga.gov/education/classroom/loanfinder/
Email Address: EdResources@nga.gov

Arts in Every Classroom, The: A Video Library, K-5

The programs in this video library show classroom teachers and arts specialists using the arts in a variety of successful ways. The 14 video programs - filmed in elementary schools around the country - along with a print guide and companion Web site, serve as a professional development resource for K-5 teachers seeking new ideas for integrating the arts into the classroom. Produced by Lavine Production Group.

Availability: All requesters
Suggested Grade: Teacher Reference
Order Number: not applicable
Production Date: 2003
Format: Streaming Video
Special Notes: Also available for purchase for $330.00.
Terms: A simple FREE registration is required to view videos.

Source: Annenberg Media
World Wide Web URL:
http://www.learner.org/resources/browse.html

Awareness Series: American Art

Short, evocative studies of the works of major artists represented in the collections of the National Gallery of Art: Copley, Catlin, Cassatt, and American Native painters. Programs are not intended as definitive studies of these artists; rather, each is designed as a starting point for group discussion of the art and artist. Segments may be used independently, in any order or combination.

Availability: Schools, community groups, homeschoolers and individuals in the United States.
Suggested Grade: 7-12
Order Number: VC 125
Format: VHS videotape
Special Notes: Programs may not be broadcast, reproduced, or transferred to another medium or format without special license from the National Gallery of Art. Closed captioned version also available as CC 125.
Terms: Borrower pays return postage. Return within 5 days of scheduled use. Book at least one month in advance, and provide alternate date. You will receive a confirmation noting our Shipping Date and your Return Date for each program. Large organizations that can provide programs to extensive audiences--such as school systems, instructional resource centers, museums, libraries, and public and instructional television stations--can arrange an Affiliate Loan for three years, with subsequent renewal to provide their audiences more immediate access to these free-loan extension programs.

Source: National Gallery of Art
Department of Education Resources
2000B South Club Drive
Landover, MD 20785
Phone: 1-202-842-6280
Fax: 1-202-842-6937
World Wide Web URL:
http://www.nga.gov/education/classroom/loanfinder/
Email Address: EdResources@nga.gov

Awareness Series: Modern Masters

Short, evocative studies of the works of major artists represented in the collections of the National Gallery of Art: Monet, Renoir, Degas, Cassatt, Gauguin, Cézanne, and Picasso. Programs are not intended as definitive studies of these artists; rather, each is designed as a starting point for group discussion of the art and artist. Segments may be used independently, in any order or combination.

Availability: Schools, community groups, homeschoolers and individuals in the United States.
Suggested Grade: 7-12
Order Number: VC 120
Format: VHS videotape
Special Notes: Programs may not be broadcast, reproduced, or transferred to another medium or format without special license from the National Gallery of Art. Closed captioned version also available as CC 120.
Terms: Borrower pays return postage. Return within 5 days of scheduled use. Book at least one month in advance, and provide alternate date. You will receive a confirmation noting our Shipping Date and your Return Date for each program. Large organizations that can provide programs to extensive audiences--such as school systems, instructional resource centers, museums, libraries, and public and instructional television stations--can arrange an Affiliate Loan for three years, with subsequent renewal to provide their audiences more immediate access to these free-loan extension programs.

Source: National Gallery of Art
Department of Education Resources
2000B South Club Drive
Landover, MD 20785
Phone: 1-202-842-6280
Fax: 1-202-842-6937
World Wide Web URL:
http://www.nga.gov/education/classroom/loanfinder/
Email Address: EdResources@nga.gov

Awareness Series: Old Masters

Short, evocative studies of the works of major artists represented in the collections of the National Gallery of Art: Rembrandt, Rubens, El Greco, Fragonard, Goya, Blake, and Turner. Programs are not intended as definitive studies of these artists; rather, each is designed as a starting point for group discussion of the art and artist. Segments may be used independently, in any order or combination.

Availability: Schools, community groups, homeschoolers and individuals in the United States.
Suggested Grade: 7-12
Order Number: VC 115
Format: VHS videotape
Special Notes: Programs may not be broadcast, reproduced, or transferred to another medium or format without special license from the National Gallery of Art. Closed captioned version also available as CC 115.

Terms: Borrower pays return postage. Return within 5 days of scheduled use. Book at least one month in advance, and provide alternate date. You will receive a confirmation noting our Shipping Date and your Return Date for each program. Large organizations that can provide programs to extensive audiences--such as school systems, instructional resource centers, museums, libraries, and public and instructional television stations--can arrange an Affiliate Loan for three years, with subsequent renewal to provide their audiences more immediate access to these free-loan extension programs.

Source: National Gallery of Art
Department of Education Resources
2000B South Club Drive
Landover, MD 20785
Phone: 1-202-842-6280
Fax: 1-202-842-6937
World Wide Web URL:
http://www.nga.gov/education/classroom/loanfinder/
Email Address: EdResources@nga.gov

Caricatures and How to Draw Them

Presents simple procedures for creating character drawings and stresses the importance of carefully observing a person.

Availability: Schools, libraries, and homeschoolers in the United States who serve the hearing impaired.
Suggested Grade: 7-13
Order Number: 24079
Production Date: 1995
Format: DVD
Special Notes: Also available as live streaming video over the Internet.
Terms: Sponsor pays all transportation costs. Return one week after receipt. Participation is limited to deaf or hard of hearing Americans, their parents, families, teachers, counselors, or others whose use would benefit a deaf or hard of hearing person. Only one person in the audience needs to be hearing impaired. You must register--which is free. These videos are all open-captioned--no special equipment is required for viewing.

Source: Described and Captioned Media Program
National Association of the Deaf
4211 Church Street Ext.
Roebuck, SC 29376
Phone: 1-800-237-6213
Fax: 1-800-538-5636
World Wide Web URL: http://www.dcmp.org

Cartoon Magic With Fran

Demonstrates step by step how to create cartoon figures. Also gives ideas for ways to use these figures in greeting cards, and others.

Availability: Schools, libraries, and homeschoolers in the United States who serve the hearing impaired.
Suggested Grade: All ages
Order Number: 13209
Production Date: 1996
Format: DVD

Terms: Sponsor pays all transportation costs. Return one week after receipt. Participation is limited to deaf or hard of hearing Americans, their parents, families, teachers, counselors, or others whose use would benefit a deaf or hard of hearing person. Only one person in the audience needs to be hearing impaired. You must register--which is free. These videos are all open-captioned--no special equipment is required for viewing.

Source: Described and Captioned Media Program
National Association of the Deaf
4211 Church Street Ext.
Roebuck, SC 29376
Phone: 1-800-237-6213
Fax: 1-800-538-5636
World Wide Web URL: http://www.dcmp.org

Chancay, the Forgotten Art
Famous pre-Columbian ceramics from Peru.
Availability: Schools, libraries, and nursing homes in the United States.
Suggested Grade: 6-12
Order Number: APPER1-video
Production Date: 1970
Format: VHS videotape
Terms: Borrowers must have a User's Agreement on file with this source--available by mail or via the Internet. Return postage is paid by borrower; return 12 days after showing. Book at least three weeks in advance. All borrowers are limited to a total of ten items per semester.
Source: Latin American Resource Center
Stone Center for Latin American Studies
Tulane University
100 Jones Hall
New Orleans, LA 70118
Phone: 1-504-862-3143
Fax: 1-504-865-6719
World Wide Web URL:
http://stonecenter.tulane.edu/pages/detail/48/
Lending-Library
Email Address: crcrts@tulane.edu

Chinese Brush Painting
Easy to follow and sure to inspire, this videotape shows how to paint in this style.
Availability: Schools, libraries, homeschoolers, and nursing homes in the United States and Canada.
Suggested Grade: 6-12
Order Number: order by title
Production Date: 1989
Format: VHS videotape
Terms: Postage is paid by borrower both ways--send $3.00 per tape to cover initial shipping to you--MONEY MUST BE SENT WITH REQUEST. Return 10 days after showing via U. S. Postal Service, library rate. Shipping is $5.00 to Canadian addresses.
Source: Center for Teaching About China
Kathleen Trescott
1214 West Schwartz
Carbondale, IL 62901

Phone: 1-618-549-1555
Email Address: trescott@midwest.net

Collage Methods
Collage: gluing paper onto paper or another background. Collagist Gerald Brommer demonstrates and explains the techniques to creating four different kinds of collages: transparent tissue paper, opaque paper, partially integrated collage, and an autobiographical photo montage. As he creates, Brommer offers suggestions and tips for a more successful product.
Availability: Schools, libraries, and homeschoolers in the United States who serve the hearing impaired.
Suggested Grade: 4-Adult
Order Number: 12338
Production Date: 1994
Format: DVD
Special Notes: Produced by Crystal Productions.
Terms: Sponsor pays all transportation costs. Return one week after receipt. Participation is limited to deaf or hard of hearing Americans, their parents, families, teachers, counselors, or others whose use would benefit a deaf or hard of hearing person. Only one person in the audience needs to be hearing impaired. You must register--which is free. These videos are all open-captioned--no special equipment is required for viewing.
Source: Described and Captioned Media Program
National Association of the Deaf
4211 Church Street Ext.
Roebuck, SC 29376
Phone: 1-800-237-6213
Fax: 1-800-538-5636
World Wide Web URL: http://www.dcmp.org

Computer Art Projects for Young People: Volume 2
Learn how to create six computer craft projects.
Availability: Schools, libraries, and homeschoolers in the United States who serve the hearing impaired.
Suggested Grade: All ages
Order Number: 11414
Production Date: 2003
Format: DVD
Terms: Sponsor pays all transportation costs. Return one week after receipt. Participation is limited to deaf or hard of hearing Americans, their parents, families, teachers, counselors, or others whose use would benefit a deaf or hard of hearing person. Only one person in the audience needs to be hearing impaired. You must register--which is free. These videos are all open-captioned--no special equipment is required for viewing.
Source: Described and Captioned Media Program
National Association of the Deaf
4211 Church Street Ext.
Roebuck, SC 29376
Phone: 1-800-237-6213
Fax: 1-800-538-5636
World Wide Web URL: http://www.dcmp.org

Courtly Art of Ancient Maya

Presents the culture and society that created the most advanced civilization of ancient Mesoamerica. Filmed in the state of Chiapas in southern Mexico, the program focuses on the courts of the Maya kingdoms of Palenque, Tonina, and Bonampak.

Availability: Schools, community groups, homeschoolers and individuals in the United States.
Suggested Grade: 7-12
Order Number: VC 171
Format: VHS videotape
Special Notes: Programs may not be broadcast, reproduced, or transferred to another medium or format without special license from the National Gallery of Art. Closed captioned version also available as CC 171.
Terms: Borrower pays return postage. Return within 5 days of scheduled use. Book at least one month in advance, and provide alternate date. You will receive a confirmation noting our Shipping Date and your Return Date for each program. Large organizations that can provide programs to extensive audiences--such as school systems, instructional resource centers, museums, libraries, and public and instructional television stations--can arrange an Affiliate Loan for three years, with subsequent renewal to provide their audiences more immediate access to these free-loan extension programs.

Source: National Gallery of Art
Department of Education Resources
2000B South Club Drive
Landover, MD 20785
Phone: 1-202-842-6280
Fax: 1-202-842-6937
World Wide Web URL:
http://www.nga.gov/education/classroom/loanfinder/
Email Address: EdResources@nga.gov

Crafting in the USA: Appalachia Region

Shows how to create five crafts that represent this region.

Availability: Schools, libraries, and homeschoolers in the United States who serve the hearing impaired.
Suggested Grade: 5-12
Order Number: 11827
Production Date: 2003
Format: DVD
Special Notes: Also available as live streaming video over the Internet.
Terms: Sponsor pays all transportation costs. Return one week after receipt. Participation is limited to deaf or hard of hearing Americans, their parents, families, teachers, counselors, or others whose use would benefit a deaf or hard of hearing person. Only one person in the audience needs to be hearing impaired. You must register--which is free. These videos are all open-captioned--no special equipment is required for viewing.

Source: Described and Captioned Media Program
National Association of the Deaf
4211 Church Street Ext.
Roebuck, SC 29376

Phone: 1-800-237-6213
Fax: 1-800-538-5636
World Wide Web URL: http://www.dcmp.org

Crafting in the USA: Folklore

Learn to make five easy crafts that represent some of the folklore and tall tale heroes of the United States.

Availability: Schools, libraries, and homeschoolers in the United States who serve the hearing impaired.
Suggested Grade: 5-12
Order Number: 11141
Production Date: 2003
Format: DVD
Special Notes: Also available as live streaming video over the Internet.
Terms: Sponsor pays all transportation costs. Return one week after receipt. Participation is limited to deaf or hard of hearing Americans, their parents, families, teachers, counselors, or others whose use would benefit a deaf or hard of hearing person. Only one person in the audience needs to be hearing impaired. You must register--which is free. These videos are all open-captioned--no special equipment is required for viewing.

Source: Described and Captioned Media Program
National Association of the Deaf
4211 Church Street Ext.
Roebuck, SC 29376
Phone: 1-800-237-6213
Fax: 1-800-538-5636
World Wide Web URL: http://www.dcmp.org

Crafting in the USA: Hawaii

Enjoy making six crafts that represent the cultures and products of Hawaii.

Availability: Schools, libraries, and homeschoolers in the United States who serve the hearing impaired.
Suggested Grade: 5-12
Order Number: 11783
Production Date: 2003
Format: DVD
Special Notes: Also available as live streaming video over the Internet.
Terms: Sponsor pays all transportation costs. Return one week after receipt. Participation is limited to deaf or hard of hearing Americans, their parents, families, teachers, counselors, or others whose use would benefit a deaf or hard of hearing person. Only one person in the audience needs to be hearing impaired. You must register--which is free. These videos are all open-captioned--no special equipment is required for viewing.

Source: Described and Captioned Media Program
National Association of the Deaf
4211 Church Street Ext.
Roebuck, SC 29376
Phone: 1-800-237-6213
Fax: 1-800-538-5636
World Wide Web URL: http://www.dcmp.org

Crafts in Less than 10 Minutes Vol. 1

Demonstrates step by step how to make numerous craft items which take very little time-bookmarks, garden gloves, lacy sun catchers, paper hearts, chenille bow, decorator mothballs, key ornaments, wine bottle covers, and oatmeal soothers.

Availability:	Schools, libraries, and homeschoolers in the United States who serve the hearing impaired.
Suggested Grade:	All ages
Order Number:	13323
Format:	DVD
Special Notes:	Also available as live streaming video over the Internet.

Terms: Sponsor pays all transportation costs. Return one week after receipt. Participation is limited to deaf or hard of hearing Americans, their parents, families, teachers, counselors, or others whose use would benefit a deaf or hard of hearing person. Only one person in the audience needs to be hearing impaired. You must register--which is free. These videos are all open-captioned--no special equipment is required for viewing.

Source: Described and Captioned Media Program
National Association of the Deaf
4211 Church Street Ext.
Roebuck, SC 29376
Phone: 1-800-237-6213
Fax: 1-800-538-5636
World Wide Web URL: http://www.dcmp.org

Crayons and Markers

Gives a brief history of writing and drawing from prehistoric humans to the present, including some writing implements. Visits a factory where crayons and markers are made, noting that one hundred million crayons are made annually.

Availability:	Schools, libraries, and homeschoolers in the United States who serve the hearing impaired.
Suggested Grade:	preK-4
Order Number:	13118
Production Date:	1994
Format:	DVD
Special Notes:	Produced by Fims for the Humanities & Sciences.

Terms: Sponsor pays all transportation costs. Return one week after receipt. Participation is limited to deaf or hard of hearing Americans, their parents, families, teachers, counselors, or others whose use would benefit a deaf or hard of hearing person. Only one person in the audience needs to be hearing impaired. You must register--which is free. These videos are all open-captioned--no special equipment is required for viewing.

Source: Described and Captioned Media Program
National Association of the Deaf
4211 Church Street Ext.
Roebuck, SC 29376
Phone: 1-800-237-6213
Fax: 1-800-538-5636
World Wide Web URL: http://www.dcmp.org

Creating Abstract Art

Abstract art: taking a recognizable object, making it as simple as possible, and distorting it to fit the artist's purpose. Step-by-step, artist Gerald Brommer shows how to create abstraction, using five methods: simplification of shapes, distortion, overlapping and fracturing shapes, vertical displacement, and contour continuation.

Availability:	Schools, libraries, and homeschoolers in the United States who serve the hearing impaired.
Suggested Grade:	6-Adult
Order Number:	12986
Production Date:	1994
Format:	DVD
Special Notes:	Produced by Crystal Productions.

Terms: Sponsor pays all transportation costs. Return one week after receipt. Participation is limited to deaf or hard of hearing Americans, their parents, families, teachers, counselors, or others whose use would benefit a deaf or hard of hearing person. Only one person in the audience needs to be hearing impaired. You must register--which is free. These videos are all open-captioned--no special equipment is required for viewing.

Source: Described and Captioned Media Program
National Association of the Deaf
4211 Church Street Ext.
Roebuck, SC 29376
Phone: 1-800-237-6213
Fax: 1-800-538-5636
World Wide Web URL: http://www.dcmp.org

Daimyo

This program explores and illustrates the dual way of the Daimyo culture of feudal Japan, one that combined the arts of war and the arts of the pen. This production examines the paradox of the warrior-aesthetic through a survey of the Daimyo arts: architecture, landscape gardening, poetry, calligraphy, painting, the tea ceremony, the No theatre and "Kendo," or swordsmanship. This unique blend of martial and aesthetic excellence was central to the shaping of Japanese culture, and its effects are present even today.

Availability:	Schools, community groups, homeschoolers and individuals in the United States.
Suggested Grade:	7-12
Order Number:	VC 205
Format:	VHS videotape
Special Notes:	Programs may not be broadcast, reproduced, or transferred to another medium or format without special license from the National Gallery of Art. Closed captioned version also available as CC 205.

Terms: Borrower pays return postage. Return within 5 days of scheduled use. Book at least one month in advance, and provide alternate date. You will receive a confirmation noting our Shipping Date and your Return Date for each program. Large organizations that can provide programs to extensive audiences--such as school systems, instructional resource centers, museums, libraries, and public and instructional television stations--can arrange an Affiliate Loan for three years, with subsequent renewal to provide their audiences more immediate access to these free-loan extension programs.

Source: National Gallery of Art
Department of Education Resources
2000B South Club Drive
Landover, MD 20785
Phone: 1-202-842-6280
Fax: 1-202-842-6937
World Wide Web URL:
http://www.nga.gov/education/classroom/loanfinder/
Email Address: EdResources@nga.gov

Doll Master and His Apprentice, The

Features the traditional Japanese art form of doll making by a master doll maker.

Availability: Schools, libraries, and nursing homes in Hawaii.
Suggested Grade: All ages
Order Number: CU-36
Production Date: 1985
Format: VHS videotape
Terms: Borrower pays return postage. A maximum of 3 videos may be borrowed per person. Return within one week of date borrowed.

Source: Consulate General of Japan, Honolulu
1742 Nuuanu Avenue
Honolulu, HI 96817-3294
Phone: 1-808-543-3111
Fax: 1-808-543-3170
World Wide Web URL:
http://www.honolulu.us.emb-japan.go.jp

Doll Master and His Apprentice, The

Features the traditional Japanese art form of doll making by a master doll maker.

Availability: Schools, libraries, homeschoolers, and nursing homes in OREGON AND SOUTHERN IDAHO ONLY. Please make requests via the web site.
Suggested Grade: All ages
Order Number: 205
Production Date: 1985
Format: VHS videotape
Terms: Borrower pays return postage. Return within three weeks after scheduled showing date. Book one month in advance if possible. Rewind the video and wrap securely for return. Be certain to indicate video number, date needed, name of your organization, and address to which video should be sent, along with phone number. Audience report enclosed with the video must be completed and returned.

Source: Consulate General of Japan, Oregon
Attn: Tamara, Video Library
1300 S. W. Fifth Avenue, Suite 2700
Portland, OR 97201
Phone: 1-503-221-1811, ext. 17
World Wide Web URL:
http://www.portland.us.emb-japan.go.jp/en/index.html
Email Address: tamara@cgjpdx.org

Drawing With Pastels

Artist Gail Price demonstrates the variety of pastels, including hard, soft, oil, iridescent, and pencil. She explains their properties and shows how they enhance a wide selection of subjects and backgrounds. Close-up photography allows a good view of drawing techniques.

Availability: Schools, libraries, and homeschoolers in the United States who serve the hearing impaired.
Suggested Grade: 4-Adult
Order Number: 12339
Production Date: 1994
Format: DVD
Special Notes: Produced by Crystal Productions.
Terms: Sponsor pays all transportation costs. Return one week after receipt. Participation is limited to deaf or hard of hearing Americans, their parents, families, teachers, counselors, or others whose use would benefit a deaf or hard of hearing person. Only one person in the audience needs to be hearing impaired. You must register--which is free. These videos are all open-captioned--no special equipment is required for viewing.

Source: Described and Captioned Media Program
National Association of the Deaf
4211 Church Street Ext.
Roebuck, SC 29376
Phone: 1-800-237-6213
Fax: 1-800-538-5636
World Wide Web URL: http://www.dcmp.org

Easy Art Projects

Artist Donna Hugh demonstrates step-by-step how easy it is to produce inexpensive and satisfying art projects.

Availability: Schools, libraries, and homeschoolers in the United States who serve the hearing impaired.
Suggested Grade: 3-7
Order Number: 12991
Production Date: 1991
Format: DVD
Terms: Sponsor pays all transportation costs. Return one week after receipt. Participation is limited to deaf or hard of hearing Americans, their parents, families, teachers, counselors, or others whose use would benefit a deaf or hard of hearing person. Only one person in the audience needs to be hearing impaired. You must register--which is free. These videos are all open-captioned--no special equipment is required for viewing.

Source: Described and Captioned Media Program
National Association of the Deaf
4211 Church Street Ext.
Roebuck, SC 29376
Phone: 1-800-237-6213
Fax: 1-800-538-5636
World Wide Web URL: http://www.dcmp.org

Easy Watercolor Techniques

Artist Donna Hugh demonstrates basic watercolor techniques in a step-by-step format. She lists needed materials and shows how to mix colors, use the brush, and outline the picture on a "voyage of discovery." The four lessons include: Watercolor Flowers, Watercolor Discovery, Desert Scene, and Opaque Watercolors. Each lesson is complete in itself.

Availability:	Schools, libraries, and homeschoolers in the United States who serve the hearing impaired.
Suggested Grade:	4-12
Order Number:	12992
Production Date:	1991
Format:	DVD
Special Notes:	Produced by Coyote Creek Productions.
Terms:	Sponsor pays all transportation costs. Return one week after receipt. Participation is limited to deaf or hard of hearing Americans, their parents, families, teachers, counselors, or others whose use would benefit a deaf or hard of hearing person. Only one person in the audience needs to be hearing impaired. You must register--which is free. These videos are all open-captioned--no special equipment is required for viewing.

Source: Described and Captioned Media Program
National Association of the Deaf
4211 Church Street Ext.
Roebuck, SC 29376
Phone: 1-800-237-6213
Fax: 1-800-538-5636
World Wide Web URL: http://www.dcmp.org

Edward Hopper

Explores the work of Edward Hopper, one of America's most-admired artists.

Availability:	Schools, community groups, homeschoolers and individuals in the United States.
Suggested Grade:	7-12
Order Number:	VC 174
Format:	VHS videotape
Special Notes:	Programs may not be broadcast, reproduced, or transferred to another medium or format without special license from the National Gallery of Art. Closed captioned.
Terms:	Borrower pays return postage. Return within 5 days of scheduled use. Book at least one month in advance, and provide alternate date. You will receive a confirmation noting our Shipping Date and your Return Date for each program. Large organizations that can provide programs to extensive audiences--such as school systems, instructional resource centers, museums, libraries, and public and instructional television stations--can arrange an Affiliate Loan for three years, with subsequent renewal to provide their audiences more immediate access to these free-loan extension programs.

Source: National Gallery of Art
Department of Education Resources
2000B South Club Drive
Landover, MD 20785
Phone: 1-202-842-6280
Fax: 1-202-842-6937
World Wide Web URL:
http://www.nga.gov/education/classroom/loanfinder/
Email Address: EdResources@nga.gov

Edward Hopper

Explores the work of Edward Hopper, one of America's most-admired artists.

Availability:	Schools, community groups, homeschoolers and individuals in the United States.
Suggested Grade:	7-12
Order Number:	DV 174
Format:	DVD
Special Notes:	Programs may not be broadcast, reproduced, or transferred to another medium or format without special license from the National Gallery of Art. Closed captioned.
Terms:	Borrower pays return postage. Return within 5 days of scheduled use. Book at least one month in advance, and provide alternate date. You will receive a confirmation noting our Shipping Date and your Return Date for each program. Large organizations that can provide programs to extensive audiences--such as school systems, instructional resource centers, museums, libraries, and public and instructional television stations--can arrange an Affiliate Loan for three years, with subsequent renewal to provide their audiences more immediate access to these free-loan extension programs.

Source: National Gallery of Art
Department of Education Resources
2000B South Club Drive
Landover, MD 20785
Phone: 1-202-842-6280
Fax: 1-202-842-6937
World Wide Web URL:
http://www.nga.gov/education/classroom/loanfinder/
Email Address: EdResources@nga.gov

Escape into Fantasy

Japanese artists of the Edo period stimulated their viewers imagination with images of murder, cruelty and sexual perversion, exploring the realm of fantasy.

Availability:	Schools, libraries and homeschoolers in Alabama, Georgia, North Carolina, South Carolina, and Virginia.
Suggested Grade:	7-12
Order Number:	521
Production Date:	1989
Format:	VHS videotape
Special Notes:	No. 8 in the "Japan: Spirit and Form" series.
Terms:	Borrower pays return postage. Two tapes may be borrowed at a time. Return within 7 days after receipt. Reservations may be made by filling the application found on the web site.

Source: Consulate General of Japan, Atlanta
Japan Information Center
One Alliance Center
3500 Lenox Road, Suite 1600
Atlanta, GA 30326
Phone: 1-404-365-9240
Fax: 1-404-240-4311
World Wide Web URL:
http://www.atlanta.us.emb-japan.go.jp
Email Address: info@cgjapanatlanta.org

Escape into Fantasy

Japanese artists of the Edo period stimulated their viewers imagination with images of murder, cruelty and sexual perversion, exploring the realm of fantasy.

Availability: Schools, libraries, and nursing homes in Hawaii.
Suggested Grade: 7-12
Order Number: CU-77
Production Date: 1989
Format: VHS videotape
Special Notes: No. 8 in the "Japan: Spirit and Form" series.
Terms: Borrower pays return postage. A maximum of 3 videos may be borrowed per person. Return within one week of date borrowed.
Source: Consulate General of Japan, Honolulu
1742 Nuuanu Avenue
Honolulu, HI 96817-3294
Phone: 1-808-543-3111
Fax: 1-808-543-3170
World Wide Web URL:
http://www.honolulu.us.emb-japan.go.jp

Escape into Fantasy

Japanese artists of the Edo period stimulated their viewers imagination with images of murder, cruelty and sexual perversion, exploring the realm of fantasy.

Availability: Schools, libraries, homeschoolers, and nursing homes in OREGON AND SOUTHERN IDAHO ONLY. Please make requests via the web site.
Suggested Grade: 7-12
Order Number: 534
Production Date: 1989
Format: VHS videotape
Special Notes: No. 8 in the "Japan: Spirit and Form" series.
Terms: Borrower pays return postage. Return within three weeks after scheduled showing date. Book one month in advance if possible. Rewind the video and wrap securely for return. Be certain to indicate video number, date needed, name of your organization, and address to which video should be sent, along with phone number. Audience report enclosed with the video must be completed and returned.
Source: Consulate General of Japan, Oregon
Attn: Tamara, Video Library
1300 S. W. Fifth Avenue, Suite 2700
Portland, OR 97201
Phone: 1-503-221-1811, ext. 17
World Wide Web URL:
http://www.portland.us.emb-japan.go.jp/en/index.html
Email Address: tamara@cgjpdx.org

Form at the Beginning

Discover the spirit behind the distinctive forms and designs present in Japanese culture. Includes Jomon (loop patterns) ware, Japan's earliest pottery tradition.

Availability: Schools, libraries, and nursing homes in Hawaii.
Suggested Grade: 7-12

Order Number: CU-70
Production Date: 1989
Format: VHS videotape
Special Notes: No. 1 in the "Japan: Spirit and Form" series.
Terms: Borrower pays return postage. A maximum of 3 videos may be borrowed per person. Return within one week of date borrowed.
Source: Consulate General of Japan, Honolulu
1742 Nuuanu Avenue
Honolulu, HI 96817-3294
Phone: 1-808-543-3111
Fax: 1-808-543-3170
World Wide Web URL:
http://www.honolulu.us.emb-japan.go.jp

Form at the Beginning

Discover the spirit behind the distinctive forms and designs present in Japanese culture. Includes Jomon (loop patterns) ware, Japan's earliest pottery tradition.

Availability: Schools, libraries, homeschoolers, and nursing homes in OREGON AND SOUTHERN IDAHO ONLY. Please make requests via the web site.
Suggested Grade: 7-12
Order Number: 527
Production Date: 1989
Format: VHS videotape
Special Notes: No. 1 in the "Japan: Spirit and Form" series.
Terms: Borrower pays return postage. Return within three weeks after scheduled showing date. Book one month in advance if possible. Rewind the video and wrap securely for return. Be certain to indicate video number, date needed, name of your organization, and address to which video should be sent, along with phone number. Audience report enclosed with the video must be completed and returned.
Source: Consulate General of Japan, Oregon
Attn: Tamara, Video Library
1300 S. W. Fifth Avenue, Suite 2700
Portland, OR 97201
Phone: 1-503-221-1811, ext. 17
World Wide Web URL:
http://www.portland.us.emb-japan.go.jp/en/index.html
Email Address: tamara@cgjpdx.org

Henri Rousseau: Jungles in Paris

Considers the art of this self-taught artist.

Availability: Schools, community groups, homeschoolers and individuals in the United States.
Suggested Grade: 7-12
Order Number: VC 173
Format: VHS videotape
Terms: Borrower pays return postage. Return within 5 days of scheduled use. Book at least one month in advance, and provide alternate date. You will receive a confirmation noting our Shipping Date and your Return Date for each program. Large organizations that can provide programs to extensive audiences--such as school systems, instructional resource centers, museums, libraries, and public and instructional television stations--can arrange

an Affiliate Loan for three years, with subsequent renewal to provide their audiences more immediate access to these free-loan extension programs.

Source: National Gallery of Art
Department of Education Resources
2000B South Club Drive
Landover, MD 20785
Phone: 1-202-842-6280
Fax: 1-202-842-6937
World Wide Web URL:
http://www.nga.gov/education/classroom/loanfinder/
Email Address: EdResources@nga.gov

Hokusai Returns

More than 500 woodblock prints were accidentally discovered at the Museum of Fine Art in Boston in 1986. This is the story of the discovery.

Availability: Schools, libraries and homeschoolers in Alabama, Georgia, North Carolina, South Carolina, and Virginia.
Suggested Grade: 7-12
Order Number: 524
Production Date: 1989
Format: VHS videotape
Special Notes: No. 11 in the "Japan: Spirit and Form" series.
Terms: Borrower pays return postage. Two tapes may be borrowed at a time. Return within 7 days after receipt. Reservations may be made by filling the application found on the web site.

Source: Consulate General of Japan, Atlanta
Japan Information Center
One Alliance Center
3500 Lenox Road, Suite 1600
Atlanta, GA 30326
Phone: 1-404-365-9240
Fax: 1-404-240-4311
World Wide Web URL:
http://www.atlanta.us.emb-japan.go.jp
Email Address: info@cgjapanatlanta.org

Hokusai Returns

More than 500 woodblock prints were accidentally discovered at the Museum of Fine Art in Boston in 1986. This is the story of the discovery.

Availability: Schools, libraries, and nursing homes in Hawaii.
Suggested Grade: 7-12
Order Number: CU-78
Production Date: 1989
Format: VHS videotape
Special Notes: No. 11 in the "Japan: Spirit and Form" series.
Terms: Borrower pays return postage. A maximum of 3 videos may be borrowed per person. Return within one week of date borrowed.

Source: Consulate General of Japan, Honolulu
1742 Nuuanu Avenue
Honolulu, HI 96817-3294
Phone: 1-808-543-3111
Fax: 1-808-543-3170

World Wide Web URL:
http://www.honolulu.us.emb-japan.go.jp

Hokusai Returns

More than 500 woodblock prints were accidentally discovered at the Museum of Fine Art in Boston in 1986. This is the story of the discovery.

Availability: Schools, libraries, homeschoolers, and nursing homes in OREGON AND SOUTHERN IDAHO ONLY. Please make requests via the web site.
Suggested Grade: 7-12
Order Number: 537
Production Date: 1989
Format: VHS videotape
Special Notes: No. 11 in the "Japan: Spirit and Form" series.
Terms: Borrower pays return postage. Return within three weeks after scheduled showing date. Book one month in advance if possible. Rewind the video and wrap securely for return. Be certain to indicate video number, date needed, name of your organization, and address to which video should be sent, along with phone number. Audience report enclosed with the video must be completed and returned.

Source: Consulate General of Japan, Oregon
Attn: Tamara, Video Library
1300 S. W. Fifth Avenue, Suite 2700
Portland, OR 97201
Phone: 1-503-221-1811, ext. 17
World Wide Web URL:
http://www.portland.us.emb-japan.go.jp/en/index.html
Email Address: tamara@cgjpdx.org

Ikebana: The Art of Flower Arrangement/The Art & Meaning of Ikebana

A young woman takes a lesson in the art of Ikebana, according to the Ohara School. She learns fundamental styles, shown with superimposed diagrams. An Ikebana exhibition of the major schools concludes the show.

Availability: Schools, libraries, and nursing homes in Hawaii.
Suggested Grade: 6-Adult
Order Number: CU-42
Production Date: 1985
Format: VHS videotape
Terms: Borrower pays return postage. A maximum of 3 videos may be borrowed per person. Return within one week of date borrowed.

Source: Consulate General of Japan, Honolulu
1742 Nuuanu Avenue
Honolulu, HI 96817-3294
Phone: 1-808-543-3111
Fax: 1-808-543-3170
World Wide Web URL:
http://www.honolulu.us.emb-japan.go.jp

Ikebana: The Art of Flower Arrangement/The Art & Meaning of Ikebana

A young woman takes a lesson in the art of Ikebana,

according to the Ohara School. She learns fundamental styles, shown with superimposed diagrams. An Ikebana exhibition of the major schools concludes the show.

Availability:	Schools, libraries, homeschoolers, and nursing homes in OREGON AND SOUTHERN IDAHO ONLY. Please make requests via the web site.
Suggested Grade:	6-Adult
Order Number:	114
Production Date:	1985
Format:	VHS videotape
Terms:	Borrower pays return postage. Return within three weeks after scheduled showing date. Book one month in advance if possible. Rewind the video and wrap securely for return. Be certain to indicate video number, date needed, name of your organization, and address to which video should be sent, along with phone number. Audience report enclosed with the video must be completed and returned.

Source: Consulate General of Japan, Oregon
Attn: Tamara, Video Library
1300 S. W. Fifth Avenue, Suite 2700
Portland, OR 97201
Phone: 1-503-221-1811, ext. 17
World Wide Web URL:
http://www.portland.us.emb-japan.go.jp/en/index.html
Email Address: tamara@cgjpdx.org

Japanese Ink Painting, The

Sumi-e or Japanese ink painting utilizes brush strokes of black ink to create a variety of artistic motifs. The video explains how ink painting has evolved into a uniquely Japanese art form by exploring works of some Japanese masters.

Availability:	Schools, libraries, and nursing homes in Illinois, Indiana, Iowa, Kansas, Minnesota, Missouri, Nebraska, North Dakota, South Dakota, and Wisconsin.
Suggested Grade:	7-Adult
Order Number:	07001
Production Date:	1989
Format:	VHS videotape
Special Notes:	No. 4 in the "Japan: Spirit and Form" series.
Terms:	Borrower pays return postage by U. S. Mail, UPS, or Federal Express, including insurance for "original" videos. Write, call, fax, or e-mail to request an application. An application form MUST be sent in one month in advance but not more than six months in advance. Include alternate titles and dates if provider can substitute titles. Send a SASE with request if you require confirmation. Return immediately after scheduled showing date. Videos may not be copied or broadcast without permission from the producer of the video. Borrower is responsible if video is lost or damaged.

Source: Consulate General of Japan at Chicago
Japan Information Center, Library
737 North Michigan Avenue, Suite 1000
Chicago, IL 60611

Phone: 1-312-280-0430
Fax: 1-312-280-6883
World Wide Web URL:
http://www.chicago.us.emb-japan.go.jp/jic.html
Email Address: jicchicago@webkddi.com

Japanese Ink Painting, The

Sumi-e or Japanese ink painting utilizes brush strokes of black ink to create a variety of artistic motifs. The video explains how ink painting has evolved into a uniquely Japanese art form by exploring works of some Japanese masters.

Availability:	Schools, libraries and homeschoolers in Alabama, Georgia, North Carolina, South Carolina, and Virginia.
Suggested Grade:	7-Adult
Order Number:	517
Production Date:	1989
Format:	VHS videotape
Special Notes:	No. 4 in the "Japan: Spirit and Form" series.
Terms:	Borrower pays return postage. Two tapes may be borrowed at a time. Return within 7 days after receipt. Reservations may be made by filling the application found on the web site.

Source: Consulate General of Japan, Atlanta
Japan Information Center
One Alliance Center
3500 Lenox Road, Suite 1600
Atlanta, GA 30326
Phone: 1-404-365-9240
Fax: 1-404-240-4311
World Wide Web URL:
http://www.atlanta.us.emb-japan.go.jp
Email Address: info@cgjapanatlanta.org

Japanese Ink Painting, The

Sumi-e or Japanese ink painting utilizes brush strokes of black ink to create a variety of artistic motifs. Ink painting has evolved into a uniquely Japanese art form.

Availability:	Schools, libraries, and nursing homes in Hawaii.
Suggested Grade:	7-12
Order Number:	CU-73
Production Date:	1989
Format:	VHS videotape
Special Notes:	No. 4 in the "Japan: Spirit and Form" series.
Terms:	Borrower pays return postage. A maximum of 3 videos may be borrowed per person. Return within one week of date borrowed.

Source: Consulate General of Japan, Honolulu
1742 Nuuanu Avenue
Honolulu, HI 96817-3294
Phone: 1-808-543-3111
Fax: 1-808-543-3170
World Wide Web URL:
http://www.honolulu.us.emb-japan.go.jp

Japanese Ink Painting, The

Sumi-e or Japanese ink painting utilizes brush strokes of

black ink to create a variety of artistic motifs. Ink painting has evolved into a uniquely Japanese art form.

Availability:	Schools, libraries, homeschoolers, and nursing homes in OREGON AND SOUTHERN IDAHO ONLY. Please make requests via the web site.
Suggested Grade:	7-12
Order Number:	530
Production Date:	1989
Format:	VHS videotape
Special Notes:	No. 4 in the "Japan: Spirit and Form" series.
Terms:	Borrower pays return postage. Return within three weeks after scheduled showing date. Book one month in advance if possible. Rewind the video and wrap securely for return. Be certain to indicate video number, date needed, name of your organization, and address to which video should be sent, along with phone number. Audience report enclosed with the video must be completed and returned.

Source: Consulate General of Japan, Oregon
Attn: Tamara, Video Library
1300 S. W. Fifth Avenue, Suite 2700
Portland, OR 97201
Phone: 1-503-221-1811, ext. 17
World Wide Web URL:
http://www.portland.us.emb-japan.go.jp/en/index.html
Email Address: tamara@cgjpdx.org

Legend of El Dorado, The

Myth and reality of gold as viewed through the pre-Columbian treasure of Bogota's Gold Museum.

Availability:	Schools, libraries, and nursing homes in the United States.
Suggested Grade:	8-Adult
Order Number:	APCOL4-video
Production Date:	1975
Format:	VHS videotape
Terms:	Borrowers must have a User's Agreement on file with this source--available by mail or via the Internet. Return postage is paid by borrower; return 12 days after showing. Book at least three weeks in advance. All borrowers are limited to a total of ten items per semester.

Source: Latin American Resource Center
Stone Center for Latin American Studies
Tulane University
100 Jones Hall
New Orleans, LA 70118
Phone: 1-504-862-3143
Fax: 1-504-865-6719
World Wide Web URL:
http://stonecenter.tulane.edu/pages/detail/48/
Lending-Library
Email Address: crcrts@tulane.edu

Los Artistas Hablan

Interviews with 5 prominent artists.

Availability:	Schools, libraries, and nursing homes in the United States.
Suggested Grade:	6-12

Language:	Spanish
Order Number:	AMLA11-video
Production Date:	1979
Format:	VHS videotape
Terms:	Borrowers must have a User's Agreement on file with this source--available by mail or via the Internet. Return postage is paid by borrower; return 12 days after showing. Book at least three weeks in advance. All borrowers are limited to a total of ten items per semester.

Source: Latin American Resource Center
Stone Center for Latin American Studies
Tulane University
100 Jones Hall
New Orleans, LA 70118
Phone: 1-504-862-3143
Fax: 1-504-865-6719
World Wide Web URL:
http://stonecenter.tulane.edu/pages/detail/48/
Lending-Library
Email Address: crcrts@tulane.edu

Manuel Jimenez - Woodcarver

Shows how a rural Mexican folk artist represents the sights and scenes of his early life using common tools.

Availability:	Schools, libraries, and nursing homes in the United States.
Suggested Grade:	6-12
Order Number:	FAMEX3-video
Production Date:	1975
Format:	VHS videotape
Terms:	Borrowers must have a User's Agreement on file with this source--available by mail or via the Internet. Return postage is paid by borrower; return 12 days after showing. Book at least three weeks in advance. All borrowers are limited to a total of ten items per semester.

Source: Latin American Resource Center
Stone Center for Latin American Studies
Tulane University
100 Jones Hall
New Orleans, LA 70118
Phone: 1-504-862-3143
Fax: 1-504-865-6719
World Wide Web URL:
http://stonecenter.tulane.edu/pages/detail/48/
Lending-Library
Email Address: crcrts@tulane.edu

Marcelo Ramos - The Fireworks Maker's Art

Mexican folk artist executes his work in highly technical, precisely timed, complex structures.

Availability:	Schools, libraries, and nursing homes in the United States.
Suggested Grade:	6-12
Order Number:	FAMEX4-video
Format:	VHS videotape
Terms:	Borrowers must have a User's Agreement on file with this source--available by mail or via the Internet. Return postage is paid by borrower; return 12 days after showing. Book at least three weeks in advance. All borrowers are limited to a total of ten items per semester.

Source: Latin American Resource Center
Stone Center for Latin American Studies
Tulane University
100 Jones Hall
New Orleans, LA 70118
Phone: 1-504-862-3143
Fax: 1-504-865-6719
World Wide Web URL:
http://stonecenter.tulane.edu/pages/detail/48/
Lending-Library
Email Address: crcrts@tulane.edu

Martin Chambi and the Heirs of the Incas

Chambi's documentary photographs of Peruvian Indians make a political as well as artistic statement.

Availability: Schools, libraries, and nursing homes in the United States.
Suggested Grade: 6-12
Order Number: AMPER2-video
Production Date: 1986
Format: VHS videotape
Terms: Borrowers must have a User's Agreement on file with this source--available by mail or via the Internet. Return postage is paid by borrower; return 12 days after showing. Book at least three weeks in advance. All borrowers are limited to a total of ten items per semester.
Source: Latin American Resource Center
Stone Center for Latin American Studies
Tulane University
100 Jones Hall
New Orleans, LA 70118
Phone: 1-504-862-3143
Fax: 1-504-865-6719
World Wide Web URL:
http://stonecenter.tulane.edu/pages/detail/48/
Lending-Library
Email Address: crcrts@tulane.edu

Matisse in Nice

Produced for the National Gallery with the exhibition, "Henri Matisse: The Early Years in Nice," this program shows the artist's profound response to the light and color of the Mediterranean and the changes that occurred in his paintings during his years in Nice, on the French Riviera. Matisse's obsession with the effects of light is seen not only in his sun drenched landscapes, but also in his exotic, colorful paintings of voluptuous nudes in richly patterned interiors.

Availability: Schools, community groups, homeschoolers and individuals in the United States.
Suggested Grade: 7-12
Order Number: VC 204
Format: VHS videotape
Special Notes: Programs may not be broadcast, reproduced, or transferred to another medium or format without special license from the National Gallery of Art. Closed captioned version also available as CC 204.

Terms: Borrower pays return postage. Return within 5 days of scheduled use. Book at least one month in advance, and provide alternate date. You will receive a confirmation noting our Shipping Date and your Return Date for each program. Large organizations that can provide programs to extensive audiences--such as school systems, instructional resource centers, museums, libraries, and public and instructional television stations--can arrange an Affiliate Loan for three years, with subsequent renewal to provide their audiences more immediate access to these free-loan extension programs.
Source: National Gallery of Art
Department of Education Resources
2000B South Club Drive
Landover, MD 20785
Phone: 1-202-842-6280
Fax: 1-202-842-6937
World Wide Web URL:
http://www.nga.gov/education/classroom/loanfinder/
Email Address: EdResources@nga.gov

Measure of All Things, The

Narrated by Christopher Plummer, this program is notable for its stunning photography of major archaeological sites in Greece. Examples of architecture, sculpture, and vase painting illustrate artistic developments during the fifth century B.C., when a newly invented political system--democracy--encouraged unprecedented creative freedom.

Availability: Schools, community groups, homeschoolers and individuals in the United States.
Suggested Grade: 7-12
Order Number: VC 154
Format: VHS videotape
Special Notes: Programs may not be broadcast, reproduced, or transferred to another medium or format without special license from the National Gallery of Art. Closed captioned version also available as CC 154.

Terms: Borrower pays return postage. Return within 5 days of scheduled use. Book at least one month in advance, and provide alternate date. You will receive a confirmation noting our Shipping Date and your Return Date for each program. Large organizations that can provide programs to extensive audiences--such as school systems, instructional resource centers, museums, libraries, and public and instructional television stations--can arrange an Affiliate Loan for three years, with subsequent renewal to provide their audiences more immediate access to these free-loan extension programs.
Source: National Gallery of Art
Department of Education Resources
2000B South Club Drive
Landover, MD 20785
Phone: 1-202-842-6280
Fax: 1-202-842-6937
World Wide Web URL:
http://www.nga.gov/education/classroom/loanfinder/
Email Address: EdResources@nga.gov

Meishu: Travels in Chinese

In this film, art history is combined with travel throughout China. It explores contacts with other cultures and beliefs caused by both natural and cultural barriers. In this way, China has developed its unique art.

Availability: Schools, libraries, homeschoolers, and nursing homes in the United States and Canada.

Suggested Grade: 8-12

Order Number: order by title

Production Date: 1988

Format: VHS videotape

Terms: Postage is paid by borrower both ways--send $3.00 per tape to cover initial shipping to you--MONEY MUST BE SENT WITH REQUEST. Return 10 days after showing via U. S. Postal Service, library rate. Shipping is $5.00 to Canadian addresses.

> **Source: Center for Teaching About China**
> **Kathleen Trescott**
> **1214 West Schwartz**
> **Carbondale, IL 62901**
> **Phone: 1-618-549-1555**
> **Email Address: trescott@midwest.net**

Mexican Murals: A Revolution on the Walls

Examines murals as examples of the marriage of art and political thought.

Availability: Schools, libraries, and nursing homes in the United States.

Suggested Grade: 6-12

Order Number: AMMEX17-video

Production Date: 1977

Format: VHS videotape

Terms: Borrowers must have a User's Agreement on file with this source--available by mail or via the Internet. Return postage is paid by borrower; return 12 days after showing. Book at least three weeks in advance. All borrowers are limited to a total of ten items per semester.

> **Source: Latin American Resource Center**
> **Stone Center for Latin American Studies**
> **Tulane University**
> **100 Jones Hall**
> **New Orleans, LA 70118**
> **Phone: 1-504-862-3143**
> **Fax: 1-504-865-6719**
> **World Wide Web URL:**
> **http://stonecenter.tulane.edu/pages/detail/48/**
> **Lending-Library**
> **Email Address: crcrts@tulane.edu**

Mobile, by Alexander Calder

The first work of art placed in the National Gallery's East Building, this mobile is also one of the last major pieces by one of America's great artists, Alexander Calder, the man who invented this form of art. The program takes us on an absorbing journey, as Calder, architect I. M. Pei, artist/engineer Paul Matisse, craftsmen, and museum officials face the challenges of producing this large technically complex piece. Having taken six years to produce, this mobile has become a tribute to the man who gave life to this form of art.

Availability: Schools, community groups, homeschoolers and individuals in the United States.

Suggested Grade: 7-12

Order Number: VC 137

Format: VHS videotape

Special Notes: Programs may not be broadcast, reproduced, or transferred to another medium or format without special license from the National Gallery of Art. Closed captioned version also available as CC 137.

Terms: Borrower pays return postage. Return within 5 days of scheduled use. Book at least one month in advance, and provide alternate date. You will receive a confirmation noting our Shipping Date and your Return Date for each program. Large organizations that can provide programs to extensive audiences--such as school systems, instructional resource centers, museums, libraries, and public and instructional television stations--can arrange an Affiliate Loan for three years, with subsequent renewal to provide their audiences more immediate access to these free-loan extension programs.

> **Source: National Gallery of Art**
> **Department of Education Resources**
> **2000B South Club Drive**
> **Landover, MD 20785**
> **Phone: 1-202-842-6280**
> **Fax: 1-202-842-6937**
> **World Wide Web URL:**
> **http://www.nga.gov/education/classroom/loanfinder/**
> **Email Address: EdResources@nga.gov**

National Gallery of Art, A Treasury of Masterpieces

J. Carter Brown, the National Gallery's director from 1969 to 1992, tells the fascinating story of the museum's beginnings and of its growth.

Availability: Schools, community groups, homeschoolers and individuals in the United States.

Suggested Grade: 7-12

Order Number: VC 208

Format: VHS videotape

Special Notes: Programs may not be broadcast, reproduced, or transferred to another medium or format without special license from the National Gallery of Art. Closed captioned version also available as CC 208.

Terms: Borrower pays return postage. Return within 5 days of scheduled use. Book at least one month in advance, and provide alternate date. You will receive a confirmation noting our Shipping Date and your Return Date for each program. Large organizations that can provide programs to extensive audiences--such as school systems, instructional resource centers, museums, libraries, and public and instructional television stations--can arrange an Affiliate Loan for three years, with subsequent renewal to provide their audiences more immediate access to these free-loan extension programs.

Source: National Gallery of Art
Department of Education Resources
2000B South Club Drive
Landover, MD 20785
Phone: 1-202-842-6280
Fax: 1-202-842-6937
World Wide Web URL:
http://www.nga.gov/education/classroom/loanfinder/
Email Address: EdResources@nga.gov

Of Time, Tombs, and Treasure: The Treasures of Tutankhamun

This program takes the viewer on a journey to Egypt and the final resting place of a young king who ruled 3,000 years ago. Narrated by J. Carter Brown, the program tells the story of the tomb's discovery in 1922 by archaeologist Howard Carter and its fabulous treasure--objects which range from magnificent jewelry to furniture, alabaster vases, gilt figurines, and the famous gold burial mask. The beauty and detail of these objects is stunning.

Availability: Schools, community groups, homeschoolers and individuals in the United States.
Suggested Grade: 7-12
Order Number: VC 132
Format: VHS videotape
Special Notes: Programs may not be broadcast, reproduced, or transferred to another medium or format without special license from the National Gallery of Art. Closed captioned version also available as CC 132.
Terms: Borrower pays return postage. Return within 5 days of scheduled use. Book at least one month in advance, and provide alternate date. You will receive a confirmation noting our Shipping Date and your Return Date for each program. Large organizations that can provide programs to extensive audiences--such as school systems, instructional resource centers, museums, libraries, and public and instructional television stations--can arrange an Affiliate Loan for three years, with subsequent renewal to provide their audiences more immediate access to these free-loan extension programs.

Source: National Gallery of Art
Department of Education Resources
2000B South Club Drive
Landover, MD 20785
Phone: 1-202-842-6280
Fax: 1-202-842-6937
World Wide Web URL:
http://www.nga.gov/education/classroom/loanfinder/
Email Address: EdResources@nga.gov

Olmec Art of Ancient Mexico

This comprehensive exhibition of Olmec art provided the opportunity to view the achievements of Mexico's earliest (1200 to 300 B.C.) and least-known civilization. Olmec objects were created in Mexico and Central America three thousand years ago, long before the great Maya, Teotihuacan, and Aztec civilizations. This program focuses on the twentieth-century discovery of powerful and dynamic Olmec art. Archival and new footage, shot on location, presents past and current archaeological finds at major Olmec sites in Mexico and shows some of the objects included in the Gallery's exhibition.

Availability: Schools, community groups, homeschoolers and individuals in the United States.
Suggested Grade: 7-12
Order Number: VC 158
Format: VHS videotape
Special Notes: Programs may not be broadcast, reproduced, or transferred to another medium or format without special license from the National Gallery of Art. Closed captioned version also available as CC 158.
Terms: Borrower pays return postage. Return within 5 days of scheduled use. Book at least one month in advance, and provide alternate date. You will receive a confirmation noting our Shipping Date and your Return Date for each program. Large organizations that can provide programs to extensive audiences--such as school systems, instructional resource centers, museums, libraries, and public and instructional television stations--can arrange an Affiliate Loan for three years, with subsequent renewal to provide their audiences more immediate access to these free-loan extension programs.

Source: National Gallery of Art
Department of Education Resources
2000B South Club Drive
Landover, MD 20785
Phone: 1-202-842-6280
Fax: 1-202-842-6937
World Wide Web URL:
http://www.nga.gov/education/classroom/loanfinder/
Email Address: EdResources@nga.gov

Origami

Origami, the centuries-old Japanese art of paper-folding, still enjoys great popularity among the young and old alike. Parents encourage this pastime at home, guiding their offspring in creating a wide variety of intricate figures. It's an invaluable aid in developing the creative imaginations of youngsters.

Availability: Schools, libraries, and nursing homes in Illinois, Indiana, Iowa, Kansas, Minnesota, Missouri, Nebraska, North Dakota, South Dakota, and Wisconsin.
Suggested Grade: 6-Adult
Order Number: 03403
Format: VHS videotape
Terms: Borrower pays return postage by U. S. Mail, UPS, or Federal Express, including insurance for "original" videos. Write, call, fax, or e-mail to request an application. An application form MUST be sent in one month in advance but not more than six months in advance. Include alternate titles and dates if provider can substitute titles. Send a SASE with request if you require confirmation.   Return immediately after scheduled showing date. Videos may not be copied or

broadcast without permission from the producer of the video. Borrower is responsible if video is lost or damaged.

Source: **Consulate General of Japan at Chicago**
Japan Information Center
Library
737 North Michigan Avenue, Suite 1000
Chicago, IL 60611
Phone: 1-312-280-0430
Fax: 1-312-280-6883
World Wide Web URL:
http://www.chicago.us.emb-japan.go.jp/jic.html
Email Address: jicchicago@webkddi.com

Past, Present and Future: Washi--Unique Japanese Paper Culture

Washi is introduced as an outstanding aspect of traditional culture. This video explores how this unique paper is incorporated into daily living in terms of production, wrapping, folding, art and other uses.

Availability: Schools, libraries and homeschoolers in Alabama, Georgia, North Carolina, South Carolina, and Virginia.
Suggested Grade: 4-12
Order Number: 319
Production Date: 1997
Format: VHS videotape
Terms: Borrower pays return postage. Two tapes may be borrowed at a time. Return within 7 days after receipt. Reservations may be made by filling the application found on the web site.

Source: **Consulate General of Japan, Atlanta**
Japan Information Center
One Alliance Center, 3500 Lenox Road, Suite 1600
Atlanta, GA 30326
Phone: 1-404-365-9240
Fax: 1-404-240-4311
World Wide Web URL:
http://www.atlanta.us.emb-japan.go.jp
Email Address: info@cgjapanatlanta.org

Past, Present and Future: Washi--Unique Japanese Paper Culture

Washi is introduced as an outstanding aspect of traditional culture. This video explores how this unique paper is incorporated into daily living in terms of production, wrapping, folding, art and other uses.

Availability: Schools, libraries, and nursing homes in Hawaii.
Suggested Grade: 4-12
Order Number: CU-128
Production Date: 1997
Format: VHS videotape
Terms: Borrower pays return postage. A maximum of 3 videos may be borrowed per person. Return within one week of date borrowed.

Source: **Consulate General of Japan, Honolulu**
1742 Nuuanu Avenue
Honolulu, HI 96817-3294

Phone: 1-808-543-3111
Fax: 1-808-543-3170
World Wide Web URL:
http://www.honolulu.us.emb-japan.go.jp

Past, Present and Future: Washi--Unique Japanese Paper Culture

Washi is introduced as an outstanding aspect of traditional culture. This video explores how this unique paper is incorporated into daily living in terms of production, wrapping, folding, art and other uses.

Availability: Schools, libraries, homeschoolers, and nursing homes .in OREGON AND SOUTHERN IDAHO ONLY. Please make requests via the web site.
Suggested Grade: 4-12
Order Number: 420
Production Date: 1997
Format: VHS videotape
Terms: Borrower pays return postage. Return within three weeks after scheduled showing date. Book one month in advance if possible. Rewind the video and wrap securely for return. Be certain to indicate video number, date needed, name of your organization, and address to which video should be sent, along with phone number. Audience report enclosed with the video must be completed and returned.

Source: **Consulate General of Japan, Oregon**
Attn: Tamara, Video Library
1300 S. W. Fifth Avenue, Suite 2700
Portland, OR 97201
Phone: 1-503-221-1811, ext. 17
World Wide Web URL:
http://www.portland.us.emb-japan.go.jp/en/index.html
Email Address: tamara@cgjpdx.org

Paul Gauguin: The Savage Dream

Filmed on location in Tahiti and the Marquesas Islands, this program explores Gauguin's obsessive search for an alternative to his own culture, culminating with his monumental artistic achievement in the South Pacific during his final years. To a great extent, the story is told in Gauguin's words, revealing his personal philosophy of art and of life.

Availability: Schools, community groups, homeschoolers and individuals in the United States.
Suggested Grade: 7-12
Order Number: VC 206
Format: VHS videotape
Special Notes: Programs may not be broadcast, reproduced, or transferred to another medium or format without special license from the National Gallery of Art. Closed captioned version also available as CC 206.
Terms: Borrower pays return postage. Return within 5 days of scheduled use. Book at least one month in advance, and provide alternate date. You will receive a confirmation noting our Shipping Date and your Return Date for each program. Large organizations that can provide programs

to extensive audiences--such as school systems, instructional resource centers, museums, libraries, and public and instructional television stations--can arrange an Affiliate Loan for three years, with subsequent renewal to provide their audiences more immediate access to these free-loan extension programs.

Source: National Gallery of Art
Department of Education Resources
2000B South Club Drive
Landover, MD 20785
Phone: 1-202-842-6280
Fax: 1-202-842-6937
World Wide Web URL:
http://www.nga.gov/education/classroom/loanfinder/
Email Address: EdResources@nga.gov

Picasso and the Circus

In this short program, a young girl strolls through the exhibition, "Picasso, The Saltimbanques." As she gazes at Picasso's pictures of jugglers, bareback riders, harlequins, and clowns, the images before her give way to scenes of a Parisian circus of the kind Picasso attended. Narration is kept to a minimum, enhancing the viewers' experience of the dual realities of the circus performances and of Picasso's art.

Availability: Schools, community groups, homeschoolers and individuals in the United States.
Suggested Grade: 4-Adult
Order Number: VC 141
Format: VHS videotape
Special Notes: Programs may not be broadcast, reproduced, or transferred to another medium or format without special license from the National Gallery of Art. Closed captioned version also available as CC 141.
Terms: Borrower pays return postage. Return within 5 days of scheduled use. Book at least one month in advance, and provide alternate date. You will receive a confirmation noting our Shipping Date and your Return Date for each program. Large organizations that can provide programs to extensive audiences--such as school systems, instructional resource centers, museums, libraries, and public and instructional television stations--can arrange an Affiliate Loan for three years, with subsequent renewal to provide their audiences more immediate access to these free-loan extension programs.

Source: National Gallery of Art
Department of Education Resources
2000B South Club Drive
Landover, MD 20785
Phone: 1-202-842-6280
Fax: 1-202-842-6937
World Wide Web URL:
http://www.nga.gov/education/classroom/loanfinder/
Email Address: EdResources@nga.gov

Pinturas de la Merced Iglesia

Documents religious art in a colonial church of Antigua, Guatemala.

Availability: Schools, libraries, and nursing homes in the United States.
Suggested Grade: 6-12
Spanish
Order Number: ACGUA3-video
Production Date: 1984
Format: VHS videotape
Terms: Borrowers must have a User's Agreement on file with this source--available by mail or via the Internet. Return postage is paid by borrower; return 12 days after showing. Book at least three weeks in advance. All borrowers are limited to a total of ten items per semester.

Source: Latin American Resource Center
Stone Center for Latin American Studies
Tulane University
100 Jones Hall
New Orleans, LA 70118
Phone: 1-504-862-3143
Fax: 1-504-865-6719
World Wide Web URL:
http://stonecenter.tulane.edu/pages/detail/48/
Lending-Library
Email Address: crcrts@tulane.edu

Place to Be, A: The Construction of the East Building of the National Gallery of Art

Traces in the detail the creation of this impressive structure from idea to completion.

Availability: Schools, community groups, homeschoolers and individuals in the United States.
Suggested Grade: 7-12
Order Number: DV 332
Format: DVD
Special Notes: Programs may not be broadcast, reproduced, or transferred to another medium or format without special license from the National Gallery of Art.
Terms: Borrower pays return postage. Return within 5 days of scheduled use. Book at least one month in advance, and provide alternate date. You will receive a confirmation noting our Shipping Date and your Return Date for each program. Large organizations that can provide programs to extensive audiences--such as school systems, instructional resource centers, museums, libraries, and public and instructional television stations--can arrange an Affiliate Loan for three years, with subsequent renewal to provide their audiences more immediate access to these free-loan extension programs.

Source: National Gallery of Art
Department of Education Resources
2000B South Club Drive
Landover, MD 20785
Phone: 1-202-842-6280
Fax: 1-202-842-6937
World Wide Web URL:
http://www.nga.gov/education/classroom/loanfinder/
Email Address: EdResources@nga.gov

FINE ARTS--ART AND HANDWORK

Place to Be, A: The Construction of the East Building of the National Gallery of Art

Traces in the detail the creation of this impressive structure from idea to completion.

Availability: Schools, community groups, homeschoolers and individuals in the United States.
Suggested Grade: 7-12
Order Number: VC 134
Format: VHS videotape
Special Notes: Programs may not be broadcast, reproduced, or transferred to another medium or format without special license from the National Gallery of Art. Closed captioned version also available as CC 134.
Terms: Borrower pays return postage. Return within 5 days of scheduled use. Book at least one month in advance, and provide alternate date. You will receive a confirmation noting our Shipping Date and your Return Date for each program. Large organizations that can provide programs to extensive audiences--such as school systems, instructional resource centers, museums, libraries, and public and instructional television stations--can arrange an Affiliate Loan for three years, with subsequent renewal to provide their audiences more immediate access to these free-loan extension programs.

Source: National Gallery of Art
Department of Education Resources
2000B South Club Drive
Landover, MD 20785
Phone: 1-202-842-6280
Fax: 1-202-842-6937
World Wide Web URL:
http://www.nga.gov/education/classroom/loanfinder/
Email Address: EdResources@nga.gov

Plunder

Looks at black market in stolen pre-Columbian antiquities.

Availability: Schools, libraries, and nursing homes in the United States.
Suggested Grade: 6-12
Order Number: APLA1-video
Production Date: 1990
Format: VHS videotape
Terms: Borrowers must have a User's Agreement on file with this source--available by mail or via the Internet. Return postage is paid by borrower; return 12 days after showing. Book at least three weeks in advance. All borrowers are limited to a total of ten items per semester.

Source: Latin American Resource Center
Stone Center for Latin American Studies
Tulane University
100 Jones Hall
New Orleans, LA 70118
Phone: 1-504-862-3143
Fax: 1-504-865-6719
World Wide Web URL:
http://stonecenter.tulane.edu/pages/detail/48/
Lending-Library
Email Address: crcrts@tulane.edu

Pompeii and the Roman Villa

Explores art and culture around the Bay of Napls before Mount Vesuvius erupted in AD 79.

Availability: Schools, community groups, homeschoolers and individuals in the United States.
Suggested Grade: 7-12
Order Number: DV 176
Format: DVD
Special Notes: Programs may not be broadcast, reproduced, or transferred to another medium or format without special license from the National Gallery of Art.
Terms: Borrower pays return postage. Return within 5 days of scheduled use. Book at least one month in advance, and provide alternate date. You will receive a confirmation noting our Shipping Date and your Return Date for each program. Large organizations that can provide programs to extensive audiences--such as school systems, instructional resource centers, museums, libraries, and public and instructional television stations--can arrange an Affiliate Loan for three years, with subsequent renewal to provide their audiences more immediate access to these free-loan extension programs.

Source: National Gallery of Art
Department of Education Resources
2000B South Club Drive
Landover, MD 20785
Phone: 1-202-842-6280
Fax: 1-202-842-6937
World Wide Web URL:
http://www.nga.gov/education/classroom/loanfinder/
Email Address: EdResources@nga.gov

Pompeii and the Roman Villa

Explores art and culture around the Bay of Napls before Mount Vesuvius erupted in AD 79.

Availability: Schools, community groups, homeschoolers and individuals in the United States.
Suggested Grade: 7-12
Order Number: VC 176
Format: VHS Videotape
Special Notes: Programs may not be broadcast, reproduced, or transferred to another medium or format without special license from the National Gallery of Art.
Terms: Borrower pays return postage. Return within 5 days of scheduled use. Book at least one month in advance, and provide alternate date. You will receive a confirmation noting our Shipping Date and your Return Date for each program. Large organizations that can provide programs to extensive audiences--such as school systems, instructional resource centers, museums, libraries, and public and instructional television stations--can arrange an Affiliate Loan for three years, with subsequent renewal to provide their audiences more immediate access to these free-loan extension programs.

Source: National Gallery of Art
Department of Education Resources
2000B South Club Drive
Landover, MD 20785

*All materials listed in this 2011-2012 edition are **BRAND NEW!***

Phone: 1-202-842-6280
Fax: 1-202-842-6937
World Wide Web URL:
http://www.nga.gov/education/classroom/loanfinder/
Email Address: EdResources@nga.gov

Rimpa School Crosses the Ocean
The Rimpa school of decorative design flourished during the Edo Period, and made a lasting mark on European art at the Paris Exhibition of 1878. Handicrafts, prints, and screens emphasized arrangement of natural forms into a visual rhythm.

Availability: Schools, libraries and homeschoolers in Alabama, Georgia, North Carolina, South Carolina, and Virginia.
Suggested Grade: 7-12
Order Number: 518
Production Date: 1989
Format: VHS videotape
Special Notes: No. 5 in the "Japan: Spirit and Form" series.
Terms: Borrower pays return postage. Two tapes may be borrowed at a time. Return within 7 days after receipt. Reservations may be made by filling the application found on the web site.
Source: Consulate General of Japan, Atlanta
Japan Information Center
One Alliance Center
3500 Lenox Road, Suite 1600
Atlanta, GA 30326
Phone: 1-404-365-9240
Fax: 1-404-240-4311
World Wide Web URL:
http://www.atlanta.us.emb-japan.go.jp
Email Address: info@cgjapanatlanta.org

Rimpa School Crosses the Ocean
The Rimpa school of decorative design flourished during the Edo Period, and made a lasting mark on European art at the Paris Exhibition of 1878. Handicrafts, prints, and screens emphasized arrangement of natural forms into a visual rhythm.

Availability: Schools, libraries, and nursing homes in Hawaii.
Suggested Grade: 7-12
Order Number: CU-74
Production Date: 1989
Format: VHS videotape
Special Notes: No. 5 in the "Japan: Spirit and Form" series.
Terms: Borrower pays return postage. A maximum of 3 videos may be borrowed per person. Return within one week of date borrowed.
Source: Consulate General of Japan, Honolulu
1742 Nuuanu Avenue
Honolulu, HI 96817-3294
Phone: 1-808-543-3111
Fax: 1-808-543-3170
World Wide Web URL:
http://www.honolulu.us.emb-japan.go.jp

Rimpa School Crosses the Ocean
The Rimpa school of decorative design flourished during the Edo Period, and made a lasting mark on European art at the Paris Exhibition of 1878. Handicrafts, prints, and screens emphasized arrangement of natural forms into a visual rhythm.

Availability: Schools, libraries, homeschoolers, and nursing homes in OREGON AND SOUTHERN IDAHO ONLY. Please make requests via the web site.
Suggested Grade: 7-12
Order Number: 531
Production Date: 1989
Format: VHS videotape
Special Notes: No. 5 in the "Japan: Spirit and Form" series.
Terms: Borrower pays return postage. Return within three weeks after scheduled showing date. Book one month in advance if possible. Rewind the video and wrap securely for return. Be certain to indicate video number, date needed, name of your organization, and address to which video should be sent, along with phone number. Audience report enclosed with the video must be completed and returned.
Source: Consulate General of Japan, Oregon
Attn: Tamara, Video Library
1300 S. W. Fifth Avenue, Suite 2700
Portland, OR 97201
Phone: 1-503-221-1811, ext. 17
World Wide Web URL:
http://www.portland.us.emb-japan.go.jp/en/index.html
Email Address: tamara@cgjpdx.org

Thousand and One Years Ago, A (Inca Art of Peru)
Learn about Inca art of long ago.

Availability: Schools, libraries, and nursing homes in the United States.
Suggested Grade: 6-12
Order Number: INC10-video
Production Date: 1968
Format: VHS videotape
Terms: Borrowers must have a User's Agreement on file with this source--available by mail or via the Internet. Return postage is paid by borrower; return 12 days after showing. Book at least three weeks in advance. All borrowers are limited to a total of ten items per semester.
Source: Latin American Resource Center
Stone Center for Latin American Studies
Tulane University
100 Jones Hall
New Orleans, LA 70118
Phone: 1-504-862-3143
Fax: 1-504-865-6719
World Wide Web URL:
http://stonecenter.tulane.edu/pages/detail/48/
Lending-Library
Email Address: crcrts@tulane.edu

Toulouse-Lautrec and Montmartre
Traces the relationship between Toulouse-Lautrec and

Montmartre's avant-garde culture, using works by the artists and his colleagues, rare archival footage and sound records, period photographs, and interviews with contemporary scholars.

Availability:	Schools, community groups, homeschoolers and individuals in the United States.
Suggested Grade:	7-12
Order Number:	VC 172
Format:	VHS videotape
Special Notes:	Programs may not be broadcast, reproduced, or transferred to another medium or format without special license from the National Gallery of Art. Closed captioned version also available as CC 172.
Terms:	Borrower pays return postage. Return within 5 days of scheduled use. Book at least one month in advance, and provide alternate date. You will receive a confirmation noting our Shipping Date and your Return Date for each program. Large organizations that can provide programs to extensive audiences--such as school systems, instructional resource centers, museums, libraries, and public and instructional television stations--can arrange an Affiliate Loan for three years, with subsequent renewal to provide their audiences more immediate access to these free-loan extension programs.

Source: National Gallery of Art
Department of Education Resources
2000B South Club Drive
Landover, MD 20785
Phone: 1-202-842-6280
Fax: 1-202-842-6937
World Wide Web URL:
http://www.nga.gov/education/classroom/loanfinder/
Email Address: EdResources@nga.gov

Tour of the Prado, A

Tour of European and Spanish paintings housed in Madrid's Prado Museum.

Availability:	Schools, libraries, and nursing homes in the United States.
Suggested Grade:	6-12
Order Number:	ASPA2-video
Production Date:	1982
Format:	VHS videotape
Terms:	Borrowers must have a User's Agreement on file with this source--available by mail or via the Internet. Return postage is paid by borrower; return 12 days after showing. Book at least three weeks in advance. All borrowers are limited to a total of ten items per semester.

Source: Latin American Resource Center
Stone Center for Latin American Studies
Tulane University
100 Jones Hall
New Orleans, LA 70118
Phone: 1-504-862-3143
Fax: 1-504-865-6719
World Wide Web URL:
http://stonecenter.tulane.edu/pages/detail/48/
Lending-Library
Email Address: crcrts@tulane.edu

Traditional Japanese Culture: Japan Arts and Crafts

Wood is used in many traditional Japanese crafts. The creation of several types of crafts such as wooden bowls, boxes, kokeshi dolls, Noh masks, Kamakura carving and lacquerware are shown here.

Availability:	Schools, libraries, and nursing homes in Illinois, Indiana, Iowa, Kansas, Minnesota, Missouri, Nebraska, North Dakota, South Dakota, and Wisconsin.
Suggested Grade:	6-12
Order Number:	03101
Production Date:	1999
Format:	VHS videotape
Terms:	Borrower pays return postage by U. S. Mail, UPS, or Federal Express, including insurance for "original" videos. Write, call, fax, or e-mail to request an application. An application form MUST be sent in one month in advance but not more than six months in advance. Include alternate titles and dates if provider can substitute titles. Send a SASE with request if you require confirmation. Return immediately after scheduled showing date. Videos may not be copied or broadcast without permission from the producer of the video. Borrower is responsible if video is lost or damaged.

Source: Consulate General of Japan at Chicago
Japan Information Center, Library
737 North Michigan Avenue, Suite 1000
Chicago, IL 60611
Phone: 1-312-280-0430
Fax: 1-312-280-6883
World Wide Web URL:
http://www.chicago.us.emb-japan.go.jp/jic.html
Email Address: jicchicago@webkddi.com

Traditional Japanese Culture: Japanese Architecture

Shows the history of Japanese wooden structures and how it affects modern architecture. Also shows how tatami mats, fusuma and sjohi panels are made.

Availability:	Schools, libraries, and nursing homes in Illinois, Indiana, Iowa, Kansas, Minnesota, Missouri, Nebraska, North Dakota, South Dakota, and Wisconsin.
Suggested Grade:	6-12
Order Number:	02002
Production Date:	1999
Format:	VHS videotape
Terms:	Borrower pays return postage by U. S. Mail, UPS, or Federal Express, including insurance for "original" videos. Write, call, fax, or e-mail to request an application. An application form MUST be sent in one month in advance but not more than six months in advance. Include alternate titles and dates if provider can substitute titles. Send a SASE with request if you require confirmation. Return immediately after scheduled showing date. Videos may not be copied or broadcast without permission from the producer of the video. Borrower is responsible if video is lost or damaged.

Source: Consulate General of Japan at Chicago
Japan Information Center
Library
737 North Michigan Avenue, Suite 1000
Chicago, IL 60611
Phone: 1-312-280-0430
Fax: 1-312-280-6883
World Wide Web URL:
http://www.chicago.us.emb-japan.go.jp/jic.html
Email Address: jicchicago@webkddi.com

Traditional Japanese Culture: Japanese Architecture

Shows the history of Japanese wooden structures and how it affects modern architecture. Also shows how tatami mats, fusuma and sjohi panels are made.

Availability: Schools, libraries and homeschoolers in Alabama, Georgia, North Carolina, South Carolina, and Virginia.
Suggested Grade: 6-12
Order Number: 155
Format: VHS videotape
Terms: Borrower pays return postage. Two tapes may be borrowed at a time. Return within 7 days after receipt. Reservations may be made by filling the application found on the web site.

Source: Consulate General of Japan, Atlanta
Japan Information Center
One Alliance Center
3500 Lenox Road, Suite 1600
Atlanta, GA 30326
Phone: 1-404-365-9240
Fax: 1-404-240-4311
World Wide Web URL:
http://www.atlanta.us.emb-japan.go.jp
Email Address: info@cgjapanatlanta.org

Traditional Japanese Culture: Japanese Architecture

Shows the history of Japanese wooden structures and how it affects modern architecture. Also shows how tatami mats, fusuma and sjohi panels are made.

Availability: Schools, libraries, and nursing homes in Hawaii.
Suggested Grade: 6-12
Order Number: CU-134
Format: VHS videotape
Terms: Borrower pays return postage. A maximum of 3 videos may be borrowed per person. Return within one week of date borrowed.

Source: Consulate General of Japan, Honolulu
1742 Nuuanu Avenue
Honolulu, HI 96817-3294
Phone: 1-808-543-3111
Fax: 1-808-543-3170
World Wide Web URL:
http://www.honolulu.us.emb-japan.go.jp

Traditional Japanese Culture: Japanese Architecture

Shows the history of Japanese wooden structures and how it affects modern architecture. Also shows how tatami mats, fusuma and sjohi panels are made.

Availability: Schools, libraries, homeschoolers, and nursing homes in Connecticut, Delaware, Maryland, New Jersey, New York, Pennsylvania, and West Virginia.
Suggested Grade: 6-12
Order Number: order by title
Format: VHS videotape
Terms: Send a blank videotape to this source and they will dub the program you desire onto it for permanent retention. You must send a self-addressed, stamped envelope with sufficient postage for return.

Source: Consulate General of Japan, New York
Audio Video Dept.
299 Park Avenue, 18th Floor
New York, NY 10171
Phone: 1-212-371-8222
Fax: 1-212-319-6357
World Wide Web URL: http://www.ny.us.emb-japan.go.jp

Traditional Japanese Culture: Japanese Architecture

Shows the history of Japanese wooden structures and how it affects modern architecture. Also shows how tatami mats, fusuma and sjohi panels are made.

Availability: Schools, libraries, homeschoolers, and nursing homes in OREGON AND SOUTHERN IDAHO ONLY. Please make requests via the web site.
Suggested Grade: 6-12
Order Number: 453
Production Date: 2000
Format: VHS videotape
Terms: Borrower pays return postage. Return within three weeks after scheduled showing date. Book one month in advance if possible. Rewind the video and wrap securely for return. Be certain to indicate video number, date needed, name of your organization, and address to which video should be sent, along with phone number. Audience report enclosed with the video must be completed and returned.

Source: Consulate General of Japan, Oregon
Attn: Tamara, Video Library
1300 S. W. Fifth Avenue, Suite 2700
Portland, OR 97201
Phone: 1-503-221-1811, ext. 17
World Wide Web URL:
http://www.portland.us.emb-japan.go.jp/en/index.html
Email Address: tamara@cgjpdx.org

Traditional Japanese Culture: Japanese Pottery & Porcelain

Briefly presents the history of Japanese ceramics and their importance as exquisite works of art.

Availability: Schools, libraries, and nursing homes in Illinois, Indiana, Iowa, Kansas, Minnesota, Missouri, Nebraska, North Dakota, South Dakota, and Wisconsin.
Suggested Grade: 6-12
Order Number: 03201

*All materials listed in this 2011-2012 edition are **BRAND NEW!***

Production Date: 1999
Format: VHS videotape
Terms: Borrower pays return postage by U. S. Mail, UPS, or Federal Express, including insurance for "original" videos. Write, call, fax, or e-mail to request an application. An application form MUST be sent in one month in advance but not more than six months in advance. Include alternate titles and dates if provider can substitute titles. Send a SASE with request if you require confirmation. Return immediately after scheduled showing date. Videos may not be copied or broadcast without permission from the producer of the video. Borrower is responsible if video is lost or damaged.

Source: **Consulate General of Japan at Chicago**
Japan Information Center
Library
737 North Michigan Avenue, Suite 1000
Chicago, IL 60611
Phone: 1-312-280-0430
Fax: 1-312-280-6883
World Wide Web URL:
http://www.chicago.us.emb-japan.go.jp/jic.html
Email Address: jicchicago@webkddi.com

Traditional Japanese Culture: Japanese Pottery & Porcelain

Briefly presents the history of Japanese ceramics and their importance as exquisite works of art.
Availability: Schools, libraries and homeschoolers in Alabama, Georgia, North Carolina, South Carolina, and Virginia.
Suggested Grade: 6-12
Order Number: 153
Format: VHS videotape
Terms: Borrower pays return postage. Two tapes may be borrowed at a time. Return within 7 days after receipt. Reservations may be made by filling the application found on the web site.

Source: **Consulate General of Japan, Atlanta**
Japan Information Center
One Alliance Center
3500 Lenox Road, Suite 1600
Atlanta, GA 30326
Phone: 1-404-365-9240
Fax: 1-404-240-4311
World Wide Web URL:
http://www.atlanta.us.emb-japan.go.jp
Email Address: info@cgjapanatlanta.org

Traditional Japanese Culture: Japanese Pottery & Porcelain

Briefly presents the history of Japanese ceramics and their importance as exquisite works of art.
Availability: Schools, libraries, homeschoolers, and nursing homes in Connecticut, Delaware, Maryland, New Jersey, New York, Pennsylvania, and West Virginia.

Suggested Grade: 6-12
Order Number: order by title
Format: VHS videotape
Terms: Send a blank videotape to this source and they will dub the program you desire onto it for permanent retention. You must send a self-addressed, stamped envelope with sufficient postage for return.

Source: **Consulate General of Japan, New York**
Audio Video Dept.
299 Park Avenue, 18th Floor
New York, NY 10171
Phone: 1-212-371-8222
Fax: 1-212-319-6357
World Wide Web URL: http://www.ny.us.emb-japan.go.jp

20th Century European Art

Five documentary programs that incorporate biographical information and more about the art and the artist: Henri Rousseau: Jungles of Paris (30 minutes); Matisse In Nice (28 minutes); Picasso and the Saltimbanques (29 minutes); Picasso and the Curcus (minutes); and, Henry Moore: A Life in Sculpture (25 minutes).
Availability: Schools, community groups, homeschoolers and individuals in the United States.
Suggested Grade: 7-12
Order Number: DV337
Format: DVD
Terms: Borrower pays return postage. Return within 5 days of scheduled use. Book at least one month in advance, and provide alternate date. You will receive a confirmation noting our Shipping Date and your Return Date for each program. Large organizations that can provide programs to extensive audiences--such as school systems, instructional resource centers, museums, libraries, and public and instructional television stations--can arrange an Affiliate Loan for three years, with subsequent renewal to provide their audiences more immediate access to these free-loan extension programs.

Source: **National Gallery of Art**
Department of Education Resources
2000B South Club Drive
Landover, MD 20785
Phone: 1-202-842-6280
Fax: 1-202-842-6937
World Wide Web URL:
http://www.nga.gov/education/classroom/loanfinder/
Email Address: EdResources@nga.gov

Walls of Mexico, The: Art and Architecture

Wall paintings of some of the most popular Mexican muralists.
Availability: Schools, libraries, and nursing homes in the United States.
Suggested Grade: 6-12
Order Number: AMMEX27-video
Format: VHS videotape

Terms: Borrowers must have a User's Agreement on file with this source--available by mail or via the Internet. Return postage is paid by borrower; return 12 days after showing. Book at least three weeks in advance. All borrowers are limited to a total of ten items per semester.

Source: Latin American Resource Center
Stone Center for Latin American Studies
Tulane University
100 Jones Hall
New Orleans, LA 70118
Phone: 1-504-862-3143
Fax: 1-504-865-6719
World Wide Web URL:
http://stonecenter.tulane.edu/pages/detail/48/
Lending-Library
Email Address: crcrts@tulane.edu

Washi--Unique Japanese Paper Culture

Washi is introduced as an outstanding aspect of traditional culture. This video explores how this unique paper is incorporated into daily living in terms of production, wrapping, folding, art and other uses.

Availability: Schools, libraries, and nursing homes in Illinois, Indiana, Iowa, Kansas, Minnesota, Missouri, Nebraska, North Dakota, South Dakota, and Wisconsin.

Suggested Grade: 4-12
Order Number: 03001
Production Date: 1997
Format: VHS videotape
Terms: Borrower pays return postage by U. S. Mail, UPS, or Federal Express, including insurance for "original" videos. Write, call, fax, or e-mail to request an application. An application form MUST be sent in one month in advance but not more than six months in advance. Include alternate titles and dates if provider can substitute titles. Send a SASE with request if you require confirmation. Return immediately after scheduled showing date. Videos may not be copied or broadcast without permission from the producer of the video. Borrower is responsible if video is lost or damaged.

Source: Consulate General of Japan at Chicago
Japan Information Center
Library
737 North Michigan Avenue, Suite 1000
Chicago, IL 60611
Phone: 1-312-280-0430
Fax: 1-312-280-6883
World Wide Web URL:
http://www.chicago.us.emb-japan.go.jp/jic.html
Email Address: jicchicago@webkddi.com

Alicia

Shows the dance and life of Alicia Alonso, one of Cuba's finest ballerinas.

Availability: Schools, libraries, and nursing homes in the United States.
Suggested Grade: 6-12
Order Number: DFCUB1-video
Production Date: 1976
Format: VHS videotape
Terms: Borrowers must have a User's Agreement on file with this source--available by mail or via the Internet. Return postage is paid by borrower; return 12 days after showing. Book at least three weeks in advance. All borrowers are limited to a total of ten items per semester.

Source: Latin American Resource Center
Stone Center for Latin American Studies
Tulane University
100 Jones Hall
New Orleans, LA 70118
Phone: 1-504-862-3143
Fax: 1-504-865-6719
World Wide Web URL:
http://stonecenter.tulane.edu/pages/detail/48/
Lending-Library
Email Address: crcrts@tulane.edu

America's Songs of Liberty

Suggests that one way citizenship may be appreciated is through learning the words and background of patriotic songs. Kyle, after hearing the national anthem sung at a baseball game, offers some history on it and three other patriotic songs. Includes "My Country "Tis of Thee," "America the Beautiful," and "This Land is Your Land."

Availability: Schools, libraries, and homeschoolers in the United States who serve the hearing impaired.
Suggested Grade: K-6
Order Number: 11436
Production Date: 2003
Format: DVD
Terms: Sponsor pays all transportation costs. Return one week after receipt. Participation is limited to deaf or hard of hearing Americans, their parents, families, teachers, counselors, or others whose use would benefit a deaf or hard of hearing person. Only one person in the audience needs to be hearing impaired. You must register--which is free. These videos are all open-captioned--no special equipment is required for viewing.

Source: Described and Captioned Media Program
National Association of the Deaf
4211 Church Street Ext.
Roebuck, SC 29376
Phone: 1-800-237-6213
Fax: 1-800-538-5636
World Wide Web URL: http://www.dcmp.org

Ballet Folclorico de la Universidad de Guardalajara

Ballet includes traditional dances of Michoacan, Veracruz, Nayarit, Oaxaca, Chapala and Jalisco.

Availability: Schools, libraries, and nursing homes in the United States.
Suggested Grade: 6-12
lANGUAGE: Spanish
Order Number: DFMEX21-video
Production Date: 1993
Format: VHS videotape
Terms: Borrowers must have a User's Agreement on file with this source--available by mail or via the Internet. Return postage is paid by borrower; return 12 days after showing. Book at least three weeks in advance. All borrowers are limited to a total of ten items per semester.

Source: Latin American Resource Center
Stone Center for Latin American Studies
Tulane University, 100 Jones Hall
New Orleans, LA 70118
Phone: 1-504-862-3143
Fax: 1-504-865-6719
World Wide Web URL:
http://stonecenter.tulane.edu/pages/detail/48/
Lending-Library
Email Address: crcrts@tulane.edu

Ballet Folklorico Nacional de Mexico

Filmed at the beautiful Palacio Bellas Artes in Mexico City.

Availability: Schools and libraries in Iowa, Illinois, Michigan, Minnesota, and Wisconsin.
Suggested Grade: 6-12
Order Number: DANMEXB21VHS
Format: VHS videotape
Terms: Borrower pays return postage. Return 8 days after showing. Book 2 weeks in advance. Order may also be picked up for those near the Center.

Source: Center for Latin American and Caribbean Studies
UW-Milwaukee
P. O. Box 413
Milwaukee, WI 53201
Phone: 1-414-229-5987
World Wide Web URL: http://www.uwm.edu/Dept/CLACS
Email Address: audvis@usm.edu

Brazilian Carnival 1985: Samba School Competition

Music, dancing, and costumes of annual Samba School competitors in Rio de Janeiro.

Availability: Schools, libraries, and nursing homes in the United States.
Suggested Grade: 6-12
Order Number: DFBRA3-video
Production Date: 1985
Format: VHS videotape
Special Notes: Available seasonally, February and March.
Terms: Borrowers must have a User's Agreement on file with this source--available by mail or via the Internet. Return postage is paid by borrower; return 12 days after showing. Book at least three weeks in advance. All borrowers are limited to a total of ten items per semester.

Source: Latin American Resource Center
Stone Center for Latin American Studies
Tulane University, 100 Jones Hall
New Orleans, LA 70118

52

Phone: 1-504-862-3143
Fax: 1-504-865-6719
World Wide Web URL:
http://stonecenter.tulane.edu/pages/detail/48/
Lending-Library
Email Address: crcrts@tulane.edu

Brazilian Music

Various Brazilian musicians taped from a TV broadcast.

Availability:	Schools, libraries, and nursing homes in the United States.
Suggested Grade:	6-12
Language:	Portuguese
Order Number:	MUBRA4-video
Format:	VHS videotape
Terms:	Borrowers must have a User's Agreement on file with this source--available by mail or via the Internet. Return postage is paid by borrower; return 12 days after showing. Book at least three weeks in advance. All borrowers are limited to a total of ten items per semester.

Source: Latin American Resource Center
Stone Center for Latin American Studies
Tulane University
100 Jones Hall
New Orleans, LA 70118
Phone: 1-504-862-3143
Fax: 1-504-865-6719
World Wide Web URL:
http://stonecenter.tulane.edu/pages/detail/48/
Lending-Library
Email Address: crcrts@tulane.edu

Buena Vista Social Club

Director Wim Wenders reveals the astonishing life stories, vibrant personalities and unforgettable music of the brilliantly talented but long overlooked performers who collaborated on the Buena Vista Social Club, a now-legendary recording of Cuban folk

Availability:	Schools and libraries in the United States and Canada.
Suggested Grade:	7-Adult
Order Number:	order by title
Production Date:	1999
Format:	VHS videotape
Terms:	Videos will typically be lent for seven days if mailed out--due date will be indicated. Films not returned within the time limit will be subject to overdue fines of $2 per video, per day. All borrowed must have a lending agreement on file. Form can be downloaded from http://isa.unc.edu/film/borrow.asplaform. Borrowers are responsible for the cost of return shipping. Materials must be returned via a shipping method that has tracking information.

Source: Latin American Film Collection
3219 Fed Ex Global Education Center
301 Pittsboro Street, CB 3205
Chapel Hill, NC 27599-3205
Email Address: LA_Films@email.unc.edu

Caribbean Music and Dance

Folk music and dance from Honduras, Grenada, Jamaica, and Haiti.

Availability:	Schools, libraries, and nursing homes in the United States.
Suggested Grade:	6-12
Order Number:	MUCARIB1-video
Production Date:	1985
Format:	VHS videotape
Terms:	Borrowers must have a User's Agreement on file with this source--available by mail or via the Internet. Return postage is paid by borrower; return 12 days after showing. Book at least three weeks in advance. All borrowers are limited to a total of ten items per semester.

Source: Latin American Resource Center
Stone Center for Latin American Studies
Tulane University
100 Jones Hall
New Orleans, LA 70118
Phone: 1-504-862-3143
Fax: 1-504-865-6719
World Wide Web URL:
http://stonecenter.tulane.edu/pages/detail/48/
Lending-Library
Email Address: crcrts@tulane.edu

Central American Peace Concert, The

Concert was held in Managua, Nicaragua in 1983, with 150 performers.

Availability:	Schools, libraries, and nursing homes in the United States.
Suggested Grade:	6-12
Languages:	Spanish with English subtitles
Order Number:	MUCA1-video
Production Date:	1983
Format:	VHS videotape
Terms:	Borrowers must have a User's Agreement on file with this source--available by mail or via the Internet. Return postage is paid by borrower; return 12 days after showing. Book at least three weeks in advance. All borrowers are limited to a total of ten items per semester.

Source: Latin American Resource Center
Stone Center for Latin American Studies
Tulane University
100 Jones Hall
New Orleans, LA 70118
Phone: 1-504-862-3143
Fax: 1-504-865-6719
World Wide Web URL:
http://stonecenter.tulane.edu/pages/detail/48/
Lending-Library
Email Address: crcrts@tulane.edu

Chinese Music in Taiwan: A Living Tradition

Kaohsiung Municipal Experimental Chinese Orchestra plays traditional Chinese folk songs, ballads, ceremonial tuns, and more as they are interpreted today in Taiwan.

Availability:	Schools, libraries, and nursing homes in the United States and Canada.

Suggested Grade: All ages
Order Number: TV002
Format: VHS videotape
Terms: Borrower pays return postage. Return with 14 days after scheduled showing, via UPS or U. S. Mail. All requests must included an educational institution affiliation, a current address, and phone number. Order through web site only.

Source: Cornell University East Asia Program
World Wide Web URL:
http://www.einaudi.cornell.edu/eastasia/outreach/video.asp
Email Address: east_asia1@cornell.edu

Chulas Fronteras

Exciting Norteno (Tex-Mex) musicians.
Availability: Schools, libraries, and nursing homes in the United States.
Suggested Grade: 6-12
Order Number: MUUS2-video
Production Date: 1976
Format: VHS videotape
Terms: Borrowers must have a User's Agreement on file with this source--available by mail or via the Internet. Return postage is paid by borrower; return 12 days after showing. Book at least three weeks in advance. All borrowers are limited to a total of ten items per semester.

Source: Latin American Resource Center
Stone Center for Latin American Studies
Tulane University
100 Jones Hall
New Orleans, LA   70118
Phone: 1-504-862-3143
Fax: 1-504-865-6719
World Wide Web URL:
http://stonecenter.tulane.edu/pages/detail/48/
Lending-Library
Email Address: crcrts@tulane.edu

Circles-Cycles: Kathak Dance

Demonstrations of both the pure dance and narrative aspects of the classical dance style of northern India by some of its greatest living performers. Miniature paintings of Kathak dancers in the Hindu and Muslim courts of northern India provide historical background.
Availability: Schools, libraries, homeschoolers, and nursing homes in the southeastern United States.
Suggested Grade: 7-12
Order Number: order by title
Production Date: 1989
Format: VHS videotape
Terms: Borrower pays return postage. Return 2 days after showing via United Parcel Service, insured. Book 2 weeks in advance.

Source: Center for South Asian Studies
University of Virginia
Video Library Coordinator
P. O. Box 400169, 110 Minor Hall
Charlottesville, VA   22904-4169

Phone: 1-434-924-8815
Email Address: southasia@virginia.edu

Dancing Girls of Lahore

The courtesans of Lahore, descended from the dancers of the Moghul courts, will be affected by Pakistan's direction as either a religious Islamic state or a more liberal, culturally Islamic society. The film presents two young women who would like to escape to new lives as film stars but must work as entertainers to support their brothers and fathers.
Availability: Schools, libraries, homeschoolers, and nursing homes in the southeastern United States.
Suggested Grade: 7-12
Order Number: order by title
Production Date: 1991
Format: VHS videotape
Terms: Borrower pays return postage. Return 2 days after showing via United Parcel Service, insured. Book 2 weeks in advance.

Source: Center for South Asian Studies
University of Virginia
Video Library Coordinator
P. O. Box 400169, 110 Minor Hall
Charlottesville, VA   22904-4169
Phone: 1-434-924-8815
Email Address: southasia@virginia.edu

Danzas Folkloricas Mexicanas

Features songs and classical dance and music.
Availability: Schools, libraries, and nursing homes in the United States.
Suggested Grade: 6-12
Language: Spanish
Order Number: DFMEX9-video
Production Date: 1988
Format: VHS videotape
Terms: Borrowers must have a User's Agreement on file with this source--available by mail or via the Internet. Return postage is paid by borrower; return 12 days after showing. Book at least three weeks in advance. All borrowers are limited to a total of ten items per semester.

Source: Latin American Resource Center
Stone Center for Latin American Studies
Tulane University
100 Jones Hall
New Orleans, LA   70118
Phone: 1-504-862-3143
Fax: 1-504-865-6719
World Wide Web URL:
http://stonecenter.tulane.edu/pages/detail/48/
Lending-Library
Email Address: crcrts@tulane.edu

Del Mero Corazon (Straight from the Heart)

Love songs from the Southwest, the heart of Chicano culture of Tex-Mex Norteno music.
Availability: Schools, libraries, and nursing homes in the United States.

Suggested Grade: 6-12
Order Number: MUUS1-video
Production Date: 1976
Format: VHS videotape
Terms: Borrowers must have a User's Agreement on file with this source--available by mail or via the Internet. Return postage is paid by borrower; return 12 days after showing. Book at least three weeks in advance. All borrowers are limited to a total of ten items per semester.
Source: **Latin American Resource Center**
Stone Center for Latin American Studies
Tulane University
100 Jones Hall
New Orleans, LA   70118
Phone: 1-504-862-3143
Fax: 1-504-865-6719
World Wide Web URL:
http://stonecenter.tulane.edu/pages/detail/48/
Lending-Library
Email Address: crcrts@tulane.edu

Ennosuke Ichikawa III: Kabuki Actor

Features a famous Japanese Kabuki actor in several performances. The Kabuki theater dates from the early 17th century and is still popular today.
Availability: Schools, libraries, and nursing homes in Hawaii.
Suggested Grade: All ages
Order Number: CU-13
Production Date: 1985
Format: VHS videotape
Terms: Borrower pays return postage. A maximum of 3 videos may be borrowed per person. Return within one week of date borrowed.
Source: **Consulate General of Japan, Honolulu**
1742 Nuuanu Avenue
Honolulu, HI   96817-3294
Phone: 1-808-543-3111
Fax: 1-808-543-3170
World Wide Web URL:
http://www.honolulu.us.emb-japan.go.jp

Ennosuke Ichikawa III: Kabuki Actor

Features a famous Japanese Kabuki actor in several performances. The Kabuki theater dates from the early 17th century and is still popular today.
Availability: Schools, libraries, homeschoolers, and nursing homes in OREGON AND SOUTHERN IDAHO ONLY. Please make requests via the web site.
Suggested Grade: All ages
Order Number: 203
Production Date: 1985
Format: VHS videotape
Terms: Borrower pays return postage. Return within three weeks after scheduled showing date. Book one month in advance if possible. Rewind the video and wrap securely for return. Be certain to indicate video number, date needed, name of your organization, and address to

which video should be sent, along with phone number. Audience report enclosed with the video must be completed and returned.
Source: **Consulate General of Japan, Oregon**
Attn: Tamara, Video Library
1300 S. W. Fifth Avenue, Suite 2700
Portland, OR   97201
Phone: 1-503-221-1811, ext. 17
World Wide Web URL:
http://www.portland.us.emb-japan.go.jp/en/index.html
Email Address: tamara@cgjpdx.org

Entrada del Gran Poder

A parade and dance/costume competition celebrated since the colonial period in La Paz, Bolivia.
Availability: Schools, libraries, and nursing homes in the United States.
Suggested Grade: 6-12
Languages: Spanish with some commentary in Quechua and Aymara
Order Number: DFBOL3-video
Production Date: 1985
Format: VHS videotape
Terms: Borrowers must have a User's Agreement on file with this source--available by mail or via the Internet. Return postage is paid by borrower; return 12 days after showing. Book at least three weeks in advance. All borrowers are limited to a total of ten items per semester.
Source: **Latin American Resource Center**
Stone Center for Latin American Studies
Tulane University
100 Jones Hall
New Orleans, LA   70118
Phone: 1-504-862-3143
Fax: 1-504-865-6719
World Wide Web URL:
http://stonecenter.tulane.edu/pages/detail/48/
Lending-Library
Email Address: crcrts@tulane.edu

Flamenco

Shows the beauty of this dance that has long been an integral part of the Spanish heart and culture.
Availability: Schools and libraries in Iowa, Illinois, Michigan, Minnesota, and Wisconsin.
Suggested Grade: 6-12
Languages: Spanish with some English subtitles
Order Number: DANSPAF61VHS
Production Date: 1994
Format: VHS videotape
Terms: Borrower pays return postage. Return 8 days after showing. Book 2 weeks in advance. Order may also be picked up for those near the Center.
Source: **Center for Latin American and Caribbean Studies**
UW-Milwaukee
P. O. Box 413
Milwaukee, WI   53201
Phone: 1-414-229-5987
World Wide Web URL: http://www.uwm.edu/Dept/CLACS
Email Address: audvis@usm.edu

Harvesting New Songs

Folkloric group Sotavento describes instruments, rhythms, and social influence of music from Colombia and Venezuela, and performs five selections.

Availability: Schools, libraries, and nursing homes in the United States.
Suggested Grade: 6-12
Order Number: MUSA2-video
Production Date: 1986
Format: VHS videotape
Terms: Borrowers must have a User's Agreement on file with this source--available by mail or via the Internet. Return postage is paid by borrower; return 12 days after showing. Book at least three weeks in advance. All borrowers are limited to a total of ten items per semester.

Source: Latin American Resource Center
Stone Center for Latin American Studies
Tulane University
100 Jones Hall
New Orleans, LA 70118
Phone: 1-504-862-3143
Fax: 1-504-865-6719
World Wide Web URL:
http://stonecenter.tulane.edu/pages/detail/48/
Lending-Library
Email Address: crcrts@tulane.edu

Harvesting New Songs - Brazil

Folkloric group Sotavento describes instruments, rhythms, and social influences of the music of Brazil, and performs three selections.

Availability: Schools, libraries, and nursing homes in the United States.
Suggested Grade: 6-12
Order Number: MUBRA7-video
Production Date: 1986
Format: VHS videotape
Terms: Borrowers must have a User's Agreement on file with this source--available by mail or via the Internet. Return postage is paid by borrower; return 12 days after showing. Book at least three weeks in advance. All borrowers are limited to a total of ten items per semester.

Source: Latin American Resource Center
Stone Center for Latin American Studies
Tulane University
100 Jones Hall
New Orleans, LA 70118
Phone: 1-504-862-3143
Fax: 1-504-865-6719
World Wide Web URL:
http://stonecenter.tulane.edu/pages/detail/48/
Lending-Library
Email Address: crcrts@tulane.edu

Heated Competition: Jonkara-Bushi

A contest in Hirosaki City, Aomori Prefecture, to appoint the national champion of young players of Tsugaru Jamisen, a traditional banjo-like musical instrument is shown.

Availability: Schools, libraries, and nursing homes in Illinois, Indiana, Iowa, Kansas, Minnesota, Missouri, Nebraska, North Dakota, South Dakota, and Wisconsin.
Suggested Grade: 6-Adult
Order Number: 09002
Production Date: 1991
Format: VHS videotape
Special Notes: Part of the "Nippon Life II" series.
Terms: Borrower pays return postage by U. S. Mail, UPS, or Federal Express, including insurance for "original" videos. Write, call, fax, or e-mail to request an application. An application form MUST be sent in one month in advance but not more than six months in advance. Include alternate titles and dates if provider can substitute titles. Send a SASE with request if you require confirmation. Return immediately after scheduled showing date. Videos may not be copied or broadcast without permission from the producer of the video. Borrower is responsible if video is lost or damaged.

Source: Consulate General of Japan at Chicago
Japan Information Center
Library
737 North Michigan Avenue, Suite 1000
Chicago, IL 60611
Phone: 1-312-280-0430
Fax: 1-312-280-6883
World Wide Web URL:
http://www.chicago.us.emb-japan.go.jp/jic.html
Email Address: jicchicago@webkddi.com

Heated Competition: Jonkara-Bushi

A contest to appoint the national champion of young players of Tsugaru Jamisen, a traditional banjo-like musical instrument.

Availability: Schools, libraries and homeschoolers in Alabama, Georgia, North Carolina, South Carolina, and Virginia.
Suggested Grade: 4-12
Order Number: 703
Production Date: 1991
Format: VHS videotape
Special Notes: Part of the "Nippon Life II" series.
Terms: Borrower pays return postage. Two tapes may be borrowed at a time. Return within 7 days after receipt. Reservations may be made by filling the application found on the web site.

Source: Consulate General of Japan, Atlanta
Japan Information Center
One Alliance Center
3500 Lenox Road, Suite 1600
Atlanta, GA 30326
Phone: 1-404-365-9240
Fax: 1-404-240-4311
World Wide Web URL:
http://www.atlanta.us.emb-japan.go.jp
Email Address: info@cgjapanatlanta.org

Heated Competition: Jonkara-Bushi

A contest to appoint the national champion of young players of Tsugaru Jamisen, a traditional banjo-like musical instrument.

Availability: Schools, libraries, homeschoolers, and nursing homes in OREGON AND SOUTHERN IDAHO ONLY. Please make requests via the web site.
Suggested Grade: 4-12
Order Number: 173
Production Date: 1991
Format: VHS videotape
Special Notes: Part of the "Nippon Life II" series.
Terms: Borrower pays return postage. Return within three weeks after scheduled showing date. Book one month in advance if possible. Rewind the video and wrap securely for return. Be certain to indicate video number, date needed, name of your organization, and address to which video should be sent, along with phone number. Audience report enclosed with the video must be completed and returned.

Source: Consulate General of Japan, Oregon
Attn: Tamara, Video Library
1300 S. W. Fifth Avenue, Suite 2700
Portland, OR 97201
Phone: 1-503-221-1811, ext. 17
World Wide Web URL:
http://www.portland.us.emb-japan.go.jp/en/index.html
Email Address: tamara@cgjpdx.org

Kabuki: Classic Theater of Japan/Noh, Drama, Bunraku: The Puppet Theater of Japan

The unique theatrical art form of Kabuki combines dance, music, and acting skills. The Noh drama, one of Japan's finest art forms is presented. Also the art of Japanese Bunraku theatre, including a description of the craft of making the large puppets.

Availability: Schools, libraries, and nursing homes in Hawaii.
Suggested Grade: 6-12
Order Number: CU-14
Production Date: 1964
Format: VHS videotape
Special Notes: Quite dated but the information is still pertinent.
Terms: Borrower pays return postage. A maximum of 3 videos may be borrowed per person. Return within one week of date borrowed.

Source: Consulate General of Japan, Honolulu
1742 Nuuanu Avenue
Honolulu, HI 96817-3294
Phone: 1-808-543-3111
Fax: 1-808-543-3170
World Wide Web URL:
http://www.honolulu.us.emb-japan.go.jp

La Rumba

History of the rumba from the plantations of colonial Cuba, to nightclubs in the United States.

Availability: Schools, libraries, and nursing homes in the United States.
Suggested Grade: 6-12
Languages: Spanish with English subtitles
Order Number: MUCUB11-video
Format: VHS videotape
Terms: Borrowers must have a User's Agreement on file with this source--available by mail or via the Internet. Return postage is paid by borrower; return 12 days after showing. Book at least three weeks in advance. All borrowers are limited to a total of ten items per semester.

Source: Latin American Resource Center
Stone Center for Latin American Studies
Tulane University
100 Jones Hall
New Orleans, LA 70118
Phone: 1-504-862-3143
Fax: 1-504-865-6719
World Wide Web URL:
http://stonecenter.tulane.edu/pages/detail/48/
Lending-Library
Email Address: crcrts@tulane.edu

Los Animales: Musica Infantil Mexicana

Review of juvenile music from 1850 to 1950 with traditional songs and digital animation.

Availability: Schools, libraries, and nursing homes in the United States.
Suggested Grade: 6-12
Language: Spanish
Order Number: MUMEX12-video
Production Date: 1995
Format: VHS videotape
Terms: Borrowers must have a User's Agreement on file with this source--available by mail or via the Internet. Return postage is paid by borrower; return 12 days after showing. Book at least three weeks in advance. All borrowers are limited to a total of ten items per semester.

Source: Latin American Resource Center
Stone Center for Latin American Studies
Tulane University, 100 Jones Hall
New Orleans, LA 70118
Phone: 1-504-862-3143
Fax: 1-504-865-6719
World Wide Web URL:
http://stonecenter.tulane.edu/pages/detail/48/
Lending-Library
Email Address: crcrts@tulane.edu

Mexican Dances (Part II)

Focuses on many dances from Mexico.

Availability: Schools and libraries in Iowa, Illinois, Michigan, Minnesota, and Wisconsin.
Suggested Grade: 4-12
Order Number: DANMEXM57VHS
Production Date: 1957
Format: VHS videotape
Terms: Borrower pays return postage. Return 8 days after showing. Book 2 weeks in advance. Order may also be picked up for those near the Center.

FINE ARTS--MUSIC AND DRAMA

Source: Center for Latin American and Caribbean Studies
UW-Milwaukee
P. O. Box 413
Milwaukee, WI 53201
Phone: 1-414-229-5987
World Wide Web URL: http://www.uwm.edu/Dept/CLACS
Email Address: audvis@usm.edu

Musica Latina I

Music videos of contemporary pop performers.

Availability: Schools, libraries, and nursing homes in the United States.
Suggested Grade: 6-12
Language: Spanish
Order Number: MULA10-video
Format: VHS videotape
Terms: Borrowers must have a User's Agreement on file with this source--available by mail or via the Internet. Return postage is paid by borrower; return 12 days after showing. Book at least three weeks in advance. All borrowers are limited to a total of ten items per semester.
Source: Latin American Resource Center
Stone Center for Latin American Studies
Tulane University
100 Jones Hall
New Orleans, LA 70118
Phone: 1-504-862-3143
Fax: 1-504-865-6719
World Wide Web URL:
http://stonecenter.tulane.edu/pages/detail/48/
Lending-Library
Email Address: crcrts@tulane.edu

Music of Latin America

Roots of Indian music, with wind and percussion, and proceeds through development of string instruments in Latin America.

Availability: Schools, libraries, and nursing homes in the United States.
Suggested Grade: 6-12
Order Number: MULA9-video
Production Date: 1987
Format: VHS videotape
Terms: Borrowers must have a User's Agreement on file with this source--available by mail or via the Internet. Return postage is paid by borrower; return 12 days after showing. Book at least three weeks in advance. All borrowers are limited to a total of ten items per semester.
Source: Latin American Resource Center
Stone Center for Latin American Studies
Tulane University
100 Jones Hall
New Orleans, LA 70118
Phone: 1-504-862-3143
Fax: 1-504-865-6719
World Wide Web URL:
http://stonecenter.tulane.edu/pages/detail/48/
Lending-Library
Email Address: crcrts@tulane.edu

Music Videos

Not the music videos we always read about, but music that depicts the culture of many countries.

Availability: All requesters
Suggested Grade: All ages
Order Number: not applicable
Format: Streaming Video
Source: National Geographic
World Wide Web URL:
http://video.nationalgeographic.com/video/

New Audiences for Mexican Music

First part of program describes popular dance music, Banda. The second part explains history of mariachi music. Part three explains Tejano music and culture.

Availability: Schools, libraries, and nursing homes in the United States.
Suggested Grade: 6-12
Order Number: MUUS5-video
Production Date: 1995
Format: VHS videotape
Terms: Borrowers must have a User's Agreement on file with this source--available by mail or via the Internet. Return postage is paid by borrower; return 12 days after showing. Book at least three weeks in advance. All borrowers are limited to a total of ten items per semester.
Source: Latin American Resource Center
Stone Center for Latin American Studies
Tulane University
100 Jones Hall
New Orleans, LA 70118
Phone: 1-504-862-3143
Fax: 1-504-865-6719
World Wide Web URL:
http://stonecenter.tulane.edu/pages/detail/48/
Lending-Library
Email Address: crcrts@tulane.edu

Not MTV: Music Videos with a Message

Five music videos from Panama and Brazil which express cultural and political viewpoints.

Availability: Schools, libraries, and nursing homes in the United States.
Suggested Grade: 6-12
Language: Some English subtitles
Order Number: MULA12-video
Production Date: 1990
Format: VHS videotape
Terms: Borrowers must have a User's Agreement on file with this source--available by mail or via the Internet. Return postage is paid by borrower; return 12 days after showing. Book at least three weeks in advance. All borrowers are limited to a total of ten items per semester.
Source: Latin American Resource Center
Stone Center for Latin American Studies
Tulane University
100 Jones Hall
New Orleans, LA 70118
Phone: 1-504-862-3143

All materials listed in this 2011-2012 edition are BRAND NEW!

Fax: 1-504-865-6719
World Wide Web URL:
http://stonecenter.tulane.edu/pages/detail/48/
Lending-Library
Email Address: crcrts@tulane.edu

Our Mexican-American Musical Heritage
Explores pre-Columbian and Spanish antecedents of Mexican music and their effect on contemporary forms.
Availability: Schools, libraries, and nursing homes in the United States.
Suggested Grade: 6-12
Order Number: HISP39-video
Format: VHS videotape
Special Notes: Includes study questions.
Terms: Borrowers must have a User's Agreement on file with this source--available by mail or via the Internet. Return postage is paid by borrower; return 12 days after showing. Book at least three weeks in advance. All borrowers are limited to a total of ten items per semester.
Source: Latin American Resource Center
Stone Center for Latin American Studies
Tulane University
100 Jones Hall
New Orleans, LA 70118
Phone: 1-504-862-3143
Fax: 1-504-865-6719
World Wide Web URL:
http://stonecenter.tulane.edu/pages/detail/48/
Lending-Library
Email Address: crcrts@tulane.edu

Raices Del Pueblo: Cantos y Danzas de Veracruz
Ballet Folklorico de la Universidad Veracruzana performs traditional regional dances.
Availability: Schools, libraries, and nursing homes in the United States.
Suggested Grade: 6-12
Language: Spanish
Order Number: DFMEX18-video
Production Date: 1990
Format: VHS videotape
Terms: Borrowers must have a User's Agreement on file with this source--available by mail or via the Internet. Return postage is paid by borrower; return 12 days after showing. Book at least three weeks in advance. All borrowers are limited to a total of ten items per semester.
Source: Latin American Resource Center
Stone Center for Latin American Studies
Tulane University
100 Jones Hall
New Orleans, LA 70118
Phone: 1-504-862-3143
Fax: 1-504-865-6719
World Wide Web URL:
http://stonecenter.tulane.edu/pages/detail/48/
Lending-Library
Email Address: crcrts@tulane.edu

Routes of Rhythm--Part II
History of popular music in Cuba.
Availability: Schools, libraries, and nursing homes in the United States.
Suggested Grade: 6-12
Order Number: MULA11-video
Format: VHS videotape
Terms: Borrowers must have a User's Agreement on file with this source--available by mail or via the Internet. Return postage is paid by borrower; return 12 days after showing. Book at least three weeks in advance. All borrowers are limited to a total of ten items per semester.
Source: Latin American Resource Center
Stone Center for Latin American Studies
Tulane University
100 Jones Hall
New Orleans, LA 70118
Phone: 1-504-862-3143
Fax: 1-504-865-6719
World Wide Web URL:
http://stonecenter.tulane.edu/pages/detail/48/
Lending-Library
Email Address: crcrts@tulane.edu

Routes of Rhythm--Part III
History of Latin American music in the United States.
Availability: Schools, libraries, and nursing homes in the United States.
Suggested Grade: 6-12
Order Number: MULA11-video
Format: VHS videotape
Terms: Borrowers must have a User's Agreement on file with this source--available by mail or via the Internet. Return postage is paid by borrower; return 12 days after showing. Book at least three weeks in advance. All borrowers are limited to a total of ten items per semester.
Source: Latin American Resource Center
Stone Center for Latin American Studies
Tulane University
100 Jones Hall
New Orleans, LA 70118
Phone: 1-504-862-3143
Fax: 1-504-865-6719
World Wide Web URL:
http://stonecenter.tulane.edu/pages/detail/48/
Lending-Library
Email Address: crcrts@tulane.edu

Salsa!
Salsa (literally hot sauce) is urban Latino music of New York, Puerto Rico, and Cuba. Here is a taste of this music.
Availability: Schools in the United States.
Suggested Grade: 7-Adult
Order Number: order by title
Production Date: 1988
Format: VHS videotape
Terms: Borrower pays return postage. Return 14 days after receipt, via USPS including insurance. All borrowers must have a current lending agreement on file with the

Outreach program. This agreement is available via the web site or may be requested via phone or fax.

Source: Center for Latin American Studies
University of Florida
319 Grinter Hall
P. O. Box 115530
Gainesville, FL 32611-5530
Phone: 1-352-392-0375
Fax: 1-352-392-7682
World Wide Web URL: http://www.latam.ufl.edu/outreach
Email Address: maryr@ufl.edu

Song for the Community, A

Shows a Japanese borough community choir prepare for a concert of Beethoven's Ninth Symphony. This is a true behind-the-scenes look at this community's effort.

Availability:	Schools, libraries, and nursing homes in Hawaii.
Suggested Grade:	7-12
Order Number:	CU-44
Production Date:	1990
Format:	VHS videotape
Terms:	Borrower pays return postage. A maximum of 3 videos may be borrowed per person. Return within one week of date borrowed.

Source: Consulate General of Japan, Honolulu
1742 Nuuanu Avenue
Honolulu, HI 96817-3294
Phone: 1-808-543-3111
Fax: 1-808-543-3170
World Wide Web URL:
http://www.honolulu.us.emb-japan.go.jp

Song for the Community, A

Shows a Japanese borough community choir prepare for a concert of Beethoven's Ninth Symphony. This is a true behind-the-scenes look at this community's effort.

Availability:	Schools, libraries, homeschoolers, and nursing homes in OREGON AND SOUTHERN IDAHO ONLY. Please make requests via the web site.
Suggested Grade:	7-12
Order Number:	169
Production Date:	1990
Format:	VHS videotape
Terms:	Borrower pays return postage. Return within three weeks after scheduled showing date. Book one month in advance if possible. Rewind the video and wrap securely for return. Be certain to indicate video number, date needed, name of your organization, and address to which video should be sent, along with phone number. Audience report enclosed with the video must be completed and returned.

Source: Consulate General of Japan, Oregon
Attn: Tamara, Video Library
1300 S. W. Fifth Avenue, Suite 2700
Portland, OR 97201
Phone: 1-503-221-1811, ext. 17

World Wide Web URL:
http://www.portland.us.emb-japan.go.jp/en/index.html
Email Address: tamara@cgjpdx.org

Sound of Millennia

A performance by the Korean National Music Company, representing Korea's many music and dance forms, was recorded at the Shrine Auditorium in Los Angeles, USA, in September of 1991 at the gala concert "Sound of Millennia," to celebrate Korea's entry to membership of the United Nations.

Availability:	Schools, libraries, and nursing homes in the United States and Canada.
Suggested Grade:	6-Adult
Order Number:	KV013
Format:	VHS videotape
Terms:	Borrower pays return postage. Return with 14 days after scheduled showing, via UPS or U. S. Mail. All requests must included an educational institution affiliation, a current address, and phone number. Order through web site only.

Source: Cornell University East Asia Program
World Wide Web URL:
http://www.einaudi.cornell.edu/eastasia/outreach/video.asp
Email Address: east_asia1@cornell.edu

Story of the National Anthem, The

Gives a brief history of how and why "The Star-Spangled Banner" was written. Notes that one person's patriotism can influence others. Students explain the words and phrases of the song and create their own class anthem.

Availability:	Schools, libraries, and homeschoolers in the United States who serve the hearing impaired.
Suggested Grade:	3-6
Order Number:	13062
Production Date:	1994
Format:	DVD
Special Notes:	Produced by New Castle Communications.
Terms:	Sponsor pays all transportation costs. Return one week after receipt. Participation is limited to deaf or hard of hearing Americans, their parents, families, teachers, counselors, or others whose use would benefit a deaf or hard of hearing person. Only one person in the audience needs to be hearing impaired. You must register--which is free. These videos are all open-captioned--no special equipment is required for viewing.

Source: Described and Captioned Media Program
National Association of the Deaf
4211 Church Street Ext.
Roebuck, SC 29376
Phone: 1-800-237-6213
Fax: 1-800-538-5636
World Wide Web URL: http://www.dcmp.org

Tango Is Also History

Development of the tango in Argentina, and its role in political and cultural history.

Availability: Schools, libraries, and nursing homes in the United States.
Suggested Grade: 6-12
Order Number: MUARG6-video
Production Date: 1983
Format: VHS videotape
Terms: Borrowers must have a User's Agreement on file with this source--available by mail or via the Internet. Return postage is paid by borrower; return 12 days after showing. Book at least three weeks in advance. All borrowers are limited to a total of ten items per semester.
Source: Latin American Resource Center
Stone Center for Latin American Studies
Tulane University
100 Jones Hall
New Orleans, LA 70118
Phone: 1-504-862-3143
Fax: 1-504-865-6719
World Wide Web URL:
http://stonecenter.tulane.edu/pages/detail/48/
Lending-Library
Email Address: crcrts@tulane.edu

Tango: Our Dance

Captures the sensuality and rituals of the complex art form of the tango, Argentina's national dance.
Availability: Schools and libraries in Iowa, Illinois, Michigan, Minnesota, and Wisconsin.
Suggested Grade: 6-12
Languages: Spanish with English subtitles
Order Number: DANARGT15.1VHS
Production Date: 1988
Format: VHS videotape
Terms: Borrower pays return postage. Return 8 days after showing. Book 2 weeks in advance. Order may also be picked up for those near the Center.
Source: Center for Latin American and Caribbean Studies
UW-Milwaukee
P. O. Box 413
Milwaukee, WI 53201
Phone: 1-414-229-5987
World Wide Web URL: http://www.uwm.edu/Dept/CLACS
Email Address: audvis@usm.edu

Tango: Our Dance

Captures the sensuality and rituals of the complex art form of the tango, Argentina's national dance.
Availability: Schools, libraries, and nursing homes in the United States.
Suggested Grade: 6-12
Spanish with English subtitles
Order Number: DFARG6-video
Production Date: 1987
Format: VHS videotape
Terms: Borrowers must have a User's Agreement on file with this source--available by mail or via the Internet. Return postage is paid by borrower; return 12 days after showing. Book at least three weeks in advance. All borrowers are limited to a total of ten items per semester.

Source: Latin American Resource Center
Stone Center for Latin American Studies
Tulane University, 100 Jones Hall
New Orleans, LA 70118
Phone: 1-504-862-3143
Fax: 1-504-865-6719
World Wide Web URL:
http://stonecenter.tulane.edu/pages/detail/48/
Lending-Library
Email Address: crcrts@tulane.edu

Theater Lives, The

Shows the Japanese puppet theater, theater in the outlying rural areas, and the lifestyles of the people in these areas. Also shows the creation of puppets and their customs.
Availability: Schools, libraries, and nursing homes in Hawaii.
Suggested Grade: 6-Adult
Order Number: CU-17
Format: VHS videotape
Terms: Borrower pays return postage. A maximum of 3 videos may be borrowed per person. Return within one week of date borrowed.
Source: Consulate General of Japan, Honolulu
1742 Nuuanu Avenue
Honolulu, HI 96817-3294
Phone: 1-808-543-3111
Fax: 1-808-543-3170
World Wide Web URL:
http://www.honolulu.us.emb-japan.go.jp

Theater Lives, The

Shows the Japanese puppet theater, theater in the outlying rural areas, and the lifestyles of the people in these areas. Also shows the creation of puppets and their customs.
Availability: Schools, libraries, homeschoolers, and nursing homes in OREGON AND SOUTHERN IDAHO ONLY. Please make requests via the web site.
Suggested Grade: 6-Adult
Order Number: 204
Production Date: 1985
Format: VHS videotape
Terms: Borrower pays return postage. Return within three weeks after scheduled showing date. Book one month in advance if possible. Rewind the video and wrap securely for return. Be certain to indicate video number, date needed, name of your organization, and address to which video should be sent, along with phone number. Audience report enclosed with the video must be completed and returned.
Source: Consulate General of Japan, Oregon
Attn: Tamara, Video Library
1300 S. W. Fifth Avenue, Suite 2700
Portland, OR 97201
Phone: 1-503-221-1811, ext. 17
World Wide Web URL:
http://www.portland.us.emb-japan.go.jp/en/index.html
Email Address: tamara@cgjpdx.org

FINE ARTS--MUSIC AND DRAMA

Traditional Japanese Culture: Japanese Dance
Shows the two basic concepts of dance which originated from dances dedicated to the gods.

Availability:	Schools, libraries, and nursing homes in Illinois, Indiana, Iowa, Kansas, Minnesota, Missouri, Nebraska, North Dakota, South Dakota, and Wisconsin.
Suggested Grade:	6-12
Order Number:	10001
Production Date:	2001
Format:	VHS videotape
Terms:	Borrower pays return postage by U. S. Mail, UPS, or Federal Express, including insurance for "original" videos. Write, call, fax, or e-mail to request an application. An application form MUST be sent in one month in advance but not more than six months in advance. Include alternate titles and dates if provider can substitute titles. Send a SASE with request if you require confirmation. Return immediately after scheduled showing date. Videos may not be copied or broadcast without permission from the producer of the video. Borrower is responsible if video is lost or damaged.

Source: Consulate General of Japan at Chicago
Japan Information Center
Library
737 North Michigan Avenue, Suite 1000
Chicago, IL 60611
Phone: 1-312-280-0430
Fax: 1-312-280-6883
World Wide Web URL:
http://www.chicago.us.emb-japan.go.jp/jic.html
Email Address: jicchicago@webkddi.com

Traditional Japanese Culture: Japanese Dance
Shows the two basic concepts of dance which originated from dances dedicated to the gods.

Availability:	Schools, libraries and homeschoolers in Alabama, Georgia, North Carolina, South Carolina, and Virginia.
Suggested Grade:	6-12
Order Number:	158
Production Date:	2001
Format:	VHS videotape
Terms:	Borrower pays return postage. Two tapes may be borrowed at a time. Return within 7 days after receipt. Reservations may be made by filling the application found on the web site.

Source: Consulate General of Japan, Atlanta
Japan Information Center
One Alliance Center
3500 Lenox Road, Suite 1600
Atlanta, GA 30326
Phone: 1-404-365-9240
Fax: 1-404-240-4311
World Wide Web URL:
http://www.atlanta.us.emb-japan.go.jp
Email Address: info@cgjapanatlanta.org

Traditional Japanese Culture: Japanese Dance
Shows the two basic concepts of dance which originated from dances dedicated to the gods.

Availability:	Schools, libraries, and nursing homes in Hawaii.
Suggested Grade:	6-12
Order Number:	CU-138
Production Date:	2001
Format:	VHS videotape
Terms:	Borrower pays return postage. A maximum of 3 videos may be borrowed per person. Return within one week of date borrowed.

Source: Consulate General of Japan, Honolulu
1742 Nuuanu Avenue
Honolulu, HI 96817-3294
Phone: 1-808-543-3111
Fax: 1-808-543-3170
World Wide Web URL:
http://www.honolulu.us.emb-japan.go.jp

Traditional Japanese Culture: Japanese Dance
Shows the two basic concepts of dance which originated from dances dedicated to the gods.

Availability:	Schools, libraries, homeschoolers, and nursing homes in Connecticut, Delaware, Maryland, New Jersey, New York, Pennsylvania, and West Virginia.
Suggested Grade:	6-12
Order Number:	order by title
Production Date:	2001
Format:	VHS videotape
Terms:	Send a blank videotape to this source and they will dub the program you desire onto it for permanent retention. You must send a self-addressed, stamped envelope with sufficient postage for return.

Source: Consulate General of Japan, New York
Audio Video Dept.
299 Park Avenue, 18th Floor
New York, NY 10171
Phone: 1-212-371-8222
Fax: 1-212-319-6357
World Wide Web URL: http://www.ny.us.emb-japan.go.jp

Traditional Japanese Culture: Japanese Dance
Shows the two basic concepts of dance which originated from dances dedicated to the gods.

Availability:	Schools, libraries, homeschoolers, and nursing homes in OREGON AND SOUTHERN IDAHO ONLY. Please make requests via the web site.
Suggested Grade:	6-12
Order Number:	447
Production Date:	1999
Format:	VHS videotape
Terms:	Borrower pays return postage. Return within three weeks after scheduled showing date. Book one month in advance if possible. Rewind the video and wrap securely for return. Be certain to indicate video number, date needed, name of your organization, and address to

which video should be sent, along with phone number. Audience report enclosed with the video must be completed and returned.

Source: **Consulate General of Japan, Oregon**
Attn: Tamara, Video Library
1300 S. W. Fifth Avenue, Suite 2700
Portland, OR 97201
Phone: 1-503-221-1811, ext. 17
World Wide Web URL:
http://www.portland.us.emb-japan.go.jp/en/index.html
Email Address: tamara@cgjpdx.org

Tradition of Performing Arts in Japan, The: The Heart of Kabuki, Noh and Bunraku

Traditional Japanese theater, including rare backstage preparations. Shows splendor of Japan's four seasons, historical visuals, and mixing of native cultures in this view of the performing arts.

Availability: Schools, libraries and homeschoolers in Alabama, Georgia, North Carolina, South Carolina, and Virginia.
Suggested Grade: 5-Adult
Order Number: 801
Production Date: 1989
Format: VHS videotape
Special Notes: Part of The Land and Its People series.
Terms: Borrower pays return postage. Two tapes may be borrowed at a time. Return within 7 days after receipt. Reservations may be made by filling the application found on the web site.

Source: **Consulate General of Japan, Atlanta**
Japan Information Center
One Alliance Center
3500 Lenox Road, Suite 1600
Atlanta, GA 30326
Phone: 1-404-365-9240
Fax: 1-404-240-4311
World Wide Web URL:
http://www.atlanta.us.emb-japan.go.jp
Email Address: info@cgjapanatlanta.org

Tradition of Performing Arts in Japan, The: The Heart of Kabuki, Noh and Bunraku

Traditional Japanese theater, including rare backstage preparations. Shows splendor of Japan's four seasons, historical visuals, and mixing of native cultures in this view of the performing arts.

Availability: Schools, libraries, and nursing homes in Hawaii.
Suggested Grade: 5-Adult
Order Number: CU-12
Production Date: 1989
Format: VHS videotape
Special Notes: Part of The Land and Its People series.
Terms: Borrower pays return postage. A maximum of 3 videos may be borrowed per person. Return within one week of date borrowed.

Source: **Consulate General of Japan, Honolulu**
1742 Nuuanu Avenue
Honolulu, HI 96817-3294
Phone: 1-808-543-3111
Fax: 1-808-543-3170
World Wide Web URL:
http://www.honolulu.us.emb-japan.go.jp

Tradition of Performing Arts in Japan, The: The Heart of Kabuki, Noh and Bunraku

Traditional Japanese theater, including rare backstage preparations. Shows splendor of Japan's four seasons, historical visuals, and mixing of native cultures in this view of the performing arts.

Availability: Schools, libraries, homeschoolers, and nursing homes in OREGON AND SOUTHERN IDAHO ONLY. Please make requests via the web site.
Suggested Grade: 5-Adult
Order Number: 180
Production Date: 1989
Format: VHS videotape
Special Notes: Part of The Land and Its People series.
Terms: Borrower pays return postage. Return within three weeks after scheduled showing date. Book one month in advance if possible. Rewind the video and wrap securely for return. Be certain to indicate video number, date needed, name of your organization, and address to which video should be sent, along with phone number. Audience report enclosed with the video must be completed and returned.

Source: **Consulate General of Japan, Oregon**
Attn: Tamara, Video Library
1300 S. W. Fifth Avenue, Suite 2700
Portland, OR 97201
Phone: 1-503-221-1811, ext. 17
World Wide Web URL:
http://www.portland.us.emb-japan.go.jp/en/index.html
Email Address: tamara@cgjpdx.org

Ashok By Any Other Name

Ashok doesn't care that he was named after a famous Indian king; he wants an American name. After several attempts to have his classmates call him by different names, Ashok learns a valuable lesson about ethnic pride from the school librarian. He returns to class to proudly announce "My name is Ashok." Based on the book by Sandra Yamate.

Availability: Schools, libraries, and homeschoolers in the United States who serve the hearing impaired.
Suggested Grade: 4-6
Order Number: 12356
Production Date: 1994
Format: DVD
Special Notes: Produced by Aims Multimedia.
Terms: Sponsor pays all transportation costs. Return one week after receipt. Participation is limited to deaf or hard of hearing Americans, their parents, families, teachers, counselors, or others whose use would benefit a deaf or hard of hearing person. Only one person in the audience needs to be hearing impaired. You must register--which is free. These videos are all open-captioned--no special equipment is required for viewing.

Source: Described and Captioned Media Program
National Association of the Deaf
4211 Church Street Ext.
Roebuck, SC 29376
Phone: 1-800-237-6213
Fax: 1-800-538-5636
World Wide Web URL: http://www.dcmp.org

Big Boys Don't Cry

Tony has problems with his schoolwork, his girlfriend, and his parents. He is disturbed with flashbacks and nightmares of a long-hidden secret. When he suspects Uncle Paul is molesting his younger brother Andy, Tony confronts painful memories of his own childhood. By sharing his secret of being sexually abused by Uncle Paul, he rescues Andy, finds a new closeness with his family, and healing begins.

Availability: Schools, libraries, and homeschoolers in the United States who serve the hearing impaired.
Suggested Grade: 8-12
Order Number: 12358
Format: DVD
Special Notes: Produced by Churchill Media.
Terms: Sponsor pays all transportation costs. Return one week after receipt. Participation is limited to deaf or hard of hearing Americans, their parents, families, teachers, counselors, or others whose use would benefit a deaf or hard of hearing person. Only one person in the audience needs to be hearing impaired. You must register--which is free. These videos are all open-captioned--no special equipment is required for viewing.

Source: Described and Captioned Media Program
National Association of the Deaf
4211 Church Street Ext.
Roebuck, SC 29376
Phone: 1-800-237-6213
Fax: 1-800-538-5636
World Wide Web URL: http://www.dcmp.org

Class Divided

This is one of the most requested programs in FRONTLINE's history. It is about an Iowa schoolteacher who, the day after Martin Luther King Jr. was murdered in 1968, gave her third-grade students a first-hand experience in the meaning of discrimination. This is the story of what she taught the children, and the impact that lesson had on their lives.

Availability: All requesters
Suggested Grade: All ages
Order Number: not applicable
Format: Streaming Video
Source: PBS
World Wide Web URL:
http://www.pbs.org/wgbh/pages/frontline/shows/
divided/etc/view.html

Don't Call Me Names

Young children learn what to do when name-calling happens to them.

Availability: Schools, libraries, and homeschoolers in the United States who serve the hearing impaired.
Suggested Grade: K-3
Order Number: 25102
Production Date: 2000
Format: Streaming Video
Special Notes: Also available as live streaming video over the Internet.
Terms: Sponsor pays all transportation costs. Return one week after receipt. Participation is limited to deaf or hard of hearing Americans, their parents, families, teachers, counselors, or others whose use would benefit a deaf or hard of hearing person. Only one person in the audience needs to be hearing impaired. You must register--which is free. These videos are all open-captioned--no special equipment is required for viewing.

Source: Described and Captioned Media Program
National Association of the Deaf
4211 Church Street Ext.
Roebuck, SC 29376
Phone: 1-800-237-6213
Fax: 1-800-538-5636
World Wide Web URL: http://www.dcmp.org

Don't Stop Before You Get Started

Gavin doesn't feel very good about himself until Nina steps out of a video and teaches him how he can change his life. Gavin learns four practical suggestions that increase his self-esteem, including taking positive risks and avoiding negative self-talk.

Availability: Schools, libraries, and homeschoolers in the United States who serve the hearing impaired.
Suggested Grade: 5-8
Order Number: 3599
Production Date: 1996
Format: DVD
Special Notes: Produced by Film Ideas, Inc.

Terms: Sponsor pays all transportation costs. Return one week after receipt. Participation is limited to deaf or hard of hearing Americans, their parents, families, teachers, counselors, or others whose use would benefit a deaf or hard of hearing person. Only one person in the audience needs to be hearing impaired. You must register--which is free. These videos are all open-captioned--no special equipment is required for viewing.

Source: Described and Captioned Media Program
National Association of the Deaf
4211 Church Street Ext.
Roebuck, SC 29376
Phone: 1-800-237-6213
Fax: 1-800-538-5636
World Wide Web URL: http://www.dcmp.org

Dying to Be Thin
Life-threatening eating disorders such as anorexia and bulimia are on the rise among America's youth.

Availability:	All requesters
Suggested Grade:	7-Adult
Order Number:	not applicable
Production Date:	2000
Format:	Streaming Video

Source: NOVA
World Wide Web URL:
http://www.pbs.org/wgbh/nova/programs/index.html

How Did That Happen?
Three realistic scenarios help young children see the connection between their actions and the consequences that follow.

Availability:	Schools, libraries, and homeschoolers in the United States who serve the hearing impaired.
Suggested Grade:	1-4
Order Number:	11982
Production Date:	2003
Format:	DVD

Terms: Sponsor pays all transportation costs. Return one week after receipt. Participation is limited to deaf or hard of hearing Americans, their parents, families, teachers, counselors, or others whose use would benefit a deaf or hard of hearing person. Only one person in the audience needs to be hearing impaired. You must register--which is free. These videos are all open-captioned--no special equipment is required for viewing.

Source: Described and Captioned Media Program
National Association of the Deaf
4211 Church Street Ext.
Roebuck, SC 29376
Phone: 1-800-237-6213
Fax: 1-800-538-5636
World Wide Web URL: http://www.dcmp.org

How to Deal With the "Jerks" In Your Life and Earn the Respect of Your Friends
High school and junior high students created and dramatized five skits that demonstrate three typical responses to familiar school situations. The responses--

passive, aggressive, and assertive--are first defined and then compared. After each response, instant replay offers discussion opportunities. The school situations include harassment; peer pressure to drink, steal, and smoke; and dating.

Availability:	Schools, libraries, and homeschoolers in the United States who serve the hearing impaired.
Suggested Grade:	7-12
Order Number:	13126
Production Date:	1994
Format:	DVD
Special Notes:	Produced by SI Video Sales Group.

Terms: Sponsor pays all transportation costs. Return one week after receipt. Participation is limited to deaf or hard of hearing Americans, their parents, families, teachers, counselors, or others whose use would benefit a deaf or hard of hearing person. Only one person in the audience needs to be hearing impaired. You must register--which is free. These videos are all open-captioned--no special equipment is required for viewing.

Source: Described and Captioned Media Program
National Association of the Deaf
4211 Church Street Ext.
Roebuck, SC 29376
Phone: 1-800-237-6213
Fax: 1-800-538-5636
World Wide Web URL: http://www.dcmp.org

How Would You Feel? Learning About Empathy
Short vignettes demonstrate empathy, the practice of seeing and feeling a situation from another person's point of view. Shows what to do, what to say, what to do about testing, and more.

Availability:	Schools, libraries, and homeschoolers in the United States who serve the hearing impaired.
Suggested Grade:	K-4
Order Number:	11986
Production Date:	2001
Format:	DVD

Terms: Sponsor pays all transportation costs. Return one week after receipt. Participation is limited to deaf or hard of hearing Americans, their parents, families, teachers, counselors, or others whose use would benefit a deaf or hard of hearing person. Only one person in the audience needs to be hearing impaired. You must register--which is free. These videos are all open-captioned--no special equipment is required for viewing.

Source: Described and Captioned Media Program
National Association of the Deaf
4211 Church Street Ext.
Roebuck, SC 29376
Phone: 1-800-237-6213
Fax: 1-800-538-5636
World Wide Web URL: http://www.dcmp.org

I'm So Frustrated
Tommy is frustrated with his building blocks project; John can't solve his math problem; and Darlene's plan to make her mother a birdhouse goes awry. How can they deal with

their frustrations? A clown learning to juggle offers practical suggestions: stop and count to ten, solve the problem one step at a time, and talk to someone and ask for help.

Availability: Schools, libraries, and homeschoolers in the United States who serve the hearing impaired.
Suggested Grade: 2-6
Order Number: 13005
Production Date: 1994
Format: DVD
Special Notes: Produced by Sunburst Communications.
Terms: Sponsor pays all transportation costs. Return one week after receipt. Participation is limited to deaf or hard of hearing Americans, their parents, families, teachers, counselors, or others whose use would benefit a deaf or hard of hearing person. Only one person in the audience needs to be hearing impaired. You must register--which is free. These videos are all open-captioned--no special equipment is required for viewing.

Source: Described and Captioned Media Program
National Association of the Deaf
4211 Church Street Ext.
Roebuck, SC 29376
Phone: 1-800-237-6213
Fax: 1-800-538-5636
World Wide Web URL: http://www.dcmp.org

It's Not Fair!

Presents three situations to help students discuss the issue of fairness.

Availability: Schools, libraries, and homeschoolers in the United States who serve the hearing impaired.
Suggested Grade: 3-6
Order Number: 13007
Production Date: 1994
Format: DVD
Special Notes: Produced by Sunburst Communications.
Terms: Sponsor pays all transportation costs. Return one week after receipt. Participation is limited to deaf or hard of hearing Americans, their parents, families, teachers, counselors, or others whose use would benefit a deaf or hard of hearing person. Only one person in the audience needs to be hearing impaired. You must register--which is free. These videos are all open-captioned--no special equipment is required for viewing.

Source: Described and Captioned Media Program
National Association of the Deaf
4211 Church Street Ext.
Roebuck, SC 29376
Phone: 1-800-237-6213
Fax: 1-800-538-5636
World Wide Web URL: http://www.dcmp.org

Leaving School

Canadian teenagers tell why they left school before graduating and how that decision impacted their lives. They share experiences of trying to find work, how the real world is different than imagined, the loss of friends, loneliness, and what they've learned. They compare the school

environment with the harsh reality of the world of work. Their advice: stay in school; education pays off.

Availability: Schools, libraries, and homeschoolers in the United States who serve the hearing impaired.
Suggested Grade: 8-12
Order Number: 12362
Production Date: 1993
Format: DVD
Special Notes: Produced by Films For the Humanitaries & Sciences.
Terms: Sponsor pays all transportation costs. Return one week after receipt. Participation is limited to deaf or hard of hearing Americans, their parents, families, teachers, counselors, or others whose use would benefit a deaf or hard of hearing person. Only one person in the audience needs to be hearing impaired. You must register--which is free. These videos are all open-captioned--no special equipment is required for viewing.

Source: Described and Captioned Media Program
National Association of the Deaf
4211 Church Street Ext.
Roebuck, SC 29376
Phone: 1-800-237-6213
Fax: 1-800-538-5636
World Wide Web URL: http://www.dcmp.org

So You Want to Be? Salesperson/Veterinarian

Young interviewers ask a salesperson and a veterinarian about job and skill requirements for their two professions.

Availability: Schools, libraries, and homeschoolers in the United States who serve the hearing impaired.
Suggested Grade: 6-10
Order Number: 12649
Production Date: 1999
Format: DVD
Special Notes: Also available as live streaming video over the Internet.
Terms: Sponsor pays all transportation costs. Return one week after receipt. Participation is limited to deaf or hard of hearing Americans, their parents, families, teachers, counselors, or others whose use would benefit a deaf or hard of hearing person. Only one person in the audience needs to be hearing impaired. You must register--which is free. These videos are all open-captioned--no special equipment is required for viewing.

Source: Described and Captioned Media Program
National Association of the Deaf
4211 Church Street Ext.
Roebuck, SC 29376
Phone: 1-800-237-6213
Fax: 1-800-538-5636
World Wide Web URL: http://www.dcmp.org

Student Workshop: All About Respect

This four-part presentation dramatizes different kinds of respect: for feelings, for rules and authority, for differences, and for self. Each scene illustrates a different issue and challenges young teenagers to analyze the situation. The host asks pertinent questions for discussion and encourages critical thinking about the role of respect.

Availability: Schools, libraries, and homeschoolers in the United States who serve the hearing impaired.
Suggested Grade: 6-9
Order Number: 13093
Production Date: 1998
Format: DVD
Special Notes: Produced by Sunburst Communications.
Terms: Sponsor pays all transportation costs. Return one week after receipt. Participation is limited to deaf or hard of hearing Americans, their parents, families, teachers, counselors, or others whose use would benefit a deaf or hard of hearing person. Only one person in the audience needs to be hearing impaired. You must register--which is free. These videos are all open-captioned--no special equipment is required for viewing.
Source: **Described and Captioned Media Program**
National Association of the Deaf
4211 Church Street Ext.
Roebuck, SC 29376
Phone: 1-800-237-6213
Fax: 1-800-538-5636
World Wide Web URL: http://www.dcmp.org

Student Workshop: Handling Your Anger
Uses a TV format to explore anger, a normal human emotion. Dramatized situations teach teenagers how to recognize anger triggers and cues, how to identify anger styles and possible consequences, and how to choose appropriate techniques for expressing and handling anger. Pauses between sections for discussion; concludes with review.

Availability: Schools, libraries, and homeschoolers in the United States who serve the hearing impaired.
Suggested Grade: 6-10
Order Number: 13094
Production Date: 1997
Format: DVD
Special Notes: Produced by Sunburst Communications.
Terms: Sponsor pays all transportation costs. Return one week after receipt. Participation is limited to deaf or hard of hearing Americans, their parents, families, teachers, counselors, or others whose use would benefit a deaf or hard of hearing person. Only one person in the audience needs to be hearing impaired. You must register--which is free. These videos are all open-captioned--no special equipment is required for viewing.
Source: **Described and Captioned Media Program**
National Association of the Deaf
4211 Church Street Ext.
Roebuck, SC 29376
Phone: 1-800-237-6213
Fax: 1-800-538-5636
World Wide Web URL: http://www.dcmp.org

Student Workshop: What To Do About Anger
A four-part interactive presentation that helps students learn how to deal with anger.

Availability: Schools, libraries, and homeschoolers in the United States who serve the hearing impaired.
Suggested Grade: 2-5
Order Number: 13095
Production Date: 1997
Format: DVD
Terms: Sponsor pays all transportation costs. Return one week after receipt. Participation is limited to deaf or hard of hearing Americans, their parents, families, teachers, counselors, or others whose use would benefit a deaf or hard of hearing person. Only one person in the audience needs to be hearing impaired. You must register--which is free. These videos are all open-captioned--no special equipment is required for viewing.
Source: **Described and Captioned Media Program**
National Association of the Deaf
4211 Church Street Ext.
Roebuck, SC 29376
Phone: 1-800-237-6213
Fax: 1-800-538-5636
World Wide Web URL: http://www.dcmp.org

Wake Up Call
Young people being sexually harassed and exploited is a serious issue today, particularly if the relationship is with someone in a trusted role, such as a teacher or boss. Lizzie finds a flexible, well-paying job, but her boss makes inappropriate and unwanted sexual overtures and innuendoes. She must decide whether to compromise her values for the chance to earn money for college.

Availability: Schools, libraries, and homeschoolers in the United States who serve the hearing impaired.
Suggested Grade: 8-Adult
Order Number: 12401
Production Date: 1996
Format: DVD
Special Notes: Produced by Aims Multimedia.
Terms: Sponsor pays all transportation costs. Return one week after receipt. Participation is limited to deaf or hard of hearing Americans, their parents, families, teachers, counselors, or others whose use would benefit a deaf or hard of hearing person. Only one person in the audience needs to be hearing impaired. You must register--which is free. These videos are all open-captioned--no special equipment is required for viewing.
Source: **Described and Captioned Media Program**
National Association of the Deaf
4211 Church Street Ext.
Roebuck, SC 29376
Phone: 1-800-237-6213
Fax: 1-800-538-5636
World Wide Web URL: http://www.dcmp.org

We Can Work It Out!
A missing orange marker, an accidental nudge at lunch, and no space at the sand table present opportunities for conflict resolution by elementary students. Christa asks Nicole about the marker and listens to her answer; Mary and Harrison talk about the nudge; Sara offers Kenny different options to

share space at the table. Presents classroom discussion opportunities between each segment and reviews strategies for resolution.

Availability: Schools, libraries, and homeschoolers in the United States who serve the hearing impaired.
Suggested Grade: 1-4
Order Number: 13031
Production Date: 1994
Format: DVD
Special Notes: Produced by Sunburst Communications.
Terms: Sponsor pays all transportation costs. Return one week after receipt. Participation is limited to deaf or hard of hearing Americans, their parents, families, teachers, counselors, or others whose use would benefit a deaf or hard of hearing person. Only one person in the audience needs to be hearing impaired. You must register--which is free. These videos are all open-captioned--no special equipment is required for viewing.
Source: Described and Captioned Media Program
National Association of the Deaf
4211 Church Street Ext.
Roebuck, SC 29376
Phone: 1-800-237-6213
Fax: 1-800-538-5636
World Wide Web URL: http://www.dcmp.org

What Might Happen Next?
Introduces simple problem-solving skills, teaching viewers to stop and think about possible consequences to actions. Three vignettes dramatize situations with potential for problems. Questions between scenes offer discussion opportunities for children. Covers issues on safety, feelings, and thinking about others.

Availability: Schools, libraries, and homeschoolers in the United States who serve the hearing impaired.
Suggested Grade: K-3
Order Number: 13097
Production Date: 1996
Format: DVD
Special Notes: Produced by Sunburst Communications.
Terms: Sponsor pays all transportation costs. Return one week after receipt. Participation is limited to deaf or hard of hearing Americans, their parents, families, teachers, counselors, or others whose use would benefit a deaf or hard of hearing person. Only one person in the audience needs to be hearing impaired. You must register--which is free. These videos are all open-captioned--no special equipment is required for viewing.
Source: Described and Captioned Media Program
National Association of the Deaf
4211 Church Street Ext.
Roebuck, SC 29376
Phone: 1-800-237-6213
Fax: 1-800-538-5636
World Wide Web URL: http://www.dcmp.org

What's Respect?
What is respect? What does it mean? Four short dramatized situations teach respect for property, rules, differences of opinions and abilities, and the environment. Each ends with discussion questions for children.

Availability: Schools, libraries, and homeschoolers in the United States who serve the hearing impaired.
Suggested Grade: 2-5
Order Number: 13098
Production Date: 1995
Format: DVD
Special Notes: Produced by Sunburst Communications.
Terms: Sponsor pays all transportation costs. Return one week after receipt. Participation is limited to deaf or hard of hearing Americans, their parents, families, teachers, counselors, or others whose use would benefit a deaf or hard of hearing person. Only one person in the audience needs to be hearing impaired. You must register--which is free. These videos are all open-captioned--no special equipment is required for viewing.
Source: Described and Captioned Media Program
National Association of the Deaf
4211 Church Street Ext.
Roebuck, SC 29376
Phone: 1-800-237-6213
Fax: 1-800-538-5636
World Wide Web URL: http://www.dcmp.org

When I Feel Afraid
What are you afraid of? How do you feel when you're afraid? What can you do about it? Explores how fears may be good or bad, and suggests giving them a true-false test. Several vignettes demonstrate how to evaluate fears and deal with them.

Availability: Schools, libraries, and homeschoolers in the United States who serve the hearing impaired.
Suggested Grade: 3-6
Order Number: 13066
Production Date: 1995
Format: DVD
Special Notes: Produced by Film Ideas, Inc.
Terms: Sponsor pays all transportation costs. Return one week after receipt. Participation is limited to deaf or hard of hearing Americans, their parents, families, teachers, counselors, or others whose use would benefit a deaf or hard of hearing person. Only one person in the audience needs to be hearing impaired. You must register--which is free. These videos are all open-captioned--no special equipment is required for viewing.
Source: Described and Captioned Media Program
National Association of the Deaf
4211 Church Street Ext.
Roebuck, SC 29376
Phone: 1-800-237-6213
Fax: 1-800-538-5636
World Wide Web URL: http://www.dcmp.org

When I Grow Up...I Want to Be a Firefighter
Elementary students learn about the important job of a firefighter.

Availability: Schools, libraries, and homeschoolers in the United States who serve the hearing impaired.

Suggested Grade: 1-4
Order Number: 13576
Production Date: 2000
Format: DVD
Terms: Sponsor pays all transportation costs. Return one week after receipt. Participation is limited to deaf or hard of hearing Americans, their parents, families, teachers, counselors, or others whose use would benefit a deaf or hard of hearing person. Only one person in the audience needs to be hearing impaired. You must register--which is free. These videos are all open-captioned--no special equipment is required for viewing.
Source: **Described and Captioned Media Program**
National Association of the Deaf
4211 Church Street Ext.
Roebuck, SC 29376
Phone: 1-800-237-6213
Fax: 1-800-538-5636
World Wide Web URL: http://www.dcmp.org

When Should You Tell? Dealing with Abuse

Karen's older cousin Tommy abused her, but at school Karen learns that it's OK to tell. She shares her feelings and reactions, and learns to trust her instincts. She learns, too, that abuse is not her fault and there are some secrets that need to be told to a trusted adult.
Availability: Schools, libraries, and homeschoolers in the United States who serve the hearing impaired.
Suggested Grade: 3-6
Order Number: 12353
Production Date: 1995
Format: DVD
Special Notes: Produced by Sunburst Communications.
Terms: Sponsor pays all transportation costs. Return one week after receipt. Participation is limited to deaf or hard of hearing Americans, their parents, families, teachers, counselors, or others whose use would benefit a deaf or hard of hearing person. Only one person in the audience needs to be hearing impaired. You must register--which is free. These videos are all open-captioned--no special equipment is required for viewing.
Source: **Described and Captioned Media Program**
National Association of the Deaf
4211 Church Street Ext.
Roebuck, SC 29376
Phone: 1-800-237-6213
Fax: 1-800-538-5636
World Wide Web URL: http://www.dcmp.org

Win-Win

Because people interact with each other, conflict exists. Five scenarios present a true-to-life look at familiar, relevant topics: violence, prejudice/discrimination, student-parent conflict, peer pressure, and sexual harassment. Each scene sets up a conflict situation, then stops to allow viewers to answer and discuss specific related questions.
Availability: Schools, libraries, and homeschoolers in the United States who serve the hearing impaired.
Suggested Grade: 7-Adult

Order Number: 1814
Production Date: 1994
Format: DVD
Special Notes: Produced by Film Ideas, Inc.
Terms: Sponsor pays all transportation costs. Return one week after receipt. Participation is limited to deaf or hard of hearing Americans, their parents, families, teachers, counselors, or others whose use would benefit a deaf or hard of hearing person. Only one person in the audience needs to be hearing impaired. You must register--which is free. These videos are all open-captioned--no special equipment is required for viewing.
Source: **Described and Captioned Media Program**
National Association of the Deaf
4211 Church Street Ext.
Roebuck, SC 29376
Phone: 1-800-237-6213
Fax: 1-800-538-5636
World Wide Web URL: http://www.dcmp.org

Yes I Can!

Illustrates situations in which young students think they cannot excel and shows them how to overcome their fears and build self-confidence.
Availability: Schools, libraries, and homeschoolers in the United States who serve the hearing impaired.
Suggested Grade: 3-6
Order Number: 13099
Production Date: 1997
Format: DVD
Terms: Sponsor pays all transportation costs. Return one week after receipt. Participation is limited to deaf or hard of hearing Americans, their parents, families, teachers, counselors, or others whose use would benefit a deaf or hard of hearing person. Only one person in the audience needs to be hearing impaired. You must register--which is free. These videos are all open-captioned--no special equipment is required for viewing.
Source: **Described and Captioned Media Program**
National Association of the Deaf
4211 Church Street Ext.
Roebuck, SC 29376
Phone: 1-800-237-6213
Fax: 1-800-538-5636
World Wide Web URL: http://www.dcmp.org

You Can Count on Me! Building Character

Failure to accept responsibility may often cause problems. Four elementary students share examples of when they each learned the meaning of responsibility.
Availability: Schools, libraries, and homeschoolers in the United States who serve the hearing impaired.
Suggested Grade: 2-5
Order Number: 13100
Production Date: 1996
Format: DVD

*All materials listed in this 2011-2012 edition are **BRAND NEW**!*

Terms: Sponsor pays all transportation costs. Return one week after receipt. Participation is limited to deaf or hard of hearing Americans, their parents, families, teachers, counselors, or others whose use would benefit a deaf or hard of hearing person. Only one person in the audience needs to be hearing impaired. You must register--which is free. These videos are all open-captioned--no special equipment is required for viewing.

Source: Described and Captioned Media Program
National Association of the Deaf
4211 Church Street Ext.
Roebuck, SC 29376
Phone: 1-800-237-6213
Fax: 1-800-538-5636
World Wide Web URL: http://www.dcmp.org

*All materials listed in this 2011-2012 edition are **BRAND NEW!***

Anemia: The Silent Shadow

Discusses iron deficiency and folic acid, identifies groups at risk, provides nutrition guidelines for prevention, and offers recipes and cooking tips.

Availability:	Staff at schools with NET, WIC, CSFP, FDPIR, CACFP, UMD or Child Nutrition Program food programs in the United States. Those not having such an affiliation should contact their library to place an interlibrary loan request.
Suggested Grade:	7-12
Languages:	English; Spanish
Order Number:	English NAL Video 2295; Spanish NAL Video 3243
Production Date:	1995
Format:	VHS videotape

Terms: Borrower pays return postage. RETURN the day after scheduled use. Book at least 4 weeks in advance. Requests must include your name, phone, mail address, eligibility program, title, NAL number, show date, and a statement, "I have read the warning on copyright restrictions and accept full responsibility for compliance." One title per request.

**Source: National Agricultural Library
Document Delivery Services Branch
4th Floor, Photo Lab
10301 Baltimore Avenue
Beltsville, MD 20705-2351
Phone: 1-301-504-5994
Fax: 1-301-504-5675
World Wide Web URL: http://www.nal.usda.gov/fnic
Email Address: lending@nal.usda.gov**

Charting a Healthier Course for the Adolescent "At Risk" of Substance Abuse

Assists the health educator in teaching students the benefits of good health versus the harmful effects of alcohol and drugs on their mental and physical health.

Availability:	Staff at schools with NET, WIC, CSFP, FDPIR, CACFP, UMD or Child Nutrition Program food programs in the United States. Those not having such an affiliation should contact their library to place an interlibrary loan request.
Suggested Grade:	Teacher Reference
Order Number:	NAL HV4999.Y68C4
Format:	VHS videotape
Special Notes:	Includes supplementary materials.

Terms: Borrower pays return postage. RETURN the day after scheduled use. Book at least 4 weeks in advance. Requests must include your name, phone, mail address, eligibility program, title, NAL number, show date, and a statement, "I have read the warning on copyright restrictions and accept full responsibility for compliance." One title per request.

**Source: National Agricultural Library
Document Delivery Services Branch
4th Floor, Photo Lab, 10301 Baltimore Avenue
Beltsville, MD 20705-2351**

Phone: 1-301-504-5994
Fax: 1-301-504-5675
World Wide Web URL: http://www.nal.usda.gov/fnic
Email Address: lending@nal.usda.gov

Come See About Nutrition and Exercise

Dr. Scott and her patient, pre-teen Julia, are accidentally shrunk and swallowed by Dr. Pancreas. While trying to escape, they learn about the Food Guide Pyramid, calories, how to read labels, metabolism, and the importance of exercise in health.

Availability:	Staff at schools with NET, WIC, CSFP, FDPIR, CACFP, UMD or Child Nutrition Program food programs in the United States. Those not having such an affiliation should contact their library to place an interlibrary loan request.
Suggested Grade:	2-6
Order Number:	NAL Video 2517
Production Date:	1996
Format:	VHS videotape
Special Notes:	Includes a teacher's guide.

Terms: Borrower pays return postage. RETURN the day after scheduled use. Book at least 4 weeks in advance. Requests must include your name, phone, mail address, eligibility program, title, NAL number, show date, and a statement, "I have read the warning on copyright restrictions and accept full responsibility for compliance." One title per request.

**Source: National Agricultural Library
Document Delivery Services Branch
4th Floor, Photo Lab
10301 Baltimore Avenue
Beltsville, MD 20705-2351
Phone: 1-301-504-5994
Fax: 1-301-504-5675
World Wide Web URL: http://www.nal.usda.gov/fnic
Email Address: lending@nal.usda.gov**

Controlling Cholesterol: Introduction to a Healthy Lifestyle

This video shows how to control cholesterol via regular exercise and watching the types of food being eaten. It discusses symptoms of heart attacks, how cholesterol affects the heart, and how you can change this process in terms of overall lifestyle.

Availability:	Staff at schools with NET, WIC, CSFP, FDPIR, CACFP, UMD or Child Nutrition Program food programs in the United States. Those not having such an affiliation should contact their library to place an interlibrary loan request.
Suggested Grade:	6-Adult
Order Number:	NAL Video 1023
Production Date:	1989
Format:	VHS videotape

Terms: Borrower pays return postage. RETURN the day after scheduled use. Book at least 4 weeks in advance. Requests must include your name, phone, mail address,

eligibility program, title, NAL number, show date, and a statement, "I have read the warning on copyright restrictions and accept full responsibility for compliance." One title per request.

Source: National Agricultural Library
Document Delivery Services Branch
4th Floor, Photo Lab
10301 Baltimore Avenue
Beltsville, MD 20705-2351
Phone: 1-301-504-5994
Fax: 1-301-504-5675
World Wide Web URL: http://www.nal.usda.gov/fnic
Email Address: lending@nal.usda.gov

Eating Disorders

Compelling interviews with several young people who suffered from anorexia nervosa, bulimia, and compulsive overeating, provide a living portrait of these devastating diseases. Experts in the field discuss treatments available, the causes and symptoms o the diseases, and techniques of prevention and detection.

Availability: Staff at schools with NET, WIC, CSFP, FDPIR, CACFP, UMD or Child Nutrition Program food programs in the United States. Those not having such an affiliation should contact their library to place an interlibrary loan request.
Suggested Grade: 7-12
Order Number: NAL Video 2273
Production Date: 1994
Format: VHS videotape
Terms: Borrower pays return postage. RETURN the day after scheduled use. Book at least 4 weeks in advance. Requests must include your name, phone, mail address, eligibility program, title, NAL number, show date, and a statement, "I have read the warning on copyright restrictions and accept full responsibility for compliance." One title per request.

Source: National Agricultural Library
Document Delivery Services Branch
4th Floor, Photo Lab
10301 Baltimore Avenue
Beltsville, MD 20705-2351
Phone: 1-301-504-5994
Fax: 1-301-504-5675
World Wide Web URL: http://www.nal.usda.gov/fnic
Email Address: lending@nal.usda.gov

Energize with Nutricise Two

Melanie Mackbee leads children in an aerobic exercise video designed for nine to twelve year olds. Nutrition concepts are interspersed throughout the video.

Availability: Staff at schools with NET, WIC, CSFP, FDPIR, CACFP, UMD or Child Nutrition Program food programs in the United States. Those not having such an affiliation should contact their library to place an interlibrary loan request.
Suggested Grade: 3-6

Order Number: NAL Video 1863
Production Date: 1993
Format: VHS videotape
Special Notes: This Contra Costa County CCTV production includes an instructional manual.
Terms: Borrower pays return postage. RETURN the day after scheduled use. Book at least 4 weeks in advance. Requests must include your name, phone, mail address, eligibility program, title, NAL number, show date, and a statement, "I have read the warning on copyright restrictions and accept full responsibility for compliance." One title per request.

Source: National Agricultural Library
Document Delivery Services Branch
4th Floor, Photo Lab, 10301 Baltimore Avenue
Beltsville, MD 20705-2351
Phone: 1-301-504-5994
Fax: 1-301-504-5675
World Wide Web URL: http://www.nal.usda.gov/fnic
Email Address: lending@nal.usda.gov

Food for Thought

Kathleen strives to win first place in the science fair while denying her symptoms of anorexia nervosa.

Availability: Staff at schools with NET, WIC, CSFP, FDPIR, CACFP, UMD or Child Nutrition Program food programs in the United States. Those not having such an affiliation should contact their library to place an interlibrary loan request.
Suggested Grade: 6-12
Order Number: NAL Video 1030
Format: VHS videotape
Terms: Borrower pays return postage. RETURN the day after scheduled use. Book at least 4 weeks in advance. Requests must include your name, phone, mail address, eligibility program, title, NAL number, show date, and a statement, "I have read the warning on copyright restrictions and accept full responsibility for compliance." One title per request.

Source: National Agricultural Library
Document Delivery Services Branch
4th Floor, Photo Lab, 10301 Baltimore Avenue
Beltsville, MD 20705-2351
Phone: 1-301-504-5994
Fax: 1-301-504-5675
World Wide Web URL: http://www.nal.usda.gov/fnic
Email Address: lending@nal.usda.gov

Getting to Know Your Heart: Lower Elementary: The American Heart Association School Site Program

This kit helps students learn the basics of heart-healthy living.

Availability: Staff at schools with NET, WIC, CSFP, FDPIR, CACFP, UMD or Child Nutrition Program food programs in the United States. Those not having such an affiliation should contact their library to place an interlibrary loan request.

*All materials listed in this 2011-2012 edition are **BRAND NEW!***

Suggested Grade: preK-6
Order Number: NAL Kit 299
Production Date: 1990
Format: VHS videotape
Special Notes: This American Heart Association kit includes 2 sound cassettes, 2 stethoscopes, 2 packages of activity cards, an alcohol prep package, a rubber tab set, and a teacher's guide.
Terms: Borrower pays return postage. RETURN the day after scheduled use. Book at least 4 weeks in advance. Requests must include your name, phone, mail address, eligibility program, title, NAL number, show date, and a statement, "I have read the warning on copyright restrictions and accept full responsibility for compliance." One title per request.

Source: National Agricultural Library
Document Delivery Services Branch
4th Floor, Photo Lab, 10301 Baltimore Avenue
Beltsville, MD 20705-2351
Phone: 1-301-504-5994
Fax: 1-301-504-5675
World Wide Web URL: http://www.nal.usda.gov/fnic
Email Address: lending@nal.usda.gov

Goofy Over Dental Health

Learn about good dental hygiene from Goofy and Dr. Molar.

Availability: Schools, libraries, and homeschoolers in the United States who serve the hearing impaired.
Suggested Grade: K-4
Order Number: 25305
Production Date: 1991
Format: Streaming Video
Special Notes: Also available as live streaming video over the Internet.
Terms: Sponsor pays all transportation costs. Return one week after receipt. Participation is limited to deaf or hard of hearing Americans, their parents, families, teachers, counselors, or others whose use would benefit a deaf or hard of hearing person. Only one person in the audience needs to be hearing impaired. You must register--which is free. These videos are all open-captioned--no special equipment is required for viewing.

Source: Described and Captioned Media Program
National Association of the Deaf
4211 Church Street Ext.
Roebuck, SC 29376
Phone: 1-800-237-6213
Fax: 1-800-538-5636
World Wide Web URL: http://www.dcmp.org

Hands Down on Germs

Designed to teach children about handwashing.

Availability: Staff at schools with NET, WIC, CSFP, FDPIR, CACFP, UMD or Child Nutrition Program food programs in the United States. Those not having such an affiliation should contact their library to place an interlibrary loan request.
Suggested Grade: K-3

Order Number: NAL Video 2806
Production Date: 1996
Format: VHS videotape
Terms: Borrower pays return postage. RETURN the day after scheduled use. Book at least 4 weeks in advance. Requests must include your name, phone, mail address, eligibility program, title, NAL number, show date, and a statement, "I have read the warning on copyright restrictions and accept full responsibility for compliance." One title per request.

Source: National Agricultural Library
Document Delivery Services Branch
4th Floor, Photo Lab
10301 Baltimore Avenue
Beltsville, MD 20705-2351
Phone: 1-301-504-5994
Fax: 1-301-504-5675
World Wide Web URL: http://www.nal.usda.gov/fnic
Email Address: lending@nal.usda.gov

Heart Decisions: Middle School

This program is designed to help middle school students see a connection between positive lifestyles and good cardiovascular health.

Availability: Staff at schools with NET, WIC, CSFP, FDPIR, CACFP, UMD or Child Nutrition Program food programs in the United States. Those not having such an affiliation should contact their library to place an interlibrary loan request.
Suggested Grade: 5-8
Order Number: NAL QP1111.6.H42
Production Date: 1989
Format: VHS videotape
Terms: Borrower pays return postage. RETURN the day after scheduled use. Book at least 4 weeks in advance. Requests must include your name, phone, mail address, eligibility program, title, NAL number, show date, and a statement, "I have read the warning on copyright restrictions and accept full responsibility for compliance." One title per request.

Source: National Agricultural Library
Document Delivery Services Branch
4th Floor, Photo Lab
10301 Baltimore Avenue
Beltsville, MD 20705-2351
Phone: 1-301-504-5994
Fax: 1-301-504-5675
World Wide Web URL: http://www.nal.usda.gov/fnic
Email Address: lending@nal.usda.gov

Heartpower

Teaches about the heart and how to keep it healthy.

Availability: Staff at schools with NET, WIC, CSFP, FDPIR, CACFP, UMD or Child Nutrition Program food programs in the United States. Those not having such an affiliation should contact their library to place an interlibrary loan request.
Suggested Grade: K-2

Order Number:	NAL Kit 358
Production Date:	1996
Format:	VHS videotape
Special Notes:	Contains a number of supplementary teaching materials. From the American Heart Association

Terms: Borrower pays return postage. RETURN the day after scheduled use. Book at least 4 weeks in advance. Requests must include your name, phone, mail address, eligibility program, title, NAL number, show date, and a statement, "I have read the warning on copyright restrictions and accept full responsibility for compliance." One title per request.

Source: National Agricultural Library
Document Delivery Services Branch
4th Floor, Photo Lab
10301 Baltimore Avenue
Beltsville, MD 20705-2351
Phone: 1-301-504-5994
Fax: 1-301-504-5675
World Wide Web URL: http://www.nal.usda.gov/fnic
Email Address: lending@nal.usda.gov

How to Avoid Weight Gain When You Stop Smoking

Discusses eating as the end result of a series of linked events and shows ex-smokers how to break those links to break the chain.

Availability:	Staff at schools with NET, WIC, CSFP, FDPIR, CACFP, UMD or Child Nutrition Program food programs in the United States. Those not having such an affiliation should contact their library to place an interlibrary loan request.
Suggested Grade:	7-12
Order Number:	NAL Video 1696
Production Date:	1992
Format:	VHS videotape

Terms: Borrower pays return postage. RETURN the day after scheduled use. Book at least 4 weeks in advance. Requests must include your name, phone, mail address, eligibility program, title, NAL number, show date, and a statement, "I have read the warning on copyright restrictions and accept full responsibility for compliance." One title per request.

Source: National Agricultural Library
Document Delivery Services Branch
4th Floor, Photo Lab
10301 Baltimore Avenue
Beltsville, MD 20705-2351
Phone: 1-301-504-5994
Fax: 1-301-504-5675
World Wide Web URL: http://www.nal.usda.gov/fnic
Email Address: lending@nal.usda.gov

How to Read the New Food Label

Explains the features of the new label and helps consumers learn to use it.

Availability:	Staff at schools with NET, WIC, CSFP, FDPIR, CACFP, UMD or Child Nutrition Program food programs in the United States. Those not having such an affiliation should contact their library to place an interlibrary loan request.
Suggested Grade:	6-Adult
Languages:	English; Spanish
Order Number:	English--NAL Video 1480; Spanish--NAL Video 1643
Format:	VHS videotape

Terms: Borrower pays return postage. RETURN the day after scheduled use. Book at least 4 weeks in advance. Requests must include your name, phone, mail address, eligibility program, title, NAL number, show date, and a statement, "I have read the warning on copyright restrictions and accept full responsibility for compliance." One title per request.

Source: National Agricultural Library
Document Delivery Services Branch
4th Floor, Photo Lab
10301 Baltimore Avenue
Beltsville, MD 20705-2351
Phone: 1-301-504-5994
Fax: 1-301-504-5675
World Wide Web URL: http://www.nal.usda.gov/fnic
Email Address: lending@nal.usda.gov

I Am Joe's Heart

This video provides information based on the latest cardiac research plus a new look at promoting cardiovascular health and a clearer understanding of how the heart functions and of the risk factors of coronary artery disease. The video demonstrates how lifestyle can seriously impair proper working of the heart and how changes in lifestyle can reduce the risk factors and stabilize existing cardiac conditions.

Availability:	Staff at schools with NET, WIC, CSFP, FDPIR, CACFP, UMD or Child Nutrition Program food programs in the United States. Those not having such an affiliation should contact their library to place an interlibrary loan request.
Suggested Grade:	6-Adult
Order Number:	NAL Video 882
Production Date:	1987
Format:	VHS videotape

Terms: Borrower pays return postage. RETURN the day after scheduled use. Book at least 4 weeks in advance. Requests must include your name, phone, mail address, eligibility program, title, NAL number, show date, and a statement, "I have read the warning on copyright restrictions and accept full responsibility for compliance." One title per request.

Source: National Agricultural Library
Document Delivery Services Branch
4th Floor, Photo Lab
10301 Baltimore Avenue
Beltsville, MD 20705-2351

Phone: 1-301-504-5994
Fax: 1-301-504-5675
World Wide Web URL: http://www.nal.usda.gov/fnic
Email Address: lending@nal.usda.gov

Lo Que Comes: Por Ti Y Tu Bebe

This program uses the novella format to teach young pregnant women about healthy eating habits during pregnancy. It includes information about weight gain and WIC (Women, Infants & Children).

Availability:	Staff at schools with NET, WIC, CSFP, FDPIR, CACFP, UMD or Child Nutrition Program food programs in the United States. Those not having such an affiliation should contact their library to place an interlibrary loan request.
Suggested Grade:	6-Adult
Language:	Spanish
Order Number:	NAL Video 1797
Production Date:	1993
Format:	VHS videotape
Special Notes:	This Philadelphia Department of Health and Ethnovision production includes a discussion guide and an English script.
Terms:	Borrower pays return postage. RETURN the day after scheduled use. Book at least 4 weeks in advance. Requests must include your name, phone, mail address, eligibility program, title, NAL number, show date, and a statement, "I have read the warning on copyright restrictions and accept full responsibility for compliance." One title per request.

Source: National Agricultural Library
Document Delivery Services Branch
4th Floor, Photo Lab
10301 Baltimore Avenue
Beltsville, MD 20705-2351
Phone: 1-301-504-5994
Fax: 1-301-504-5675
World Wide Web URL: http://www.nal.usda.gov/fnic
Email Address: lending@nal.usda.gov

My Father, My Brother, and Me

A journalist set off on a personal journey to understand Parkinson's disease as it has taken a large toll on his family.

Availability:	All requesters
Suggested Grade:	All ages
Order Number:	not applicable
Format:	Streaming Video

Source: PBS
World Wide Web URL:
http://www.pbs.org/wgbh/pages/frontline/parkinsons/view/

Parker's Brain Storm Video

A children's book designed to help prepare a child for brain surgery--adapted to video.

Availability:	All requesters
Suggested Grade:	preK-2
Order Number:	not applicable
Format:	Streaming Video

Source: Children's Brain Tumor Foundation Inc.
274 Madison Avenue, Suite 1004
New York, NY 10016
Phone: 1-212-448-9494
Fax: 1-212-448-1022
World Wide Web URL: http://www.cbtf.org
Email Address: jriester@cbtf.org

Posture

What is good posture? What does it tell the world about a person? Describes in detail the components of correct standing, sitting, and lying postures. Demonstrates and contrasts good and poor posture. Depicts how the line of gravity test is used to evaluate an individual's posture. Stresses the relationship between good posture and an individual's physical and mental well-being.

Availability:	Schools, libraries, and homeschoolers in the United States who serve the hearing impaired.
Suggested Grade:	3-6
Order Number:	2321
Production Date:	1987
Format:	DVD
Special Notes:	Produced by New Dimension Media.
Terms:	Sponsor pays all transportation costs. Return one week after receipt. Participation is limited to deaf or hard of hearing Americans, their parents, families, teachers, counselors, or others whose use would benefit a deaf or hard of hearing person. Only one person in the audience needs to be hearing impaired. You must register--which is free. These videos are all open-captioned--no special equipment is required for viewing.

Source: Described and Captioned Media Program
National Association of the Deaf
4211 Church Street Ext.
Roebuck, SC 29376
Phone: 1-800-237-6213
Fax: 1-800-538-5636
World Wide Web URL: http://www.dcmp.org

Ralphie's Class Presents: A Healthy Heart

Through the use of puppets, this program teaches children the concept of what a heart is, what it means to us, and how to take care of one's blood pressure, the importance of watching one's weight and controlling stress.

Availability:	Staff at schools with NET, WIC, CSFP, FDPIR, CACFP, UMD or Child Nutrition Program food programs in the United States. Those not having such an affiliation should contact their library to place an interlibrary loan request.
Suggested Grade:	preK-6
Order Number:	NAL Video 1849
Production Date:	1993
Format:	VHS videotape
Special Notes:	This United Learning kit includes a teacher's guide and 4 duplicating masters.
Terms:	Borrower pays return postage. RETURN the day after scheduled use. Book at least 4 weeks in advance. Requests must include your name, phone, mail address,

eligibility program, title, NAL number, show date, and a statement, "I have read the warning on copyright restrictions and accept full responsibility for compliance." One title per request.

Source: National Agricultural Library
Document Delivery Services Branch
4th Floor, Photo Lab, 10301 Baltimore Avenue
Beltsville, MD 20705-2351
Phone: 1-301-504-5994
Fax: 1-301-504-5675
World Wide Web URL: http://www.nal.usda.gov/fnic
Email Address: lending@nal.usda.gov

Science Goes on a Diet

Shows a translucency test to detect fat in foods, calorie calculation of a peanut using a calorimeter, color expenditure, and more.

Availability: Staff at schools with NET, WIC, CSFP, FDPIR, CACFP, UMD or Child Nutrition Program food programs in the United States. Those not having such an affiliation should contact their library to place an interlibrary loan request.
Suggested Grade: 7-12
Order Number: NAL Video 1889
Format: VHS videotape
Terms: Borrower pays return postage. RETURN the day after scheduled use. Book at least 4 weeks in advance. Requests must include your name, phone, mail address, eligibility program, title, NAL number, show date, and a statement, "I have read the warning on copyright restrictions and accept full responsibility for compliance." One title per request.

Source: National Agricultural Library
Document Delivery Services Branch
4th Floor, Photo Lab, 10301 Baltimore Avenue
Beltsville, MD 20705-2351
Phone: 1-301-504-5994
Fax: 1-301-504-5675
World Wide Web URL: http://www.nal.usda.gov/fnic
Email Address: lending@nal.usda.gov

Sick Around the World

Can the U. S. learn anything from the rest of the world about how to run a health care system?

Availability: All requesters
Suggested Grade: 7-Adult
Order Number: not applicable
Production Date: 2008
Format: Streaming Video
Source: PBS
World Wide Web URL: http://www.pbs.org/wgbh/pages/frontline/sickaroundtheworld/

Smart Moves for Your Health

This program is designed to help motivate teenagers to make wise decisions about their eating and exercise habits to improve their overall health. It presents a 4-step model to follow to plan improvements in those habits.

Availability: Staff at schools with NET, WIC, CSFP, FDPIR, CACFP, UMD or Child Nutrition Program food programs in the United States. Those not having such an affiliation should contact their library to place an interlibrary loan request.
Suggested Grade: 6-12
Order Number: NAL Video 1170
Production Date: 1990
Format: VHS videotape
Terms: Borrower pays return postage. RETURN the day after scheduled use. Book at least 4 weeks in advance. Requests must include your name, phone, mail address, eligibility program, title, NAL number, show date, and a statement, "I have read the warning on copyright restrictions and accept full responsibility for compliance." One title per request.

Source: National Agricultural Library
Document Delivery Services Branch
4th Floor, Photo Lab
10301 Baltimore Avenue
Beltsville, MD 20705-2351
Phone: 1-301-504-5994
Fax: 1-301-504-5675
World Wide Web URL: http://www.nal.usda.gov/fnic
Email Address: lending@nal.usda.gov

Start Smart

Discusses the benefits of a school breakfast program.

Availability: Staff at schools with NET, WIC, CSFP, FDPIR, CACFP, UMD or Child Nutrition Program food programs in the United States. Those not having such an affiliation should contact their library to place an interlibrary loan request.
Suggested Grade: preK-6
Order Number: NAL Video 1587
Production Date: 1989
Format: VHS videotape
Special Notes: An Illinois State Board of Education program.
Terms: Borrower pays return postage. RETURN the day after scheduled use. Book at least 4 weeks in advance. Requests must include your name, phone, mail address, eligibility program, title, NAL number, show date, and a statement, "I have read the warning on copyright restrictions and accept full responsibility for compliance." One title per request.

Source: National Agricultural Library
Document Delivery Services Branch
4th Floor, Photo Lab
10301 Baltimore Avenue
Beltsville, MD 20705-2351
Phone: 1-301-504-5994
Fax: 1-301-504-5675
World Wide Web URL: http://www.nal.usda.gov/fnic
Email Address: lending@nal.usda.gov

Truth About Alcohol, The

Designed to provide middle school students with facts about alcohol such as what alcohol is, how it acts on the body, and why young people are so vulnerable to its dangers. It focuses on situations adolescents can relate to in their own lives: peer pressure to drink, problems caused by drinking and driving, and the emotional trauma of living with a parent who abuses alcohol.

Availability: Staff at schools with NET, WIC, CSFP, FDPIR, CACFP, UMD or Child Nutrition Program food programs in the United States. Those not having such an affiliation should contact their library to place an interlibrary loan request.
Suggested Grade: 5-8
Order Number: NAL Video 1148
Production Date: 1991
Format: VHS videotape
Terms: Borrower pays return postage. RETURN the day after scheduled use. Book at least 4 weeks in advance. Requests must include your name, phone, mail address, eligibility program, title, NAL number, show date, and a statement, "I have read the warning on copyright restrictions and accept full responsibility for compliance." One title per request.

Source: National Agricultural Library
Document Delivery Services Branch
4th Floor, Photo Lab
10301 Baltimore Avenue
Beltsville, MD 20705-2351
Phone: 1-301-504-5994
Fax: 1-301-504-5675
World Wide Web URL: http://www.nal.usda.gov/fnic
Email Address: lending@nal.usda.gov

War on Germs, The

Teaches proper handwashing techniques.

Availability: Staff at schools with NET, WIC, CSFP, FDPIR, CACFP, UMD or Child Nutrition Program food programs in the United States. Those not having such an affiliation should contact their library to place an interlibrary loan request.
Suggested Grade: 4-12
Order Number: NAL Video 2808
Production Date: 1997
Format: VHS videotape
Terms: Borrower pays return postage. RETURN the day after scheduled use. Book at least 4 weeks in advance. Requests must include your name, phone, mail address, eligibility program, title, NAL number, show date, and a statement, "I have read the warning on copyright restrictions and accept full responsibility for compliance." One title per request.

Source: National Agricultural Library
Document Delivery Services Branch
4th Floor, Photo Lab
10301 Baltimore Avenue
Beltsville, MD 20705-2351
Phone: 1-301-504-5994
Fax: 1-301-504-5675
World Wide Web URL: http://www.nal.usda.gov/fnic
Email Address: lending@nal.usda.gov

Wash Your Hands

A clever scenario that teaches a young man how to wash his hands properly.

Availability: Staff at schools with NET, WIC, CSFP, FDPIR, CACFP, UMD or Child Nutrition Program food programs in the United States. Those not having such an affiliation should contact their library to place an interlibrary loan request.
Suggested Grade: 2-6
English; Spanish
Order Number: English--NAL 2291; Spanish--NAL 2292
Production Date: 1995
Format: VHS videotape
Terms: Borrower pays return postage. RETURN the day after scheduled use. Book at least 4 weeks in advance. Requests must include your name, phone, mail address, eligibility program, title, NAL number, show date, and a statement, "I have read the warning on copyright restrictions and accept full responsibility for compliance." One title per request.

Source: National Agricultural Library
Document Delivery Services Branch
4th Floor, Photo Lab
10301 Baltimore Avenue
Beltsville, MD 20705-2351
Phone: 1-301-504-5994
Fax: 1-301-504-5675
World Wide Web URL: http://www.nal.usda.gov/fnic
Email Address: lending@nal.usda.gov

Weight: Maintaining a Healthy Balance

Teaches viewers a variety of skills to help them control their weight.

Availability: Staff at schools with NET, WIC, CSFP, FDPIR, CACFP, UMD or Child Nutrition Program food programs in the United States. Those not having such an affiliation should contact their library to place an interlibrary loan request.
Suggested Grade: 6-12
Order Number: NAL Video 2294
Production Date: 1996
Format: VHS videotape
Terms: Borrower pays return postage. RETURN the day after scheduled use. Book at least 4 weeks in advance. Requests must include your name, phone, mail address, eligibility program, title, NAL number, show date, and a statement, "I have read the warning on copyright restrictions and accept full responsibility for compliance." One title per request.

Source: National Agricultural Library
Document Delivery Services Branch
4th Floor, Photo Lab
10301 Baltimore Avenue
Beltsville, MD 20705-2351
Phone: 1-301-504-5994
Fax: 1-301-504-5675
World Wide Web URL: http://www.nal.usda.gov/fnic
Email Address: lending@nal.usda.gov

Weight Management: Steps for Lasting Success
Demonstrates weight management skills.

Availability:	Staff at schools with NET, WIC, CSFP, FDPIR, CACFP, UMD or Child Nutrition Program food programs in the United States. Those not having such an affiliation should contact their library to place an interlibrary loan request.
Suggested Grade:	6-12
Order Number:	NAL Video 2188
Production Date:	1995
Format:	VHS videotape
Terms:	Borrower pays return postage. RETURN the day after scheduled use. Book at least 4 weeks in advance. Requests must include your name, phone, mail address, eligibility program, title, NAL number, show date, and a statement, "I have read the warning on copyright restrictions and accept full responsibility for compliance." One title per request.

Source: National Agricultural Library
Document Delivery Services Branch
4th Floor, Photo Lab
10301 Baltimore Avenue
Beltsville, MD 20705-2351
Phone: 1-301-504-5994
Fax: 1-301-504-5675
World Wide Web URL: http://www.nal.usda.gov/fnic
Email Address: lending@nal.usda.gov

AIDS: Stopping the Spread of HIV

Sexually active people need to be knowledgeable about AIDS and HIV. Reviews how a person contracts HIV, what AIDS does to the body, how to practice safer sex, which activities increase risk, when to be tested for HIV, and the importance of planning ahead. Clearly and succinctly addresses the issue of sex and HIV. NOTE: Uses specific terminology.

Availability:	Schools, libraries, and homeschoolers in the United States who serve the hearing impaired.
Suggested Grade:	8-Adult
Order Number:	13068
Production Date:	1996
Format:	DVD
Special Notes:	Produced by Aims Multimedia.

Terms: Sponsor pays all transportation costs. Return one week after receipt. Participation is limited to deaf or hard of hearing Americans, their parents, families, teachers, counselors, or others whose use would benefit a deaf or hard of hearing person. Only one person in the audience needs to be hearing impaired. You must register--which is free. These videos are all open-captioned--no special equipment is required for viewing.

Source: Described and Captioned Media Program
National Association of the Deaf
4211 Church Street Ext.
Roebuck, SC 29376
Phone: 1-800-237-6213
Fax: 1-800-538-5636
World Wide Web URL: http://www.dcmp.org

Be a Food Groupie--And Care About Healthy Eating

Centers around five characters: Orange, Broccoli, Bread, Milk, and Peanut Food Groupie. Each character represents one of five food groups as established by USDA. The characters explain where the foods they represent come from and how each food group helps children stay healthy. Children are advised to eat a variety of foods from all the food groups.

Availability:	Staff at schools with NET, WIC, CSFP, FDPIR, CACFP, UMD or Child Nutrition Program food programs in the United States. Those not having such an affiliation should contact their library to place an interlibrary loan request.
Suggested Grade:	preK-6
Order Number:	NAL Kit 141
Production Date:	1992
Format:	Set of 3 VHS videotapes
Special Notes:	Includes 5 plush representations of food characters, hanging mobile, storybook, poster, sticker cards, parent letters, and a teacher's guide.

Terms: Borrower pays return postage. RETURN the day after scheduled use. Book at least 4 weeks in advance. Requests must include your name, phone, mail address, eligibility program, title, NAL number, show date, and a statement, "I have read the warning on copyright restrictions and accept full responsibility for compliance." One title per request.

Source: National Agricultural Library
Document Delivery Services Branch
4th Floor, Photo Lab
10301 Baltimore Avenue
Beltsville, MD 20705-2351
Phone: 1-301-504-5994
Fax: 1-301-504-5675
World Wide Web URL: http://www.nal.usda.gov/fnic
Email Address: lending@nal.usda.gov

Bread Comes to Life

Watch bread being made from start to finish.

Availability:	Schools, libraries, and homeschoolers in the United States who serve the hearing impaired.
Suggested Grade:	PreK-6
Order Number:	11178
Production Date:	2002
Format:	DVD
Special Notes:	Also available as live streaming video over the Internet.

Terms: Sponsor pays all transportation costs. Return one week after receipt. Participation is limited to deaf or hard of hearing Americans, their parents, families, teachers, counselors, or others whose use would benefit a deaf or hard of hearing person. Only one person in the audience needs to be hearing impaired. You must register--which is free. These videos are all open-captioned--no special equipment is required for viewing.

Source: Described and Captioned Media Program
National Association of the Deaf
4211 Church Street Ext.
Roebuck, SC 29376
Phone: 1-800-237-6213
Fax: 1-800-538-5636
World Wide Web URL: http://www.dcmp.org

Catchoo and Gesundheit

Designed to teach children about the importance of vitamins and minerals in the diet, this animated cartoon depicts the scrawny lifestyle of Catchoo, the alley cat and Gesundheit, the ally rat.

Availability:	Staff at schools with NET, WIC, CSFP, FDPIR, CACFP, UMD or Child Nutrition Program food programs in the United States. Those not having such an affiliation should contact their library to place an interlibrary loan request.
Suggested Grade:	preK-4
Order Number:	NAL Video 140
Format:	VHS videotape

Terms: Borrower pays return postage. RETURN the day after scheduled use. Book at least 4 weeks in advance. Requests must include your name, phone, mail address, eligibility program, title, NAL number, show date, and a statement, "I have read the warning on copyright restrictions and accept full responsibility for compliance." One title per request.

Source: National Agricultural Library
Document Delivery Services Branch
4th Floor, Photo Lab
10301 Baltimore Avenue
Beltsville, MD 20705-2351
Phone: 1-301-504-5994
Fax: 1-301-504-5675
World Wide Web URL: http://www.nal.usda.gov/fnic
Email Address: lending@nal.usda.gov

Chances and Choices with Food

Includes lesson plans that encourage critical thinking. Concepts deal with food safety.

Availability:	Staff at schools with NET, WIC, CSFP, FDPIR, CACFP, UMD or Child Nutrition Program food programs in the United States. Those not having such an affiliation should contact their library to place an interlibrary loan request.
Suggested Grade:	4-6
Order Number:	NAL Video 2230
Production Date:	1992
Format:	VHS videotape
Special Notes:	Includes other supplementary material.
Terms:	Borrower pays return postage. RETURN the day after scheduled use. Book at least 4 weeks in advance. Requests must include your name, phone, mail address, eligibility program, title, NAL number, show date, and a statement, "I have read the warning on copyright restrictions and accept full responsibility for compliance." One title per request.

Source: National Agricultural Library
Document Delivery Services Branch
4th Floor, Photo Lab
10301 Baltimore Avenue
Beltsville, MD 20705-2351
Phone: 1-301-504-5994
Fax: 1-301-504-5675
World Wide Web URL: http://www.nal.usda.gov/fnic
Email Address: lending@nal.usda.gov

Chocolate

Ms. Jennings and a group of students explore chocolate's history and how it is made. They learn about each of the three main ingredients--cocoa, sugar, and milk--and finally arrive at the chocolate factory. Shows the process from cleaning the cocoa beans to blending in the milk and sugar to making different forms of chocolate.

Availability:	Schools, libraries, and homeschoolers in the United States who serve the hearing impaired.
Suggested Grade:	4-8
Order Number:	13113
Production Date:	1998
Format:	DVD
Special Notes:	Produced by Oakleaf Productions.
Terms:	Sponsor pays all transportation costs. Return one week after receipt. Participation is limited to deaf or hard of hearing Americans, their parents, families, teachers, counselors, or others whose use would benefit a deaf or hard of hearing person. Only one person in the audience needs to be hearing impaired. You must register--which is free. These videos are all open-captioned--no special equipment is required for viewing.

Source: Described and Captioned Media Program
National Association of the Deaf
4211 Church Street Ext.
Roebuck, SC 29376
Phone: 1-800-237-6213
Fax: 1-800-538-5636
World Wide Web URL: http://www.dcmp.org

Contemporary Nutrition: An Interactive Look at the Food Guide Pyramid

Provides basic guidelines on proper nutrition and diet. Using a four-level pyramid diagram, the program's menu explores the six food groups, their effects on our health, and how much we should consume from each group. Viewers answer varied questions within each segment. CC option. PC REQUIREMENTS: Windows 95 or higher, 16MB RAM, 40MB Free hard disk space, 2X CD-ROM drive, 256-color VGA display, SoundBlaster(tm) compatible sound card with speakers

Availability:	Schools, libraries, and homeschoolers in the United States who serve the hearing impaired.
Suggested Grade:	8-12
Order Number:	9002
Production Date:	1997
Format:	DVD
Special Notes:	Produced by Cambridge Educational.
Terms:	Sponsor pays all transportation costs. Return one week after receipt. Participation is limited to deaf or hard of hearing Americans, their parents, families, teachers, counselors, or others whose use would benefit a deaf or hard of hearing person. Only one person in the audience needs to be hearing impaired. You must register--which is free. These videos are all open-captioned--no special equipment is required for viewing.

Source: Described and Captioned Media Program
National Association of the Deaf
4211 Church Street Ext.
Roebuck, SC 29376
Phone: 1-800-237-6213
Fax: 1-800-538-5636
World Wide Web URL: http://www.dcmp.org

Cooking Basics: Meat

Discusses what meat is (pork, veal, beef, and lamb), its nutritional value, and various cuts of meat. Details labeling information on meat before demonstrating ways to cook both tender and tough cuts.

Availability:	Schools, libraries, and homeschoolers in the United States who serve the hearing impaired.
Suggested Grade:	6-Adult
Order Number:	11427
Production Date:	2001
Format:	DVD

Special Notes: Also available as live streaming video over the Internet.

Terms: Sponsor pays all transportation costs. Return one week after receipt. Participation is limited to deaf or hard of hearing Americans, their parents, families, teachers, counselors, or others whose use would benefit a deaf or hard of hearing person. Only one person in the audience needs to be hearing impaired. You must register--which is free. These videos are all open-captioned--no special equipment is required for viewing.

Source: Described and Captioned Media Program
National Association of the Deaf
4211 Church Street Ext.
Roebuck, SC 29376
Phone: 1-800-237-6213
Fax: 1-800-538-5636
World Wide Web URL: http://www.dcmp.org

Crunchy Critter Club, The

The nutrition education goals of these videos for early childhood programs include: to develop a positive attitude about trying new foods; to identify a wide variety of foods and their important relationship to health; to participate in cooking activities which enhance physical and social development; reinforce curricular content area; follow sanitation and safety principles; and to make eating an enjoyable experience.

Availability: Staff at schools with NET, WIC, CSFP, FDPIR, CACFP, UMD or Child Nutrition Program food programs in the United States. Those not having such an affiliation should contact their library to place an interlibrary loan request.

Suggested Grade: preK-6
Order Number: NAL Video 460
Production Date: 1991
Format: Set of 2 VHS videotapes
Special Notes: This Georgia State production includes a teacher's guide and a guidebook.

Terms: Borrower pays return postage. RETURN the day after scheduled use. Book at least 4 weeks in advance. Requests must include your name, phone, mail address, eligibility program, title, NAL number, show date, and a statement, "I have read the warning on copyright restrictions and accept full responsibility for compliance." One title per request.

Source: National Agricultural Library
Document Delivery Services Branch
4th Floor, Photo Lab, 10301 Baltimore Avenue
Beltsville, MD 20705-2351
Phone: 1-301-504-5994
Fax: 1-301-504-5675
World Wide Web URL: http://www.nal.usda.gov/fnic
Email Address: lending@nal.usda.gov

Dudley and Dee Dee in Nutrition Land

Cartoon Characters Dudley, Dee Dee, and friend get to nutrition land and discover how eating foods from five food groups will keep your teeth healthy and your body strong.

Availability: Staff at schools with NET, WIC, CSFP, FDPIR, CACFP, UMD or Child Nutrition Program food programs in the United States. Those not having such an affiliation should contact their library to place an interlibrary loan request.

Suggested Grade: preK-6
Order Number: NAL Video 2288
Format: VHS videotape
Special Notes: This is a Startoons and American Dental Association production.

Terms: Borrower pays return postage. RETURN the day after scheduled use. Book at least 4 weeks in advance. Requests must include your name, phone, mail address, eligibility program, title, NAL number, show date, and a statement, "I have read the warning on copyright restrictions and accept full responsibility for compliance." One title per request.

Source: National Agricultural Library
Document Delivery Services Branch
4th Floor, Photo Lab
10301 Baltimore Avenue
Beltsville, MD 20705-2351
Phone: 1-301-504-5994
Fax: 1-301-504-5675
World Wide Web URL: http://www.nal.usda.gov/fnic
Email Address: lending@nal.usda.gov

Every Day, Lots of Ways: An Interdisciplinary Nutrition Curriculum for Kindergarten-Sixth Grade

This program uses core subjects to promote fresh, frozen and canned vegetables and fruits, vegetable and fruit juices, and dried fruits. It is part of a campaign to reduce the risk of cancer and other chronic diseases such as heart disease.

Availability: Staff at schools with NET, WIC, CSFP, FDPIR, CACFP, UMD or Child Nutrition Program food programs in the United States. Those not having such an affiliation should contact their library to place an interlibrary loan request.

Suggested Grade: preK-6
Order Number: NAL Kit 245
Production Date: 1993
Format: Set of 2 VHS videotapes
Special Notes: Includes teaching materials.

Terms: Borrower pays return postage. RETURN the day after scheduled use. Book at least 4 weeks in advance. Requests must include your name, phone, mail address, eligibility program, title, NAL number, show date, and a statement, "I have read the warning on copyright restrictions and accept full responsibility for compliance." One title per request.

Source: National Agricultural Library
Document Delivery Services Branch
4th Floor, Photo Lab, 10301 Baltimore Avenue
Beltsville, MD 20705-2351
Phone: 1-301-504-5994
Fax: 1-301-504-5675
World Wide Web URL: http://www.nal.usda.gov/fnic
Email Address: lending@nal.usda.gov

HOME ECONOMICS

15 Minute Noodle

Demonstrates the basics of cooking pasta and shows how to quickly create five different dishes.

Availability:	Schools, libraries, and homeschoolers in the United States who serve the hearing impaired.
Suggested Grade:	6-Adult
Order Number:	11452
Production Date:	2000
Format:	DVD
Special Notes:	Also available as live streaming video over the Internet.
Terms:	Sponsor pays all transportation costs. Return one week after receipt. Participation is limited to deaf or hard of hearing Americans, their parents, families, teachers, counselors, or others whose use would benefit a deaf or hard of hearing person. Only one person in the audience needs to be hearing impaired. You must register--which is free. These videos are all open-captioned--no special equipment is required for viewing.

Source: Described and Captioned Media Program
National Association of the Deaf
4211 Church Street Ext.
Roebuck, SC 29376
Phone: 1-800-237-6213
Fax: 1-800-538-5636
World Wide Web URL: http://www.dcmp.org

Food: A Multi-Cultural Feast

Discusses how the food we eat in the United States is multi-cultural in its origin. The origins of a number of foods are illustrated.

Availability:	Schools, libraries, and homeschoolers in the United States who serve the hearing impaired.
Suggested Grade:	3-6
Order Number:	10943
Production Date:	1998
Format:	DVD
Special Notes:	Also available as live streaming video over the Internet.
Terms:	Sponsor pays all transportation costs. Return one week after receipt. Participation is limited to deaf or hard of hearing, Americans, their parents, families, teachers, counselors, or others whose use would benefit a deaf or hard of hearing person. Only one person in the audience needs to be hearing impaired. You must register--which is free. These videos are all open-captioned--no special equipment is required for viewing.

Source: Described and Captioned Media Program
National Association of the Deaf
4211 Church Street Ext.
Roebuck, SC 29376
Phone: 1-800-237-6213
Fax: 1-800-538-5636
World Wide Web URL: http://www.dcmp.org

Foodessence: Myths & Taboos

Presents differences in cultures and religions regarding food. Includes a segment of the Jewish law against pork and shows a very brief breastfeeding scene.

Availability:	Schools, libraries, and homeschoolers in the United States who serve the hearing impaired.
Suggested Grade:	4-8
Order Number:	8725
Production Date:	1998
Format:	DVD
Special Notes:	Also available as live streaming video over the Internet.
Terms:	Sponsor pays all transportation costs. Return one week after receipt. Participation is limited to deaf or hard of hearing Americans, their parents, families, teachers, counselors, or others whose use would benefit a deaf or hard of hearing person. Only one person in the audience needs to be hearing impaired. You must register--which is free. These videos are all open-captioned--no special equipment is required for viewing.

Source: Described and Captioned Media Program
National Association of the Deaf
4211 Church Street Ext.
Roebuck, SC 29376
Phone: 1-800-237-6213
Fax: 1-800-538-5636
World Wide Web URL: http://www.dcmp.org

Food Safety Express: An Educational Program for Preschool Children

This program contains five video vignettes featuring puppets who introduce food safety topics in an entertaining way for children. It discusses the importance of washing hands, using clean dishes and utensils, ways to open food containers so that food stays clean, and the storage of cold foods.

Availability:	Staff at schools with NET, WIC, CSFP, FDPIR, CACFP, UMD or Child Nutrition Program food programs in the United States. Those not having such an affiliation should contact their library to place an interlibrary loan request.
Suggested Grade:	preK-6
Order Number:	NAL Kit 269
Production Date:	1993
Format:	VHS videotape
Special Notes:	This University of Missouri kit includes 5 parent newsletters, a teacher's manual, an activity manual and a final report.
Terms:	Borrower pays return postage. RETURN the day after scheduled use. Book at least 4 weeks in advance. Requests must include your name, phone, mail address, eligibility program, title, NAL number, show date, and a statement, "I have read the warning on copyright restrictions and accept full responsibility for compliance." One title per request.

Source: National Agricultural Library
Document Delivery Services Branch
4th Floor, Photo Lab
10301 Baltimore Avenue
Beltsville, MD 20705-2351
Phone: 1-301-504-5994
Fax: 1-301-504-5675

*All materials listed in this 2011-2012 edition are **BRAND NEW!***

World Wide Web URL: http://www.nal.usda.gov/fnic
Email Address: lending@nal.usda.gov

For Goodness Sake!

This program presents healthful alternatives to meat, use of non-fat dry milk to enhance the nutrient value of many meals, many uses of rice and of broccoli.

Availability:	Staff at schools with NET, WIC, CSFP, FDPIR, CACFP, UMD or Child Nutrition Program food programs in the United States. Those not having such an affiliation should contact their library to place an interlibrary loan request.
Suggested Grade:	7-12
Order Number:	NAL Video 1275
Production Date:	1987
Format:	VHS videotape
Terms:	Borrower pays return postage. RETURN the day after scheduled use. Book at least 4 weeks in advance. Requests must include your name, phone, mail address, eligibility program, title, NAL number, show date, and a statement, "I have read the warning on copyright restrictions and accept full responsibility for compliance." One title per request.

Source: National Agricultural Library
Document Delivery Services Branch
4th Floor, Photo Lab
10301 Baltimore Avenue
Beltsville, MD 20705-2351
Phone: 1-301-504-5994
Fax: 1-301-504-5675
World Wide Web URL: http://www.nal.usda.gov/fnic
Email Address: lending@nal.usda.gov

Glorious Fruit: A Fresh Look at Fruit Preparation

The United Fresh Fruit and Vegetable Association developed this nutrition education program to increase consumer awareness of the attributes of fresh fruits. Objectives for participants are to: analyze their current fruit intake habits; identify 3 benefits of eating fresh fruits; choose and store at least 5 fresh fruits to maintain optimal quality; list 5 methods to prepare fresh fruits; create a recipe using fresh fruit; describe one fruit that is new to them; and demonstrate 3 ways to decorate with fruit.

Availability:	Staff at schools with NET, WIC, CSFP, FDPIR, CACFP, UMD or Child Nutrition Program food programs in the United States. Those not having such an affiliation should contact their library to place an interlibrary loan request.
Suggested Grade:	4-12
Order Number:	NAL Video 343
Format:	VHS videotape
Special Notes:	Includes a folder containing activities to be conducted during 4 sessions, and worksheets that can be reproduced.
Terms:	Borrower pays return postage. RETURN the day after scheduled use. Book at least 4 weeks in advance. Requests must include your name, phone, mail address,

eligibility program, title, NAL number, show date, and a statement, "I have read the warning on copyright restrictions and accept full responsibility for compliance." One title per request.

Source: National Agricultural Library
Document Delivery Services Branch
4th Floor, Photo Lab
10301 Baltimore Avenue
Beltsville, MD 20705-2351
Phone: 1-301-504-5994
Fax: 1-301-504-5675
World Wide Web URL: http://www.nal.usda.gov/fnic
Email Address: lending@nal.usda.gov

Good Food Diner, The

This video teaches children how to choose healthy foods to make them feel better and give them energy. It stresses the importance of breakfast.

Availability:	Staff at schools with NET, WIC, CSFP, FDPIR, CACFP, UMD or Child Nutrition Program food programs in the United States. Those not having such an affiliation should contact their library to place an interlibrary loan request.
Suggested Grade:	preK-6
Order Number:	NAL Video 1630
Production Date:	1992
Format:	VHS videotape
Terms:	Borrower pays return postage. RETURN the day after scheduled use. Book at least 4 weeks in advance. Requests must include your name, phone, mail address, eligibility program, title, NAL number, show date, and a statement, "I have read the warning on copyright restrictions and accept full responsibility for compliance." One title per request.

Source: National Agricultural Library
Document Delivery Services Branch
4th Floor, Photo Lab
10301 Baltimore Avenue
Beltsville, MD 20705-2351
Phone: 1-301-504-5994
Fax: 1-301-504-5675
World Wide Web URL: http://www.nal.usda.gov/fnic
Email Address: lending@nal.usda.gov

Goofy Over Health

This program introduces children to the issues of health and nutrition using live action and Disney animation. The program explores issues such as the importance of exercise, nutrition, and sleep for maintaining good health.

Availability:	Staff at schools with NET, WIC, CSFP, FDPIR, CACFP, UMD or Child Nutrition Program food programs in the United States. Those not having such an affiliation should contact their library to place an interlibrary loan request.
Suggested Grade:	preK-6
Order Number:	NAL Video 1630
Production Date:	1991

Format: VHS videotape
Special Notes: This Disney Educational Productions video includes 2 discussion guides.
Terms: Borrower pays return postage. RETURN the day after scheduled use. Book at least 4 weeks in advance. Requests must include your name, phone, mail address, eligibility program, title, NAL number, show date, and a statement, "I have read the warning on copyright restrictions and accept full responsibility for compliance." One title per request.

Source: National Agricultural Library
Document Delivery Services Branch
4th Floor, Photo Lab
10301 Baltimore Avenue
Beltsville, MD 20705-2351
Phone: 1-301-504-5994
Fax: 1-301-504-5675
World Wide Web URL: http://www.nal.usda.gov/fnic
Email Address: lending@nal.usda.gov

Happy, Healthy Holidays

Looks at the special foods prepared during the holidays and tells how to prepare them properly.

Availability: Staff at schools with NET, WIC, CSFP, FDPIR, CACFP, UMD or Child Nutrition Program food programs in the United States. Those not having such an affiliation should contact their library to place an interlibrary loan request.
Suggested Grade: 6-Adult
Order Number: NAL Video 2475
Production Date: 1996
Format: VHS videotape
Terms: Borrower pays return postage. RETURN the day after scheduled use. Book at least 4 weeks in advance. Requests must include your name, phone, mail address, eligibility program, title, NAL number, show date, and a statement, "I have read the warning on copyright restrictions and accept full responsibility for compliance." One title per request.

Source: National Agricultural Library
Document Delivery Services Branch
4th Floor, Photo Lab, 10301 Baltimore Avenue
Beltsville, MD 20705-2351
Phone: 1-301-504-5994
Fax: 1-301-504-5675
World Wide Web URL: http://www.nal.usda.gov/fnic
Email Address: lending@nal.usda.gov

Heartcare Program, The: Dietary Management of Cholesterol

Describes how to revise your eating habits for a healthier life.

Availability: Staff at schools with NET, WIC, CSFP, FDPIR, CACFP, UMD or Child Nutrition Program food programs in the United States. Those not having such an affiliation should contact their library to place an interlibrary loan request.

Suggested Grade: 7-12
Order Number: NAL Video 2057
Production Date: 1994
Format: Set of 4 VHS videotapes
Terms: Borrower pays return postage. RETURN the day after scheduled use. Book at least 4 weeks in advance. Requests must include your name, phone, mail address, eligibility program, title, NAL number, show date, and a statement, "I have read the warning on copyright restrictions and accept full responsibility for compliance." One title per request.

Source: National Agricultural Library
Document Delivery Services Branch
4th Floor, Photo Lab, 10301 Baltimore Avenue
Beltsville, MD 20705-2351
Phone: 1-301-504-5994
Fax: 1-301-504-5675
World Wide Web URL: http://www.nal.usda.gov/fnic
Email Address: lending@nal.usda.gov

Heartcare: Skills for Lowering Your Blood Cholesterol

This program describes how to revise your eating habits for a healthier life.

Availability: Staff at schools with NET, WIC, CSFP, FDPIR, CACFP, UMD or Child Nutrition Program food programs in the United States. Those not having such an affiliation should contact their library to place an interlibrary loan request.
Suggested Grade: 7-12
Order Number: NAL Video 1086
Production Date: 1988
Format: VHS videotape
Terms: Borrower pays return postage. RETURN the day after scheduled use. Book at least 4 weeks in advance. Requests must include your name, phone, mail address, eligibility program, title, NAL number, show date, and a statement, "I have read the warning on copyright restrictions and accept full responsibility for compliance." One title per request.

Source: National Agricultural Library
Document Delivery Services Branch
4th Floor, Photo Lab, 10301 Baltimore Avenue
Beltsville, MD 20705-2351
Phone: 1-301-504-5994
Fax: 1-301-504-5675
World Wide Web URL: http://www.nal.usda.gov/fnic
Email Address: lending@nal.usda.gov

Herschel the Rabbit

Stresses the importance of including vegetables in one's daily diet to provide the body with energy and to help the body grow.

Availability: Staff at schools with NET, WIC, CSFP, FDPIR, CACFP, UMD or Child Nutrition Program food programs in the United States. Those not having such an affiliation should contact their library to place an interlibrary loan request.

Suggested Grade: preK-6
Order Number: NAL Video 1785
Production Date: 1992
Format: VHS videotape
Special Notes: This is a Collie Craft production.
Terms: Borrower pays return postage. RETURN the day after scheduled use. Book at least 4 weeks in advance. Requests must include your name, phone, mail address, eligibility program, title, NAL number, show date, and a statement, "I have read the warning on copyright restrictions and accept full responsibility for compliance." One title per request.

Source: National Agricultural Library
Document Delivery Services Branch
4th Floor, Photo Lab
10301 Baltimore Avenue
Beltsville, MD   20705-2351
Phone: 1-301-504-5994
Fax: 1-301-504-5675
World Wide Web URL: http://www.nal.usda.gov/fnic
Email Address: lending@nal.usda.gov

Hip to Be Fit--A Production of California Raisins

Through music and fast-paced action, Kristi and her friends, the California Raisins, show kids that a healthy, well-balanced diet and plenty of exercise can make them champions in the classroom and on the playground.
Availability: Staff at schools with NET, WIC, CSFP, FDPIR, CACFP, UMD or Child Nutrition Program food programs in the United States. Those not having such an affiliation should contact their library to place an interlibrary loan request.
Suggested Grade: preK-6
Order Number: NAL Video 1765
Production Date: 1993
Format: VHS videotape
Special Notes: This is a Wright Group production.
Terms: Borrower pays return postage. RETURN the day after scheduled use. Book at least 4 weeks in advance. Requests must include your name, phone, mail address, eligibility program, title, NAL number, show date, and a statement, "I have read the warning on copyright restrictions and accept full responsibility for compliance." One title per request.

Source: National Agricultural Library
Document Delivery Services Branch
4th Floor, Photo Lab
10301 Baltimore Avenue
Beltsville, MD   20705-2351
Phone: 1-301-504-5994
Fax: 1-301-504-5675
World Wide Web URL: http://www.nal.usda.gov/fnic
Email Address: lending@nal.usda.gov

How to Lower Your Cholesterol: A Simple Dietary Approach

Discusses what cholesterol is and what the dietary sources of cholesterol are. Suggestions are given for low fat meals and what foods may be substituted for saturated fat. Lists of substitutes are provided. Methods of lowering cholesterol in the diet are discussed.
Availability: Staff at schools with NET, WIC, CSFP, FDPIR, CACFP, UMD or Child Nutrition Program food programs in the United States. Those not having such an affiliation should contact their library to place an interlibrary loan request.
Suggested Grade: 7-12
Order Number: NAL Video 452
Production Date: 1988
Format: VHS videotape
Terms: Borrower pays return postage. RETURN the day after scheduled use. Book at least 4 weeks in advance. Requests must include your name, phone, mail address, eligibility program, title, NAL number, show date, and a statement, "I have read the warning on copyright restrictions and accept full responsibility for compliance." One title per request.

Source: National Agricultural Library
Document Delivery Services Branch
4th Floor, Photo Lab
10301 Baltimore Avenue
Beltsville, MD   20705-2351
Phone: 1-301-504-5994
Fax: 1-301-504-5675
World Wide Web URL: http://www.nal.usda.gov/fnic
Email Address: lending@nal.usda.gov

Janey Junkfood's Fresh Adventure

This program teaches children, through juggling and rap music, how to balance their diet. Children learn how to see through the hype of television commercials, how to read food labels, and how they can choose healthier snacks at home, school and on the run.
Availability: Staff at schools with NET, WIC, CSFP, FDPIR, CACFP, UMD or Child Nutrition Program food programs in the United States. Those not having such an affiliation should contact their library to place an interlibrary loan request.
Suggested Grade: preK-6
Order Number: NAL Video 1414
Production Date: 1992
Format: VHS videotape
Special Notes: This Foodplay, Jamaica Plain, MA, production includes an activity guide.
Terms: Borrower pays return postage. RETURN the day after scheduled use. Book at least 4 weeks in advance. Requests must include your name, phone, mail address, eligibility program, title, NAL number, show date, and a statement, "I have read the warning on copyright restrictions and accept full responsibility for compliance." One title per request.

Source: National Agricultural Library
Document Delivery Services Branch
4th Floor, Photo Lab, 10301 Baltimore Avenue
Beltsville, MD   20705-2351

Phone: 1-301-504-5994
Fax: 1-301-504-5675
World Wide Web URL: http://www.nal.usda.gov/fnic
Email Address: lending@nal.usda.gov

Kellogg's Fit to Be

Tells the story of nine-year-old Michael who improved his physical fitness by eating more nutritionally and exercising daily. Instead of junk food, he began to eat a balanced diet including fruit. Michael also began to exercise with his friends.

Availability: Staff at schools with NET, WIC, CSFP, FDPIR, CACFP, UMD or Child Nutrition Program food programs in the United States. Those not having such an affiliation should contact their library to place an interlibrary loan request.

Suggested Grade: preK-6
Order Number: NAL Video 620
Production Date: 1989
Format: VHS videotape
Terms: Borrower pays return postage. RETURN the day after scheduled use. Book at least 4 weeks in advance. Requests must include your name, phone, mail address, eligibility program, title, NAL number, show date, and a statement, "I have read the warning on copyright restrictions and accept full responsibility for compliance." One title per request.
Source: National Agricultural Library
Document Delivery Services Branch
4th Floor, Photo Lab
10301 Baltimore Avenue
Beltsville, MD 20705-2351
Phone: 1-301-504-5994
Fax: 1-301-504-5675
World Wide Web URL: http://www.nal.usda.gov/fnic
Email Address: lending@nal.usda.gov

La Piramide de la Alimentacion

Describes the Food Guide Pyramid and discusses the reason for the Pyramid design.

Availability: Staff at schools with NET, WIC, CSFP, FDPIR, CACFP, UMD or Child Nutrition Program food programs in the United States. Those not having such an affiliation should contact their library to place an interlibrary loan request.

Suggested Grade: 7-12
Spanish
Order Number: NAL Video 1783
Production Date: 1994
Format: VHS videotape
Terms: Borrower pays return postage. RETURN the day after scheduled use. Book at least 4 weeks in advance. Requests must include your name, phone, mail address, eligibility program, title, NAL number, show date, and a statement, "I have read the warning on copyright restrictions and accept full responsibility for compliance." One title per request.

Source: National Agricultural Library
Document Delivery Services Branch
4th Floor, Photo Lab
10301 Baltimore Avenue
Beltsville, MD 20705-2351
Phone: 1-301-504-5994
Fax: 1-301-504-5675
World Wide Web URL: http://www.nal.usda.gov/fnic
Email Address: lending@nal.usda.gov

Lifesteps: Weight Management

A program that helps participants develop new eating habits through behavior modification.

Availability: Staff at schools with NET, WIC, CSFP, FDPIR, CACFP, UMD or Child Nutrition Program food programs in the United States. Those not having such an affiliation should contact their library to place an interlibrary loan request.

Suggested Grade: 6-12
Order Number: NAL Kit 205
Production Date: 1994
Format: Set of 2 VHS videotapes
Special Notes: Includes a teacher's guide and many other supplemental teaching aids.
Terms: Borrower pays return postage. RETURN the day after scheduled use. Book at least 4 weeks in advance. Requests must include your name, phone, mail address, eligibility program, title, NAL number, show date, and a statement, "I have read the warning on copyright restrictions and accept full responsibility for compliance." One title per request.
Source: National Agricultural Library
Document Delivery Services Branch
4th Floor, Photo Lab
10301 Baltimore Avenue
Beltsville, MD 20705-2351
Phone: 1-301-504-5994
Fax: 1-301-504-5675
World Wide Web URL: http://www.nal.usda.gov/fnic
Email Address: lending@nal.usda.gov

Lower Your Cholesterol Now!

Shows how to make wiser nutritional choices to lower saturated fat, cholesterol and calories. Tips are provided for reading labels, for shopping and cooking for a cholesterol-lowering diet. The program is divided into six segments: oils; meats, fish and poultry; lunch meat and frozen dinners; dairy and eggs; desserts and more; fruits, vegetables and grains.

Availability: Staff at schools with NET, WIC, CSFP, FDPIR, CACFP, UMD or Child Nutrition Program food programs in the United States. Those not having such an affiliation should contact their library to place an interlibrary loan request.

Suggested Grade: 7-Adult
Order Number: NAL Video 2094
Production Date: 1994

Format: VHS videotape
Terms: Borrower pays return postage. RETURN the day after scheduled use. Book at least 4 weeks in advance. Requests must include your name, phone, mail address, eligibility program, title, NAL number, show date, and a statement, "I have read the warning on copyright restrictions and accept full responsibility for compliance." One title per request.

Source: National Agricultural Library
Document Delivery Services Branch
4th Floor, Photo Lab
10301 Baltimore Avenue
Beltsville, MD 20705-2351
Phone: 1-301-504-5994
Fax: 1-301-504-5675
World Wide Web URL: http://www.nal.usda.gov/fnic
Email Address: lending@nal.usda.gov

Lowfat Lifestyle on the Go

This video and recipe book provide information on achieving and maintaining a low-fat diet. The materials explain how to avoid fat in your diet, reveal the names of commonly used fats and oils, show how to shop smartly in the supermarket, and teach how to prepare tasty low fat recipes that are quick to fix.

Availability: Staff at schools with NET, WIC, CSFP, FDPIR, CACFP, UMD or Child Nutrition Program food programs in the United States. Those not having such an affiliation should contact their library to place an interlibrary loan request.
Suggested Grade: 7-12
Order Number: NAL Video 462
Production Date: 1989
Format: VHS videotape
Special Notes: Includes a recipe book.
Terms: Borrower pays return postage. RETURN the day after scheduled use. Book at least 4 weeks in advance. Requests must include your name, phone, mail address, eligibility program, title, NAL number, show date, and a statement, "I have read the warning on copyright restrictions and accept full responsibility for compliance." One title per request.

Source: National Agricultural Library
Document Delivery Services Branch
4th Floor, Photo Lab
10301 Baltimore Avenue
Beltsville, MD 20705-2351
Phone: 1-301-504-5994
Fax: 1-301-504-5675
World Wide Web URL: http://www.nal.usda.gov/fnic
Email Address: lending@nal.usda.gov

Low-Fat New Mexican Chile Dishes

Demonstrates recipes for a variety of traditional Mexican dishes reduced in fat by at least one-third. Includes the preparation of enchiladas, burritos, refried beans, tortillas, caldillo, and corn bread.

Availability: Staff at schools with NET, WIC, CSFP, FDPIR, CACFP, UMD or Child Nutrition Program food programs in the United States. Those not having such an affiliation should contact their library to place an interlibrary loan request.
Suggested Grade: 7-12
Languages: English; Spanish
Order Number: English NAL Video 2846; Spanish NAL Video 2891
Production Date: 1994
Format: VHS videotape
Terms: Borrower pays return postage. RETURN the day after scheduled use. Book at least 4 weeks in advance. Requests must include your name, phone, mail address, eligibility program, title, NAL number, show date, and a statement, "I have read the warning on copyright restrictions and accept full responsibility for compliance." One title per request.

Source: National Agricultural Library
Document Delivery Services Branch
4th Floor, Photo Lab, 10301 Baltimore Avenue
Beltsville, MD 20705-2351
Phone: 1-301-504-5994
Fax: 1-301-504-5675
World Wide Web URL: http://www.nal.usda.gov/fnic
Email Address: lending@nal.usda.gov

New Lean Life Food Series, The

Addresses the issue of too much fat in the American diet.

Availability: Staff at schools with NET, WIC, CSFP, FDPIR, CACFP, UMD or Child Nutrition Program food programs in the United States. Those not having such an affiliation should contact their library to place an interlibrary loan request.
Suggested Grade: 7-12
Order Number: NAL Video 2069
Production Date: 1995
Format: VHS videotape
Terms: Borrower pays return postage. RETURN the day after scheduled use. Book at least 4 weeks in advance. Requests must include your name, phone, mail address, eligibility program, title, NAL number, show date, and a statement, "I have read the warning on copyright restrictions and accept full responsibility for compliance." One title per request.

Source: National Agricultural Library
Document Delivery Services Branch
4th Floor, Photo Lab, 10301 Baltimore Avenue
Beltsville, MD 20705-2351
Phone: 1-301-504-5994
Fax: 1-301-504-5675
World Wide Web URL: http://www.nal.usda.gov/fnic
Email Address: lending@nal.usda.gov

Nifty Nutrition with Skill Integration Activities

A developmentally appropriate curriculum with sequential nutrition and health concepts based on the U. S. Dietary Guidelines and Food Guide Pyramid. Basic language, math, social studies, science, art and health skills are integrated into the curriculum and coded to each lesson.

Availability: Staff at schools with NET, WIC, CSFP, FDPIR, CACFP, UMD or Child Nutrition Program food programs in the United States. Those not having such an affiliation should contact their library to place an interlibrary loan request.

Suggested Grade: preK-6
Order Number: NAL Kit 229
Production Date: 1995
Format: Set of 7 VHS videotapes
Special Notes: This Arkansas Department of Education kit includes 7 teacher guides.
Terms: Borrower pays return postage. RETURN the day after scheduled use. Book at least 4 weeks in advance. Requests must include your name, phone, mail address, eligibility program, title, NAL number, show date, and a statement, "I have read the warning on copyright restrictions and accept full responsibility for compliance." One title per request.

**Source: National Agricultural Library
Document Delivery Services Branch
4th Floor, Photo Lab
10301 Baltimore Avenue
Beltsville, MD 20705-2351
Phone: 1-301-504-5994
Fax: 1-301-504-5675
World Wide Web URL: http://www.nal.usda.gov/fnic
Email Address: lending@nal.usda.gov**

Nutritional Rap

Simulates a television program on the "N-TV" network.

Availability: Staff at schools with NET, WIC, CSFP, FDPIR, CACFP, UMD or Child Nutrition Program food programs in the United States. Those not having such an affiliation should contact their library to place an interlibrary loan request.

Suggested Grade: preK-6
Order Number: NAL Video 1492
Production Date: 1992
Format: VHS videotape
Special Notes: Accompanied by a pamphlet.
Terms: Borrower pays return postage. RETURN the day after scheduled use. Book at least 4 weeks in advance. Requests must include your name, phone, mail address, eligibility program, title, NAL number, show date, and a statement, "I have read the warning on copyright restrictions and accept full responsibility for compliance." One title per request.

**Source: National Agricultural Library
Document Delivery Services Branch
4th Floor, Photo Lab
10301 Baltimore Avenue
Beltsville, MD 20705-2351
Phone: 1-301-504-5994
Fax: 1-301-504-5675
World Wide Web URL: http://www.nal.usda.gov/fnic
Email Address: lending@nal.usda.gov**

Nutrition and Me

This is a curriculum-based health package for students. It focuses on three areas: categories of foods as organized in the Food Pyramid; digestion of food, with emphasis on the influence of food on growth; and the food industry. It is structured to involve student participation, as well as written follow-up activities.

Availability: Staff at schools with NET, WIC, CSFP, FDPIR, CACFP, UMD or Child Nutrition Program food programs in the United States. Those not having such an affiliation should contact their library to place an interlibrary loan request.

Suggested Grade: 4-6
Order Number: NAL Kit 217
Production Date: 1993
Format: Set of 3 VHS videotapes
Special Notes: This Churchill Media kit includes 10 transparencies, a wall chart, 2 books, 7 duplicating master sheets, and a classroom guide.
Terms: Borrower pays return postage. RETURN the day after scheduled use. Book at least 4 weeks in advance. Requests must include your name, phone, mail address, eligibility program, title, NAL number, show date, and a statement, "I have read the warning on copyright restrictions and accept full responsibility for compliance." One title per request.

**Source: National Agricultural Library
Document Delivery Services Branch
4th Floor, Photo Lab
10301 Baltimore Avenue
Beltsville, MD 20705-2351
Phone: 1-301-504-5994
Fax: 1-301-504-5675
World Wide Web URL: http://www.nal.usda.gov/fnic
Email Address: lending@nal.usda.gov**

Nutrition Kit Eating Sensibly in the 1990's

This video and its accompanying teaching materials present the dietary guidelines for Americans as prepared by the U. S. Department of Health and Human Services. The guidelines covered in these materials are: eat a variety of food; avoid too much sugar; avoid too much fat, saturated fat, and cholesterol; and eat foods with adequate starch and fiber.

Availability: Staff at schools with NET, WIC, CSFP, FDPIR, CACFP, UMD or Child Nutrition Program food programs in the United States. Those not having such an affiliation should contact their library to place an interlibrary loan request.

Suggested Grade: 4-12
Order Number: NAL Video 535
Production Date: 1987
Format: VHS videotape
Terms: Borrower pays return postage. RETURN the day after scheduled use. Book at least 4 weeks in advance. Requests must include your name, phone, mail address,

eligibility program, title, NAL number, show date, and a statement, "I have read the warning on copyright restrictions and accept full responsibility for compliance." One title per request.

> **Source: National Agricultural Library**
> **Document Delivery Services Branch**
> **4th Floor, Photo Lab**
> **10301 Baltimore Avenue**
> **Beltsville, MD 20705-2351**
> **Phone: 1-301-504-5994**
> **Fax: 1-301-504-5675**
> **World Wide Web URL: http://www.nal.usda.gov/fnic**
> **Email Address: lending@nal.usda.gov**

Nutrition Labeling

This program discusses the nature of nutrients, what has to be included on nutrition labels, what information can be found on nutrition labels, and the meaning of the term U. S. RDA.

Availability:	Staff at schools with NET, WIC, CSFP, FDPIR, CACFP, UMD or Child Nutrition Program food programs in the United States. Those not having such an affiliation should contact their library to place an interlibrary loan request.
Suggested Grade:	preK-6
Order Number:	NAL Video 1474
Production Date:	1989
Format:	VHS videotape
Special Notes:	This is a WIC Program, Austin, Texas.
Terms:	Borrower pays return postage. RETURN the day after scheduled use. Book at least 4 weeks in advance. Requests must include your name, phone, mail address, eligibility program, title, NAL number, show date, and a statement, "I have read the warning on copyright restrictions and accept full responsibility for compliance." One title per request.

> **Source: National Agricultural Library**
> **Document Delivery Services Branch**
> **4th Floor, Photo Lab**
> **10301 Baltimore Avenue**
> **Beltsville, MD 20705-2351**
> **Phone: 1-301-504-5994**
> **Fax: 1-301-504-5675**
> **World Wide Web URL: http://www.nal.usda.gov/fnic**
> **Email Address: lending@nal.usda.gov**

Nutrition News: The Family Health Project

This video contains 11 news reports on nutrition topics: The Family Health Project; cavity research; surimi (imitation crab); teen weight management; aloe vera juice; clean and lean meat standards; ethnic food inspection, light desserts; and future food

Availability:	Staff at schools with NET, WIC, CSFP, FDPIR, CACFP, UMD or Child Nutrition Program food programs in the United States. Those not having such an affiliation should contact their library to place an interlibrary loan request.

Suggested Grade:	4-12
Order Number:	NAL Video 627
Production Date:	1989
Format:	VHS videotape
Terms:	Borrower pays return postage. RETURN the day after scheduled use. Book at least 4 weeks in advance. Requests must include your name, phone, mail address, eligibility program, title, NAL number, show date, and a statement, "I have read the warning on copyright restrictions and accept full responsibility for compliance." One title per request.

> **Source: National Agricultural Library**
> **Document Delivery Services Branch**
> **4th Floor, Photo Lab**
> **10301 Baltimore Avenue**
> **Beltsville, MD 20705-2351**
> **Phone: 1-301-504-5994**
> **Fax: 1-301-504-5675**
> **World Wide Web URL: http://www.nal.usda.gov/fnic**
> **Email Address: lending@nal.usda.gov**

Operation Risk

Designed to assist in teaching the hows and whys of safe food handling.

Availability:	Staff at schools with NET, WIC, CSFP, FDPIR, CACFP, UMD or Child Nutrition Program food programs in the United States. Those not having such an affiliation should contact their library to place an interlibrary loan request.
Suggested Grade:	3-5
Order Number:	NAL Kit 288
Production Date:	1993
Format:	VHS videotape
Special Notes:	Includes a teacher's guide.
Terms:	Borrower pays return postage. RETURN the day after scheduled use. Book at least 4 weeks in advance. Requests must include your name, phone, mail address, eligibility program, title, NAL number, show date, and a statement, "I have read the warning on copyright restrictions and accept full responsibility for compliance." One title per request.

> **Source: National Agricultural Library**
> **Document Delivery Services Branch**
> **4th Floor, Photo Lab, 10301 Baltimore Avenue**
> **Beltsville, MD 20705-2351**
> **Phone: 1-301-504-5994**
> **Fax: 1-301-504-5675**
> **World Wide Web URL: http://www.nal.usda.gov/fnic**
> **Email Address: lending@nal.usda.gov**

Preparation and the Dietary Guidelines

Demonstrates how to prepare foods that are tasty and nutritious while supporting the dietary guidelines.

Availability:	Staff at schools with NET, WIC, CSFP, FDPIR, CACFP, UMD or Child Nutrition Program food programs in the United States. Those not having such an affiliation should contact their library to place an interlibrary loan request.

Suggested Grade: 6-12
Order Number: NAL Video 1642
Production Date: 1993
Format: VHS videotape
Terms: Borrower pays return postage. RETURN the day after scheduled use. Book at least 4 weeks in advance. Requests must include your name, phone, mail address, eligibility program, title, NAL number, show date, and a statement, "I have read the warning on copyright restrictions and accept full responsibility for compliance." One title per request.

Source: National Agricultural Library
Document Delivery Services Branch
4th Floor, Photo Lab
10301 Baltimore Avenue
Beltsville, MD 20705-2351
Phone: 1-301-504-5994
Fax: 1-301-504-5675
World Wide Web URL: http://www.nal.usda.gov/fnic
Email Address: lending@nal.usda.gov

Read Before You Eat!

A videotape quiz that teaches viewers some fine points of food labeling.
Availability: Staff at schools with NET, WIC, CSFP, FDPIR, CACFP, UMD or Child Nutrition Program food programs in the United States. Those not having such an affiliation should contact their library to place an interlibrary loan request.
Suggested Grade: 6-12
Order Number: NAL Video 2205
Format: VHS videotape
Terms: Borrower pays return postage. RETURN the day after scheduled use. Book at least 4 weeks in advance. Requests must include your name, phone, mail address, eligibility program, title, NAL number, show date, and a statement, "I have read the warning on copyright restrictions and accept full responsibility for compliance." One title per request.

Source: National Agricultural Library
Document Delivery Services Branch
4th Floor, Photo Lab
10301 Baltimore Avenue
Beltsville, MD 20705-2351
Phone: 1-301-504-5994
Fax: 1-301-504-5675
World Wide Web URL: http://www.nal.usda.gov/fnic
Email Address: lending@nal.usda.gov

Safe Food for Children

Provides information on safe food handling for child care providers.
Availability: Staff at schools with NET, WIC, CSFP, FDPIR, CACFP, UMD or Child Nutrition Program food programs in the United States. Those not having such an affiliation should contact their library to place an interlibrary loan request.
Suggested Grade: Teacher Reference

Order Number: NAL Kit 231
Production Date: 1993
Format: Set of 2 VHS videotapes
Special Notes: Includes leader's guides. One video is for viewing by students, one is teacher material.
Terms: Borrower pays return postage. RETURN the day after scheduled use. Book at least 4 weeks in advance. Requests must include your name, phone, mail address, eligibility program, title, NAL number, show date, and a statement, "I have read the warning on copyright restrictions and accept full responsibility for compliance." One title per request.

Source: National Agricultural Library
Document Delivery Services Branch
4th Floor, Photo Lab
10301 Baltimore Avenue
Beltsville, MD 20705-2351
Phone: 1-301-504-5994
Fax: 1-301-504-5675
World Wide Web URL: http://www.nal.usda.gov/fnic
Email Address: lending@nal.usda.gov

Seven Most Popular Nutrition Myths

Attempts to put to rest seven of the most popular nutrition myths.
Availability: Staff at schools with NET, WIC, CSFP, FDPIR, CACFP, UMD or Child Nutrition Program food programs in the United States. Those not having such an affiliation should contact their library to place an interlibrary loan request.
Suggested Grade: 7-12
Order Number: NAL Video 1586
Production Date: 1992
Format: VHS videotape
Special Notes: A National Health Video production.
Terms: Borrower pays return postage. RETURN the day after scheduled use. Book at least 4 weeks in advance. Requests must include your name, phone, mail address, eligibility program, title, NAL number, show date, and a statement, "I have read the warning on copyright restrictions and accept full responsibility for compliance." One title per request.

Source: National Agricultural Library
Document Delivery Services Branch
4th Floor, Photo Lab
10301 Baltimore Avenue
Beltsville, MD 20705-2351
Phone: 1-301-504-5994
Fax: 1-301-504-5675
World Wide Web URL: http://www.nal.usda.gov/fnic
Email Address: lending@nal.usda.gov

Shopping for Health: Smart Choices at the Supermarket

Features five guidelines for making smart choices at the supermarket as well as tips for moving toward a healthier, plant-based eating style.

*All materials listed in this 2011-2012 edition are **BRAND NEW!***

Availability: Staff at schools with NET, WIC, CSFP, FDPIR, CACFP, UMD or Child Nutrition Program food programs in the United States. Those not having such an affiliation should contact their library to place an interlibrary loan request.

Suggested Grade: 7-Adult
Order Number: NAL Video 2614
Production Date: 1997
Format: VHS videotape
Terms: Borrower pays return postage. RETURN the day after scheduled use. Book at least 4 weeks in advance. Requests must include your name, phone, mail address, eligibility program, title, NAL number, show date, and a statement, "I have read the warning on copyright restrictions and accept full responsibility for compliance." One title per request.

Source: National Agricultural Library
Document Delivery Services Branch
4th Floor, Photo Lab
10301 Baltimore Avenue
Beltsville, MD 20705-2351
Phone: 1-301-504-5994
Fax: 1-301-504-5675
World Wide Web URL: http://www.nal.usda.gov/fnic
Email Address: lending@nal.usda.gov

Shopping for Women's Health: Reduce Your Risks of Osteoporosis and Breast Cancer

Educates women about general nutrition that can help reduce the risk of osteoporosis and breast cancer.

Availability: Staff at schools with NET, WIC, CSFP, FDPIR, CACFP, UMD or Child Nutrition Program food programs in the United States. Those not having such an affiliation should contact their library to place an interlibrary loan request.

Suggested Grade: 7-Adult
Order Number: NAL Video 2620
Production Date: 1997
Format: VHS videotape
Terms: Borrower pays return postage. RETURN the day after scheduled use. Book at least 4 weeks in advance. Requests must include your name, phone, mail address, eligibility program, title, NAL number, show date, and a statement, "I have read the warning on copyright restrictions and accept full responsibility for compliance." One title per request.

Source: National Agricultural Library
Document Delivery Services Branch
4th Floor, Photo Lab
10301 Baltimore Avenue
Beltsville, MD 20705-2351
Phone: 1-301-504-5994
Fax: 1-301-504-5675
World Wide Web URL: http://www.nal.usda.gov/fnic
Email Address: lending@nal.usda.gov

Shopping Smart: Consumer's Guide to Healthy Food Selection

The setting for this video is the supermarket. From the produce counter to the deli, this program explores every corner of the grocery store to help the shoppers make wise nutritional choices. Some of the country's leading nutritionists answer commonly asked questions and clarify packaging claims and label terms.

Availability: Staff at schools with NET, WIC, CSFP, FDPIR, CACFP, UMD or Child Nutrition Program food programs in the United States. Those not having such an affiliation should contact their library to place an interlibrary loan request.

Suggested Grade: 7-12
Order Number: NAL Video 636
Production Date: 1988
Format: VHS videotape
Terms: Borrower pays return postage. RETURN the day after scheduled use. Book at least 4 weeks in advance. Requests must include your name, phone, mail address, eligibility program, title, NAL number, show date, and a statement, "I have read the warning on copyright restrictions and accept full responsibility for compliance." One title per request.

Source: National Agricultural Library
Document Delivery Services Branch
4th Floor, Photo Lab, 10301 Baltimore Avenue
Beltsville, MD 20705-2351
Phone: 1-301-504-5994
Fax: 1-301-504-5675
World Wide Web URL: http://www.nal.usda.gov/fnic
Email Address: lending@nal.usda.gov

Shopping Smart for a Healthy Heart

This video discusses the effects on the heart of a diet high in cholesterol and fat in the context of shopping for food at a supermarket. The program gives tips on shopping for oils, shortenings, eggs, dairy products, vegetables, meats, fish, bakery products and cereals. Some cooking tips are also provided.

Availability: Staff at schools with NET, WIC, CSFP, FDPIR, CACFP, UMD or Child Nutrition Program food programs in the United States. Those not having such an affiliation should contact their library to place an interlibrary loan request.

Suggested Grade: 7-12
Languages: English; Spanish
Order Number: English--NAL 780; Spanish--NAL 781
Production Date: 1989
Format: VHS videotape
Terms: Borrower pays return postage. RETURN the day after scheduled use. Book at least 4 weeks in advance. Requests must include your name, phone, mail address, eligibility program, title, NAL number, show date, and a statement, "I have read the warning on copyright restrictions and accept full responsibility for compliance." One title per request.

Source: National Agricultural Library
Document Delivery Services Branch
4th Floor, Photo Lab
10301 Baltimore Avenue
Beltsville, MD 20705-2351
Phone: 1-301-504-5994
Fax: 1-301-504-5675
World Wide Web URL: http://www.nal.usda.gov/fnic
Email Address: lending@nal.usda.gov

Shop Right for Good Nutrition

This program assists consumers in the selection and purchase of food. The role of food labels and how to understand them is discussed. The regulation by the FDA and USDA of certain terms used to describe food is also examined.

Availability: Staff at schools with NET, WIC, CSFP, FDPIR, CACFP, UMD or Child Nutrition Program food programs in the United States. Those not having such an affiliation should contact their library to place an interlibrary loan request.
Suggested Grade: 7-12
Order Number: NAL Video 578
Production Date: 1989
Format: VHS videotape
Terms: Borrower pays return postage. RETURN the day after scheduled use. Book at least 4 weeks in advance. Requests must include your name, phone, mail address, eligibility program, title, NAL number, show date, and a statement, "I have read the warning on copyright restrictions and accept full responsibility for compliance." One title per request.

Source: National Agricultural Library
Document Delivery Services Branch
4th Floor, Photo Lab
10301 Baltimore Avenue
Beltsville, MD 20705-2351
Phone: 1-301-504-5994
Fax: 1-301-504-5675
World Wide Web URL: http://www.nal.usda.gov/fnic
Email Address: lending@nal.usda.gov

Shop Smart: Reading Food Labels

Information about food labeling and how labels can help make food choices for a healthy diet.

Availability: Staff at schools with NET, WIC, CSFP, FDPIR, CACFP, UMD or Child Nutrition Program food programs in the United States. Those not having such an affiliation should contact their library to place an interlibrary loan request.
Suggested Grade: 7-Adult
Order Number: NAL Video 1823
Format: VHS videotape
Terms: Borrower pays return postage. RETURN the day after scheduled use. Book at least 4 weeks in advance. Requests must include your name, phone, mail address, eligibility program, title, NAL number, show date, and

a statement, "I have read the warning on copyright restrictions and accept full responsibility for compliance." One title per request.

Source: National Agricultural Library
Document Delivery Services Branch
4th Floor, Photo Lab, 10301 Baltimore Avenue
Beltsville, MD 20705-2351
Phone: 1-301-504-5994
Fax: 1-301-504-5675
World Wide Web URL: http://www.nal.usda.gov/fnic
Email Address: lending@nal.usda.gov

Snackology: How to Have Your Snacks and Eat Them Too

This video teaches how to evaluate common snack foods in order to identify those that are "least damaging" to a well-balanced diet. This video discusses minimizing fat and calorie damage in everyday snack food. Cookies, ice cream and frozen desserts, popcorn, chips and munchies, snack pies and pastries, candy, and their ingredients are examined.

Availability: Staff at schools with NET, WIC, CSFP, FDPIR, CACFP, UMD or Child Nutrition Program food programs in the United States. Those not having such an affiliation should contact their library to place an interlibrary loan request.
Suggested Grade: 4-12
Order Number: NAL Video 532
Format: VHS videotape
Terms: Borrower pays return postage. RETURN the day after scheduled use. Book at least 4 weeks in advance. Requests must include your name, phone, mail address, eligibility program, title, NAL number, show date, and a statement, "I have read the warning on copyright restrictions and accept full responsibility for compliance." One title per request.

Source: National Agricultural Library
Document Delivery Services Branch
4th Floor, Photo Lab, 10301 Baltimore Avenue
Beltsville, MD 20705-2351
Phone: 1-301-504-5994
Fax: 1-301-504-5675
World Wide Web URL: http://www.nal.usda.gov/fnic
Email Address: lending@nal.usda.gov

Sports Nutrition: Fueling a Winner

This program dispels some popular nutrition myths and educates the athlete regarding proper nutrition. It shows how the athlete's diet differs from the normal diet and how to calculate amounts of food to eat to maintain weight in spite of heavy exercise. Also discussed is the importance of water.

Availability: Staff at schools with NET, WIC, CSFP, FDPIR, CACFP, UMD or Child Nutrition Program food programs in the United States. Those not having such an affiliation should contact their library to place an interlibrary loan request.

*All materials listed in this 2011-2012 edition are **BRAND NEW**!*

Suggested Grade: 7-12
Order Number: NAL Video 862
Production Date: 1989
Format: VHS videotape
Terms: Borrower pays return postage. RETURN the day after scheduled use. Book at least 4 weeks in advance. Requests must include your name, phone, mail address, eligibility program, title, NAL number, show date, and a statement, "I have read the warning on copyright restrictions and accept full responsibility for compliance." One title per request.

Source: National Agricultural Library
Document Delivery Services Branch
4th Floor, Photo Lab
10301 Baltimore Avenue
Beltsville, MD 20705-2351
Phone: 1-301-504-5994
Fax: 1-301-504-5675
World Wide Web URL: http://www.nal.usda.gov/fnic
Email Address: lending@nal.usda.gov

Supermarket Savvy

Presents guidelines for using the nutrition information on food product labels to select healthier foods at the supermarket.

Availability: Staff at schools with NET, WIC, CSFP, FDPIR, CACFP, UMD or Child Nutrition Program food programs in the United States. Those not having such an affiliation should contact their library to place an interlibrary loan request.
Suggested Grade: 7-12
Order Number: NAL Video 330
Production Date: 1987
Format: VHS videotape
Terms: Borrower pays return postage. RETURN the day after scheduled use. Book at least 4 weeks in advance. Requests must include your name, phone, mail address, eligibility program, title, NAL number, show date, and a statement, "I have read the warning on copyright restrictions and accept full responsibility for compliance." One title per request.

Source: National Agricultural Library
Document Delivery Services Branch
4th Floor, Photo Lab
10301 Baltimore Avenue
Beltsville, MD 20705-2351
Phone: 1-301-504-5994
Fax: 1-301-504-5675
World Wide Web URL: http://www.nal.usda.gov/fnic
Email Address: lending@nal.usda.gov

Understanding the New Food Label: An Overview from the Consumer Perspective

Panelists with expertise in food labeling discuss three aspects of the new food labels including: nutrition claims on labels, new features of the label, and efforts by USDA and FDA to educate consumers with regard to the new label.

Availability: Staff at schools with NET, WIC, CSFP, FDPIR, CACFP, UMD or Child Nutrition Program food programs in the United States. Those not having such an affiliation should contact their library to place an interlibrary loan request.
Suggested Grade: 7-12
Order Number: NAL Video 1565
Production Date: 1993
Format: VHS videotape
Terms: Borrower pays return postage. RETURN the day after scheduled use. Book at least 4 weeks in advance. Requests must include your name, phone, mail address, eligibility program, title, NAL number, show date, and a statement, "I have read the warning on copyright restrictions and accept full responsibility for compliance." One title per request.

Source: National Agricultural Library
Document Delivery Services Branch
4th Floor, Photo Lab
10301 Baltimore Avenue
Beltsville, MD 20705-2351
Phone: 1-301-504-5994
Fax: 1-301-504-5675
World Wide Web URL: http://www.nal.usda.gov/fnic
Email Address: lending@nal.usda.gov

We're a Family

Families come in different forms. Some are traditional, some blended or step, and some are single parent. Presents the concept that, no matter the structure, families are made of people who care for, love, listen to, and share time with each other.

Availability: Schools, libraries, and homeschoolers in the United States who serve the hearing impaired.
Suggested Grade: 1-6
Order Number: 12350
Production Date: 1992
Format: DVD
Special Notes: Produced by Sunburst Communications.
Terms: Sponsor pays all transportation costs. Return one week after receipt. Participation is limited to deaf or hard of hearing Americans, their parents, families, teachers, counselors, or others whose use would benefit a deaf or hard of hearing person. Only one person in the audience needs to be hearing impaired. You must register--which is free. These videos are all open-captioned--no special equipment is required for viewing.

Source: Described and Captioned Media Program
National Association of the Deaf
4211 Church Street Ext.
Roebuck, SC 29376
Phone: 1-800-237-6213
Fax: 1-800-538-5636
World Wide Web URL: http://www.dcmp.org

We're Growing Up!

Talks matter-of-factly about human growth and discusses the physical changes adolescents undergo. Reviews male and female anatomy and sexual development. Emphasizes and encourages emotional maturity and responsible choices.

Availability:	Schools, libraries, and homeschoolers in the United States who serve the hearing impaired.
Suggested Grade:	5-8
Order Number:	12832
Production Date:	1995
Format:	DVD
Special Notes:	Produced by Marsh Media.
Terms:	Sponsor pays all transportation costs. Return one week after receipt. Participation is limited to deaf or hard of hearing Americans, their parents, families, teachers, counselors, or others whose use would benefit a deaf or hard of hearing person. Only one person in the audience needs to be hearing impaired. You must register--which is free. These videos are all open-captioned--no special equipment is required for viewing.

Source: Described and Captioned Media Program
National Association of the Deaf
4211 Church Street Ext.
Roebuck, SC 29376
Phone: 1-800-237-6213
Fax: 1-800-538-5636
World Wide Web URL: http://www.dcmp.org

ABC's of Teaching ABC's, The

Parents are shown how to incorporate teaching the ABCs into a child's daily activities.

Availability: Schools, libraries, and homeschoolers in the United States who serve the hearing impaired.
Suggested Grade: Adult
Order Number: 13150
Production Date: 1992
Format: DVD
Terms: Sponsor pays all transportation costs. Return one week after receipt. Participation is limited to deaf or hard of hearing Americans, their parents, families, teachers, counselors, or others whose use would benefit a deaf or hard of hearing person. Only one person in the audience needs to be hearing impaired. You must register--which is free. These videos are all open-captioned--no special equipment is required for viewing.

Source: Described and Captioned Media Program
National Association of the Deaf
4211 Church Street Ext.
Roebuck, SC 29376
Phone: 1-800-237-6213
Fax: 1-800-538-5636
World Wide Web URL: http://www.dcmp.org

Aesop's Fables

Presents animated versions of several fables.

Availability: Schools, libraries, and homeschoolers in the United States who serve the hearing impaired.
Suggested Grade: K-4
Order Number: 12825
Production Date: 1996
Format: DVD
Terms: Sponsor pays all transportation costs. Return one week after receipt. Participation is limited to deaf or hard of hearing Americans, their parents, families, teachers, counselors, or others whose use would benefit a deaf or hard of hearing person. Only one person in the audience needs to be hearing impaired. You must register--which is free. These videos are all open-captioned--no special equipment is required for viewing.

Source: Described and Captioned Media Program
National Association of the Deaf
4211 Church Street Ext.
Roebuck, SC 29376
Phone: 1-800-237-6213
Fax: 1-800-538-5636
World Wide Web URL: http://www.dcmp.org

Amazing Bone, The

A fun tale about a pig who finds an enchanted bone.

Availability: Schools, libraries, and homeschoolers in the United States who serve the hearing impaired.
Suggested Grade: K-3
Order Number: 11150
Production Date: 1985
Format: DVD
Special Notes: Also available as live streaming video over the Internet.

Terms: Sponsor pays all transportation costs. Return one week after receipt. Participation is limited to deaf or hard of hearing Americans, their parents, families, teachers, counselors, or others whose use would benefit a deaf or hard of hearing person. Only one person in the audience needs to be hearing impaired. You must register--which is free. These videos are all open-captioned--no special equipment is required for viewing.

Source: Described and Captioned Media Program
National Association of the Deaf
4211 Church Street Ext.
Roebuck, SC 29376
Phone: 1-800-237-6213
Fax: 1-800-538-5636
World Wide Web URL: http://www.dcmp.org

Amazing Grace

A story about a girl who is discouraged from doing what she wants because she's a girl and African-American.

Availability: Schools, libraries, and homeschoolers in the United States who serve the hearing impaired.
Suggested Grade: K-3
Order Number: 11616
Production Date: 1994
Format: DVD
Special Notes: Also available as live streaming video over the Internet.

Terms: Sponsor pays all transportation costs. Return one week after receipt. Participation is limited to deaf or hard of hearing Americans, their parents, families, teachers, counselors, or others whose use would benefit a deaf or hard of hearing person. Only one person in the audience needs to be hearing impaired. You must register--which is free. These videos are all open-captioned--no special equipment is required for viewing.

Source: Described and Captioned Media Program
National Association of the Deaf
4211 Church Street Ext.
Roebuck, SC 29376
Phone: 1-800-237-6213
Fax: 1-800-538-5636
World Wide Web URL: http://www.dcmp.org

Between the Lions: Clickety-Clack, Clickety-Clack!

The special magic of some lions who live in the library will teach students the short "i" sound.

Availability: Schools, libraries, and homeschoolers in the United States who serve the hearing impaired.
Suggested Grade: preK-4
Order Number: 10855
Production Date: 2000
Format: DVD
Special Notes: Also available as live streaming video over the Internet.

Terms: Sponsor pays all transportation costs. Return one week after receipt. Participation is limited to deaf or hard of hearing Americans, their parents, families, teachers, counselors, or others whose use would benefit a deaf or hard of hearing person. Only one person in the audience needs to be hearing impaired. You must register--which is free. These videos are all open-captioned--no special equipment is required for viewing.

Source: Described and Captioned Media Program
National Association of the Deaf
4211 Church Street Ext.
Roebuck, SC 29376
Phone: 1-800-237-6213
Fax: 1-800-538-5636
World Wide Web URL: http://www.dcmp.org

By the Light of the Halloween Moon

A cumulative story about a girl who refuses to be scared by a cat, a witch, a bat, and other assorted Halloween friends.

Availability:	Schools, libraries, and homeschoolers in the United States who serve the hearing impaired.
Suggested Grade:	preK-3
Order Number:	10863
Production Date:	1997
Format:	DVD
Special Notes:	Also available as live streaming video over the Internet.
Terms:	Sponsor pays all transportation costs. Return one week after receipt. Participation is limited to deaf or hard of hearing Americans, their parents, families, teachers, counselors, or others whose use would benefit a deaf or hard of hearing person. Only one person in the audience needs to be hearing impaired. You must register--which is free. These videos are all open-captioned--no special equipment is required for viewing.

Source: Described and Captioned Media Program
National Association of the Deaf
4211 Church Street Ext.
Roebuck, SC 29376
Phone: 1-800-237-6213
Fax: 1-800-538-5636
World Wide Web URL: http://www.dcmp.org

Charlie Needs a Cloak

Charlie the shepherd shears his sheep and makes a new coat for winter. Each step is described.

Availability:	Schools, libraries, and homeschoolers in the United States who serve the hearing impaired.
Suggested Grade:	K-3
Languages:	English; Spanish
Order Number:	English 11664; Spanish 12288\ormat: D V D
Special Notes:	Also available as live streaming video over the Internet.
Terms:	Sponsor pays all transportation costs. Return one week after receipt. Participation is limited to deaf or hard of hearing Americans, their parents, families, teachers, counselors, or others whose use would benefit a deaf or hard of hearing person. Only one person in the audience needs to be hearing impaired. You must register--which is free. These videos are all open-captioned--no special equipment is required for viewing.

Source: Described and Captioned Media Program
National Association of the Deaf
4211 Church Street Ext.
Roebuck, SC 29376

Phone: 1-800-237-6213
Fax: 1-800-538-5636
World Wide Web URL: http://www.dcmp.org

Cuentos Populares Latinoamericanos

Six fables relating morals through humor and art.

Availability:	Schools, libraries, and nursing homes in the United States.
Suggested Grade:	6-12
Language:	Simple Spanish
Order Number:	LG7-video
Production Date:	1992
Format:	VHS videotape
Terms:	Borrowers must have a User's Agreement on file with this source--available by mail or via the Internet. Return postage is paid by borrower; return 12 days after showing. Book at least three weeks in advance. All borrowers are limited to a total of ten items per semester.

Source: Latin American Resource Center
Stone Center for Latin American Studies
Tulane University
100 Jones Hall
New Orleans, LA 70118
Phone: 1-504-862-3143
Fax: 1-504-865-6719
World Wide Web URL:
http://stonecenter.tulane.edu/pages/detail/48/
Lending-Library
Email Address: crcrts@tulane.edu

Essay What?

Four teenagers compete in an essay writing contest judged by Aristotle, Shakespeare, and Mark Twain. Identifies the four essay types and their key elements.

Availability:	Schools, libraries, and homeschoolers in the United States who serve the hearing impaired.
Suggested Grade:	8-12
Order Number:	11641
Production Date:	2000
Format:	DVD
Special Notes:	Also available as live streaming video over the Internet.
Terms:	Sponsor pays all transportation costs. Return one week after receipt. Participation is limited to deaf or hard of hearing Americans, their parents, families, teachers, counselors, or others whose use would benefit a deaf or hard of hearing person. Only one person in the audience needs to be hearing impaired. You must register--which is free. These videos are all open-captioned--no special equipment is required for viewing.

Source: Described and Captioned Media Program
National Association of the Deaf
4211 Church Street Ext.
Roebuck, SC 29376
Phone: 1-800-237-6213
Fax: 1-800-538-5636
World Wide Web URL: http://www.dcmp.org

*All materials listed in this 2011-2012 edition are **BRAND NEW!***

Heritage: Spanish-Speakers and Bilingualism
Examines different kinds of Spanish spoken in the U. S. and their relationship to Spanish in Latin America.

Availability:	Schools, libraries, and nursing homes in the United States.
Suggested Grade:	6-12
Order Number:	LANHISP1-video
Production Date:	1991
Format:	VHS videotape
Terms:	Borrowers must have a User's Agreement on file with this source--available by mail or via the Internet. Return postage is paid by borrower; return 12 days after showing. Book at least three weeks in advance. All borrowers are limited to a total of ten items per semester.

Source: Latin American Resource Center
Stone Center for Latin American Studies
Tulane University
100 Jones Hall
New Orleans, LA 70118
Phone: 1-504-862-3143
Fax: 1-504-865-6719
World Wide Web URL:
http://stonecenter.tulane.edu/pages/detail/48/
Lending-Library
Email Address: crcrts@tulane.edu

In the Night Kitchen
Presents the animated story of a little boy who dreams he falls out of his bed in the middle of the night and finds himself in a magical place called the night kitchen. From the book written and illustrated by Maurice Sendak.

Availability:	Schools, libraries, and homeschoolers in the United States who serve the hearing impaired.
Suggested Grade:	preK-3
Language:	Spanish
Order Number:	12011
Production Date:	1987
Format:	DVD
Terms:	Sponsor pays all transportation costs. Return one week after receipt. Participation is limited to deaf or hard of hearing Americans, their parents, families, teachers, counselors, or others whose use would benefit a deaf or hard of hearing person. Only one person in the audience needs to be hearing impaired. You must register--which is free. These videos are all open-captioned--no special equipment is required for viewing.

Source: Described and Captioned Media Program
National Association of the Deaf
4211 Church Street Ext.
Roebuck, SC 29376
Phone: 1-800-237-6213
Fax: 1-800-538-5636
World Wide Web URL: http://www.dcmp.org

Learn English Videos
Learn the English words for animals, fruit, entertainment and fun, food, and the more.

Availability:	All requesters
Suggested Grade:	All ages
Order Number:	not applicable
Format:	Streaming Video

Source: Jacob Richman
World Wide Web URL:
http://www.my-english-dictionary.com/videos.htm

Learn Hebrew Videos
Learn the Hebrews words for animals, fruit, entertainment and fun, food, and the human body.

Availability:	All requesters
Suggested Grade:	All ages
Order Number:	not applicable
Format:	Streaming Video

Source: Jacob Richman
World Wide Web URL:
http://www.my-hebrew-dictionary.com/videos.htm

Learn Spanish Videos
Learn some popular Spanish words.

Availability:	All requesters
Suggested Grade:	All ages
Order Number:	not applicable
Format:	Streaming Video

Source: Jacob Richman
World Wide Web URL:
http://www.learn-spanish.co.il/videos/index.html

Little Red Riding Hood
Little Red Riding Coat disobeys her mother's instructions when she goes to her grandmother's house and suffers the consequences. A Chinese version of the familiar fairy tale. Narrated by Robert Guillaume.

Availability:	Schools, libraries, and homeschoolers in the United States who serve the hearing impaired.
Suggested Grade:	4-6
Order Number:	12417
Production Date:	1995
Format:	DVD
Special Notes:	Produced by Ambrose Video Publishing, Inc..
Terms:	Sponsor pays all transportation costs. Return one week after receipt. Participation is limited to deaf or hard of hearing Americans, their parents, families, teachers, counselors, or others whose use would benefit a deaf or hard of hearing person. Only one person in the audience needs to be hearing impaired. You must register--which is free. These videos are all open-captioned--no special equipment is required for viewing.

Source: Described and Captioned Media Program
National Association of the Deaf
4211 Church Street Ext.
Roebuck, SC 29376
Phone: 1-800-237-6213
Fax: 1-800-538-5636
World Wide Web URL: http://www.dcmp.org

Living Language Spanish
Helps with five situations: airport, hotel, street, restaurant, and department store.

Availability: Schools, libraries, and nursing homes in the United States.
Suggested Grade: 6-12
Order Number: LANSPA9-video
Production Date: 1984
Format: VHS videotape
Terms: Borrowers must have a User's Agreement on file with this source--available by mail or via the Internet. Return postage is paid by borrower; return 12 days after showing. Book at least three weeks in advance. All borrowers are limited to a total of ten items per semester.

Source: Latin American Resource Center
Stone Center for Latin American Studies
Tulane University
100 Jones Hall
New Orleans, LA 70118
Phone: 1-504-862-3143
Fax: 1-504-865-6719
World Wide Web URL:
http://stonecenter.tulane.edu/pages/detail/48/
Lending-Library
Email Address: crcrts@tulane.edu

Mexican Sign Language

Instructional video demonstrating more than one thousand words in Mexican Sign Language. The manual alphabet and number signs are shown. Each word is voiced and captioned in both Spanish and English and is signed twice. The instruction is divided into 10 lessons.

Availability: Schools, libraries, and homeschoolers in the United States who serve the hearing impaired.
Suggested Grade: All ages
Spanish
Order Number: 12879
Format: DVD
Special Notes: Produced by Signing Fiesta.
Terms: Sponsor pays all transportation costs. Return one week after receipt. Participation is limited to deaf or hard of hearing Americans, their parents, families, teachers, counselors, or others whose use would benefit a deaf or hard of hearing person. Only one person in the audience needs to be hearing impaired. You must register--which is free. These videos are all open-captioned--no special equipment is required for viewing.

Source: Described and Captioned Media Program
National Association of the Deaf
4211 Church Street Ext.
Roebuck, SC 29376
Phone: 1-800-237-6213
Fax: 1-800-538-5636
World Wide Web URL: http://www.dcmp.org

Monty

Monty is a sleepy alligator-taxi who ferries Arthur the frog, Doris the duck, and Tom the rabbit across the river to and from school. When Monty decides he's tired of their back-seat driving, he takes a vacation, leaving them to find their own way across on the book by James Stevenson.

Availability: Schools, libraries, and homeschoolers in the United States who serve the hearing impaired.
Suggested Grade: preK-4
Order Number: 12346
Production Date: 1992
Format: DVD
Special Notes: Produced by Weston Woods Studios.
Terms: Sponsor pays all transportation costs. Return one week after receipt. Participation is limited to deaf or hard of hearing Americans, their parents, families, teachers, counselors, or others whose use would benefit a deaf or hard of hearing person. Only one person in the audience needs to be hearing impaired. You must register--which is free. These videos are all open-captioned--no special equipment is required for viewing.

Source: Described and Captioned Media Program
National Association of the Deaf
4211 Church Street Ext.
Roebuck, SC 29376
Phone: 1-800-237-6213
Fax: 1-800-538-5636
World Wide Web URL: http://www.dcmp.org

Most Wonderful Egg In the World, The

Three hens quarrel about which of them is the most beautiful. Unable to settle their dispute, they ask the king for his advice. He offers to make a princess of the one who lays the most wonderful egg. After laying three spectacular eggs, the king declares all three of them princesses. This animated version is based on the book by Helme Heine.

Availability: Schools, libraries, and homeschoolers in the United States who serve the hearing impaired.
Suggested Grade: preK-6
Order Number: 12333
Production Date: 1986
Format: DVD
Special Notes: Also available as live streaming video over the Internet.
Terms: Sponsor pays all transportation costs. Return one week after receipt. Participation is limited to deaf or hard of hearing Americans, their parents, families, teachers, counselors, or others whose use would benefit a deaf or hard of hearing person. Only one person in the audience needs to be hearing impaired. You must register--which is free. These videos are all open-captioned--no special equipment is required for viewing.

Source: Described and Captioned Media Program
National Association of the Deaf
4211 Church Street Ext.
Roebuck, SC 29376
Phone: 1-800-237-6213
Fax: 1-800-538-5636
World Wide Web URL: http://www.dcmp.org

Myths & Legends of Ancient Rome

Explores the legend of Romulus and Remus, twin boys who founded Rome on seven hills. Briefly relates how Perseus, son of Jupiter, used his shield as a mirror to safely slay Medusa, a monster who turned anyone who looked on her to stone. Recounts the story of Psyche and Cupid, a story of broken promises and forgiveness. Each legend ends with thought and discussion questions.

Availability: Schools, libraries, and homeschoolers in the United States who serve the hearing impaired.
Suggested Grade: 6-10
Order Number: 13012
Production Date: 1996
Format: DVD
Special Notes: Produced by United Learning, Inc.
Terms: Sponsor pays all transportation costs. Return one week after receipt. Participation is limited to deaf or hard of hearing Americans, their parents, families, teachers, counselors, or others whose use would benefit a deaf or hard of hearing person. Only one person in the audience needs to be hearing impaired. You must register--which is free. These videos are all open-captioned--no special equipment is required for viewing.
Source: Described and Captioned Media Program
National Association of the Deaf
4211 Church Street Ext.
Roebuck, SC 29376
Phone: 1-800-237-6213
Fax: 1-800-538-5636
World Wide Web URL: http://www.dcmp.org

Narrative Writing 1: Structures--What is a Narrative?
Discusses the three-act structure of a classical narrative with examples.

Availability: Schools, libraries, and homeschoolers in the United States who serve the hearing impaired.
Suggested Grade: 8-Adult
Order Number: 11610
Production Date: 2002
Format: DVD
Special Notes: Also available as live streaming video over the Internet.
Terms: Sponsor pays all transportation costs. Return one week after receipt. Participation is limited to deaf or hard of hearing Americans, their parents, families, teachers, counselors, or others whose use would benefit a deaf or hard of hearing person. Only one person in the audience needs to be hearing impaired. You must register--which is free. These videos are all open-captioned--no special equipment is required for viewing.
Source: Described and Captioned Media Program
National Association of the Deaf
4211 Church Street Ext.
Roebuck, SC 29376
Phone: 1-800-237-6213
Fax: 1-800-538-5636
World Wide Web URL: http://www.dcmp.org

Noisy Nora
Noisy Nora, the middle mouse child, bangs windows, slams doors and knocks over furniture, trying to get her parents' attention. When that fails, she hides until her parents begin to look for her. Then she appears with a monumental crash! Based on the book by Rosemary Wells. Animated.

Availability: Schools, libraries, and homeschoolers in the United States who serve the hearing impaired.
Suggested Grade: preK-6
Order Number: 13626
Production Date: 1994
Format: DVD
Special Notes: Produced by Weston Woods Studios.
Terms: Sponsor pays all transportation costs. Return one week after receipt. Participation is limited to deaf or hard of hearing Americans, their parents, families, teachers, counselors, or others whose use would benefit a deaf or hard of hearing person. Only one person in the audience needs to be hearing impaired. You must register--which is free. These videos are all open-captioned--no special equipment is required for viewing.
Source: Described and Captioned Media Program
National Association of the Deaf
4211 Church Street Ext.
Roebuck, SC 29376
Phone: 1-800-237-6213
Fax: 1-800-538-5636
World Wide Web URL: http://www.dcmp.org

Princess and the Pea, The
The queen searches for the perfect princess for her son by devising a test that only a true princess can pass. A Korean version of a familiar fairy tale.

Availability: Schools, libraries, and homeschoolers in the United States who serve the hearing impaired.
Suggested Grade: 4-6
Order Number: 12421
Production Date: 1995
Format: DVD
Special Notes: Produced by Ambrose Video Publishing, Inc..
Terms: Sponsor pays all transportation costs. Return one week after receipt. Participation is limited to deaf or hard of hearing Americans, their parents, families, teachers, counselors, or others whose use would benefit a deaf or hard of hearing person. Only one person in the audience needs to be hearing impaired. You must register--which is free. These videos are all open-captioned--no special equipment is required for viewing.
Source: Described and Captioned Media Program
National Association of the Deaf
4211 Church Street Ext.
Roebuck, SC 29376
Phone: 1-800-237-6213
Fax: 1-800-538-5636
World Wide Web URL: http://www.dcmp.org

Punctuation: Program 6--Introduction to Punctuation and the End Marks
Gives clear rules and examples of how to use punctuation.

Availability: Schools, libraries, and homeschoolers in the United States who serve the hearing impaired.
Suggested Grade: 6-12
Order Number: 11622
Production Date: 2000
Format: DVD

*All materials listed in this 2011-2012 edition are **BRAND NEW!***

LANGUAGE ARTS

Special Notes: Also available as live streaming video over the Internet.
Terms: Sponsor pays all transportation costs. Return one week after receipt. Participation is limited to deaf or hard of hearing Americans, their parents, families, teachers, counselors, or others whose use would benefit a deaf or hard of hearing person. Only one person in the audience needs to be hearing impaired. You must register--which is free. These videos are all open-captioned--no special equipment is required for viewing.

Source: Described and Captioned Media Program
National Association of the Deaf
4211 Church Street Ext.
Roebuck, SC 29376
Phone: 1-800-237-6213
Fax: 1-800-538-5636
World Wide Web URL: http://www.dcmp.org

Teaching Foreign Languages K-12: A Library of Classroom Practices

A video library illustrating effective instruction and assessment strategies for teaching foreign languages. The language classrooms shown in this library include Spanish, French, German, Japanese, Italian, Latin, Russian, and Chinese.

Availability: All requesters
Suggested Grade: Teacher Reference
Order Number: not applicable
Production Date: 2003
Format: Streaming Video
Special Notes: Also available for purchase for $555.00.
Terms: A simple FREE registration is required to view videos.

Source: Annenberg Media
World Wide Web URL:
http://www.learner.org/resources/browse.html

Teaching Reading K-2: A Library of Classroom Practices

This video library features the teaching practices of a diverse cross-section of kindergarten through second grade teachers from across the country.

Availability: All requesters
Suggested Grade: Teacher Reference
Order Number: not applicable
Production Date: 2002
Format: Streaming Video
Special Notes: Also available for purchase for $295.00.
Terms: A simple FREE registration is required to view videos.

Source: Annenberg Media
World Wide Web URL:
http://www.learner.org/resources/browse.html

Verso Negro: Black Verse of the Spanish Caribbean

Examines Afro-Caribbean poetry, and its history and living legacy, as personified today by poets both in the Caribbean and the United States.

Availability: Schools and libraries in Iowa, Illinois, Michigan, Minnesota, and Wisconsin.
Suggested Grade: 6-12
Order Number: AFRICACARV61VHS
Production Date: 1999
Format: VHS videotape
Terms: Borrower pays return postage. Return 8 days after showing. Book 2 weeks in advance. Order may also be picked up for those near the Center.

Source: Center for Latin American and Caribbean Studies
UW-Milwaukee
P. O. Box 413
Milwaukee, WI 53201
Phone: 1-414-229-5987
World Wide Web URL: http://www.uwm.edu/Dept/CLACS
Email Address: audvis@usm.edu

Writing: Uses and Importance

Writing is a very important and powerful tool used in everyday life. Shows different ways to write and lists many specific uses of writing.

Availability: Schools, libraries, and homeschoolers in the United States who serve the hearing impaired.
Suggested Grade: 4-8
Order Number: 13067
Production Date: 1996
Format: DVD
Terms: Sponsor pays all transportation costs. Return one week after receipt. Participation is limited to deaf or hard of hearing Americans, their parents, families, teachers, counselors, or others whose use would benefit a deaf or hard of hearing person. Only one person in the audience needs to be hearing impaired. You must register--which is free. These videos are all open-captioned--no special equipment is required for viewing.

Source: Described and Captioned Media Program
National Association of the Deaf
4211 Church Street Ext.
Roebuck, SC 29376
Phone: 1-800-237-6213
Fax: 1-800-538-5636
World Wide Web URL: http://www.dcmp.org

*All materials listed in this 2011-2012 edition are **BRAND NEW!***

Algebra: A Piece of Cake! Part One

While making a cake, a teenage cook teaches some algebraic concepts.

Availability: Schools, libraries, and homeschoolers in the United States who serve the hearing impaired.
Suggested Grade: 7-9
Order Number: 11084
Production Date: 2001
Format: DVD
Terms: Sponsor pays all transportation costs. Return one week after receipt. Participation is limited to deaf or hard of hearing Americans, their parents, families, teachers, counselors, or others whose use would benefit a deaf or hard of hearing person. Only one person in the audience needs to be hearing impaired. You must register--which is free. These videos are all open-captioned--no special equipment is required for viewing.

> **Source: Described and Captioned Media Program**
> **National Association of the Deaf**
> **4211 Church Street Ext.**
> **Roebuck, SC 29376**
> **Phone: 1-800-237-6213**
> **Fax: 1-800-538-5636**
> **World Wide Web URL: http://www.dcmp.org**

Algebra: A Piece of Cake! Part Two

While making a cake, a teenage cook teaches some algebraic concepts.

Availability: Schools, libraries, and homeschoolers in the United States who serve the hearing impaired.
Suggested Grade: 7-9
Order Number: 10955
Production Date: 2001
Format: DVD
Terms: Sponsor pays all transportation costs. Return one week after receipt. Participation is limited to deaf or hard of hearing Americans, their parents, families, teachers, counselors, or others whose use would benefit a deaf or hard of hearing person. Only one person in the audience needs to be hearing impaired. You must register--which is free. These videos are all open-captioned--no special equipment is required for viewing.

> **Source: Described and Captioned Media Program**
> **National Association of the Deaf**
> **4211 Church Street Ext.**
> **Roebuck, SC 29376**
> **Phone: 1-800-237-6213**
> **Fax: 1-800-538-5636**
> **World Wide Web URL: http://www.dcmp.org**

All About Angles

What are angles? Why are they important? What are "degrees"? How are angles measured? What is a protractor and how is it used? What are the four kinds of angles? Three lessons use animated graphics to answer these questions. Gives practice problems and reviews concepts.

Availability: Schools, libraries, and homeschoolers in the United States who serve the hearing impaired.
Suggested Grade: 7-12

Order Number: 12977
Production Date: 1992
Format: DVD
Special Notes: Produced by Allied Video Corporation.
Terms: Sponsor pays all transportation costs. Return one week after receipt. Participation is limited to deaf or hard of hearing Americans, their parents, families, teachers, counselors, or others whose use would benefit a deaf or hard of hearing person. Only one person in the audience needs to be hearing impaired. You must register--which is free. These videos are all open-captioned--no special equipment is required for viewing.

> **Source: Described and Captioned Media Program**
> **National Association of the Deaf**
> **4211 Church Street Ext.**
> **Roebuck, SC 29376**
> **Phone: 1-800-237-6213**
> **Fax: 1-800-538-5636**
> **World Wide Web URL: http://www.dcmp.org**

All-Star Elf

Mathica, the elf, serves as judge of the All-Star Games. Hare leaves the foot race and enters other competitions, confident he will still win the race. As she judges Hare's results, Mathica uses math concepts such as estimating, units of measurement, linear and volume measurement, and graphs. To his dismay, Hare loses the foot race.

Availability: Schools, libraries, and homeschoolers in the United States who serve the hearing impaired.
Suggested Grade: 4-6
Order Number: 12334
Production Date: 1993
Format: DVD
Special Notes: Produced by ACG/United Learning.
Terms: Sponsor pays all transportation costs. Return one week after receipt. Participation is limited to deaf or hard of hearing Americans, their parents, families, teachers, counselors, or others whose use would benefit a deaf or hard of hearing person. Only one person in the audience needs to be hearing impaired. You must register--which is free. These videos are all open-captioned--no special equipment is required for viewing.

> **Source: Described and Captioned Media Program**
> **National Association of the Deaf**
> **4211 Church Street Ext.**
> **Roebuck, SC 29376**
> **Phone: 1-800-237-6213**
> **Fax: 1-800-538-5636**
> **World Wide Web URL: http://www.dcmp.org**

Apple Blossom Teaches Addition Facts Through 18

Apple Blossom the dragon and her three friends unpack her boxes, learning addition facts as they unwrap books, hats, and other possessions. Pauses for viewer participation in problem solving. Stresses addition by making sets of 10 when adding numbers.

Availability: Schools, libraries, and homeschoolers in the United States who serve the hearing impaired.
Suggested Grade: 1-3

MATHEMATICS

Order Number: 13105
Production Date: 1998
Format: DVD
Special Notes: Produced by SVE & Churchill Media.
Terms: Sponsor pays all transportation costs. Return one week after receipt. Participation is limited to deaf or hard of hearing Americans, their parents, families, teachers, counselors, or others whose use would benefit a deaf or hard of hearing person. Only one person in the audience needs to be hearing impaired. You must register--which is free. These videos are all open-captioned--no special equipment is required for viewing.

Source: Described and Captioned Media Program
National Association of the Deaf
4211 Church Street Ext.
Roebuck, SC 29376
Phone: 1-800-237-6213
Fax: 1-800-538-5636
World Wide Web URL: http://www.dcmp.org

Basic Math: Adding and Subtracting Fractions

Defines prime and composite numbers, as they relate to factors and explains finding the lowest common denominator.

Availability: Schools, libraries, and homeschoolers in the United States who serve the hearing impaired.
Suggested Grade: 4-8
Order Number: 11640
Production Date: 2001
Format: DVD
Special Notes: Also available as live streaming video over the Internet.
Terms: Sponsor pays all transportation costs. Return one week after receipt. Participation is limited to deaf or hard of hearing Americans, their parents, families, teachers, counselors, or others whose use would benefit a deaf or hard of hearing person. Only one person in the audience needs to be hearing impaired. You must register--which is free. These videos are all open-captioned--no special equipment is required for viewing.

Source: Described and Captioned Media Program
National Association of the Deaf
4211 Church Street Ext.
Roebuck, SC 29376
Phone: 1-800-237-6213
Fax: 1-800-538-5636
World Wide Web URL: http://www.dcmp.org

Basic Math: Dividing Integers

Clearly shows how to perform this mathematical function.

Availability: Schools, libraries, and homeschoolers in the United States who serve the hearing impaired.
Suggested Grade: 7-12
Order Number: 11671
Production Date: 2001
Format: DVD
Terms: Sponsor pays all transportation costs. Return one week after receipt. Participation is limited to deaf or hard of hearing Americans, their parents, families, teachers, counselors, or others whose use would benefit a deaf or

hard of hearing person. Only one person in the audience needs to be hearing impaired. You must register--which is free. These videos are all open-captioned--no special equipment is required for viewing.

Source: Described and Captioned Media Program
National Association of the Deaf
4211 Church Street Ext.
Roebuck, SC 29376
Phone: 1-800-237-6213
Fax: 1-800-538-5636
World Wide Web URL: http://www.dcmp.org

Basic Math: Fraction Basics

Covers basic fraction terminology, reducing fractions, and common factors.

Availability: Schools, libraries, and homeschoolers in the United States who serve the hearing impaired.
Suggested Grade: 4-8
Order Number: 11666
Production Date: 2001
Format: DVD
Special Notes: Also available as live streaming video over the Internet.
Terms: Sponsor pays all transportation costs. Return one week after receipt. Participation is limited to deaf or hard of hearing Americans, their parents, families, teachers, counselors, or others whose use would benefit a deaf or hard of hearing person. Only one person in the audience needs to be hearing impaired. You must register--which is free. These videos are all open-captioned--no special equipment is required for viewing.

Source: Described and Captioned Media Program
National Association of the Deaf
4211 Church Street Ext.
Roebuck, SC 29376
Phone: 1-800-237-6213
Fax: 1-800-538-5636
World Wide Web URL: http://www.dcmp.org

Basic Math: Integers and Addition

Covers definitions of terms and discusses the number line, positive and negative integers, and addition of single- and multiple digit numbers.

Availability: Schools, libraries, and homeschoolers in the United States who serve the hearing impaired.
Suggested Grade: 7-12
Order Number: 11673
Production Date: 2001
Format: DVD
Terms: Sponsor pays all transportation costs. Return one week after receipt. Participation is limited to deaf or hard of hearing Americans, their parents, families, teachers, counselors, or others whose use would benefit a deaf or hard of hearing person. Only one person in the audience needs to be hearing impaired. You must register--which is free. These videos are all open-captioned--no special equipment is required for viewing.

*All materials listed in this 2011-2012 edition are **BRAND NEW!***

Source: Described and Captioned Media Program
National Association of the Deaf
4211 Church Street Ext.
Roebuck, SC 29376
Phone: 1-800-237-6213
Fax: 1-800-538-5636
World Wide Web URL: http://www.dcmp.org

Chicka Chicka 1 2 3

One hundred and one numbers race each other up the apple tree. As the numbers pile up, bad bumblebee comes buzzing. Which number will save the day? Gives children practice counting numbers through singing and music.

Availability: Schools, libraries, and homeschoolers in the United States who serve the hearing impaired.
Suggested Grade: preK-3
Order Number: 11999
Production Date: 2004
Format: DVD
Terms: Sponsor pays all transportation costs. Return one week after receipt. Participation is limited to deaf or hard of hearing Americans, their parents, families, teachers, counselors, or others whose use would benefit a deaf or hard of hearing person. Only one person in the audience needs to be hearing impaired. You must register--which is free. These videos are all open-captioned--no special equipment is required for viewing.

Source: Described and Captioned Media Program
National Association of the Deaf
4211 Church Street Ext.
Roebuck, SC 29376
Phone: 1-800-237-6213
Fax: 1-800-538-5636
World Wide Web URL: http://www.dcmp.org

Factoring Is Fantastic: Part One--Common Factors

Demonstrates how to factor algebraic expressions.

Availability: Schools, libraries, and homeschoolers in the United States who serve the hearing impaired.
Suggested Grade: 6-12
Order Number: 10787
Format: DVD
Special Notes: Also available as live streaming video over the Internet.
Terms: Sponsor pays all transportation costs. Return one week after receipt. Participation is limited to deaf or hard of hearing Americans, their parents, families, teachers, counselors, or others whose use would benefit a deaf or hard of hearing person. Only one person in the audience needs to be hearing impaired. You must register--which is free. These videos are all open-captioned--no special equipment is required for viewing.

Source: Described and Captioned Media Program
National Association of the Deaf
4211 Church Street Ext.
Roebuck, SC 29376
Phone: 1-800-237-6213
Fax: 1-800-538-5636
World Wide Web URL: http://www.dcmp.org

Factoring Is Fantastic: Part Two-_Quadratic Trinomials

Lots of information about solving quadratic trinomials.

Availability: Schools, libraries, and homeschoolers in the United States who serve the hearing impaired.
Suggested Grade: 6-12
Order Number: 10801
Production Date: 2002
Format: DVD
Special Notes: Also available as live streaming video over the Internet.
Terms: Sponsor pays all transportation costs. Return one week after receipt. Participation is limited to deaf or hard of hearing Americans, their parents, families, teachers, counselors, or others whose use would benefit a deaf or hard of hearing person. Only one person in the audience needs to be hearing impaired. You must register--which is free. These videos are all open-captioned--no special equipment is required for viewing.

Source: Described and Captioned Media Program
National Association of the Deaf
4211 Church Street Ext.
Roebuck, SC 29376
Phone: 1-800-237-6213
Fax: 1-800-538-5636
World Wide Web URL: http://www.dcmp.org

Fractions and All Their Parts-Part I

What are fractions? How are they named? What is a "numerator" and a "denominator"? Lesson one defines and illustrates "fraction". Lesson two covers naming fractions and defines "numerator" and "denominator". Lesson three demonstrates how to find the fraction of a number. Reviews each section.

Availability: Schools, libraries, and homeschoolers in the United States who serve the hearing impaired.
Suggested Grade: 4-8
Order Number: 3245
Production Date: 1992
Format: DVD
Special Notes: Produced by Allied Video Corporation.
Terms: Sponsor pays all transportation costs. Return one week after receipt. Participation is limited to deaf or hard of hearing Americans, their parents, families, teachers, counselors, or others whose use would benefit a deaf or hard of hearing person. Only one person in the audience needs to be hearing impaired. You must register--which is free. These videos are all open-captioned--no special equipment is required for viewing.

Source: Described and Captioned Media Program
National Association of the Deaf
4211 Church Street Ext.
Roebuck, SC 29376
Phone: 1-800-237-6213
Fax: 1-800-538-5636
World Wide Web URL: http://www.dcmp.org

Fractions and All Their Parts-Part II

What are equivalent fractions? How do you simplify a

fraction? What is a mixed number? What is an improper fraction? After reviewing terminology, three lessons clarify each question with definitions and sample problems. Demonstrates how to change improper fractions to mixed numbers. Sample problems and reviews intersperse the lessons.

Availability: Schools, libraries, and homeschoolers in the United States who serve the hearing impaired.
Suggested Grade: 4-8
Order Number: 3246
Production Date: 1992
Format: DVD
Special Notes: Produced by Allied Video Corporation.
Terms: Sponsor pays all transportation costs. Return one week after receipt. Participation is limited to deaf or hard of hearing Americans, their parents, families, teachers, counselors, or others whose use would benefit a deaf or hard of hearing person. Only one person in the audience needs to be hearing impaired. You must register--which is free. These videos are all open-captioned--no special equipment is required for viewing.

Source: Described and Captioned Media Program
National Association of the Deaf
4211 Church Street Ext.
Roebuck, SC 29376
Phone: 1-800-237-6213
Fax: 1-800-538-5636
World Wide Web URL: http://www.dcmp.org

How Much Is a Million?

Marvelosissimo the Mathematical Magician uses stars, goldfish, and kids to make the concepts of a million, a billion, and a trillion clear and not quite so intimidating.

Availability: Schools, libraries, and homeschoolers in the United States who serve the hearing impaired.
Suggested Grade: K-3
Order Number: 11642
Production Date: 2000
Format: DVD
Special Notes: Also available as live streaming video over the Internet.
Terms: Sponsor pays all transportation costs. Return one week after receipt. Participation is limited to deaf or hard of hearing Americans, their parents, families, teachers, counselors, or others whose use would benefit a deaf or hard of hearing person. Only one person in the audience needs to be hearing impaired. You must register--which is free. These videos are all open-captioned--no special equipment is required for viewing.

Source: Described and Captioned Media Program
National Association of the Deaf
4211 Church Street Ext.
Roebuck, SC 29376
Phone: 1-800-237-6213
Fax: 1-800-538-5636
World Wide Web URL: http://www.dcmp.org

Hunting the Hidden Dimension

Mysteriously beautiful fractals are shaking up the world of mathematics and deepening our understanding of nature.

Availability: All requesters
Suggested Grade: 7-Adult
Order Number: not applicable
Production Date: 2008
Format: Streaming Video
Source: NOVA
World Wide Web URL:
http://www.pbs.org/wgbh/nova/programs/index.html

Number Crunching

Defines and illustrates statistical terms: bell curve, mean, median, mode, range, and standard deviation. Shows how to mathematically determine each to interpret data.

Availability: Schools, libraries, and homeschoolers in the United States who serve the hearing impaired.
Suggested Grade: 8-10
Order Number: 11453
Production Date: 2003
Format: DVD
Special Notes: Also available as live streaming video over the Internet.
Terms: Sponsor pays all transportation costs. Return one week after receipt. Participation is limited to deaf or hard of hearing Americans, their parents, families, teachers, counselors, or others whose use would benefit a deaf or hard of hearing person. Only one person in the audience needs to be hearing impaired. You must register--which is free. These videos are all open-captioned--no special equipment is required for viewing.

Source: Described and Captioned Media Program
National Association of the Deaf
4211 Church Street Ext.
Roebuck, SC 29376
Phone: 1-800-237-6213
Fax: 1-800-538-5636
World Wide Web URL: http://www.dcmp.org

Spheres and Circles

Describes a circle and sphere and shows examples in everyday life.

Availability: Schools, libraries, and homeschoolers in the United States who serve the hearing impaired.
Suggested Grade: K-4
Order Number: 12652
Production Date: 1997
Format: DVD
Special Notes: Also available as live streaming video over the Internet.
Terms: Sponsor pays all transportation costs. Return one week after receipt. Participation is limited to deaf or hard of hearing Americans, their parents, families, teachers, counselors, or others whose use would benefit a deaf or hard of hearing person. Only one person in the audience needs to be hearing impaired. You must register--which is free. These videos are all open-captioned--no special equipment is required for viewing.

Source: Described and Captioned Media Program
National Association of the Deaf
4211 Church Street Ext.
Roebuck, SC 29376
Phone: 1-800-237-6213
Fax: 1-800-538-5636
World Wide Web URL: http://www.dcmp.org

Surprises in Mind

This documentary uncovers a surprise: Mathematical creativity--expressed in art, architecture, and music and valued by industry--is built into the brain and can flourish under the right conditions.

Availability: All requesters
Suggested Grade: Teacher Reference
Order Number: not applicable
Production Date: 2001
Format: Streaming Video
Terms: A simple FREE registration is required to view videos.
**Source: Annenberg Media
World Wide Web URL:
http://www.learner.org/resources/browse.html**

Teaching Math: A Video Library, K-4

See how the National Council of Teachers of Mathematics standards are used in elementary classrooms across America.

Availability: All requesters
Suggested Grade: Teacher Reference
Order Number: not applicable
Production Date: 1997
Format: Streaming Video
Special Notes: Also available for purchase for $375.00.
Terms: A simple FREE registration is required to view videos.
**Source: Annenberg Media
World Wide Web URL:
http://www.learner.org/resources/browse.html**

What is Area?

What is area? Lesson one defines and clarifies what "area" means and also teaches the concept of square units. Lessons two, three, and four develop formulas for the area of a rectangle, parallelogram, and triangle. Working sample problems help clarify the formulas. Each animated lesson concludes with practice problems.

Availability: Schools, libraries, and homeschoolers in the United States who serve the hearing impaired.
Suggested Grade: 5-9
Order Number: 13034
Production Date: 1992
Format: DVD
Special Notes: Produced by Allied Video Corporation.
Terms: Sponsor pays all transportation costs. Return one week after receipt. Participation is limited to deaf or hard of hearing Americans, their parents, families, teachers, counselors, or others whose use would benefit a deaf or hard of hearing person. Only one person in the audience needs to be hearing impaired. You must register--which

is free. These videos are all open-captioned--no special equipment is required for viewing.
**Source: Described and Captioned Media Program
National Association of the Deaf
4211 Church Street Ext.
Roebuck, SC 29376
Phone: 1-800-237-6213
Fax: 1-800-538-5636
World Wide Web URL: http://www.dcmp.org**

Word Problems? No Problem!

Junior high students discover how to work through mathematical word problems, identifying specific steps in the process.

Availability: Schools, libraries, and homeschoolers in the United States who serve the hearing impaired.
Suggested Grade: 5-9
Order Number: 11817
Production Date: 2001
Format: DVD
Terms: Sponsor pays all transportation costs. Return one week after receipt. Participation is limited to deaf or hard of hearing Americans, their parents, families, teachers, counselors, or others whose use would benefit a deaf or hard of hearing person. Only one person in the audience needs to be hearing impaired. You must register--which is free. These videos are all open-captioned--no special equipment is required for viewing.
**Source: Described and Captioned Media Program
National Association of the Deaf
4211 Church Street Ext.
Roebuck, SC 29376
Phone: 1-800-237-6213
Fax: 1-800-538-5636
World Wide Web URL: http://www.dcmp.org**

World of Circles, The

What are circles? What is a "radius"? What does "diameter" mean? How can it be measured? What do "circumference" and "pi" mean? How can I find the area of a circle? Uses animated graphics to clearly define and illustrate a circle and its parts. Sample problems reinforce concepts. Shows how to use a compass.

Availability: Schools, libraries, and homeschoolers in the United States who serve the hearing impaired.
Suggested Grade: 5-9
Order Number: 12354
Production Date: 1992
Format: DVD
Special Notes: Produced by Allied Video Corporation.
Terms: Sponsor pays all transportation costs. Return one week after receipt. Participation is limited to deaf or hard of hearing Americans, their parents, families, teachers, counselors, or others whose use would benefit a deaf or hard of hearing person. Only one person in the audience needs to be hearing impaired. You must register--which is free. These videos are all open-captioned--no special equipment is required for viewing.

Source: **Described and Captioned Media Program**
National Association of the Deaf
4211 Church Street Ext.
Roebuck, SC 29376
Phone: 1-800-237-6213
Fax: 1-800-538-5636
World Wide Web URL: http://www.dcmp.org

XY Encounter, The

Max and Keisha stumble on a secret Web site that reveals an alien in their city. They solve clues to locate him by using graphs, geometry, number sequence, and fractions, only to discover the alien has to go home for dinner.

Availability: Schools, libraries, and homeschoolers in the United States who serve the hearing impaired.
Suggested Grade: 6-9
Order Number: 13581
Production Date: 2000
Format: DVD
Terms: Sponsor pays all transportation costs. Return one week after receipt. Participation is limited to deaf or hard of hearing Americans, their parents, families, teachers, counselors, or others whose use would benefit a deaf or hard of hearing person. Only one person in the audience needs to be hearing impaired. You must register--which is free. These videos are all open-captioned--no special equipment is required for viewing.

Source: **Described and Captioned Media Program**
National Association of the Deaf
4211 Church Street Ext.
Roebuck, SC 29376
Phone: 1-800-237-6213
Fax: 1-800-538-5636
World Wide Web URL: http://www.dcmp.org

*All materials listed in this 2011-2012 edition are **BRAND NEW!***

Balloons

Animation and newsreel footage explore a brief history of balloons, airships, and dirigibles. Presents a balloon quiz at the end.

Availability: Schools, libraries, and homeschoolers in the United States who serve the hearing impaired.
Suggested Grade: preK-4
Order Number: 12403
Format: DVD
Terms: Sponsor pays all transportation costs. Return one week after receipt. Participation is limited to deaf or hard of hearing Americans, their parents, families, teachers, counselors, or others whose use would benefit a deaf or hard of hearing person. Only one person in the audience needs to be hearing impaired. You must register--which is free. These videos are all open-captioned--no special equipment is required for viewing.

Source: Described and Captioned Media Program
National Association of the Deaf
4211 Church Street Ext.
Roebuck, SC 29376
Phone: 1-800-237-6213
Fax: 1-800-538-5636
World Wide Web URL: http://www.dcmp.org

Bass Fishing on Lake Champlain

An episode of "The Real Fishing Show."

Availability: All requesters
Suggested Grade: 6-Adult
Order Number: not applicable
Format: Streaming Video

Source: Vermont Department of Fish and Wildlife
World Wide Web URL:
http://www.myoutdoortv.com/explore-the-u.s./vermont.html

Budo: The Martial Arts/The Art of Karate

Introduces the art and philosophy of the representative martial arts of Japan: Judo, Karate, and Aikido.

Availability: Schools, libraries and homeschoolers in Alabama, Georgia, North Carolina, South Carolina, and Virginia.
Suggested Grade: 6-Adult
Order Number: 102
Production Date: 1982
Format: VHS videotape
Terms: Borrower pays return postage. Two tapes may be borrowed at a time. Return within 7 days after receipt. Reservations may be made by filling the application found on the web site.

Source: Consulate General of Japan, Atlanta
Japan Information Center
One Alliance Center
3500 Lenox Road, Suite 1600
Atlanta, GA 30326
Phone: 1-404-365-9240
Fax: 1-404-240-4311
World Wide Web URL:
http://www.atlanta.us.emb-japan.go.jp
Email Address: info@cgjapanatlanta.org

Budo: The Martial Arts/The Art of Karate

Introduces the art and philosophy of the representative martial arts of Japan: Judo, Karate, and Aikido.

Availability: Schools, libraries, and nursing homes in Hawaii.
Suggested Grade: 6-Adult
Order Number: SP-2
Production Date: 1982
Format: VHS videotape
Terms: Borrower pays return postage. A maximum of 3 videos may be borrowed per person. Return within one week of date borrowed.

Source: Consulate General of Japan, Honolulu
1742 Nuuanu Avenue
Honolulu, HI 96817-3294
Phone: 1-808-543-3111
Fax: 1-808-543-3170
World Wide Web URL:
http://www.honolulu.us.emb-japan.go.jp

Budo: The Martial Arts/The Art of Karate

Introduces the art and philosophy of the representative martial arts of Japan: Judo, Karate, and Aikido.

Availability: Schools, libraries, homeschoolers, and nursing homes in OREGON AND SOUTHERN IDAHO ONLY. Please make requests via the web site.
Suggested Grade: 6-Adult
Order Number: 109
Production Date: 1982
Format: VHS videotape
Terms: Borrower pays return postage. Return within three weeks after scheduled showing date. Book one month in advance if possible. Rewind the video and wrap securely for return. Be certain to indicate video number, date needed, name of your organization, and address to which video should be sent, along with phone number. Audience report enclosed with the video must be completed and returned.

Source: Consulate General of Japan, Oregon
Attn: Tamara, Video Library
1300 S. W. Fifth Avenue, Suite 2700
Portland, OR 97201
Phone: 1-503-221-1811, ext. 17
World Wide Web URL:
http://www.portland.us.emb-japan.go.jp/en/index.html
Email Address: tamara@cgjpdx.org

Eddie's Last Fight

An endearing portrait of Edward Townsend Jr., known as Eddie, who raised six world champion boxers in Japan.

Availability: Schools, libraries and homeschoolers in Alabama, Georgia, North Carolina, South Carolina, and Virginia.
Suggested Grade: 7-Adult
Order Number: 513
Production Date: 1988
Format: VHS videotape
Special Notes: Tape 13 of the "Document Japan" series.

Terms: Borrower pays return postage. Two tapes may be borrowed at a time. Return within 7 days after receipt. Reservations may be made by filling the application found on the web site.

Source: Consulate General of Japan, Atlanta
Japan Information Center
One Alliance Center
3500 Lenox Road, Suite 1600
Atlanta, GA 30326
Phone: 1-404-365-9240
Fax: 1-404-240-4311
World Wide Web URL:
http://www.atlanta.us.emb-japan.go.jp
Email Address: info@cgjapanatlanta.org

Eddie's Last Fight: The Old Trainer/19 Year Old Champion

An endearing portrait of Edward Townsend Jr., known as Eddie, who raised six world champion boxers in Japan.

Availability: Schools, libraries, and nursing homes in Hawaii.
Suggested Grade: 7-12
Order Number: CU-69
Production Date: 1988
Format: VHS videotape
Special Notes: Tape 13 of the "Document Japan" series.
Terms: Borrower pays return postage. A maximum of 3 videos may be borrowed per person. Return within one week of date borrowed.

Source: Consulate General of Japan, Honolulu
1742 Nuuanu Avenue
Honolulu, HI 96817-3294
Phone: 1-808-543-3111
Fax: 1-808-543-3170
World Wide Web URL:
http://www.honolulu.us.emb-japan.go.jp

Eddie's Last Fight: The Old Trainer/19 Year Old Champion

An endearing portrait of Edward Townsend Jr., known as Eddie, who raised six world champion boxers in Japan.

Availability: Schools, libraries, homeschoolers, and nursing homes in OREGON AND SOUTHERN IDAHO ONLY. Please make requests via the web site.
Suggested Grade: 7-12
Order Number: 513
Production Date: 1988
Format: VHS videotape
Special Notes: Tape 13 of the "Document Japan" series.
Terms: Borrower pays return postage. Return within three weeks after scheduled showing date. Book one month in advance if possible. Rewind the video and wrap securely for return. Be certain to indicate video number, date needed, name of your organization, and address to which video should be sent, along with phone number. Audience report enclosed with the video must be completed and returned.

Source: Consulate General of Japan, Oregon
Attn: Tamara, Video Library
1300 S. W. Fifth Avenue, Suite 2700
Portland, OR 97201
Phone: 1-503-221-1811, ext. 17
World Wide Web URL:
http://www.portland.us.emb-japan.go.jp/en/index.html
Email Address: tamara@cgjpdx.org

Exercise: It's Good for You!

Explains why exercise is important for a healthy body, how a balanced diet and staying active are beneficial, and that bathing and getting plenty of rest are good for you.

Availability: Schools, libraries, and homeschoolers in the United States who serve the hearing impaired.
Suggested Grade: 1-4
Order Number: 11140
Production Date: 2003
Format: DVD
Special Notes: Also available as live streaming video over the Internet.
Terms: Sponsor pays all transportation costs. Return one week after receipt. Participation is limited to deaf or hard of hearing Americans, their parents, families, teachers, counselors, or others whose use would benefit a deaf or hard of hearing person. Only one person in the audience needs to be hearing impaired. You must register--which is free. These videos are all open-captioned--no special equipment is required for viewing.

Source: Described and Captioned Media Program
National Association of the Deaf
4211 Church Street Ext.
Roebuck, SC 29376
Phone: 1-800-237-6213
Fax: 1-800-538-5636
World Wide Web URL: http://www.dcmp.org

Fervor! The Giant Kite Battle of Ensyu

For three days Hamamatsu city was full of the excitement of a Kite Competition with 1,500 kites and 2.7 million participants. Three towns take part in the competition and flies a kite with a unique design of the town, and competitions to cut other's string are held.

Availability: Schools, libraries and homeschoolers in Alabama, Georgia, North Carolina, South Carolina, and Virginia.
Suggested Grade: 7-Adult
Order Number: 702
Production Date: 1991
Format: VHS videotape
Special Notes: No. 2 of the "Nippon Life II" series.
Terms: Borrower pays return postage. Two tapes may be borrowed at a time. Return within 7 days after receipt. Reservations may be made by filling the application found on the web site.

Source: Consulate General of Japan, Atlanta
Japan Information Center
One Alliance Center, 3500 Lenox Road, Suite 1600
Atlanta, GA 30326

Phone: 1-404-365-9240
Fax: 1-404-240-4311
World Wide Web URL:
http://www.atlanta.us.emb-japan.go.jp
Email Address: info@cgjapanatlanta.org

Fervor! The Giant Kite Battle of Ensyu

For three days Hamamatsu city was full of the excitement of a Kite Competition with 1,500 kites and 2.7 million participants. Three towns take part in the competition and flies a kite with a unique design of the town, and competitions to cut other's string are held

Availability: Schools, libraries, and nursing homes in Hawaii.
Suggested Grade: 7-Adult
Order Number: Cu-51
Format: VHS videotape
Terms: Borrower pays return postage. A maximum of 3 videos may be borrowed per person. Return within one week of date borrowed.
  Source: Consulate General of Japan, Honolulu
  1742 Nuuanu Avenue
  Honolulu, HI 96817-3294
  Phone: 1-808-543-3111
  Fax: 1-808-543-3170
  World Wide Web URL:
  http://www.honolulu.us.emb-japan.go.jp

Fervor! The Giant Kite Battle of Ensyu

For three days Hamamatsu city was full of the excitement of a Kite Competition with 1,500 kites and 2.7 million participants. Three towns take part in the competition and flies a kite with a unique design of the town, and competitions to cut other's string are held.

Availability: Schools, libraries, homeschoolers, and nursing homes in OREGON AND SOUTHERN IDAHO ONLY. Please make requests via the web site.
Suggested Grade: 6-12
Order Number: 172
Production Date: 1991
Format: VHS videotape
Special Notes: No. 2 of the "Nippon Life II" series.
Terms: Borrower pays return postage. Return within three weeks after scheduled showing date. Book one month in advance if possible. Rewind the video and wrap securely for return. Be certain to indicate video number, date needed, name of your organization, and address to which video should be sent, along with phone number. Audience report enclosed with the video must be completed and returned.
  Source: Consulate General of Japan, Oregon
  Attn: Tamara, Video Library
  1300 S. W. Fifth Avenue, Suite 2700
  Portland, OR 97201
  Phone: 1-503-221-1811, ext. 17
  World Wide Web URL:
  http://www.portland.us.emb-japan.go.jp/en/index.html
  Email Address: tamara@cgjpdx.org

Kyudo

Kyudo is the Japanese sport of archery. This program looks at this sport in Japan.

Availability: Schools, libraries, and nursing homes in Illinois, Indiana, Iowa, Kansas, Minnesota, Missouri, Nebraska, North Dakota, South Dakota, and Wisconsin.
Suggested Grade: All ages
Order Number: 18004
Production Date: 1994
Format: VHS videotape
Terms: Borrower pays return postage by U. S. Mail, UPS, or Federal Express, including insurance for "original" videos. Write, call, fax, or e-mail to request an application. An application form MUST be sent in one month in advance but not more than six months in advance. Include alternate titles and dates if provider can substitute titles. Send a SASE with request if you require confirmation. Return immediately after scheduled showing date. Videos may not be copied or broadcast without permission from the producer of the video. Borrower is responsible if video is lost or damaged.
  Source: Consulate General of Japan at Chicago
  Japan Information Center, Library
  737 North Michigan Avenue, Suite 1000
  Chicago, IL 60611
  Phone: 1-312-280-0430
  Fax: 1-312-280-6883
  World Wide Web URL:
  http://www.chicago.us.emb-japan.go.jp/jic.html
  Email Address: jicchicago@webkddi.com

Magic of Crankbaits, The

A demonstration of the effectiveness of crankbaits for catching bass and northern pike.

Availability: All requesters
Suggested Grade: 6-Adult
Order Number: not applicable
Format: Streaming Video
  Source: Vermont Department of Fish and Wildlife
  World Wide Web URL:
  http://www.myoutdoortv.com/explore-the-u.s./vermont.html

Managing Vermont's Furbearer Animals: Dispelling Misconceptions About Regulated Trapping

An inside look on fur trappers and how important trapping is.

Availability: All requesters
Suggested Grade: 6-Adult
Order Number: not applicable
Format: Streaming Video
  Source: Vermont Department of Fish and Wildlife
  World Wide Web URL:
  http://www.myoutdoortv.com/explore-the-u.s./vermont.html

Marathon Challenge

Explore what it takes-physically and mentally-for novice runners to make it through a classic test of endurance.

Availability: All requesters
Suggested Grade: 7-Adult
Order Number: not applicable
Production Date: 2007
Format: Streaming Video
Source: NOVA
World Wide Web URL:
http://www.pbs.org/wgbh/nova/programs/index.html

Tai Chi for Health

Five segments present the Yang Long Form from the beginner's level.
Availability: Schools, libraries, homeschoolers, and nursing homes in the United States and Canada.
Suggested Grade: 6-12
Order Number: order by title
Format: VHS videotape
Terms: Postage is paid by borrower both ways--send $3.00 per tape to cover initial shipping to you--MONEY MUST BE SENT WITH REQUEST. Return 10 days after showing via U. S. Postal Service, library rate. Shipping is $5.00 to Canadian addresses.
Source: Center for Teaching About China
Kathleen Trescott
1214 West Schwartz
Carbondale, IL 62901
Phone: 1-618-549-1555
Email Address: trescott@midwest.net

Tai Chi: Healing Dance

Follow the 36 step training course to help obtain benefits to the mind and body.
Availability: Schools, libraries, homeschoolers, and nursing homes in the United States and Canada.
Suggested Grade: 6-12
Order Number: order by title
Production Date: 1995
Format: VHS videotape
Terms: Postage is paid by borrower both ways--send $3.00 per tape to cover initial shipping to you--MONEY MUST BE SENT WITH REQUEST. Return 10 days after showing via U. S. Postal Service, library rate. Shipping is $5.00 to Canadian addresses.
Source: Center for Teaching About China
Kathleen Trescott
1214 West Schwartz
Carbondale, IL 62901
Phone: 1-618-549-1555
Email Address: trescott@midwest.net

Traditional Japanese Sports: Judo

Reports on the popular and traditional Japanese sport of Judo.
Availability: Schools, libraries, homeschoolers, and nursing homes in Connecticut, Delaware, Maryland, New Jersey, New York, Pennsylvania, and West Virginia.

Suggested Grade: All ages
Order Number: order by title
Format: VHS videotape
Terms: Send a blank videotape to this source and they will dub the program you desire onto it for permanent retention. You must send a self-addressed, stamped envelope with sufficient postage for return.
Source: Consulate General of Japan, New York
Audio Video Dept.
299 Park Avenue, 18th Floor
New York, NY 10171
Phone: 1-212-371-8222
Fax: 1-212-319-6357
World Wide Web URL: http://www.ny.us.emb-japan.go.jp

Traditional Japanese Sports: Karatedo

The Japanese form of self-defense, Karatedo has developed into a major sport.
Availability: Schools, libraries, homeschoolers, and nursing homes in Connecticut, Delaware, Maryland, New Jersey, New York, Pennsylvania, and West Virginia.
Suggested Grade: All ages
Order Number: order by title
Production Date: 1997
Format: VHS videotape
Terms: Send a blank videotape to this source and they will dub the program you desire onto it for permanent retention. You must send a self-addressed, stamped envelope with sufficient postage for return.
Source: Consulate General of Japan, New York
Audio Video Dept.
299 Park Avenue, 18th Floor
New York, NY 10171
Phone: 1-212-371-8222
Fax: 1-212-319-6357
World Wide Web URL: http://www.ny.us.emb-japan.go.jp

Traditional Japanese Sports: Kendo

History of martial arts leading to the present-day Kendo, with scenes of training and contests, as well as the moral instruction that accompanies this art.
Availability: Schools, libraries, homeschoolers, and nursing homes in Connecticut, Delaware, Maryland, New Jersey, New York, Pennsylvania, and West Virginia.
Suggested Grade: All ages
Order Number: order by title
Production Date: 1997
Format: VHS videotape
Terms: Send a blank videotape to this source and they will dub the program you desire onto it for permanent retention. You must send a self-addressed, stamped envelope with sufficient postage for return.
Source: Consulate General of Japan, New York
Audio Video Dept.
299 Park Avenue, 18th Floor
New York, NY 10171
Phone: 1-212-371-8222

Fax: 1-212-319-6357
World Wide Web URL: http://www.ny.us.emb-japan.go.jp

Traditional Japanese Sports: Kendo

History of martial arts leading to the present-day Kendo, with scenes of training and contests, as well as the moral instruction that accompanies this art.

Availability: Schools, libraries, homeschoolers, and nursing homes in OREGON AND SOUTHERN IDAHO ONLY. Please make requests via the web site.
Suggested Grade: All ages
Order Number: 216
Production Date: 1985
Format: VHS videotape
Terms: Borrower pays return postage. Return within three weeks after scheduled showing date. Book one month in advance if possible. Rewind the video and wrap securely for return. Be certain to indicate video number, date needed, name of your organization, and address to which video should be sent, along with phone number. Audience report enclosed with the video must be completed and returned.

Source: Consulate General of Japan, Oregon
Attn: Tamara, Video Library
1300 S. W. Fifth Avenue, Suite 2700
Portland, OR 97201
Phone: 1-503-221-1811, ext. 17
World Wide Web URL:
http://www.portland.us.emb-japan.go.jp/en/index.html
Email Address: tamara@cgjpdx.org

Traditional Japanese Sports: Kyudo

Kyudo is the Japanese sport of archery. This program looks at this sport in Japan.

Availability: Schools, libraries, homeschoolers, and nursing homes in Connecticut, Delaware, Maryland, New Jersey, New York, Pennsylvania, and West Virginia.
Suggested Grade: All ages
Order Number: order by title
Production Date: 1997
Format: VHS videotape
Terms: Send a blank videotape to this source and they will dub the program you desire onto it for permanent retention. You must send a self-addressed, stamped envelope with sufficient postage for return.

Source: Consulate General of Japan, New York
Audio Video Dept.
299 Park Avenue, 18th Floor
New York, NY 10171
Phone: 1-212-371-8222
Fax: 1-212-319-6357
World Wide Web URL: http://www.ny.us.emb-japan.go.jp

Traditional Japanese Sports: Kyudo

Kyudo is the Japanese sport of archery. This program looks at this sport in Japan.

Availability: Schools, libraries, homeschoolers, and nursing homes in OREGON AND SOUTHERN IDAHO ONLY. Please make requests via the web site.
Suggested Grade: All ages
Order Number: 443
Production Date: 1997
Format: VHS videotape
Terms: Borrower pays return postage. Return within three weeks after scheduled showing date. Book one month in advance if possible. Rewind the video and wrap securely for return. Be certain to indicate video number, date needed, name of your organization, and address to which video should be sent, along with phone number. Audience report enclosed with the video must be completed and returned.

Source: Consulate General of Japan, Oregon
Attn: Tamara, Video Library
1300 S. W. Fifth Avenue, Suite 2700
Portland, OR 97201
Phone: 1-503-221-1811, ext. 17
World Wide Web URL:
http://www.portland.us.emb-japan.go.jp/en/index.html
Email Address: tamara@cgjpdx.org

Traditional Japanese Sports: Naginata

In the Middle Ages, the "naginata," a long-handled sword, was the weapon of the infantry. Interestingly, this martial art is practiced today mainly by women. This video shows more about this sport.

Availability: Schools, libraries, homeschoolers, and nursing homes in Connecticut, Delaware, Maryland, New Jersey, New York, Pennsylvania, and West Virginia.
Suggested Grade: 6-Adult
Order Number: order by title
Format: VHS videotape
Terms: Send a blank videotape to this source and they will dub the program you desire onto it for permanent retention. You must send a self-addressed, stamped envelope with sufficient postage for return.

Source: Consulate General of Japan, New York
Audio Video Dept.
299 Park Avenue, 18th Floor
New York, NY 10171
Phone: 1-212-371-8222
Fax: 1-212-319-6357
World Wide Web URL: http://www.ny.us.emb-japan.go.jp

Traditional Japanese Sports: Sumo

Reports on the popular and traditional Japanese sport of Sumo wrestling.

Availability: Schools, libraries, homeschoolers, and nursing homes in Connecticut, Delaware, Maryland, New Jersey, New York, Pennsylvania, and West Virginia.
Suggested Grade: All ages
Order Number: order by title
Production Date: 1997

Format: VHS videotape
Terms: Send a blank videotape to this source and they will dub the program you desire onto it for permanent retention. You must send a self-addressed, stamped envelope with sufficient postage for return.

Source: Consulate General of Japan, New York
Audio Video Dept.
299 Park Avenue, 18th Floor
New York, NY 10171
Phone: 1-212-371-8222
Fax: 1-212-319-6357
World Wide Web URL: http://www.ny.us.emb-japan.go.jp

Traditional Japanese Sports: Sumo

Reports on the popular and traditional Japanese sport of Sumo wrestling.

Availability: Schools, libraries, homeschoolers, and nursing homes in OREGON AND SOUTHERN IDAHO ONLY. Please make requests via the web site.
Suggested Grade: All ages
Order Number: 215
Production Date: 1985
Format: VHS videotape
Terms: Borrower pays return postage. Return within three weeks after scheduled showing date. Book one month in advance if possible. Rewind the video and wrap securely for return. Be certain to indicate video number, date needed, name of your organization, and address to which video should be sent, along with phone number. Audience report enclosed with the video must be completed and returned.

Source: Consulate General of Japan, Oregon
Attn: Tamara, Video Library
1300 S. W. Fifth Avenue, Suite 2700
Portland, OR 97201
Phone: 1-503-221-1811, ext. 17
World Wide Web URL:
http://www.portland.us.emb-japan.go.jp/en/index.html
Email Address: tamara@cgjpdx.org

What They Say About Hunting

Slices through the emotion and rhetoric that often dominate hunting debates to provide viewers with facts about the role of hunting in conservation of wildlife.

Availability: Schools, libraries, homeschoolers, and nursing homes in the United States and Canada.
Suggested Grade: 7-12
Order Number: 522
Format: VHS videotape
Special Notes: May be retained permanently. Cleared for TV broadcast.

Source: National Shooting Sports Foundation
11 Mile Hill Road
Newtown, CT 06470-2359
Phone: 1-203-426-1320
World Wide Web URL: http://www.nssf.org/safety
Email Address: literature@nssf.org

Wildlife for Tomorrow

Shows how wildlife managers work to prevent wildlife from becoming endangered and how regulated hunting fits into the overall conservation picture.

Availability: Schools, libraries, homeschoolers, and nursing homes in the United States and Canada.
Suggested Grade: 4-7
Order Number: 502
Format: VHS videotape
Special Notes: May be retained permanently. Cleared for TV broadcast.

Source: National Shooting Sports Foundation
11 Mile Hill Road
Newtown, CT 06470-2359
Phone: 1-203-426-1320
World Wide Web URL: http://www.nssf.org/safety
Email Address: literature@nssf.org

Working the Shoreline

Learn how to fish along the shoreline.

Availability: All requesters
Suggested Grade: 6-Adult
Order Number: not applicable
Format: Streaming Video

Source: Vermont Department of Fish and Wildlife
World Wide Web URL:
http://www.myoutdoortv.com/explore-the-u.s./vermont.html

Young Baseball Heroes

A high school team prepares for a great tournament at Koshen Stadium.

Availability: Schools, libraries and homeschoolers in Alabama, Georgia, North Carolina, South Carolina, and Virginia.
Suggested Grade: 6-Adult
Order Number: 403
Format: VHS videotape
Special Notes: Part of the "Faces of Japan" series.
Terms: Borrower pays return postage. Two tapes may be borrowed at a time. Return within 7 days after receipt. Reservations may be made by filling the application found on the web site.

Source: Consulate General of Japan, Atlanta
Japan Information Center
One Alliance Center
3500 Lenox Road, Suite 1600
Atlanta, GA 30326
Phone: 1-404-365-9240
Fax: 1-404-240-4311
World Wide Web URL:
http://www.atlanta.us.emb-japan.go.jp
Email Address: info@cgjapanatlanta.org

Young Baseball Heroes

A high school team prepares for a great tournament at Koshen Stadium.

Availability: Schools, libraries, homeschoolers, and nursing homes in OREGON AND SOUTHERN IDAHO ONLY. Please make requests via the web site.

Suggested Grade: 6-Adult

Order Number: 516

Format: VHS videotape

Special Notes: Part of the "Faces of Japan" series.

Terms: Borrower pays return postage. Return within three weeks after scheduled showing date. Book one month in advance if possible. Rewind the video and wrap securely for return. Be certain to indicate video number, date needed, name of your organization, and address to which video should be sent, along with phone number. Audience report enclosed with the video must be completed and returned.

Source: Consulate General of Japan, Oregon
Attn: Tamara, Video Library
1300 S. W. Fifth Avenue, Suite 2700
Portland, OR 97201
Phone: 1-503-221-1811, ext. 17
World Wide Web URL:
http://www.portland.us.emb-japan.go.jp/en/index.html
Email Address: tamara@cgjpdx.org

RELIGION AND PHILOSOPHY

Annual Festivities and Ceremonies--Beliefs in Daily Life

While Japanese people, in general, have no fixed or exclusive religious affiliation, they do, at times, express belief very fervently, invoking the deity or creed appropriate to the situation or festivity, whether it be Buddhism, Christianity or one of the various Shinto deities. This video focuses on the belief as expressed in ceremonial occasions and annual celebrations.

Availability: Schools, libraries, and nursing homes in Illinois, Indiana, Iowa, Kansas, Minnesota, Missouri, Nebraska, North Dakota, South Dakota, and Wisconsin.
Suggested Grade: 4-12
Order Number: 13010
Production Date: 1991
Format: VHS videotape
Special Notes: No. 13 of the "Nippon the Land and Its People" series.
Terms: Borrower pays return postage by U. S. Mail, UPS, or Federal Express, including insurance for "original" videos. Write, call, fax, or e-mail to request an application. An application form MUST be sent in one month in advance but not more than six months in advance. Include alternate titles and dates if provider can substitute titles. Send a SASE with request if you require confirmation. Return immediately after scheduled showing date. Videos may not be copied or broadcast without permission from the producer of the video. Borrower is responsible if video is lost or damaged.

Source: Consulate General of Japan at Chicago
Japan Information Center
Library
737 North Michigan Avenue, Suite 1000
Chicago, IL 60611
Phone: 1-312-280-0430
Fax: 1-312-280-6883
World Wide Web URL:
http://www.chicago.us.emb-japan.go.jp/jic.html
Email Address: jicchicago@webkddi.com

Annual Festivities and Ceremonies--Beliefs in Daily Life

While Japanese people, in general, have no fixed or exclusive religious affiliation, they do, at times, express belief very fervently, invoking the deity or creed appropriate to the situation or festivity, whether it be Buddhism, Christianity or one of the various Shinto deities. This video focuses on the belief as expressed in ceremonial occasions and annual celebrations.

Availability: Schools, libraries and homeschoolers in Alabama, Georgia, North Carolina, South Carolina, and Virginia.
Suggested Grade: 4-12
Order Number: 811
Production Date: 1991
Format: VHS videotape

Special Notes: No. 13 of the "Nippon the Land and Its People" series.
Terms: Borrower pays return postage. Two tapes may be borrowed at a time. Return within 7 days after receipt. Reservations may be made by filling the application found on the web site.

Source: Consulate General of Japan, Atlanta
Japan Information Center
One Alliance Center
3500 Lenox Road, Suite 1600
Atlanta, GA 30326
Phone: 1-404-365-9240
Fax: 1-404-240-4311
World Wide Web URL:
http://www.atlanta.us.emb-japan.go.jp
Email Address: info@cgjapanatlanta.org

Annual Festivities and Ceremonies--Beliefs in Daily Life

Focuses on the belief as expressed in ceremonial occasions and annual celebrations, fervently invoking the deity or creed appropriate to the situation or festivity.

Availability: Schools, libraries, and nursing homes in Hawaii.
Suggested Grade: 4-12
Order Number: CU-11
Production Date: 1991
Format: VHS videotape
Special Notes: No. 13 of the "Nippon the Land and Its People" series.
Terms: Borrower pays return postage. A maximum of 3 videos may be borrowed per person. Return within one week of date borrowed.

Source: Consulate General of Japan, Honolulu
1742 Nuuanu Avenue
Honolulu, HI 96817-3294
Phone: 1-808-543-3111
Fax: 1-808-543-3170
World Wide Web URL:
http://www.honolulu.us.emb-japan.go.jp

Annual Festivities and Ceremonies--Beliefs in Daily Life

Focuses on the belief as expressed in ceremonial occasions and annual celebrations, fervently invoking the deity or creed appropriate to the situation or festivity.

Availability: Schools, libraries, homeschoolers, and nursing homes in OREGON AND SOUTHERN IDAHO ONLY. Please make requests via the web site.
Suggested Grade: 4-12
Order Number: 303
Production Date: 1991
Format: VHS videotape
Special Notes: No. 13 of the "Nippon the Land and Its People" series.
Terms: Borrower pays return postage. Return within three weeks after scheduled showing date. Book one month in advance if possible. Rewind the video and wrap securely for return. Be certain to indicate video number, date needed, name of your organization, and address to

*All materials listed in this 2011-2012 edition are **BRAND NEW!***

which video should be sent, along with phone number. Audience report enclosed with the video must be completed and returned.

Source: Consulate General of Japan, Oregon
Attn: Tamara, Video Library
1300 S. W. Fifth Avenue, Suite 2700
Portland, OR 97201
Phone: 1-503-221-1811, ext. 17
World Wide Web URL:
http://www.portland.us.emb-japan.go.jp/en/index.html
Email Address: tamara@cgjpdx.org

Annual Festivities and Ceremonies--Beliefs in Daily Life
Focuses on the belief as expressed in ceremonial occasions and annual celebrations, fervently invoking the deity or creed appropriate to the situation or festivity.

Availability: Schools, libraries, and nursing homes in the United States and Canada.
Suggested Grade: 4-12
Order Number: JV0267
Format: VHS videotape
Terms: Borrower pays return postage. Return with 14 days after scheduled showing, via UPS or U. S. Mail. All requests must included an educational institution affiliation, a current address, and phone number. Order through web site only.

Source: Cornell University East Asia Program
World Wide Web URL:
http://www.einaudi.cornell.edu/eastasia/outreach/video.asp
Email Address: east_asia1@cornell.edu

Crucified and Risen Christ, The
The story relates Jesus' appearance to some of his disciples after his resurrection and finally his ascension.

Availability: All requesters
Suggested Grade: 7-12
Order Number: not applicable
Format: Streaming video

Source: Dawn Video Services
4804 Laurel Canyon Blvd., 724
Valley Village, CA 91607
Phone: 1-888-440-3296
Fax: 1-818-762-9428
World Wide Web URL: http://www.dawnbible.com/

Dalai Lama on Death and Dying, The
The Dalai Lama speaks on the process and stages of dying, detailing subtle levels of consciousness through which a dying person passes. A lecture videotaped in Montreal.

Availability: Schools, libraries, homeschoolers, and nursing homes in the southeastern United States.
Suggested Grade: 7-12
Order Number: order by title
Production Date: 1980
Format: VHS videotape
Terms: Borrower pays return postage. Return 2 days after showing via United Parcel Service, insured. Book 2 weeks in advance.

Source: Center for South Asian Studies
University of Virginia
Video Library Coordinator
P. O. Box 400169, 110 Minor Hall
Charlottesville, VA 22904-4169
Phone: 1-434-924-8815
Email Address: southasia@virginia.edu

Diya
Follows the life history of a diya, a small terra cotta oil lamp used in Diwali puja ceremonies and other religions ceremonies in India. Looks at the everyday experiences of those who make, sell, and use them.

Availability: Schools, libraries, homeschoolers, and nursing homes in the southeastern United States.
Suggested Grade: 7-12
Order Number: order by title
Production Date: 2001
Format: VHS videotape
Terms: Borrower pays return postage. Return 2 days after showing via United Parcel Service, insured. Book 2 weeks in advance.

Source: Center for South Asian Studies
University of Virginia
Video Library Coordinator
P. O. Box 400169, 110 Minor Hall
Charlottesville, VA 22904-4169
Phone: 1-434-924-8815
Email Address: southasia@virginia.edu

Dream Is Certain, The
Prophetic dreams and visions come into view as various scenes of Daniel's exciting life unfold. More than 2,500 years of past and present world events were forecast.

Availability: All requesters
Suggested Grade: 7-12
Order Number: not applicable
Format: Streaming video

Source: Dawn Video Services
4804 Laurel Canyon Blvd., 724
Valley Village, CA 91607
Phone: 1-888-440-3296
Fax: 1-818-762-9428
World Wide Web URL: http://www.dawnbible.com/

Everlasting Life Promised by God
A Christian woman and an unbelieving husband have a conflict especially at church-going time on Sunday.

Availability: All requesters
Suggested Grade: 7-12
Order Number: not applicable
Format: Streaming video

Source: Dawn Video Services
4804 Laurel Canyon Blvd., 724
Valley Village, CA 91607
Phone: 1-888-440-3296
Fax: 1-818-762-9428
World Wide Web URL: http://www.dawnbible.com/

*All materials listed in this 2011-2012 edition are **BRAND NEW!***

RELIGION AND PHILOSOPHY

Exploring the Mandala

A computer simulation of the relationship between a two-dimensional mandala--represented here by a sand mandala--and the type of three-dimensional mandala visualized in meditation by Tibetan yogis.

Availability: Schools,   libraries, homeschoolers, and nursing homes in the southeastern United States.
Suggested Grade: 7-12
Order Number: order by title
Production Date: 1992
Format: VHS videotape
Terms: Borrower pays return postage. Return 2 days after showing via United Parcel Service, insured. Book 2 weeks in advance.

Source: Center for South Asian Studies
University of Virginia
Video Library Coordinator
P. O. Box 400169, 110 Minor Hall
Charlottesville, VA 22904-4169
Phone: 1-434-924-8815
Email Address: southasia@virginia.edu

Four Holy Men: Renunciation in Indian Society

Focuses on four sadhus: the administrator of a Ramakrishna Mission hospital; a traditional guru who heads a monastery; a recluse; a scholar who is the founder of a national political party.

Availability: Schools,   libraries, homeschoolers, and nursing homes in the southeastern United States.
Suggested Grade: 7-12
Order Number: order by title
Format: VHS videotape
Terms: Borrower pays return postage. Return 2 days after showing via United Parcel Service, insured. Book 2 weeks in advance.

Source: Center for South Asian Studies
University of Virginia
Video Library Coordinator
P. O. Box 400169, 110 Minor Hall
Charlottesville, VA 22904-4169
Phone: 1-434-924-8815
Email Address: southasia@virginia.edu

Fourth Stage, The: A Hindu's Quest for Release

A newly retired newspaper editor decides whether or not to enter the classical Hindu fourth stage of life and renounce the world.

Availability: Schools,   libraries, homeschoolers, and nursing homes in the southeastern United States.
Suggested Grade: 7-12
Order Number: order by title
Production Date: 1984
Format: VHS videotape
Terms: Borrower pays return postage. Return 2 days after showing via United Parcel Service, insured. Book 2 weeks in advance.

Source: Center for South Asian Studies
University of Virginia
Video Library Coordinator
P. O. Box 400169, 110 Minor Hall
Charlottesville, VA 22904-4169
Phone: 1-434-924-8815
Email Address: southasia@virginia.edu

God Has a Plan

A modern version of the Cain and Abel story followed by a panel discussion setting forth God's plan for the redemption and recovery of mankind from death.

Availability: All requesters
Suggested Grade: 7-12
Order Number: not applicable
Format: Streaming video

Source: Dawn Video Services
4804 Laurel Canyon Blvd., 724
Valley Village, CA 91607
Phone: 1-888-440-3296
Fax: 1-818-762-9428
World Wide Web URL: http://www.dawnbible.com/

God So Loved

Nicodemus, who visited Jesus by night, and Joseph of Arimathaea, who furnished a burial place for Jesus, reveal the great love they had for him.

Availability: All requesters
Suggested Grade: 7-12
Order Number: not applicable
Format: Streaming video

Source: Dawn Video Services
4804 Laurel Canyon Blvd., 724
Valley Village, CA 91607
Phone: 1-888-440-3296
Fax: 1-818-762-9428
World Wide Web URL: http://www.dawnbible.com/

His Holiness the Dalai Lama

A series of lectures entitled "Emptiness and Great Compassion: The Psychology of Selflessness," in which the Dalai Lama teaches his synthesis of the entire Buddhist path to enlightenment. The lectures were delivered at Harvard University in 1981.

Availability: Schools,   libraries, homeschoolers, and nursing homes in the southeastern United States.
Suggested Grade: 7-12
Order Number: order by title
Format: Set of 8 VHS videotapes
Terms: Borrower pays return postage. Return 2 days after showing via United Parcel Service, insured. Book 2 weeks in advance.

Source: Center for South Asian Studies
University of Virginia
Video Library Coordinator
P. O. Box 400169, 110 Minor Hall
Charlottesville, VA 22904-4169

All materials listed in this 2011-2012 edition are BRAND NEW!

Phone: 1-434-924-8815
Email Address: southasia@virginia.edu

History of Voodoo, A

Basic explanation of some of the deities associated with various forms of voodoo, while debunking some of the myths that have been created.

Availability: Schools, libraries, and nursing homes in the United States.
Suggested Grade: 6-12
Order Number: R1-video
Production Date: 1996
Format: VHS videotape
Terms: Borrowers must have a User's Agreement on file with this source--available by mail or via the Internet. Return postage is paid by borrower; return 12 days after showing. Book at least three weeks in advance. All borrowers are limited to a total of ten items per semester.
Source: Latin American Resource Center
Stone Center for Latin American Studies
Tulane University
100 Jones Hall
New Orleans, LA 70118
Phone: 1-504-862-3143
Fax: 1-504-865-6719
World Wide Web URL:
http://stonecenter.tulane.edu/pages/detail/48/
Lending-Library
Email Address: crcrts@tulane.edu

Hosay Trinidad

A documentary of the Islamic muharram rituals performed on the island of Trinidad.

Availability: Schools and libraries in the United States.
Suggested Grade: 7-Adult
Order Number: SA118
Production Date: 1998
Format: VHS videotape
Terms: Borrower pays return postage. Return 3 days after showing via UPS. Book at least 2 weeks in advance.
Source: Syracuse University, South Asia Center
Video Library and Teaching Resources
346F Eggers Hall
The Maxwell School
Syracuse, NY 13244

How a Hindu Worships: At the Home Shrine

Two videos that discusses the Hindu religious ritual worship.

Availability: Schools and libraries in the United States.
Suggested Grade: 7-Adult
Order Number: SA54
Format: VHS videotape
Terms: Borrower pays return postage. Return 3 days after showing via UPS. Book at least 2 weeks in advance.
Source: Syracuse University, South Asia Center
Video Library and Teaching Resources
346F Eggers Hall, The Maxwell School
Syracuse, NY 13244

I Am a Monk

The daily life and education of a Buddhist monk in Thailand, as exemplified by an American who has lived in a Bangkok monastery for eight years.

Availability: Schools, libraries, homeschoolers, and nursing homes in the southeastern United States.
Suggested Grade: 7-12
Order Number: order by title
Format: VHS videotape
Terms: Borrower pays return postage. Return 2 days after showing via United Parcel Service, insured. Book 2 weeks in advance.
Source: Center for South Asian Studies
University of Virginia
Video Library Coordinator
P. O. Box 400169, 110 Minor Hall
Charlottesville, VA 22904-4169
Phone: 1-434-924-8815
Email Address: southasia@virginia.edu

Kashmir Story, The

Describes the suffering and the aspirations of all Kashmiris--Sunni and Shia Muslims, Hindus and Buddhists, nomadic, children, their parents, boys with guns and the families whose loved ones are no more. Highlights the differences of religious perceptions that have overpowered peace in the state and the legacies of the Kashmiri tradition.

Availability: Schools and libraries in the United States.
Suggested Grade: 7-Adult
Order Number: SA43
Format: VHS videotape
Terms: Borrower pays return postage. Return 3 days after showing via UPS. Book at least 2 weeks in advance.
Source: Syracuse University, South Asia Center
Video Library and Teaching Resources
346F Eggers Hall
The Maxwell School
Syracuse, NY 13244

King Does Not Lie, The: The Initiation of a Shango Priest

Shows Afro-Cuban religion, Santeria, as a Puerto Rican community of santeros gather for the initiation of a priest of Shango.

Availability: Schools, libraries, and nursing homes in the United States.
Suggested Grade: 6-12
Order Number: RPUE1-video
Production Date: 1993
Format: VHS videotape
Terms: Borrowers must have a User's Agreement on file with this source--available by mail or via the Internet. Return postage is paid by borrower; return 12 days after showing. Book at least three weeks in advance. All borrowers are limited to a total of ten items per semester.

Source: Latin American Resource Center
Stone Center for Latin American Studies
Tulane University
100 Jones Hall
New Orleans, LA 70118
Phone: 1-504-862-3143
Fax: 1-504-865-6719
World Wide Web URL:
http://stonecenter.tulane.edu/pages/detail/48/
Lending-Library
Email Address: crcrts@tulane.edu

Life Restored and Death Destroyed

The Apostle Paul is interviewed by the historian, Luke, and Paul's strong conviction concerning the resurrection is revealed.

Availability: All requesters
Suggested Grade: 7-12
Order Number: not applicable
Format: Streaming Video
Source: Dawn Video Services
4804 Laurel Canyon Blvd., 724
Valley Village, CA 91607
Phone: 1-888-440-3296
Fax: 1-818-762-9428
World Wide Web URL: http://www.dawnbible.com/

Loving Krishna

Two major festivals, the celebration of Krishna's birth and the great Chariot Festival, held in a small historic town where worship and daily life are intertwined, along with arts and crafts, and bazaar exchanges.

Availability: Schools, libraries, homeschoolers, and nursing homes in the southeastern United States.
Suggested Grade: 7-12
Order Number: order by title
Production Date: 1985
Format: VHS videotape
Terms: Borrower pays return postage. Return 2 days after showing via United Parcel Service, insured. Book 2 weeks in advance.
Source: Center for South Asian Studies
University of Virginia
Video Library Coordinator
P. O. Box 400169, 110 Minor Hall
Charlottesville, VA 22904-4169
Phone: 1-434-924-8815
Email Address: southasia@virginia.edu

Maha Kumbh: A Mythic Confluence

Filmed in Allahabad, this program captures the 2001 Maha Kumbh festival--a 43-day event that drew tens of millions of devotees to the confluence of the Ganges, Yamuna, and mythic Saraswati Rivers to honor the creation story of Hinduism and to pray for release from the cycle of reincarnation.

Availability: Schools and libraries in the United States.
Suggested Grade: 7-Adult
Order Number: SA129
Production Date: 2001
Format: VHS videotape
Special Notes: Contains brief glimpses of nudity.
Terms: Borrower pays return postage. Return 3 days after showing via UPS. Book at least 2 weeks in advance.
Source: Syracuse University, South Asia Center
Video Library and Teaching Resources
346F Eggers Hall
The Maxwell School
Syracuse, NY 13244

Mananitas a la Virgen

Documentary coverage of the ceremonial Mananitas a la Virgen on the feast day of the Virgin of Guadalupe.

Availability: Schools, libraries, and nursing homes in the United States.
Suggested Grade: 6-12
Languages: Spanish
Order Number: RLA6-video
Production Date: 1985
Format: VHS videotape
Terms: Borrowers must have a User's Agreement on file with this source--available by mail or via the Internet. Return postage is paid by borrower; return 12 days after showing. Book at least three weeks in advance. All borrowers are limited to a total of ten items per semester.
Source: Latin American Resource Center
Stone Center for Latin American Studies
Tulane University
100 Jones Hall
New Orleans, LA 70118
Phone: 1-504-862-3143
Fax: 1-504-865-6719
World Wide Web URL:
http://stonecenter.tulane.edu/pages/detail/48/
Lending-Library
Email Address: crcrts@tulane.edu

Marx for Beginners

Cartoon chronicles trends in philosophy and political thought from ancient Egyptians to Karl Marx.

Availability: Schools, libraries, and nursing homes in the United States.
Suggested Grade: 6-12
Order Number: HC2-video
Format: VHS videotape
Terms: Borrowers must have a User's Agreement on file with this source--available by mail or via the Internet. Return postage is paid by borrower; return 12 days after showing. Book at least three weeks in advance. All borrowers are limited to a total of ten items per semester.
Source: Latin American Resource Center
Stone Center for Latin American Studies
Tulane University
100 Jones Hall
New Orleans, LA 70118
Phone: 1-504-862-3143

*All materials listed in this 2011-2012 edition are **BRAND NEW!***

Fax: 1-504-865-6719
World Wide Web URL:
http://stonecenter.tulane.edu/pages/detail/48/
Lending-Library
Email Address: crcrts@tulane.edu

Messianic Kingdom, The

The Apostles James and John recall the time when they requested Jesus to let them sit, one on his right hand, and the other on his left hand in the kingdom.

Availability: All requesters
Suggested Grade: 7-12
Order Number: not applicable
Format: Streaming video

Source: Dawn Video Services
4804 Laurel Canyon Blvd., 724
Valley Village, CA 91607
Phone: 1-888-440-3296
Fax: 1-818-762-9428
World Wide Web URL: http://www.dawnbible.com/

Mythology of Ancient Mexico

Development of successive pre-Columbian civilizations in Mexico and their religious beliefs and practices.

Availability: Schools, libraries, and nursing homes in the United States.
Suggested Grade: 6-12
Order Number: LPMEX1-video
Production Date: 1991
Format: VHS videotape
Terms: Borrowers must have a User's Agreement on file with this source--available by mail or via the Internet. Return postage is paid by borrower; return 12 days after showing. Book at least three weeks in advance. All borrowers are limited to a total of ten items per semester.

Source: Latin American Resource Center
Stone Center for Latin American Studies
Tulane University
100 Jones Hall
New Orleans, LA 70118
Phone: 1-504-862-3143
Fax: 1-504-865-6719
World Wide Web URL:
http://stonecenter.tulane.edu/pages/detail/48/
Lending-Library
Email Address: crcrts@tulane.edu

Nganga Kiyangala

History, rites, and practices of Nganga and Bantu-based belief systems brought to Cuba by African slaves from the Congo.

Availability: Schools, libraries, and nursing homes in the United States.
Suggested Grade: 6-12
Languages: Spanish with English subtitles
Order Number: RCUB4-video
Production Date: 1991
Format: VHS videotape

Terms: Borrowers must have a User's Agreement on file with this source--available by mail or via the Internet. Return postage is paid by borrower; return 12 days after showing. Book at least three weeks in advance. All borrowers are limited to a total of ten items per semester.

Source: Latin American Resource Center
Stone Center for Latin American Studies
Tulane University
100 Jones Hall
New Orleans, LA 70118
Phone: 1-504-862-3143
Fax: 1-504-865-6719
World Wide Web URL:
http://stonecenter.tulane.edu/pages/detail/48/
Lending-Library
Email Address: crcrts@tulane.edu

Observing the Breath

An exposition of a traditional meditation technique from the Theravada school of Buddhism.

Availability: Schools, libraries, homeschoolers, and nursing homes in the southeastern United States.
Suggested Grade: 7-12
Order Number: order by title
Production Date: 1983
Format: VHS videotape
Terms: Borrower pays return postage. Return 2 days after showing via United Parcel Service, insured. Book 2 weeks in advance.

Source: Center for South Asian Studies
University of Virginia
Video Library Coordinator
P. O. Box 400169, 110 Minor Hall
Charlottesville, VA 22904-4169
Phone: 1-434-924-8815
Email Address: southasia@virginia.edu

Old Made Young, The

Two elderly men and their young doctor discuss God's provision for health and life in Christ's kingdom. Quotes from the Bible are used to construct a promise of "the good life" for all mankind.

Availability: All requesters
Suggested Grade: 7-12
Order Number: not applicable
Format: Streaming video

Source: Dawn Video Services
4804 Laurel Canyon Blvd., 724
Valley Village, CA 91607
Phone: 1-888-440-3296
Fax: 1-818-762-9428
World Wide Web URL: http://www.dawnbible.com/

Requiem for a Faith

This focuses on the efforts of Tibetans in exile in a refugee camp in India to preserve a major tradition of Mahayana Buddhism.

Availability: Schools, libraries, homeschoolers, and nursing homes in the southeastern United States.
Suggested Grade: 7-12
Order Number: order by title
Production Date: 1972
Format: VHS videotape
Terms: Borrower pays return postage. Return 2 days after showing via United Parcel Service, insured. Book 2 weeks in advance.

Source: Center for South Asian Studies
University of Virginia
Video Library Coordinator
P. O. Box 400169, 110 Minor Hall
Charlottesville, VA 22904-4169
Phone: 1-434-924-8815
Email Address: southasia@virginia.edu

Sadhus: India's Holy Men

This three-part mini-series explores the lives of three of the most controversial sadhus of Hindu India. Part 1: The Rolling Saint, follows Lotan Baba's 2500-mile penance across India. Part 2: The Living God, focuses on Jayendra Saraswati, arguably the most influential man in India. Part 3: Living with the Dead, concentrates on Ram Nath, a member of the rare and extreme "aghori" sadhu sect, who ritually pollutes himself in order to worship.

Availability: Schools, libraries, homeschoolers, and nursing homes in the southeastern United States.
Suggested Grade: 7-12
Order Number: order by title
Production Date: 1995
Format: Set of 3 VHS videotapes
Terms: Borrower pays return postage. Return 2 days after showing via United Parcel Service, insured. Book 2 weeks in advance.

Source: Center for South Asian Studies
University of Virginia
Video Library Coordinator
P. O. Box 400169, 110 Minor Hall
Charlottesville, VA 22904-4169
Phone: 1-434-924-8815
Email Address: southasia@virginia.edu

Sathya Sai Baba: Aura of Divinity

Five thousand years ago, the ancient scriptures of the Mahabharata prophesied that in this age of spiritual and moral decline, political corruption, crime and falsehood, a holy man would appear in order to put us all on the righteous path. Sri Sathya Si Baba claims to be such a man.

Availability: Schools, libraries, homeschoolers, and nursing homes in the southeastern United States.
Suggested Grade: 7-12
Order Number: order by title
Format: VHS videotape

Terms: Borrower pays return postage. Return 2 days after showing via United Parcel Service, insured. Book 2 weeks in advance.

Source: Center for South Asian Studies
University of Virginia
Video Library Coordinator
P. O. Box 400169, 110 Minor Hall
Charlottesville, VA 22904-4169
Phone: 1-434-924-8815
Email Address: southasia@virginia.edu

Sermon on the Mount, The

Matthew and "doubting" Thomas recall many of the truths Jesus presented in his Sermon on the Mount, and determine to be worthy of a position with Jesus in His kingdom..

Availability: All requesters
Suggested Grade: 7-12
Order Number: not applicable
Format: Streaming video

Source: Dawn Video Services
4804 Laurel Canyon Blvd., 724
Valley Village, CA 91607
Phone: 1-888-440-3296
Fax: 1-818-762-9428
World Wide Web URL: http://www.dawnbible.com/

Sound of Wisdom: A Festival of Sacred Chant

A meeting of Tibetan and Western musical traditions at the Cathedral of St. John the Divine in New York City. Eleven Buddhist monks of the Gyuto Tantric College, each of them capable of chanting a three-note chord, perform ritual chants, accompanied by traditional Tibetan instruments.

Availability: Schools, libraries, homeschoolers, and nursing homes in the southeastern United States.
Suggested Grade: 7-12
Order Number: order by title
Production Date: 1987
Format: VHS videotape
Terms: Borrower pays return postage. Return 2 days after showing via United Parcel Service, insured. Book 2 weeks in advance.

Source: Center for South Asian Studies
University of Virginia
Video Library Coordinator
P. O. Box 400169, 110 Minor Hall
Charlottesville, VA 22904-4169
Phone: 1-434-924-8815
Email Address: southasia@virginia.edu

Tales of Pabuji: A Rajasthani Tradition

Explores the 600 year tradition in Rajasthan of the epic of Lord Pabuji, patron saint of camel herders, and the everyday life of the Rebaris of Rajasthan.

Availability: Schools, libraries, homeschoolers, and nursing homes in the southeastern United States.
Suggested Grade: 7-12

Order Number: order by title
Production Date: 1996
Format: VHS videotape
Terms: Borrower pays return postage. Return 2 days after showing via United Parcel Service, insured. Book 2 weeks in advance.

> **Source: Center for South Asian Studies**
> **University of Virginia**
> **Video Library Coordinator**
> **P. O. Box 400169, 110 Minor Hall**
> **Charlottesville, VA 22904-4169**
> **Phone: 1-434-924-8815**
> **Email Address: southasia@virginia.edu**

Tantra of Gyuto

Tibetan Buddhist monks use sound to effect a specific change in the individual and his environment. Reversing their centuries-old practice of secrecy, they have allowed certain chants to be heard.

Availability: Schools, libraries, homeschoolers, and nursing homes in the southeastern United States.
Suggested Grade: 7-12
Order Number: order by title
Production Date: 1985
Format: VHS videotape
Terms: Borrower pays return postage. Return 2 days after showing via United Parcel Service, insured. Book 2 weeks in advance.

> **Source: Center for South Asian Studies**
> **University of Virginia**
> **Video Library Coordinator**
> **P. O. Box 400169, 110 Minor Hall**
> **Charlottesville, VA 22904-4169**
> **Phone: 1-434-924-8815**
> **Email Address: southasia@virginia.edu**

Teaching Come and See! Parish Edition

Specially developed for Parish Schools of Religion, grades K through 6, this program is an in-service video that affirms catechists in their ministry, challenges them to a new vision of mission, and explores the developments of mission in their teaching.

Availability: Schools, libraries, homeschoolers, church groups, nursing homes, and service clubs in the United States
Suggested Grade: Teacher Reference
Order Number: order by title
Format: VHS videotape
Terms: Borrower pays return postage. Return within 21 days after receipt. Book at least 3 weeks in advance. You will be notified as soon as possible, if your order cannot be filled. All videos are cleared for television broadcast use.

> **Source: Columban Fathers Mission Society**
> **Mission Education Department**
> **Attn: Connie Wacha**
> **P. O. Box 10**
> **St. Columbans, NE 68056**

> **Phone: 1-402-291-1920**
> **Fax: 1-402-715-5575**
> **World Wide Web URL: http://columban.org/missioned**

Trip to Awareness: A Jain Pilgrimage to India

The essentials of Jainism are presented during a pilgrimage, by American students of the Jain master Munishri Chitrabhanu, to the main Jain temples of India.

Availability: Schools, libraries, homeschoolers, and nursing homes in the southeastern United States.
Suggested Grade: 7-12
Order Number: order by title
Format: VHS videotape
Terms: Borrower pays return postage. Return 2 days after showing via United Parcel Service, insured. Book 2 weeks in advance.

> **Source: Center for South Asian Studies**
> **University of Virginia**
> **Video Library Coordinator**
> **P. O. Box 400169, 110 Minor Hall**
> **Charlottesville, VA 22904-4169**
> **Phone: 1-434-924-8815**
> **Email Address: southasia@virginia.edu**

Valley of the Gods: Worship in Katmandu

Captures the celebration of religious traditions in elaborate ceremonies in Katmandu. Most of the population participates in these festivals, which stem from Hindu, Buddhist, and Muslim faiths and are sometimes intertwined.

Availability: Schools, libraries, homeschoolers, and nursing homes in the southeastern United States.
Suggested Grade: 7-12
Order Number: order by title
Production Date: 1995
Format: VHS videotape
Terms: Borrower pays return postage. Return 2 days after showing via United Parcel Service, insured. Book 2 weeks in advance.

> **Source: Center for South Asian Studies**
> **University of Virginia**
> **Video Library Coordinator**
> **P. O. Box 400169, 110 Minor Hall**
> **Charlottesville, VA 22904-4169**
> **Phone: 1-434-924-8815**
> **Email Address: southasia@virginia.edu**

Vision for Justice

This program includes two programs dealing with "World Poverty" and "World Hunger."

Availability: Schools, libraries, homeschoolers, church groups, nursing homes, and service clubs in the United States.
Suggested Grade: 7-12
Order Number: order by title
Format: VHS videotape
Special Notes: Includes lesson plans, posters, student gifts, worksheets and prayer services.

*All materials listed in this 2011-2012 edition are **BRAND NEW**!*

Terms: Borrower pays return postage. Return within 21 days after receipt. Book at least 3 weeks in advance. You will be notified as soon as possible, if your order cannot be filled. All videos are cleared for television broadcast use.

Source: Columban Fathers Mission Society
Mission Education Department
Attn: Connie Wacha
P. O. Box 10
St. Columbans, NE 68056
Phone: 1-402-291-1920
Fax: 1-402-715-5575
World Wide Web URL: http://columban.org/missioned

Visualization of Padmasambhava, The

A traditional meditation according to the Nyingma school of Tiebetan Buddhism.

Availability: Schools, libraries, homeschoolers, and nursing homes in the southeastern United States.
Suggested Grade: 7-12
Order Number: order by title
Production Date: 1983
Format: VHS videotape
Terms: Borrower pays return postage. Return 2 days after showing via United Parcel Service, insured. Book 2 weeks in advance.

Source: Center for South Asian Studies
University of Virginia
Video Library Coordinator
P. O. Box 400169, 110 Minor Hall
Charlottesville, VA 22904-4169
Phone: 1-434-924-8815
Email Address: southasia@virginia.edu

Wheel of Life, The

Focuses on a Tibetan Buddhist painting of a wheel held in the jaws of Death; its iconography is traditionally used to teach the types of happy and bad rebirth in the round of death and rebirth, as well as the causes of suffering.

Availability: Schools, libraries, homeschoolers, and nursing homes in the southeastern United States.
Suggested Grade: 7-12
Order Number: order by title
Production Date: 1991
Format: VHS videotape
Terms: Borrower pays return postage. Return 2 days after showing via United Parcel Service, insured. Book 2 weeks in advance.

Source: Center for South Asian Studies
University of Virginia
Video Library Coordinator
P. O. Box 400169, 110 Minor Hall
Charlottesville, VA 22904-4169
Phone: 1-434-924-8815
Email Address: southasia@virginia.edu

When the Dead Live Again

A member of a family is taken away in death and the age-old question arises, "Why must the good suffer and die?"

Availability: All requesters
Suggested Grade: 7-12
Order Number: not applicable
Format: Streaming video

Source: Dawn Video Services
4804 Laurel Canyon Blvd., 724
Valley Village, CA 91607
Phone: 1-888-440-3296
Fax: 1-818-762-9428
World Wide Web URL: http://www.dawnbible.com/

Why God Permits Evil

Two friends threatened by business disappointment and experiencing death in their families, search for the reason why a God of love permits so much suffering.

Availability: All requesters
Suggested Grade: 7-12
Order Number: not applicable
Format: Streaming video

Source: Dawn Video Services
4804 Laurel Canyon Blvd., 724
Valley Village, CA 91607
Phone: 1-888-440-3296
Fax: 1-818-762-9428
World Wide Web URL: http://www.dawnbible.com/

Women and Islam

Leila Ahmed, professor of women's studies at Amherst, argues the case for revision of the widely-held views in the Islamic world about the role of women, using examples from history and the role played by women in the contemporary world. She explains the origin of the veil and discusses the issue of marriage and women's rights within marriage.

Availability: Schools, libraries, homeschoolers, and nursing homes in the southeastern United States.
Suggested Grade: 7-12
Order Number: order by title
Production Date: 1994
Format: VHS videotape
Terms: Borrower pays return postage. Return 2 days after showing via United Parcel Service, insured. Book 2 weeks in advance.

Source: Center for South Asian Studies
University of Virginia
Video Library Coordinator
P. O. Box 400169, 110 Minor Hall
Charlottesville, VA 22904-4169
Phone: 1-434-924-8815
Email Address: southasia@virginia.edu

Balancing Act

Environmental enhancement is a major effort of the State Water Contractors. Learn what types of projects are being developed to offset environmental impacts of State Water Project construction and operation.

Availability: Schools,   libraries, homeschoolers, and nursing homes in the United States.
Suggested Grade: 6-Adult
Order Number: order by title
Format: DVD
Special Notes: A number of titles from this organization are included on this DVD.
Terms: Borrower pays return postage. Return within 14 days after scheduled use, via UPS or Federal Express. Book at least 14 days in advance and include alternate date. Requests should include title(s), format, name of responsible person, organizational affiliation, phone, and complete delivery address. No part of any program can be used or duplicated without prior written permission. All programs are available for purchase at a nominal fee. May be available in other formats; inquire if interested. Online video previews are available.
Source: California Department of Water Resources
Attn: Video Library, Room 204-22
P. O. Box 942836
Sacramento, CA 94236-0001
Phone: 1-916-653-4893
Fax: 1-916-653-3310
World Wide Web URL: http://www.water.ca.gov/
Email Address: www.publicawillm@water.ca.gov

Balancing Act

Environmental enhancement is a major effort of the State Water Contractors. Learn what types of projects are being developed to offset environmental impacts of State Water Project construction and operation.

Availability: Schools,   libraries, homeschoolers, and nursing homes in the United States.
Suggested Grade: 6-Adult
Order Number: order by title
Format: VHS videotape
Special Notes: Closed captioned.
Terms: Borrower pays return postage. Return within 14 days after scheduled use, via UPS or Federal Express. Book at least 14 days in advance and include alternate date. Requests should include title(s), format, name of responsible person, organizational affiliation, phone, and complete delivery address. No part of any program can be used or duplicated without prior written permission. All programs are available for purchase at a nominal fee. May be available in other formats; inquire if interested. Online video previews are available.
Source: California Department of Water Resources
Attn: Video Library, Room 204-22
P. O. Box 942836
Sacramento, CA 94236-0001
Phone: 1-916-653-4893

Fax: 1-916-653-3310
World Wide Web URL: http://www.water.ca.gov/
Email Address: www.publicawillm@water.ca.gov

Big Energy Gamble, The

Can California's ambitious plan to cut greenhouse gases actually succeed?

Availability: All requesters
Suggested Grade: 7-Adult
Order Number: not applicable
Production Date: 2009
Format: Streaming Video
Source: NOVA
World Wide Web URL:
http://www.pbs.org/wgbh/nova/programs/index.html

Can Tropical Rainforests Be Saved?

Discussion on the use of trees as currency, sovereign rights of nations and indigenous people, and medical and economic use for forest flora.

Availability: Schools   and   libraries   in Iowa, Illinois, Michigan, Minnesota, and Wisconsin.
Suggested Grade: 6-12
Order Number: ENVRFS16VHS
Production Date: 1991
Format: VHS videotape
Terms: Borrower pays return postage. Return 8 days after showing. Book 2 weeks in advance. Order may also be picked up for those near the Center.
Source: Center for Latin American and Caribbean Studies
UW-Milwaukee
P. O. Box 413
Milwaukee, WI 53201
Phone: 1-414-229-5987
World Wide Web URL: http://www.uwm.edu/Dept/CLACS
Email Address: audvis@usm.edu

Can Tropical Rainforests Be Saved?

Discussion on the use of trees as currency, sovereign rights of nations and indigenous people, and medical and economic use for forest flora.

Availability: Schools in the United States.
Suggested Grade: 6-12
Order Number: order by title
Format: VHS videotape
Terms: Borrower pays return postage. Return 14 days after receipt, via USPS including insurance. All borrowers must have a current lending agreement on file with the Outreach program. This agreement is available via the web site or may be requested via phone or fax.
Source: Center for Latin American Studies
University of Florida
319 Grinter Hall
P. O. Box 115530
Gainesville, FL 32611-5530
Phone: 1-352-392-0375
Fax: 1-352-392-7682
World Wide Web URL: http://www.latam.ufl.edu/outreach
Email Address: maryr@ufl.edu

Challenge of Global Warming, The

Scientifically looks at ways to dispose of air polluting carbon.

Availability:	Schools, libraries, and nursing homes in Hawaii.
Suggested Grade:	6-12
Order Number:	NA-29
Format:	VHS videotape
Terms:	Borrower pays return postage. A maximum of 3 videos may be borrowed per person. Return within one week of date borrowed.

Source: Consulate General of Japan, Honolulu
1742 Nuuanu Avenue
Honolulu, HI 96817-3294
Phone: 1-808-543-3111
Fax: 1-808-543-3170
World Wide Web URL:
http://www.honolulu.us.emb-japan.go.jp

Coastal Growth: A Delicate Balance

Looks at the environmental, social, and economic impact of development of barrier islands and wetlands in Virginia.

Availability:	Schools, libraries, and homeschoolers in Connecticut, Maine, Massachusetts, New Hampshire, Rhode Island, and Vermont.
Suggested Grade:	7-12
Order Number:	VID 245
Format:	VHS videotape
Terms:	Borrower pays return postage. Return within three weeks of receipt. If the tape you request is available, it will be mailed within 5 business days. If not, you will be notified that this video is already out on loan. No more than three titles may be borrowed by one requestor at a time. No reservations for a specific date will be accepted. It is most efficient to order via the web site.

Source: U. S. Environmental Protection Agency, Region 1
Customer Service Center
One Congress Street, Suite 1100
Boston, MA 02214
World Wide Web URL:
http://yosemite.epa.gov/r1/videolen.nsf/

Earth to Kids

Children and their families are shown how to evaluate products for their environmental impact. The video provides information about brand-name products that are poor environmental choices and suggests alternatives.

Availability:	Schools, libraries, homeschoolers, and nursing homes in the United States.
Suggested Grade:	4-12
Order Number:	order by title
Production Date:	1991
Format:	VHS videotape
Terms:	Borrower pays return postage. Return the day after scheduled showing, via UPS or Priority Mail, insured for $100.00. Book 4 weeks in advance and include an alternate date. Order should include name of person responsible for handling the video, and complete mailing address. Please mention this Guide when

ordering. Tapes may not be duplicated, edited or exhibited for a fee.

Source: Church World Service
Film & Video Library
28606 Phillips Street, P. O. Box 968
Elkhart, IN 46515
Phone: 1-800-297-1516, ext. 338
Fax: 1-574-262-0966
World Wide Web URL: http://www.churchworldservice.org
Email Address: videos@churchworldservice.org

Emas Park

Examines animal and plant life found in this national park in the high plains of Brazil.

Availability:	Schools, libraries, and nursing homes in the United States.
Suggested Grade:	6-12
Order Number:	GEBRA4-video
Production Date:	1985
Format:	VHS videotape
Terms:	Borrowers must have a User's Agreement on file with this source--available by mail or via the Internet. Return postage is paid by borrower; return 12 days after showing. Book at least three weeks in advance. All borrowers are limited to a total of ten items per semester.

Source: Latin American Resource Center
Stone Center for Latin American Studies
Tulane University
100 Jones Hall
New Orleans, LA 70118
Phone: 1-504-862-3143
Fax: 1-504-865-6719
World Wide Web URL:
http://stonecenter.tulane.edu/pages/detail/48/
Lending-Library
Email Address: crcrts@tulane.edu

Emergency Flood-Fighting Techniques

To train flood-fighters, experts from the Department of Water Resources demonstrate various emergency flood fighting techniques. Although the program concentrates on levee protection, viewers also learn how sandbags are used to protect structures from flood waters.

Availability:	Schools, libraries, homeschoolers, and nursing homes in the United States.
Suggested Grade:	6-Adult
Order Number:	order by title
Format:	DVD
Special Notes:	A number of titles from this organization are included on this DVD.
Terms:	Borrower pays return postage. Return within 14 days after scheduled use, via UPS or Federal Express. Book at least 14 days in advance and include alternate date. Requests should include title(s), format, name of responsible person, organizational affiliation, phone, and complete delivery address. No part of any program can be used or duplicated without prior written permission. All programs are available for purchase at a nominal fee. May be available in other formats;

inquire if interested. Online video previews are available.

Source: California Department of Water Resources
Attn: Video Library, Room 204-22
P. O. Box 942836
Sacramento, CA 94236-0001
Phone: 1-916-653-4893
Fax: 1-916-653-3310
World Wide Web URL: http://www.water.ca.gov/
Email Address: www.publicawillm@water.ca.gov

Emergency Flood-Fighting Techniques

To train flood-fighters, experts from the Department of Water Resources demonstrate various emergency flood fighting techniques. Although the program concentrates on levee protection, viewers also learn how sandbags are used to protect structures from flood waters.

Availability: Schools, libraries, homeschoolers, and nursing homes in the United States.
Suggested Grade: 6-Adult
Order Number: order by title
Format: VHS videotape
Terms: Borrower pays return postage. Return within 14 days after scheduled use, via UPS or Federal Express. Book at least 14 days in advance and include alternate date. Requests should include title(s), format, name of responsible person, organizational affiliation, phone, and complete delivery address. No part of any program can be used or duplicated without prior written permission. All programs are available for purchase at a nominal fee. May be available in other formats; inquire if interested. Online video previews are available.

Source: California Department of Water Resources
Attn: Video Library, Room 204-22
P. O. Box 942836
Sacramento, CA 94236-0001
Phone: 1-916-653-4893
Fax: 1-916-653-3310
World Wide Web URL: http://www.water.ca.gov/
Email Address: www.publicawillm@water.ca.gov

Environmental Dog

Ralphie the Dog, poisoned when he snacks on powdered cleanser, becomes Environmental Dog, and teaches his human family to be careful with the energy and materials they use. This program makes learning about environmental issues fun.

Availability: Schools, libraries, homeschoolers, and nursing homes in the United States.
Suggested Grade: 2-8
Order Number: order by title
Production Date: 1990
Format: VHS videotape
Terms: Borrower pays return postage. Return the day after scheduled showing, via UPS or Priority Mail, insured for $100.00. Book 4 weeks in advance and include an alternate date. Order should include name of person responsible for handling the video, and complete

mailing address. Please mention this Guide when ordering. Tapes may not be duplicated, edited or exhibited for a fee.

Source: Church World Service
Film & Video Library
28606 Phillips Street, P. O. Box 968
Elkhart, IN 46515
Phone: 1-800-297-1516, ext. 338
Fax: 1-574-262-0966
World Wide Web URL: http://www.churchworldservice.org
Email Address: videos@churchworldservice.org

Environment Videos

Lots of videos about our environment and how to take care of it.

Availability: All requesters
Suggested Grade: All ages
Order Number: not applicable
Format: Streaming Video
Source: National Geographic
World Wide Web URL:
http://video.nationalgeographic.com/video/

Environment Latest Approaches

Covers various aspects of preserving nature and the environment.

Availability: Schools, libraries, and nursing homes in Hawaii.
Suggested Grade: 6-12
Order Number: NA-27
Format: VHS videotape
Terms: Borrower pays return postage. A maximum of 3 videos may be borrowed per person. Return within one week of date borrowed.

Source: Consulate General of Japan, Honolulu
1742 Nuuanu Avenue
Honolulu, HI 96817-3294
Phone: 1-808-543-3111
Fax: 1-808-543-3170
World Wide Web URL:
http://www.honolulu.us.emb-japan.go.jp

Fifty Simple Things Kids Can Do to Save the Earth

This CBS Schoolbreak Special shows some of the things kids can do to help save the environment. The first part is on "Water and Resources," and includes the cleaning-up and restocking of a stream that had turned into an unofficial dump. The second part is on "Greenlife, Wildlife, Energy and Air." Its message includes a boy in West Palm Beach, Florida, who is helping to save the gentle manatee. It also looks at kids trying to save sea turtles and the rainforest, and efforts at recycling, reducing energy use, and planting trees.

Availability: Schools, libraries, homeschoolers, and nursing homes in the United States.
Suggested Grade: K-8
Order Number: order by title
Production Date: 1992
Format: VHS videotape

SCIENCE--ENVIRONMENTAL EDUCATION

Terms: Borrower pays return postage. Return the day after scheduled showing, via UPS or Priority Mail, insured for $100.00. Book 4 weeks in advance and include an alternate date. Order should include name of person responsible for handling the video, and complete mailing address. Please mention this Guide when ordering. Tapes may not be duplicated, edited or exhibited for a fee.

Source: Church World Service
Film & Video Library
28606 Phillips Street, P. O. Box 968
Elkhart, IN 46515
Phone: 1-800-297-1516, ext. 338
Fax: 1-574-262-0966
World Wide Web URL: http://www.churchworldservice.org
Email Address: videos@churchworldservice.org

Flight from the Marshes

Explores the fight to save the red-crested Japanese crane from extinction.

Availability: Schools, libraries, and nursing homes in Hawaii.
Suggested Grade: 6-12
Order Number: NA-6
Production Date: 1984
Format: VHS videotape
Terms: Borrower pays return postage. A maximum of 3 videos may be borrowed per person. Return within one week of date borrowed.

Source: Consulate General of Japan, Honolulu
1742 Nuuanu Avenue
Honolulu, HI 96817-3294
Phone: 1-808-543-3111
Fax: 1-808-543-3170
World Wide Web URL:
http://www.honolulu.us.emb-japan.go.jp

Flight from the Marshes

Explores the fight to save the red-crested Japanese crane from extinction.

Availability: Schools, libraries, homeschoolers, and nursing homes in OREGON AND SOUTHERN IDAHO ONLY. Please make requests via the web site.
Suggested Grade: 6-12
Order Number: 202
Production Date: 1985
Format: VHS videotape
Terms: Borrower pays return postage. Return within three weeks after scheduled showing date. Book one month in advance if possible. Rewind the video and wrap securely for return. Be certain to indicate video number, date needed, name of your organization, and address to which video should be sent, along with phone number. Audience report enclosed with the video must be completed and returned.

Source: Consulate General of Japan, Oregon
Attn: Tamara, Video Library
1300 S. W. Fifth Avenue, Suite 2700
Portland, OR 97201

Phone: 1-503-221-1811, ext. 17
World Wide Web URL:
http://www.portland.us.emb-japan.go.jp/en/index.html
Email Address: tamara@cgjpdx.org

Forest Family Forever!

1000-year-old Grandfather Tree shares his knowledge about rainforests' plant and animal life, destruction, and importance to world ecology.

Availability: Schools, libraries, and homeschoolers in the United States who serve the hearing impaired.
Suggested Grade: 2-6
Order Number: 11346
Production Date: 2001
Format: DVD
Special Notes: Also available as live streaming video over the Internet.
Terms: Sponsor pays all transportation costs. Return one week after receipt. Participation is limited to deaf or hard of hearing Americans, their parents, families, teachers, counselors, or others whose use would benefit a deaf or hard of hearing person. Only one person in the audience needs to be hearing impaired. You must register--which is free. These videos are all open-captioned--no special equipment is required for viewing.

Source: Described and Captioned Media Program
National Association of the Deaf
4211 Church Street Ext.
Roebuck, SC 29376
Phone: 1-800-237-6213
Fax: 1-800-538-5636
World Wide Web URL: http://www.dcmp.org

From Whaling to Watching: The Northern Right Whale

Shows spectacular footage of these rare whales and helps us realize the role we all have to play in protecting the most endangered of the large whales.

Availability: Schools, libraries, and homeschoolers in Connecticut, Maine, Massachusetts, New Hampshire, Rhode Island, and Vermont.
Suggested Grade: 6-12
Order Number: VID 299
Production Date: 1997
Format: VHS videotape
Terms: Borrower pays return postage. Return within three weeks of receipt. If the tape you request is available, it will be mailed within 5 business days. If not, you will be notified that this video is already out on loan. No more than three titles may be borrowed by one requestor at a time. No reservations for a specific date will be accepted. It is most efficient to order via the web site.

Source: U. S. Environmental Protection Agency, Region 1
Customer Service Center
One Congress Street, Suite 1100
Boston, MA 02214
World Wide Web URL:
http://yosemite.epa.gov/r1/videolen.nsf/

126

*All materials listed in this 2011-2012 edition are **BRAND NEW**!*

Galapagos: My Fragile World

Evolutionary processes on the Galapagos Islands, both human and animal, as seen by a long-time resident.

Availability: Schools, libraries, and nursing homes in the United States.
Suggested Grade: 6-12
Order Number: GEECU1-video
Production Date: 1988
Format: VHS videotape
Terms: Borrowers must have a User's Agreement on file with this source--available by mail or via the Internet. Return postage is paid by borrower; return 12 days after showing. Book at least three weeks in advance. All borrowers are limited to a total of ten items per semester.

Source: Latin American Resource Center
Stone Center for Latin American Studies
Tulane University
100 Jones Hall
New Orleans, LA 70118
Phone: 1-504-862-3143
Fax: 1-504-865-6719
World Wide Web URL:
http://stonecenter.tulane.edu/pages/detail/48/
Lending-Library
Email Address: crcrts@tulane.edu

Get Ready, Get Set, Grow!

The Brooklyn Children's Garden, where generations of children have gotten dirt under their fingernails, introduces students to the wonders of plant growth, and the basics of gardening, engendering respect for the natural world. After all, "Only plants can make food!"

Availability: Schools, libraries, homeschoolers, and nursing homes in the United States.
Suggested Grade: 1-8
Order Number: order by title
Production Date: 1986
Format: VHS videotape
Special Notes: Accompanied by information for children and adults on how to start a community garden.
Terms: Borrower pays return postage. Return the day after scheduled showing, via UPS or Priority Mail, insured for $100.00. Book 4 weeks in advance and include an alternate date. Order should include name of person responsible for handling the video, and complete mailing address. Please mention this Guide when ordering. Tapes may not be duplicated, edited or exhibited for a fee.

Source: Church World Service
Film & Video Library
28606 Phillips Street, P. O. Box 968
Elkhart, IN 46515
Phone: 1-800-297-1516, ext. 338
Fax: 1-574-262-0966
World Wide Web URL: http://www.churchworldservice.org
Email Address: videos@churchworldservice.org

Ground Water Banking on the Future

California's largest reservoir of water was created millions of years ago and lies just a few feet under the ground. The importance of ground water is the subject of this program.

Availability: Schools, libraries, homeschoolers, and nursing homes in the United States.
Suggested Grade: 6-Adult
Order Number: order by title
Format: VHS videotape
Terms: Borrower pays return postage. Return within 14 days after scheduled use, via UPS or Federal Express. Book at least 14 days in advance and include alternate date. Requests should include title(s), format, name of responsible person, organizational affiliation, phone, and complete delivery address. No part of any program can be used or duplicated without prior written permission. All programs are available for purchase at a nominal fee. May be available in other formats; inquire if interested. Online video previews are available.

Source: California Department of Water Resources
Attn: Video Library, Room 204-22
P. O. Box 942836
Sacramento, CA 94236-0001
Phone: 1-916-653-4893
Fax: 1-916-653-3310
World Wide Web URL: http://www.water.ca.gov/
Email Address: www.publicawillm@water.ca.gov

Ground Water Banking on the Future

California's largest reservoir of water was created millions of years ago and lies just a few feet under the ground. The importance of ground water is the subject of this program.

Availability: Schools, libraries, homeschoolers, and nursing homes in the United States.
Suggested Grade: 6-Adult
Order Number: order by title
Format: DVD
Terms: Borrower pays return postage. Return within 14 days after scheduled use, via UPS or Federal Express. Book at least 14 days in advance and include alternate date. Requests should include title(s), format, name of responsible person, organizational affiliation, phone, and complete delivery address. No part of any program can be used or duplicated without prior written permission. All programs are available for purchase at a nominal fee. May be available in other formats; inquire if interested. Online video previews are available.

Source: California Department of Water Resources
Attn: Video Library, Room 204-22
P. O. Box 942836
Sacramento, CA 94236-0001
Phone: 1-916-653-4893
Fax: 1-916-653-3310
World Wide Web URL: http://www.water.ca.gov/
Email Address: www.publicawillm@water.ca.gov

Heat

A far-reaching investigation into America's energy landscape and what can be done to save our planet--and

All materials listed in this 2011-2012 edition are BRAND NEW!

127

what it will take.

Availability: All requesters
Suggested Grade: 7-Adult
Order Number: not applicable
Production Date: 2008
Format: Streaming Video

Source: PBS
World Wide Web URL:
http://www.pbs.org/wgbh/pages/frontline/heat/view/

Helping Our Feathered Friends

Explores Japan's dedication to bird watching and the preservation of habitats.

Availability: Schools, libraries and homeschoolers in Alabama, Georgia, North Carolina, South Carolina, and Virginia.
Suggested Grade: 6-12
Order Number: 019
Production Date: 1992
Format: VHS videotape
Terms: Borrower pays return postage. Two tapes may be borrowed at a time. Return within 7 days after receipt. Reservations may be made by filling the application found on the web site.

Source: Consulate General of Japan, Atlanta
Japan Information Center
One Alliance Center
3500 Lenox Road, Suite 1600
Atlanta, GA 30326
Phone: 1-404-365-9240
Fax: 1-404-240-4311
World Wide Web URL:
http://www.atlanta.us.emb-japan.go.jp
Email Address: info@cgjapanatlanta.org

Helping Our Feathered Friends

Explores Japan's dedication to bird watching and the preservation of habitats.

Availability: Schools, libraries, and nursing homes in Hawaii.
Suggested Grade: 6-12
Order Number: NA-5
Production Date: 1992
Format: VHS videotape
Terms: Borrower pays return postage. A maximum of 3 videos may be borrowed per person. Return within one week of date borrowed.

Source: Consulate General of Japan, Honolulu
1742 Nuuanu Avenue
Honolulu, HI 96817-3294
Phone: 1-808-543-3111
Fax: 1-808-543-3170
World Wide Web URL:
http://www.honolulu.us.emb-japan.go.jp

Helping Our Feathered Friends

Explores Japan's dedication to bird watching and the preservation of habitats.

Availability: Schools, libraries, homeschoolers, and nursing homes in OREGON AND SOUTHERN IDAHO ONLY. Please make requests via the web site.
Suggested Grade: 6-12
Order Number: 193
Production Date: 1992
Format: VHS videotape
Terms: Borrower pays return postage. Return within three weeks after scheduled showing date. Book one month in advance if possible. Rewind the video and wrap securely for return. Be certain to indicate video number, date needed, name of your organization, and address to which video should be sent, along with phone number. Audience report enclosed with the video must be completed and returned.

Source: Consulate General of Japan, Oregon
Attn: Tamara, Video Library
1300 S. W. Fifth Avenue, Suite 2700
Portland, OR 97201
Phone: 1-503-221-1811, ext. 17
World Wide Web URL:
http://www.portland.us.emb-japan.go.jp/en/index.html
Email Address: tamara@cgjpdx.org

How the Waste Was Won

Explains how to conquer waste disposal problems.

Availability: Schools, libraries, and homeschoolers in Connecticut, Maine, Massachusetts, New Hampshire, Rhode Island, and Vermont.
Suggested Grade: All ages
Order Number: RL 29
Production Date: 1990
Format: VHS videotape
Terms: Borrower pays return postage. Return within three weeks of receipt. If the tape you request is available, it will be mailed within 5 business days. If not, you will be notified that this video is already out on loan. No more than three titles may be borrowed by one requestor at a time. No reservations for a specific date will be accepted. It is most efficient to order via the web site.

Source: U. S. Environmental Protection Agency, Region 1
Customer Service Center
One Congress Street, Suite 1100
Boston, MA 02214
World Wide Web URL:
http://yosemite.epa.gov/r1/videolen.nsf/

IAQ Tools for Schools Walkthrough Video: 4 Schools Making a Difference

Shows the difference four schools are making in improving air quality.

Availability: Schools, libraries, and homeschoolers in Connecticut, Maine, Massachusetts, New Hampshire, Rhode Island, and Vermont.
Suggested Grade: All ages
Order Number: VID 354
Production Date: 2001
Format: VHS videotape

Terms: Borrower pays return postage. Return within three weeks of receipt. If the tape you request is available, it will be mailed within 5 business days. If not, you will be notified that this video is already out on loan. No more than three titles may be borrowed by one requestor at a time. No reservations for a specific date will be accepted. It is most efficient to order via the web site.

Source: U. S. Environmental Protection Agency, Region 1
Customer Service Center
One Congress Street, Suite 1100
Boston, MA 02214
World Wide Web URL:
http://yosemite.epa.gov/r1/videolen.nsf/

In Partnership with Earth: Pollution Prevention for the 1990s

Late singer John Denver hosts this informative program on pollution and its effect on our earth. We learn that the future looks more promising as we begin to generate less pollution.

Availability: Schools, libraries, and homeschoolers in Connecticut, Maine, Massachusetts, New Hampshire, Rhode Island, and Vermont.
Suggested Grade: 6-Adult
Order Number: VID 053
Production Date: 1990
Format: VHS videotape
Terms: Borrower pays return postage. Return within three weeks of receipt. If the tape you request is available, it will be mailed within 5 business days. If not, you will be notified that this video is already out on loan. No more than three titles may be borrowed by one requestor at a time. No reservations for a specific date will be accepted. It is most efficient to order via the web site.

Source: U. S. Environmental Protection Agency, Region 1
Customer Service Center
One Congress Street, Suite 1100
Boston, MA 02214
World Wide Web URL:
http://yosemite.epa.gov/r1/videolen.nsf/

Jungle

Development and industrialization of the rain forests.

Availability: Schools, libraries, and nursing homes in the United States.
Suggested Grade: 6-12
Order Number: GESA5-video
Production Date: 1985
Format: VHS videotape
Terms: Borrowers must have a User's Agreement on file with this source--available by mail or via the Internet. Return postage is paid by borrower; return 12 days after showing. Book at least three weeks in advance. All borrowers are limited to a total of ten items per semester.

Source: Latin American Resource Center
Stone Center for Latin American Studies
Tulane University, 100 Jones Hall
New Orleans, LA 70118
Phone: 1-504-862-3143

Fax: 1-504-865-6719
World Wide Web URL:
http://stonecenter.tulane.edu/pages/detail/48/
Lending-Library
Email Address: crcrts@tulane.edu

Last Ancient Forests, The/Save America's Forests

Discusses how and why we must save our forests before these markers of history are gone.

Availability: All requesters through interlibrary loan.
Suggested Grade: 4-12
Order Number: 585.7 (200) L277 1999 VIDEOC
Production Date: 1999
Format: VHS videotape
Terms: These videotapes are available through interlibrary loan only. Simply request the specific video by name and number at your local public library, university library, or company library. The librarian will submit your request using an ALA interlibrary loan form, and the videos will be mailed to your library for your use. Interlibrary loans are limited to two videos at a time. The address listed below is for the ALA loan form only--your librarian must submit requests to this address.

Source: U. S. Geological Survey Library
345 Middlefield Road, MS 955
Menlo Park, CA 94025

Lead Paint Poisoning: The Thief of Childhood

Profiles several families in and around the Boston area and their experiences with lead paint poisoning in the home. Information on prevention and removal of lead paint is provided by experts in the field.

Availability: Schools, libraries, and homeschoolers in Connecticut, Maine, Massachusetts, New Hampshire, Rhode Island, and Vermont.
Suggested Grade: 4-Adult
Order Number: VID 316
Format: VHS videotape
Terms: Borrower pays return postage. Return within three weeks of receipt. If the tape you request is available, it will be mailed within 5 business days. If not, you will be notified that this video is already out on loan. No more than three titles may be borrowed by one requestor at a time. No reservations for a specific date will be accepted. It is most efficient to order via the web site.

Source: U. S. Environmental Protection Agency, Region 1
Customer Service Center
One Congress Street, Suite 1100
Boston, MA 02214
World Wide Web URL:
http://yosemite.epa.gov/r1/videolen.nsf/

Protecting Our Global Home--Japan's Ecological Contributions

The Japanese respect for nature is emphasized. The video talks about the endangered species and their protection, whale-watching, and the present push to control and diminish air pollution.

Availability: Schools, libraries and homeschoolers in Alabama, Georgia, North Carolina, South Carolina, and Virginia.
Suggested Grade: 6-12
Order Number: 014
Production Date: 1992
Format: VHS videotape
Terms: Borrower pays return postage. Two tapes may be borrowed at a time. Return within 7 days after receipt. Reservations may be made by filling the application found on the web site.

Source: Consulate General of Japan, Atlanta
Japan Information Center
One Alliance Center
3500 Lenox Road, Suite 1600
Atlanta, GA 30326
Phone: 1-404-365-9240
Fax: 1-404-240-4311
World Wide Web URL:
http://www.atlanta.us.emb-japan.go.jp
Email Address: info@cgjapanatlanta.org

Protecting Our Global Home--Japan's Ecological Contributions

The Japanese respect for nature is emphasized. The video talks about the endangered species and their protection, whale-watching, and the present push to control and diminish air pollution.
Availability: Schools, libraries, and nursing homes in Hawaii.
Suggested Grade: 6-12
Order Number: NA-1
Production Date: 1992
Format: VHS videotape
Terms: Borrower pays return postage. A maximum of 3 videos may be borrowed per person. Return within one week of date borrowed.

Source: Consulate General of Japan, Honolulu
1742 Nuuanu Avenue
Honolulu, HI 96817-3294
Phone: 1-808-543-3111
Fax: 1-808-543-3170
World Wide Web URL:
http://www.honolulu.us.emb-japan.go.jp

Protecting Our Habitat: Recycling at the Grassroots

Shows the different steps to recycling in Japan.
Availability: Schools, libraries and homeschoolers in Alabama, Georgia, North Carolina, South Carolina, and Virginia.
Suggested Grade: 6-12
Order Number: 020
Production Date: 1992
Format: VHS videotape
Terms: Borrower pays return postage. Two tapes may be borrowed at a time. Return within 7 days after receipt. Reservations may be made by filling the application found on the web site.

Source: Consulate General of Japan, Atlanta
Japan Information Center
One Alliance Center
3500 Lenox Road, Suite 1600
Atlanta, GA 30326
Phone: 1-404-365-9240
Fax: 1-404-240-4311
World Wide Web URL:
http://www.atlanta.us.emb-japan.go.jp
Email Address: info@cgjapanatlanta.org

Protecting Our Habitat: Recycling at the Grassroots

Shows the different steps to recycling in Japan.
Availability: Schools, libraries, and nursing homes in Hawaii.
Suggested Grade: 6-12
Order Number: NA-2
Production Date: 1992
Format: VHS videotape
Terms: Borrower pays return postage. A maximum of 3 videos may be borrowed per person. Return within one week of date borrowed.

Source: Consulate General of Japan, Honolulu
1742 Nuuanu Avenue
Honolulu, HI 96817-3294
Phone: 1-808-543-3111
Fax: 1-808-543-3170
World Wide Web URL:
http://www.honolulu.us.emb-japan.go.jp

Protecting Our Habitat: Recycling at the Grassroots

Shows the different steps to recycling in Japan.
Availability: Schools, libraries, homeschoolers, and nursing homes in OREGON AND SOUTHERN IDAHO ONLY. Please make requests via the web site.
Suggested Grade: 6-12
Order Number: 195
Format: VHS videotape
Terms: Borrower pays return postage. Return within three weeks after scheduled showing date. Book one month in advance if possible. Rewind the video and wrap securely for return. Be certain to indicate video number, date needed, name of your organization, and address to which video should be sent, along with phone number. Audience report enclosed with the video must be completed and returned.

Source: Consulate General of Japan, Oregon
Attn: Tamara, Video Library
1300 S. W. Fifth Avenue, Suite 2700
Portland, OR 97201
Phone: 1-503-221-1811, ext. 17
World Wide Web URL:
http://www.portland.us.emb-japan.go.jp/en/index.html
Email Address: tamara@cgjpdx.org

Rain Forest

Problems of deforestation in the rain forests of Costa Rica and elsewhere.

Availability: Schools, libraries, and nursing homes in the United States.
Suggested Grade: 6-12
Order Number: GECOS1-video
Production Date: 1986
Format: VHS videotape
Terms: Borrowers must have a User's Agreement on file with this source--available by mail or via the Internet. Return postage is paid by borrower; return 12 days after showing. Book at least three weeks in advance. All borrowers are limited to a total of ten items per semester.
Source: Latin American Resource Center
Stone Center for Latin American Studies
Tulane University
100 Jones Hall
New Orleans, LA 70118
Phone: 1-504-862-3143
Fax: 1-504-865-6719
World Wide Web URL:
http://stonecenter.tulane.edu/pages/detail/48/
Lending-Library
Email Address: crcrts@tulane.edu

Rain Forest Connections

Shows forest destruction in Central and South America, causes, and possible solutions and consequences for Louisiana and the rest of the United States.
Availability: Schools, libraries, and nursing homes in the United States.
Suggested Grade: 6-12
Order Number: GELA7-Video
Production Date: 1985
Format: VHS videotape
Terms: Borrowers must have a User's Agreement on file with this source--available by mail or via the Internet. Return postage is paid by borrower; return 12 days after showing. Book at least three weeks in advance. All borrowers are limited to a total of ten items per semester.
Source: Latin American Resource Center
Stone Center for Latin American Studies
Tulane University
100 Jones Hall
New Orleans, LA 70118
Phone: 1-504-862-3143
Fax: 1-504-865-6719
World Wide Web URL:
http://stonecenter.tulane.edu/pages/detail/48/
Lending-Library
Email Address: crcrts@tulane.edu

Recycle This! Rock 'n Roll & Recycling

Set to rock and roll music, this video emphasizes that recycling helps protect the environment, save energy, reduce waste, and conserve resources.
Availability: Schools, libraries, and homeschoolers in Connecticut, Maine, Massachusetts, New Hampshire, Rhode Island, and Vermont.
Suggested Grade: 1-5
Order Number: VID 079

Format: VHS videotape
Special Notes: Produced by the Dow Chemical Company.
Terms: Borrower pays return postage. Return within three weeks of receipt. If the tape you request is available, it will be mailed within 5 business days. If not, you will be notified that this video is already out on loan. No more than three titles may be borrowed by one requestor at a time. No reservations for a specific date will be accepted. It is most efficient to order via the web site.
Source: U. S. Environmental Protection Agency, Region 1
Customer Service Center
One Congress Street, Suite 1100
Boston, MA 02214
World Wide Web URL:
http://yosemite.epa.gov/r1/videolen.nsf/

Reviving Our Rain Forests--The Mission of Professor Akira Miyawaki

Professor Miyawaki was instrumental in developing a personal reforestation program in Japan; here is an interview with him.
Availability: Schools, libraries and homeschoolers in Alabama, Georgia, North Carolina, South Carolina, and Virginia.
Suggested Grade: 6-12
Order Number: 021
Production Date: 1992
Format: VHS videotape
Terms: Borrower pays return postage. Two tapes may be borrowed at a time. Return within 7 days after receipt. Reservations may be made by filling the application found on the web site.
Source: Consulate General of Japan, Atlanta
Japan Information Center
One Alliance Center, 3500 Lenox Road, Suite 1600
Atlanta, GA 30326
Phone: 1-404-365-9240
Fax: 1-404-240-4311
World Wide Web URL:
http://www.atlanta.us.emb-japan.go.jp
Email Address: info@cgjapanatlanta.org

Reviving Our Rain Forests--The Mission of Professor Akira Miyawaki

Professor Miyawaki was instrumental in developing a personal reforestation program in Japan; here is an interview with him.
Availability: Schools, libraries, and nursing homes in Hawaii.
Suggested Grade: 6-12
Order Number: NA-4
Production Date: 1992
Format: VHS videotape
Terms: Borrower pays return postage. A maximum of 3 videos may be borrowed per person. Return within one week of date borrowed.
Source: Consulate General of Japan, Honolulu
1742 Nuuanu Avenue
Honolulu, HI 96817-3294

Phone: 1-808-543-3111
Fax: 1-808-543-3170
World Wide Web URL:
http://www.honolulu.us.emb-japan.go.jp

Reviving Our Rain Forests--The Mission of Professor Akira Miyawaki

Professor Miyawaki was instrumental in developing a personal reforestation program in Japan; here is an interview with him.

Availability:	Schools, libraries, homeschoolers, and nursing homes in OREGON AND SOUTHERN IDAHO ONLY. Please make requests via the web site.
Suggested Grade:	6-12
Order Number:	194
Production Date:	1992
Format:	VHS videotape
Terms:	Borrower pays return postage. Return within three weeks after scheduled showing date. Book one month in advance if possible. Rewind the video and wrap securely for return. Be certain to indicate video number, date needed, name of your organization, and address to which video should be sent, along with phone number. Audience report enclosed with the video must be completed and returned.

Source: Consulate General of Japan, Oregon
Attn: Tamara, Video Library
1300 S. W. Fifth Avenue, Suite 2700
Portland, OR 97201
Phone: 1-503-221-1811, ext. 17
World Wide Web URL:
http://www.portland.us.emb-japan.go.jp/en/index.html
Email Address: tamara@cgjpdx.org

Rotten Truth, The

The PBS series "3-2-1 Contact" takes viewers on a visit to the fictitious "Museum of Modern Garbage" and to landfill sites to dramatize the mounting waste problem, and the need for consumers to change their habits.

Availability:	Schools, libraries, homeschoolers, and nursing homes in the United States.
Suggested Grade:	All ages
Order Number:	order by title
Production Date:	1990
Format:	VHS videotape
Terms:	Borrower pays return postage. Return the day after scheduled showing, via UPS or Priority Mail, insured for $100.00. Book 4 weeks in advance and include an alternate date. Order should include name of person responsible for handling the video, and complete mailing address. Please mention this Guide when ordering. Tapes may not be duplicated, edited or exhibited for a fee.

Source: Church World Service
Film & Video Library
28606 Phillips Street, P. O. Box 968
Elkhart, IN 46515
Phone: 1-800-297-1516, ext. 338

Fax: 1-574-262-0966
World Wide Web URL: http://www.churchworldservice.org
Email Address: videos@churchworldservice.org

Saved by the Sun

Is it time to take solar energy seriously?

Availability:	All requesters
Suggested Grade:	7-Adult
Order Number:	not applicable
Production Date:	2007
Format:	Streaming Video

Source: NOVA
World Wide Web URL:
http://www.pbs.org/wgbh/nova/programs/index.html

Science in Focus: Energy

Video programs, print guide, and Web site providing a workshop for elementary school teachers to help them provide a solid foundation, enabling them to distinguish between the way "energy" is commonly understood and its meaning in science.

Availability:	All requesters
Suggested Grade:	Teacher Reference
Order Number:	not applicable
Production Date:	2002
Format:	Streaming Video
Terms:	A simple FREE registration is required to view videos.

Source: Annenberg Media
World Wide Web URL:
http://www.learner.org/resources/browse.html

Secret of the Missing Seeds, The

Tells about a wicked king, Gongel the Gloomy, whose strange treasure is not gold--but seeds. Every year the king's soldiers gather up all of the seeds throughout the kingdom of Middleland and take them away to his guarded castle. Soon Middleland becomes barren and desolate. To save Middleland, four brave youngsters, Rudy, Suki, Maria and Fred, set out to discover why the Kingdom of Middleland is desolate and hungry.

Availability:	Schools, libraries, homeschoolers, and nursing homes in the United States.
Suggested Grade:	K-6
Order Number:	order by title
Production Date:	1981
Format:	VHS videotape
Terms:	Borrower pays return postage. Return the day after scheduled showing, via UPS or Priority Mail, insured for $100.00. Book 4 weeks in advance and include an alternate date. Order should include name of person responsible for handling the video, and complete mailing address. Please mention this Guide when ordering. Tapes may not be duplicated, edited or exhibited for a fee.

Source: Church World Service
Film & Video Library
28606 Phillips Street, P. O. Box 968
Elkhart, IN 46515

Phone: 1-800-297-1516, ext. 338
Fax: 1-574-262-0966
World Wide Web URL: http://www.churchworldservice.org
Email Address: videos@churchworldservice.org

Self Service

This abstract, humorous, and thought-provoking animated video looks at humankind's tendency to "get the most out of everything," even to the point of using it all up in the process. This program would be good for starting discussion on resource usage an our obligation to the planet that supports us. Mosquitos are the animator's metaphor for avaricious humankind.

Availability: Schools, libraries, homeschoolers, and nursing homes in the United States.
Suggested Grade: All ages
Order Number: order by title
Format: VHS videotape
Terms: Borrower pays return postage. Return the day after scheduled showing, via UPS or Priority Mail, insured for $100.00. Book 4 weeks in advance and include an alternate date. Order should include name of person responsible for handling the video, and complete mailing address. Please mention this Guide when ordering. Tapes may not be duplicated, edited or exhibited for a fee.

Source: Church World Service
Film & Video Library
28606 Phillips Street, P. O. Box 968
Elkhart, IN 46515
Phone: 1-800-297-1516, ext. 338
Fax: 1-574-262-0966
World Wide Web URL: http://www.churchworldservice.org
Email Address: videos@churchworldservice.org

Simple Things You Can Do to Save Energy

A highly entertaining introduction to energy conservation for kids. The video follows 12-year-old Sarah as she takes viewers on an unusual tour through a home where light bulbs talk, an energy-sucking beast lives in the basement, and kids are blown away by hurricane-force drafts. Through these amusing occurrences, and the help of a wacky game show host, this program teaches valuable lessons about energy use and provides many practical conservation tips.

Availability: Schools, libraries, homeschoolers, and nursing homes in the United States.
Suggested Grade: 2-8
Order Number: order by title
Format: VHS videotape
Terms: Borrower pays return postage. Return the day after scheduled showing, via UPS or Priority Mail, insured for $100.00. Book 4 weeks in advance and include an alternate date. Order should include name of person responsible for handling the video, and complete mailing address. Please mention this Guide when ordering. Tapes may not be duplicated, edited or exhibited for a fee.

Source: Church World Service
Film & Video Library
28606 Phillips Street, P. O. Box 968
Elkhart, IN 46515
Phone: 1-800-297-1516, ext. 338
Fax: 1-574-262-0966
World Wide Web URL: http://www.churchworldservice.org
Email Address: videos@churchworldservice.org

Simple Things You Can Do to Save Energy in Your School

This video shows kids what they can do to help their schools save energy loss from inefficient heating, lighting, and air conditioning. It encourages them to talk to maintenance personnel and others to help eliminate school-wide energy-wasters, and to work at the classroom level on simple energy-saving projects.

Availability: Schools, libraries, homeschoolers, and nursing homes in the United States.
Suggested Grade: 2-8
Order Number: order by title
Format: VHS videotape
Special Notes: Sequel to "Simple Things You Can Do to Save Energy."
Terms: Borrower pays return postage. Return the day after scheduled showing, via UPS or Priority Mail, insured for $100.00. Book 4 weeks in advance and include an alternate date. Order should include name of person responsible for handling the video, and complete mailing address. Please mention this Guide when ordering. Tapes may not be duplicated, edited or exhibited for a fee.

Source: Church World Service
Film & Video Library
28606 Phillips Street, P. O. Box 968
Elkhart, IN 46515
Phone: 1-800-297-1516, ext. 338
Fax: 1-574-262-0966
World Wide Web URL: http://www.churchworldservice.org
Email Address: videos@churchworldservice.org

Songbird Story

When songbirds disappear from their neighborhood, two young people fly along one of the bird migration routes in an animated dream to the tropical rain forest where they see how quickly the rain forests in Central and South America are being cut down to make way for people and development. They learn that they have no time to waste in saving the songbirds.

Availability: Schools, libraries, homeschoolers, and nursing homes in the United States.
Suggested Grade: All ages
Order Number: order by title
Production Date: 1994
Format: VHS videotape
Terms: Borrower pays return postage. Return the day after scheduled showing, via UPS or Priority Mail, insured for $100.00. Book 4 weeks in advance and include an

alternate date. Order should include name of person responsible for handling the video, and complete mailing address. Please mention this Guide when ordering. Tapes may not be duplicated, edited or exhibited for a fee.

Source: **Church World Service**
Film & Video Library
28606 Phillips Street, P. O. Box 968
Elkhart, IN   46515
Phone: 1-800-297-1516, ext. 338
Fax: 1-574-262-0966
World Wide Web URL: http://www.churchworldservice.org
Email Address: videos@churchworldservice.org

Understanding Ecology: What Is an Ecosystem?

Explains the differences between ecosystems and other ecological units and looks at the connections between various aspects of an ecosystem and how pollution disrupts its natural order.

Availability:	Schools, libraries, and homeschoolers in Connecticut, Maine, Massachusetts, New Hampshire, Rhode Island, and Vermont.
Suggested Grade:	4-8
Order Number:	VID 276a
Production Date:	1993
Format:	VHS videotape
Terms:	Borrower pays return postage. Return within three weeks of receipt. If the tape you request is available, it will be mailed within 5 business days. If not, you will be notified that this video is already out on loan. No more than three titles may be borrowed by one requestor at a time. No reservations for a specific date will be accepted. It is most efficient to order via the web site.

Source: **U. S. Environmental Protection Agency, Region 1**
Customer Service Center
One Congress Street, Suite 1100
Boston, MA   02214
World Wide Web URL:
http://yosemite.epa.gov/r1/videolen.nsf/

Un-Endangered Species, The

Explores the growth and success of wildlife management, examining its role in saving many species.

Availability:	Schools, libraries, homeschoolers, and nursing homes in the United States and Canada.
Suggested Grade:	7-12
Order Number:	512
Format:	VHS videotape
Special Notes:	May be retained permanently. Cleared for TV broadcast.

Source: **National Shooting Sports Foundation**
11 Mile Hill Road
Newtown, CT   06470-2359
Phone: 1-203-426-1320
World Wide Web URL: http://www.nssf.org/safety
Email Address: literature@nssf.org

World Heritage--Shirakami Forest 1997

UNESCO certified Shirakami Mountain Forest, which borders Aomori and Akita prefectures, as a world heritage. This 17,000 hectacre forest area is among nature's most priceless treasures--a heritage that must be preserved for future generations.

Availability:	Schools, libraries, and nursing homes in Hawaii.
Suggested Grade:	6-12
Order Number:	NA-28
Format:	VHS videotape
Terms:	Borrower pays return postage. A maximum of 3 videos may be borrowed per person. Return within one week of date borrowed.

Source: **Consulate General of Japan, Honolulu**
1742 Nuuanu Avenue
Honolulu, HI   96817-3294
Phone: 1-808-543-3111
Fax: 1-808-543-3170
World Wide Web URL:
http://www.honolulu.us.emb-japan.go.jp

All About the Earth

Tells children what makes the third planet from the sun so special.

Availability: All requesters through interlibrary loan.
Suggested Grade: K-4
Order Number: 735.1 A44 1999 VIDEOC
Production Date: 1999
Format: VHS videotape
Terms: These videotapes are available through interlibrary loan only. Simply request the specific video by name and number at your local public library, university library, or company library. The librarian will submit your request using an ALA interlibrary loan form, and the videos will be mailed to your library for your use. Interlibrary loans are limited to two videos at a time. The address listed below is for the ALA loan form only--your librarian must submit requests to this address.

Source: U. S. Geological Survey Library
345 Middlefield Road, MS 955
Menlo Park, CA 94025

Arctic Dinosaurs

Experts in Alaska investigate how dinosaurs managed to thrive in polar regions.

Availability: All requesters
Suggested Grade: 7-Adult
Order Number: not applicable
Production Date: 2008
Format: Streaming Video

Source: NOVA
World Wide Web URL:
http://www.pbs.org/wgbh/nova/programs/index.html

Avalanche!

A team of scientists triggers an avalanche onto themselves in order to study its power and effects.

Availability: All requesters through interlibrary loan.
Suggested Grade: 4-12
Order Number: 245 A9242 1997 VIDEOC
Production Date: 1997
Format: VHS videotape
Terms: These videotapes are available through interlibrary loan only. Simply request the specific video by name and number at your local public library, university library, or company library. The librarian will submit your request using an ALA interlibrary loan form, and the videos will be mailed to your library for your use. Interlibrary loans are limited to two videos at a time. The address listed below is for the ALA loan form only--your librarian must submit requests to this address.

Source: U. S. Geological Survey Library
345 Middlefield Road, MS 955
Menlo Park, CA 94025

Being An Explorer

What are explorers? What do they do? What skills do they need? Is exploring done today? How can students be explorers? Following a summary of the 18-month Lewis and Clark expedition, elementary students learn about Will Steger, contemporary arctic explorer. Emphasizes the importance of keeping a journal to record what is seen and heard. Students explore nearby woods and share their discoveries.

Availability: Schools, libraries, and homeschoolers in the United States who serve the hearing impaired.
Suggested Grade: 3-6
Order Number: 13038
Production Date: 1996
Format: DVD
Special Notes: Produced by New Castle Communications.
Terms: Sponsor pays all transportation costs. Return one week after receipt. Participation is limited to deaf or hard of hearing Americans, their parents, families, teachers, counselors, or others whose use would benefit a deaf or hard of hearing person. Only one person in the audience needs to be hearing impaired. You must register--which is free. These videos are all open-captioned--no special equipment is required for viewing.

Source: Described and Captioned Media Program
National Association of the Deaf
4211 Church Street Ext.
Roebuck, SC 29376
Phone: 1-800-237-6213
Fax: 1-800-538-5636
World Wide Web URL: http://www.dcmp.org

Biomes

Offers general information and descriptions of nine of the most common terrestrial biomes, five of the main marine biomes, and two of the standing water biomes.

Availability: All requesters through interlibrary loan.
Suggested Grade: 6-12
Order Number: 919 B5653 1998 VIDEOC
Production Date: 1998
Format: VHS videotape
Terms: These videotapes are available through interlibrary loan only. Simply request the specific video by name and number at your local public library, university library, or company library. The librarian will submit your request using an ALA interlibrary loan form, and the videos will be mailed to your library for your use. Interlibrary loans are limited to two videos at a time. The address listed below is for the ALA loan form only--your librarian must submit requests to this address.

Source: U. S. Geological Survey Library
345 Middlefield Road, MS 955
Menlo Park, CA 94025

Cracking the Code of Life

Follow the race to decode the human genome and see how this newfound knowledge is already changing medicine.

Availability: All requesters
Suggested Grade: 7-Adult
Order Number: not applicable
Production Date: 2001
Format: Streaming Video

Source: NOVA
World Wide Web URL:
http://www.pbs.org/wgbh/nova/programs/index.html

Curse of T. Rex

A documentary on the legal battle surrounding "Sue," a magnificent Tyrannosaurus Rex fossil, found in the South Dakota badlands.

Availability: All requesters through interlibrary loan.
Suggested Grade: 4-12
Order Number: 675 C8773 1997 VIDEOC
Production Date: 1997
Format: VHS videotape
Special Notes: Closed captioned for the hearing impaired.
Terms: These videotapes are available through interlibrary loan only. Simply request the specific video by name and number at your local public library, university library, or company library. The librarian will submit your request using an ALA interlibrary loan form, and the videos will be mailed to your library for your use. Interlibrary loans are limited to two videos at a time. The address listed below is for the ALA loan form only--your librarian must submit requests to this address.
Source: U. S. Geological Survey Library
345 Middlefield Road, MS 955
Menlo Park, CA 94025

Discovering the Connection: The Day the Earth Caught Fire

A rebroadcast of a lecture held on March 13, 2008 about this topic.

Availability: All requesters
Suggested Grade: 7-12
Order Number: not applicable
Production Date: 2008
Format: Streaming Video
Source: Smithsonian National Air and Space Museum
World Wide Web URL:
http://www.nasm.si.edu/webcasts/archive.cfm

Don't Feed the Bears

Learn how to prevent having black bears in your backyard by following these easy steps.

Availability: All requesters
Suggested Grade: 6-Adult
Order Number: not applicable
Format: Streaming Video
Source: Vermont Department of Fish and Wildlife
World Wide Web URL:
http://www.myoutdoortv.com/explore-the-u.s./vermont.html

Evening with the Apollo 8 Astronauts, An

A rebroadcast of a lecture feature Frank Borman, Jim Lovell, and Bill Anders from November 13, 2008.

Availability: All requesters
Suggested Grade: 9-12
Order Number: not applicable
Production Date: 2008

Format: Streaming Video
Source: Smithsonian National Air and Space Museum
World Wide Web URL:
http://www.nasm.si.edu/webcasts/archive.cfm

Forecasting Space Weather

A rebroadcast of a lecture held on June 17, 2008 about this topic.

Availability: All requesters
Suggested Grade: 7-12
Order Number: not applicable
Production Date: 2008
Format: Streaming Video
Source: Smithsonian National Air and Space Museum
World Wide Web URL:
http://www.nasm.si.edu/webcasts/archive.cfm

Indian Ocean Experiment

Provides results for an international experiment conducted in the Indian Ocean that helped scientists unravel mysteries about climate processes related to air pollution and global warming.

Availability: All requesters through interlibrary loan.
Suggested Grade: 6-Adult
Order Number: S (276) Un5aa v.6 no.3 VIDEOC
Production Date: 2000
Format: VHS videotape
Terms: These videotapes are available through interlibrary loan only. Simply request the specific video by name and number at your local public library, university library, or company library. The librarian will submit your request using an ALA interlibrary loan form, and the videos will be mailed to your library for your use. Interlibrary loans are limited to two videos at a time. The address listed below is for the ALA loan form only--your librarian must submit requests to this address.
Source: U. S. Geological Survey Library
345 Middlefield Road, MS 955
Menlo Park, CA 94025

Is There Life on Mars?

The decades-long search for life on the Red Planet heats up with the discovery of frozen water.

Availability: All requesters
Suggested Grade: 7-Adult
Order Number: not applicable
Format: Streaming Video
Source: NOVA
World Wide Web URL:
http://www.pbs.org/wgbh/nova/programs/index.html

Journey Through Our Eyes, A

Introduces students to the miracle of vision...the anatomy of the eye...and the importance of regular and safe eye care. Commonly asked questions such as "How do your eyes work?", "What is glaucoma?" and "How do eyeglasses help you see?" are answered, and common vision problems, eye diseases, and the importance of eye safety are discussed.

Availability: Teachers, librarians, and group leaders in the United States.
Suggested Grade: 4-7
Order Number: order by title
Format: CD-ROM
Special Notes: May be retained permanently. Closed captioned with a detailed teacher's guide, educational poster, and hands-on activities.
Terms: It is asked that you complete a brief survey included with each program. Videos may not be duplicated--copies will be provided if you need them. Mail and FAX requests must be on school letterhead and contain a statement of total school enrollment, estimated number of student viewers, classes/subjects in which video is used and audience grade level (must match audience specified in description). Allow at least four weeks for delivery.
Source: American Optometric Association
Please forward all requests on official letterhead to:
Video Placement Worldwide
25 Second Street North
St. Petersburg, FL 33701
Fax: 1-813-823-2955
World Wide Web URL: http://www.vpw.com

Kids Videos
Educational videos that make learning fun for kids on all sorts of topics.
Availability: All requesters
Suggested Grade: K-6
Order Number: not applicable
Format: Streaming Video
Source: National Geographic
World Wide Web URL:
http://video.nationalgeographic.com/video/

New Worlds, Yellowstone, and Life in the Universe
A rebroadcast of a lecture held on December 11, 2007 about this topic.
Availability: All requesters
Suggested Grade: 7-12
Order Number: not applicable
Production Date: 2008
Format: Streaming Video
Source: Smithsonian National Air and Space Museum
World Wide Web URL:
http://www.nasm.si.edu/webcasts/archive.cfm

Out of the Inferno
Examine the terrifying and often unpredictable variety of a volcano's moods, from vast, swirling mudflows to the ash-clouds that choked the life from ancient Pompeii.
Availability: All requesters through interlibrary loan.
Suggested Grade: 5-12
Order Number: 220 097 1998 VIDEOC
Production Date: 1998
Format: VHS videotape
Terms: These videotapes are available through interlibrary loan only. Simply request the specific video by name and

number at your local public library, university library, or company library. The librarian will submit your request using an ALA interlibrary loan form, and the videos will be mailed to your library for your use. Interlibrary loans are limited to two videos at a time. The address listed below is for the ALA loan form only--your librarian must submit requests to this address.
Source: U. S. Geological Survey Library
345 Middlefield Road, MS 955
Menlo Park, CA 94025

Periodic Table of Videos
Short videos about all 118 elements in the periodic table.
Availability: All requesters
Suggested Grade: 4-Adult
Order Number: not applicable
Format: Streaming Videos
Source: University of Nottingham
World Wide Web URL: http://www.periodicvideos.com/

Plants
Part of the Branches on the Tree of Life series. Uses crisp graphic animation to describe the molecular-level mechanisms of photosynthesis.
Availability: Schools, libraries, and homeschoolers in the United States who serve the hearing impaired.
Suggested Grade: 8-12
Order Number: 30499
Production Date: 2008
Format: DVD
Special Notes: Also available as live streaming video over the Internet.
Terms: Sponsor pays all transportation costs. Return one week after receipt. Participation is limited to deaf or hard of hearing Americans, their parents, families, teachers, counselors, or others whose use would benefit a deaf or hard of hearing person. Only one person in the audience needs to be hearing impaired. You must register--which is free. These videos are all open-captioned--no special equipment is required for viewing.
Source: Described and Captioned Media Program
National Association of the Deaf
4211 Church Street Ext.
Roebuck, SC 29376
Phone: 1-800-237-6213
Fax: 1-800-538-5636
World Wide Web URL: http://www.dcmp.org

Round Rocks: Teaching Earth Science as a Process of Discovery
An example of how to effectively teach earth science.
Availability: All requesters through interlibrary loan.
Suggested Grade: 4-12
Order Number: 204 R682 1997 VIDEOC
Production Date: 1997
Format: VHS videotape
Special Notes: Includes a teacher's guide.
Terms: These videotapes are available through interlibrary loan only. Simply request the specific video by name and

number at your local public library, university library, or company library. The librarian will submit your request using an ALA interlibrary loan form, and the videos will be mailed to your library for your use. Interlibrary loans are limited to two videos at a time. The address listed below is for the ALA loan form only--your librarian must submit requests to this address.

Source: U. S. Geological Survey Library
345 Middlefield Road, MS 955
Menlo Park, CA 94025

Science and Space Videos

Learn more about aerospace education and our solar system with this collection of videos.

Availability:	All requesters
Suggested Grade:	All ages
Order Number:	not applicable
Format:	Streaming Video

Source: National Geographic
World Wide Web URL:
http://video.nationalgeographic.com/video/

Secondary School Small DVD Pack

Reveals the animal abuse involved in the "specimen" industry and describes a number of reusable, humane, cost-effective, and high-tech alternatives to animal dissection.

Availability:	Schools and libraries in the United States and Canada.
Suggested Grade:	6-Adult
Order Number:	order by title
Format:	Set of 2 DVDs
Special Notes:	May be retained permanently.

Source: TeachKind.org
501 Front Street
Norfolk, VA 23510
Phone: 1-757-962-8242
World Wide Web URL: http://www.teachkind.org
Email Address: info@teachkind.org

Simple Machines

Real-life examples demonstrate the function and purpose of the six simple machines: the inclined plane, the wedge, the screw, the lever, the wheel and axle, and the pulley.

Availability:	Schools, libraries, and homeschoolers in the United States who serve the hearing impaired.
Suggested Grade:	4-8
Order Number:	12926
Production Date:	1999
Format:	DVD
Terms:	Sponsor pays all transportation costs. Return one week after receipt. Participation is limited to deaf or hard of hearing Americans, their parents, families, teachers, counselors, or others whose use would benefit a deaf or hard of hearing person. Only one person in the audience needs to be hearing impaired. You must register--which is free. These videos are all open-captioned--no special equipment is required for viewing.

Source: Described and Captioned Media Program
National Association of the Deaf
4211 Church Street Ext.
Roebuck, SC 29376
Phone: 1-800-237-6213
Fax: 1-800-538-5636
World Wide Web URL: http://www.dcmp.org

Space Shuttle Disaster

An investigation uncovers the human failures and design flaws behind the 2003 Columbia tragedy.

Availability:	All requesters
Suggested Grade:	7-Adult
Order Number:	not applicable
Production Date:	2008
Format:	Streaming Video

Source: NOVA
World Wide Web URL:
http://www.pbs.org/wgbh/nova/programs/index.html

To the Moon

Presents the story behind the Apollo space program, including the historic walk on the moon in 1969.

Availability:	All requesters through interlibrary loan.
Suggested Grade:	4-12
Order Number:	739 T6 1999 VIDEOC
Production Date:	1999
Format:	VHS videotape
Terms:	These videotapes are available through interlibrary loan only. Simply request the specific video by name and number at your local public library, university library, or company library. The librarian will submit your request using an ALA interlibrary loan form, and the videos will be mailed to your library for your use. Interlibrary loans are limited to two videos at a time. The address listed below is for the ALA loan form only--your librarian must submit requests to this address.

Source: U. S. Geological Survey Library
345 Middlefield Road, MS 955
Menlo Park, CA 94025

Understanding Volcanic Hazards

An understanding into this monumental geologic hazard.

Availability:	All requesters through interlibrary loan.
Suggested Grade:	4-Adult
Order Number:	220 U523 1955 VIDEOC
Production Date:	1995
Format:	VHS videotape
Terms:	These videotapes are available through interlibrary loan only. Simply request the specific video by name and number at your local public library, university library, or company library. The librarian will submit your request using an ALA interlibrary loan form, and the videos will be mailed to your library for your use. Interlibrary loans are limited to two videos at a time. The address listed below is for the ALA loan form only--your librarian must submit requests to this address.

Source: U. S. Geological Survey Library
345 Middlefield Road, MS 955
Menlo Park, CA 94025

Visit to the Feather River Hatchery, A

This video features Maria, who talks about her trip to the Fish Hatchery to her classmates in a "show and tell" format. It shows the hatchery and the life cycle of the salmon, as Maria tells of her experiences on the tour.

Availability: Schools, libraries, homeschoolers, and nursing homes in the United States.
Suggested Grade: 4-8
Order Number: order by title
Format: DVD
Special Notes: A number of titles from this organization are included on this DVD.
Terms: Borrower pays return postage. Return within 14 days after scheduled use, via UPS or Federal Express. Book at least 14 days in advance and include alternate date. Requests should include title(s), format, name of responsible person, organizational affiliation, phone, and complete delivery address. No part of any program can be used or duplicated without prior written permission. All programs are available for purchase at a nominal fee. May be available in other formats; inquire if interested. Online video previews are available.

Source: California Department of Water Resources
Attn: Video Library, Room 204-22
P. O. Box 942836
Sacramento, CA 94236-0001
Phone: 1-916-653-4893
Fax: 1-916-653-3310
World Wide Web URL: http://www.water.ca.gov/
Email Address: www.publicawillm@water.ca.gov

Visit to the Feather River Hatchery, A

This video features Maria, who talks about her trip to the Fish Hatchery to her classmates in a "show and tell" format. It shows the hatchery and the life cycle of the salmon, as Maria tells of her experiences on the tour.

Availability: Schools, libraries, homeschoolers, and nursing homes in the United States.
Suggested Grade: 4-8
Order Number: order by title
Format: VHS videotape
Special Notes: Closed captioned.
Terms: Borrower pays return postage. Return within 14 days after scheduled use, via UPS or Federal Express. Book at least 14 days in advance and include alternate date. Requests should include title(s), format, name of responsible person, organizational affiliation, phone, and complete delivery address. No part of any program can be used or duplicated without prior written permission. All programs are available for purchase at a nominal fee. May be available in other formats; inquire if interested. Online video previews are available.

Source: California Department of Water Resources
Attn: Video Library, Room 204-22
P. O. Box 942836
Sacramento, CA 94236-0001
Phone: 1-916-653-4893
Fax: 1-916-653-3310
World Wide Web URL: http://www.water.ca.gov/
Email Address: www.publicawillm@water.ca.gov

Voyage to the Moon

A student narrator briefly discusses the moon's gravity, orbit, rotation, and phases, and then reviews the United States' space mission to the moon. Uses NASA footage, computer graphics, and the radio transmissions between NASA and Apollo 11 to vividly present the historic landing. Challenges viewers to set goals to explore our solar system.

Availability: Schools, libraries, and homeschoolers in the United States who serve the hearing impaired.
Suggested Grade: 4-8
Order Number: 13030
Format: DVD
Special Notes: Produced by United Learning, Inc.
Terms: Sponsor pays all transportation costs. Return one week after receipt. Participation is limited to deaf or hard of hearing Americans, their parents, families, teachers, counselors, or others whose use would benefit a deaf or hard of hearing person. Only one person in the audience needs to be hearing impaired. You must register--which is free. These videos are all open-captioned--no special equipment is required for viewing.

Source: Described and Captioned Media Program
National Association of the Deaf
4211 Church Street Ext.
Roebuck, SC 29376
Phone: 1-800-237-6213
Fax: 1-800-538-5636
World Wide Web URL: http://www.dcmp.org

Water Cycle, The--Grades K-6

Illustrates the water cycle which helps ensure a continuing supply of this natural resource.

Availability: Schools, libraries, homeschoolers, and nursing homes in the United States.
Suggested Grade: K-6
Order Number: order by title
Format: DVD
Special Notes: A number of titles from this organization are included on this DVD.
Terms: Borrower pays return postage. Return within 14 days after scheduled use, via UPS or Federal Express. Book at least 14 days in advance and include alternate date. Requests should include title(s), format, name of responsible person, organizational affiliation, phone, and complete delivery address. No part of any program can be used or duplicated without prior written permission. All programs are available for purchase at a nominal fee. May be available in other formats; inquire if interested. Online video previews are available.

Source: California Department of Water Resources
Attn: Video Library, Room 204-22, P. O. Box 942836
Sacramento, CA 94236-0001
Phone: 1-916-653-4893
Fax: 1-916-653-3310
World Wide Web URL: http://www.water.ca.gov/
Email Address: www.publicawillm@water.ca.gov

Water Cycle, The--Grades K-6

Illustrates the water cycle which helps ensure a continuing supply of this natural resource.

Availability: Schools, libraries, homeschoolers, and nursing homes in the United States.
Suggested Grade: K-6
Order Number: order by title
Format: VHS videotape
Terms: Borrower pays return postage. Return within 14 days after scheduled use, via UPS or Federal Express. Book at least 14 days in advance and include alternate date. Requests should include title(s), format, name of responsible person, organizational affiliation, phone, and complete delivery address. No part of any program can be used or duplicated without prior written permission. All programs are available for purchase at a nominal fee. May be available in other formats; inquire if interested. Online video previews are available.
Source: California Department of Water Resources
Attn: Video Library, Room 204-22
P. O. Box 942836
Sacramento, CA 94236-0001
Phone: 1-916-653-4893
Fax: 1-916-653-3310
World Wide Web URL: http://www.water.ca.gov/
Email Address: www.publicawillm@water.ca.gov

Water: Who Needs It?

Answers this question.

Availability: Schools, libraries, homeschoolers, and nursing homes in the United States.
Suggested Grade: K-6
Order Number: order by title
Format: DVD
Special Notes: A number of titles from this organization are included on this DVD.
Terms: Borrower pays return postage. Return within 14 days after scheduled use, via UPS or Federal Express. Book at least 14 days in advance and include alternate date. Requests should include title(s), format, name of responsible person, organizational affiliation, phone, and complete delivery address. No part of any program can be used or duplicated without prior written permission. All programs are available for purchase at a nominal fee. May be available in other formats; inquire if interested. Online video previews are available.
Source: California Department of Water Resources
Attn: Video Library, Room 204-22
P. O. Box 942836
Sacramento, CA 94236-0001

Phone: 1-916-653-4893
Fax: 1-916-653-3310
World Wide Web URL: http://www.water.ca.gov/
Email Address: www.publicawillm@water.ca.gov

Water: Who Needs It?

Answers this question.

Availability: Schools, libraries, homeschoolers, and nursing homes in the United States.
Suggested Grade: K-6
Order Number: order by title
Format: VHS videotape
Terms: Borrower pays return postage. Return within 14 days after scheduled use, via UPS or Federal Express. Book at least 14 days in advance and include alternate date. Requests should include title(s), format, name of responsible person, organizational affiliation, phone, and complete delivery address. No part of any program can be used or duplicated without prior written permission. All programs are available for purchase at a nominal fee. May be available in other formats; inquire if interested. Online video previews are available.
Source: California Department of Water Resources
Attn: Video Library, Room 204-22
P. O. Box 942836
Sacramento, CA 94236-0001
Phone: 1-916-653-4893
Fax: 1-916-653-3310
World Wide Web URL: http://www.water.ca.gov/
Email Address: www.publicawillm@water.ca.gov

What's Inside Your Body? Heart & Blood/Digestion & Respiration

Young students discuss the heart, blood, makeup of the lungs, and the complex digestive system.

Availability: Schools, libraries, and homeschoolers in the United States who serve the hearing impaired.
Suggested Grade: 2-7
Order Number: 12933
Production Date: 1999
Format: DVD
Terms: Sponsor pays all transportation costs. Return one week after receipt. Participation is limited to deaf or hard of hearing Americans, their parents, families, teachers, counselors, or others whose use would benefit a deaf or hard of hearing person. Only one person in the audience needs to be hearing impaired. You must register--which is free. These videos are all open-captioned--no special equipment is required for viewing.
Source: Described and Captioned Media Program
National Association of the Deaf
4211 Church Street Ext.
Roebuck, SC 29376
Phone: 1-800-237-6213
Fax: 1-800-538-5636
World Wide Web URL: http://www.dcmp.org

Work and Energy

Offers a fundamental look at the basic concepts of work and energy.

Availability:	Schools, libraries, and homeschoolers in the United States who serve the hearing impaired.
Suggested Grade:	7-12
Order Number:	13121
Production Date:	1998
Format:	DVD

Terms: Sponsor pays all transportation costs. Return one week after receipt. Participation is limited to deaf or hard of hearing Americans, their parents, families, teachers, counselors, or others whose use would benefit a deaf or hard of hearing person. Only one person in the audience needs to be hearing impaired. You must register--which is free. These videos are all open-captioned--no special equipment is required for viewing.

**Source: Described and Captioned Media Program
National Association of the Deaf
4211 Church Street Ext.
Roebuck, SC 29376
Phone: 1-800-237-6213
Fax: 1-800-538-5636
World Wide Web URL: http://www.dcmp.org**

SCIENCE--NATURE STUDY

Amazing Coral Reef, The
Describes how coral reefs form and their importance to the sea life they sustain. Gives characteristics of hard and soft coral and shows examples, pointing out that both grow extremely slowly.

Availability: Schools, libraries, and homeschoolers in the United States who serve the hearing impaired.
Suggested Grade: 3-9
Order Number: 11463
Production Date: 2004
Format: DVD
Special Notes: Also available as live streaming video over the Internet.
Terms: Sponsor pays all transportation costs. Return one week after receipt. Participation is limited to deaf or hard of hearing Americans, their parents, families, teachers, counselors, or others whose use would benefit a deaf or hard of hearing person. Only one person in the audience needs to be hearing impaired. You must register--which is free. These videos are all open-captioned--no special equipment is required for viewing.

Source: Described and Captioned Media Program
National Association of the Deaf
4211 Church Street Ext.
Roebuck, SC 29376
Phone: 1-800-237-6213
Fax: 1-800-538-5636
World Wide Web URL: http://www.dcmp.org

Animal Life Spans
How long do animals usually live? What about dogs, elephants, big or small animals? What are some factors that influence life span? Shows how scientists determine the age of animals in the wild. Using long- and short-lived animals, concludes that environment, size, food, shelter, a place to have and care for young, number of babies, and maturity rate all affect an animal's life span.

Availability: Schools, libraries, and homeschoolers in the United States who serve the hearing impaired.
Suggested Grade: 4-8
Order Number: 12979
Production Date: 1992
Format: DVD
Special Notes: Produced by National Geographic Society.
Terms: Sponsor pays all transportation costs. Return one week after receipt. Participation is limited to deaf or hard of hearing Americans, their parents, families, teachers, counselors, or others whose use would benefit a deaf or hard of hearing person. Only one person in the audience needs to be hearing impaired. You must register--which is free. These videos are all open-captioned--no special equipment is required for viewing.

Source: Described and Captioned Media Program
National Association of the Deaf
4211 Church Street Ext.
Roebuck, SC 29376
Phone: 1-800-237-6213
Fax: 1-800-538-5636
World Wide Web URL: http://www.dcmp.org

Animals of the Rainforest
Brings to life the signs and sounds of the rainforest.

Availability: Schools in the United States.
Suggested Grade: 3-6
Order Number: order by title
Format: VHS videotape
Terms: Borrower pays return postage. Return 14 days after receipt, via USPS including insurance. All borrowers must have a current lending agreement on file with the Outreach program. This agreement is available via the web site or may be requested via phone or fax.

Source: Center for Latin American Studies
University of Florida
319 Grinter Hall
P. O. Box 115530
Gainesville, FL 32611-5530
Phone: 1-352-392-0375
Fax: 1-352-392-7682
World Wide Web URL: http://www.latam.ufl.edu/outreach
Email Address: maryr@ufl.edu

Animals on the Ice Floe: Shiretoko in Mid-Winter
In winter, the sea along the Shiretoko peninsula in Hokkaido is surrounded with ice. This highlights some of the animals such as eagles and seals that live on the ice floe.

Availability: Schools, libraries and homeschoolers in Alabama, Georgia, North Carolina, South Carolina, and Virginia.
Suggested Grade: 4-Adult
Order Number: 511
Production Date: 1988
Format: VHS videotape
Special Notes: No. 11 of the "Document Japan" series.
Terms: Borrower pays return postage. Two tapes may be borrowed at a time. Return within 7 days after receipt. Reservations may be made by filling the application found on the web site.

Source: Consulate General of Japan, Atlanta
Japan Information Center
One Alliance Center
3500 Lenox Road, Suite 1600
Atlanta, GA 30326
Phone: 1-404-365-9240
Fax: 1-404-240-4311
World Wide Web URL:
http://www.atlanta.us.emb-japan.go.jp
Email Address: info@cgjapanatlanta.org

Animals on the Ice Floe: Shiretoko in Mid-Winter
In winter, the sea along the Shiretoko peninsula in Hokkaido is surrounded with ice. This highlights some of the animals such as eagles and seals that live on the ice floe.

Availability: Schools, libraries, and nursing homes in Hawaii.
Suggested Grade: 4-Adult
Order Number: NA-15
Production Date: 1988
Format: VHS videotape
Special Notes: No. 11 of the "Document Japan" series.

Terms: Borrower pays return postage. A maximum of 3 videos may be borrowed per person. Return within one week of date borrowed.

Source: Consulate General of Japan, Honolulu
1742 Nuuanu Avenue
Honolulu, HI 96817-3294
Phone: 1-808-543-3111
Fax: 1-808-543-3170
World Wide Web URL:
http://www.honolulu.us.emb-japan.go.jp

Animals on the Ice Floe: Shiretoko in Mid-Winter

In winter, the sea along the Shiretoko peninsula in Hokkaido is surrounded with ice. This highlights some of the animals such as eagles and seals that live on the ice floe.

Availability: Schools, libraries, homeschoolers, and nursing homes in OREGON AND SOUTHERN IDAHO ONLY. Please make requests via the web site.
Suggested Grade: 4-Adult
Order Number: 511
Production Date: 1988
Format: VHS videotape
Special Notes: No. 11 of the "Document Japan" series.
Terms: Borrower pays return postage. Return within three weeks after scheduled showing date. Book one month in advance if possible. Rewind the video and wrap securely for return. Be certain to indicate video number, date needed, name of your organization, and address to which video should be sent, along with phone number. Audience report enclosed with the video must be completed and returned.

Source: Consulate General of Japan, Oregon
Attn: Tamara, Video Library
1300 S. W. Fifth Avenue, Suite 2700
Portland, OR 97201
Phone: 1-503-221-1811, ext. 17
World Wide Web URL:
http://www.portland.us.emb-japan.go.jp/en/index.html
Email Address: tamara@cgjpdx.org

Animals Videos

A number of videos about animals.
Availability: All requesters
Suggested Grade: All ages
Order Number: not applicable
Format: Streaming Video
Source: National Geographic
World Wide Web URL:
http://video.nationalgeographic.com/video/

Ape Genius

Experts zero in on what separates humans from our closest living relatives.
Availability: All requesters
Suggested Grade: 7-Adult
Order Number: not applicable
Production Date: 2008
Format: Streaming Video

Source: NOVA
World Wide Web URL:
http://www.pbs.org/wgbh/nova/programs/index.html

At Home With Zoo Animals

How do zoos make animals feel at home? Good zoos try to re-create animals' native environments and provide the right food in a natural manner. Animals need the right amount of space. Good zoos also help endangered animals survive through captive breeding programs and reintroduction into the wild. Compares animals in captivity with those in the wild.

Availability: Schools, libraries, and homeschoolers in the United States who serve the hearing impaired.
Suggested Grade: preK-6
Order Number: 12982
Production Date: 1992
Format: DVD
Special Notes: Produced by National Geographic Society.
Terms: Sponsor pays all transportation costs. Return one week after receipt. Participation is limited to deaf or hard of hearing Americans, their parents, families, teachers, counselors, or others whose use would benefit a deaf or hard of hearing person. Only one person in the audience needs to be hearing impaired. You must register--which is free. These videos are all open-captioned--no special equipment is required for viewing.

Source: Described and Captioned Media Program
National Association of the Deaf
4211 Church Street Ext.
Roebuck, SC 29376
Phone: 1-800-237-6213
Fax: 1-800-538-5636
World Wide Web URL: http://www.dcmp.org

Big Green Caterpillar, The

Two elementary students find an egglike object on a leaf, and, with advice from their teacher, provide the right environment for it to grow. They watch as a caterpillar emerges.

Availability: Schools, libraries, and homeschoolers in the United States who serve the hearing impaired.
Suggested Grade: 2-5
Order Number: 13039
Production Date: 1994
Format: DVD
Terms: Sponsor pays all transportation costs. Return one week after receipt. Participation is limited to deaf or hard of hearing Americans, their parents, families, teachers, counselors, or others whose use would benefit a deaf or hard of hearing person. Only one person in the audience needs to be hearing impaired. You must register--which is free. These videos are all open-captioned--no special equipment is required for viewing.

Source: Described and Captioned Media Program
National Association of the Deaf
4211 Church Street Ext.
Roebuck, SC 29376
Phone: 1-800-237-6213

Fax: 1-800-538-5636
World Wide Web URL: http://www.dcmp.org

Carnivorous Plants

Animals usually eat plants, but where soil is poor and nutrients scarce, some plants have adapted and feed on insects in order to survive. Excellent photography shows how these carnivorous plants trap and digest their food. Classifies the plants as a passive, semiactive, or active trap. Shows the cobra lily, pitcher plant, Cephalotus, sundew, Venus flytrap, and others. Notes that the "trap" is a modified leaf, not a flower.

Availability: Schools, libraries, and homeschoolers in the United States who serve the hearing impaired.
Suggested Grade: 6-10
Order Number: 13042
Production Date: 1993
Format: DVD
Special Notes: Produced by Stanton Films.
Terms: Sponsor pays all transportation costs. Return one week after receipt. Participation is limited to deaf or hard of hearing Americans, their parents, families, teachers, counselors, or others whose use would benefit a deaf or hard of hearing person. Only one person in the audience needs to be hearing impaired. You must register--which is free. These videos are all open-captioned--no special equipment is required for viewing.

Source: Described and Captioned Media Program
National Association of the Deaf
4211 Church Street Ext.
Roebuck, SC 29376
Phone: 1-800-237-6213
Fax: 1-800-538-5636
World Wide Web URL: http://www.dcmp.org

Fight for Survival: The Fish Owl of Northern Japan

The Blakistons fish owl which lives in Hokkaido, Japan's northernmost island, is an endangered species. This program unveils the life of the fish owl.

Availability: Schools, libraries, and nursing homes in Hawaii.
Suggested Grade: 6-12
Order Number: NA-19
Production Date: 1993
Format: VHS videotape
Terms: Borrower pays return postage. A maximum of 3 videos may be borrowed per person. Return within one week of date borrowed.

Source: Consulate General of Japan, Honolulu
1742 Nuuanu Avenue
Honolulu, HI 96817-3294
Phone: 1-808-543-3111
Fax: 1-808-543-3170
World Wide Web URL:
http://www.honolulu.us.emb-japan.go.jp

Four-Winged Dinosaur

Surprising fossils from northeastern China spur a debate over how birds evolved.

Availability: All requesters
Suggested Grade: 7-Adult
Order Number: not applicable
Production Date: 2008
Format: Streaming Video

Source: NOVA
World Wide Web URL:
http://www.pbs.org/wgbh/nova/programs/index.html

Funny Crabs in the Mangrove, The

At least 70 species of crab live in the Iri-omote Island mangrove in Japan. This video looks at these animals and some of their strange and funny behaviors.

Availability: Schools, libraries, and nursing homes in Hawaii.
Suggested Grade: 4-12
Order Number: NA-22
Production Date: 1993
Format: VHS videotape
Terms: Borrower pays return postage. A maximum of 3 videos may be borrowed per person. Return within one week of date borrowed.

Source: Consulate General of Japan, Honolulu
1742 Nuuanu Avenue
Honolulu, HI 96817-3294
Phone: 1-808-543-3111
Fax: 1-808-543-3170
World Wide Web URL:
http://www.honolulu.us.emb-japan.go.jp

Galapagos of the East, The: Ogasawara Islands

Examines the creatures that live on these islands in the middle of the Pacific Ocean.

Availability: Schools, libraries, and nursing homes in Hawaii.
Suggested Grade: 4-12
Order Number: NA-21
Production Date: 1993
Format: VHS videotape
Terms: Borrower pays return postage. A maximum of 3 videos may be borrowed per person. Return within one week of date borrowed.

Source: Consulate General of Japan, Honolulu
1742 Nuuanu Avenue
Honolulu, HI 96817-3294
Phone: 1-808-543-3111
Fax: 1-808-543-3170
World Wide Web URL:
http://www.honolulu.us.emb-japan.go.jp

Galapagos of the East, The: Ogasawara Islands

Examines the creatures that live on these islands in the middle of the Pacific Ocean.

Availability: Schools, libraries, homeschoolers, and nursing homes in OREGON AND SOUTHERN IDAHO ONLY. Please make requests via the web site.
Suggested Grade: 4-12

Order Number: 404
Production Date: 1993
Format: VHS videotape
Terms: Borrower pays return postage. Return within three weeks after scheduled showing date. Book one month in advance if possible. Rewind the video and wrap securely for return. Be certain to indicate video number, date needed, name of your organization, and address to which video should be sent, along with phone number. Audience report enclosed with the video must be completed and returned.

Source: Consulate General of Japan, Oregon
Attn: Tamara, Video Library
1300 S. W. Fifth Avenue, Suite 2700
Portland, OR 97201
Phone: 1-503-221-1811, ext. 17
World Wide Web URL:
http://www.portland.us.emb-japan.go.jp/en/index.html
Email Address: tamara@cgjpdx.org

Giant Sea Turtles

Explores the life of the giant leatherback sea turtle.
Availability: Schools, libraries, and homeschoolers in the United States who serve the hearing impaired.
Suggested Grade: 4-10
Order Number: 8735
Production Date: 1999
Format: DVD
Special Notes: Also available as live streaming video over the Internet.
Terms: Sponsor pays all transportation costs. Return one week after receipt. Participation is limited to deaf or hard of hearing Americans, their parents, families, teachers, counselors, or others whose use would benefit a deaf or hard of hearing person. Only one person in the audience needs to be hearing impaired. You must register--which is free. These videos are all open-captioned--no special equipment is required for viewing.

Source: Described and Captioned Media Program
National Association of the Deaf
4211 Church Street Ext.
Roebuck, SC 29376
Phone: 1-800-237-6213
Fax: 1-800-538-5636
World Wide Web URL: http://www.dcmp.org

Incredible Journey of the Butterflies, The

Follow the 2,000-mile migration of monarchs to a sanctuary in the highlands of Mexico.
Availability: All requesters
Suggested Grade: 4-Adult
Order Number: not applicable
Production Date: 2009
Format: Streaming Video
Source: NOVA
World Wide Web URL:
http://www.pbs.org/wgbh/nova/programs/index.html

Kids Discover Dolphins

Presents lots of information about these mammals of the sea.
Availability: Schools, libraries, and homeschoolers in the United States who serve the hearing impaired.
Suggested Grade: 2-5
Order Number: 11154
Production Date: 2001
Format: DVD
Special Notes: Also available as live streaming video over the Internet.
Terms: Sponsor pays all transportation costs. Return one week after receipt. Participation is limited to deaf or hard of hearing Americans, their parents, families, teachers, counselors, or others whose use would benefit a deaf or hard of hearing person. Only one person in the audience needs to be hearing impaired. You must register--which is free. These videos are all open-captioned--no special equipment is required for viewing.

Source: Described and Captioned Media Program
National Association of the Deaf
4211 Church Street Ext.
Roebuck, SC 29376
Phone: 1-800-237-6213
Fax: 1-800-538-5636
World Wide Web URL: http://www.dcmp.org

Little Duck Tale, A

The drama of a spotbill duck family and their survival is filmed in the heart of Tokyo. A unique documentary on animal behavior.
Availability: Schools, libraries, and nursing homes in Hawaii.
Suggested Grade: All ages
Order Number: NA-10
Production Date: 1990
Format: VHS videotape
Terms: Borrower pays return postage. A maximum of 3 videos may be borrowed per person. Return within one week of date borrowed.

Source: Consulate General of Japan, Honolulu
1742 Nuuanu Avenue
Honolulu, HI 96817-3294
Phone: 1-808-543-3111
Fax: 1-808-543-3170
World Wide Web URL:
http://www.honolulu.us.emb-japan.go.jp

Little Duck Tale, A

The drama of a spotbill duck family and their survival is filmed in the heart of Tokyo. A unique documentary on animal behavior.
Availability: Schools, libraries, homeschoolers, and nursing homes in OREGON AND SOUTHERN IDAHO ONLY. Please make requests via the web site.
Suggested Grade: All ages
Order Number: 168
Production Date: 1990

Format: VHS videotape

Terms: Borrower pays return postage. Return within three weeks after scheduled showing date. Book one month in advance if possible. Rewind the video and wrap securely for return. Be certain to indicate video number, date needed, name of your organization, and address to which video should be sent, along with phone number. Audience report enclosed with the video must be completed and returned.

Source: **Consulate General of Japan, Oregon**
Attn: Tamara, Video Library
1300 S. W. Fifth Avenue, Suite 2700
Portland, OR 97201
Phone: 1-503-221-1811, ext. 17
World Wide Web URL:
http://www.portland.us.emb-japan.go.jp/en/index.html
Email Address: tamara@cgjpdx.org

Lizard Kings

Meet the monitors, the largest, fiercest and craftiest lizards on Earth.

Availability: All requesters
Suggested Grade: 7-Adult
Order Number: not applicable
Production Date: 2009
Format: Streaming Video
Source: NOVA
World Wide Web URL:
http://www.pbs.org/wgbh/nova/programs/index.html

Lord of the Ants

Naturalist E.O. Wilson's fascination with little creatures has led him to some very big ideas

Availability: All requesters
Suggested Grade: 7-Adult
Order Number: not applicable
Production Date: 2008
Format: Streaming Video
Source: NOVA
World Wide Web URL:
http://www.pbs.org/wgbh/nova/programs/index.html

Ocean Animal Emergency

Wildlife veterinarians struggle to save injured seals and sea lions on the California coast.

Availability: All requesters
Suggested Grade: 7-Adult
Order Number: not applicable
Production Date: 2008
Format: Streaming Video
Source: NOVA
World Wide Web URL:
http://www.pbs.org/wgbh/nova/programs/index.html

Sables in the Northern Land

The Sarobetsu Moor in northern Hokkaido is featured in this video--it is the habitat of the sable. This video documents these animals in Japan.

Availability: Schools, libraries, and nursing homes in Hawaii.
Suggested Grade: 6-12
Order Number: NA-20
Production Date: 1993
Format: VHS videotape
Terms: Borrower pays return postage. A maximum of 3 videos may be borrowed per person. Return within one week of date borrowed.

Source: **Consulate General of Japan, Honolulu**
1742 Nuuanu Avenue
Honolulu, HI 96817-3294
Phone: 1-808-543-3111
Fax: 1-808-543-3170
World Wide Web URL:
http://www.honolulu.us.emb-japan.go.jp

Sables in the Northern Land

The Sarobetsu Moor in northern Hokkaido is featured in this video--it is the habitat of the sable. This video documents these animals in Japan.

Availability: Schools, libraries, homeschoolers, and nursing homes in OREGON AND SOUTHERN IDAHO ONLY. Please make requests via the web site.
Suggested Grade: 6-12
Order Number: 406
Production Date: 1993
Format: VHS videotape
Terms: Borrower pays return postage. Return within three weeks after scheduled showing date. Book one month in advance if possible. Rewind the video and wrap securely for return. Be certain to indicate video number, date needed, name of your organization, and address to which video should be sent, along with phone number. Audience report enclosed with the video must be completed and returned.

Source: **Consulate General of Japan, Oregon**
Attn: Tamara, Video Library
1300 S. W. Fifth Avenue, Suite 2700
Portland, OR 97201
Phone: 1-503-221-1811, ext. 17
World Wide Web URL:
http://www.portland.us.emb-japan.go.jp/en/index.html
Email Address: tamara@cgjpdx.org

Sea Lions: Lessons on the Beach

A community of sea lions annually visits an island in the Gulf of California, where the babies are born and must be taught to swim. Compares seals and sea lions. Details physical characteristics, diet, behaviors, and enemies. The only enemy this "grizzly bear of the sea" cannot fight is fishing boats.

Availability: Schools, libraries, and homeschoolers in the United States who serve the hearing impaired.
Suggested Grade: 2-6
Order Number: 13022
Production Date: 1993
Format: DVD

Special Notes: Produced by ACG/United Learning.

Terms: Sponsor pays all transportation costs. Return one week after receipt. Participation is limited to deaf or hard of hearing Americans, their parents, families, teachers, counselors, or others whose use would benefit a deaf or hard of hearing person. Only one person in the audience needs to be hearing impaired. You must register--which is free. These videos are all open-captioned--no special equipment is required for viewing.

Source: Described and Captioned Media Program
National Association of the Deaf
4211 Church Street Ext.
Roebuck, SC 29376
Phone: 1-800-237-6213
Fax: 1-800-538-5636
World Wide Web URL: http://www.dcmp.org

Starting Life

Where do baby animals come from? What do they look like? A family visits a farm in spring and learns the answers. Shows a duckling hatch and a lamb and calf being born. Viewers decide which creatures are born from eggs and which are born live. Later that spring, the family has a new baby.

Availability: Schools, libraries, and homeschoolers in the United States who serve the hearing impaired.

Suggested Grade: K-4
Order Number: 13025
Production Date: 1993
Format: DVD
Special Notes: Produced by ACG/United Learning.

Terms: Sponsor pays all transportation costs. Return one week after receipt. Participation is limited to deaf or hard of hearing Americans, their parents, families, teachers, counselors, or others whose use would benefit a deaf or hard of hearing person. Only one person in the audience needs to be hearing impaired. You must register--which is free. These videos are all open-captioned--no special equipment is required for viewing.

Source: Described and Captioned Media Program
National Association of the Deaf
4211 Church Street Ext.
Roebuck, SC 29376
Phone: 1-800-237-6213
Fax: 1-800-538-5636
World Wide Web URL: http://www.dcmp.org

Vertebrates

A brief introduction to this classification of animals.

Availability: Schools, libraries, and homeschoolers in the United States who serve the hearing impaired.

Suggested Grade: 6-9
Order Number: 13431
Production Date: 1997
Format: DVD
Special Notes: Also available as live streaming video over the Internet.

Terms: Sponsor pays all transportation costs. Return one week after receipt. Participation is limited to deaf or hard of hearing Americans, their parents, families, teachers, counselors, or others whose use would benefit a deaf or hard of hearing person. Only one person in the audience needs to be hearing impaired. You must register--which is free. These videos are all open-captioned--no special equipment is required for viewing.

Source: Described and Captioned Media Program
National Association of the Deaf
4211 Church Street Ext.
Roebuck, SC 29376
Phone: 1-800-237-6213
Fax: 1-800-538-5636
World Wide Web URL: http://www.dcmp.org

Wild Birds of Taiwan

Located in the northwest Pacific, in tropical and subtropical zones, Taiwan is a common stopping-off point for migrating birds, and home to 400 species of birds, 14 endemic species found nowhere else. Chinese bulbuls like people and follow them from the lowlands to the highlands. Features splendid photography.

Availability: Schools, libraries, and nursing homes in the United States and Canada.

Suggested Grade: All ages
Order Number: TV013
Format: VHS videotape

Terms: Borrower pays return postage. Return with 14 days after scheduled showing, via UPS or U. S. Mail. All requests must included an educational institution affiliation, a current address, and phone number. Order through web site only.

Source: Cornell University East Asia Program
World Wide Web URL:
http://www.einaudi.cornell.edu/eastasia/outreach/video.asp
Email Address: east_asia1@cornell.edu

All materials listed in this 2011-2012 edition are BRAND NEW!

SOCIAL STUDIES--GEOGRAPHY--US

Adventure in Glen Canyon
On the Utah and Arizona border lies Glen Canyon, Lake Powell. Until 1950, Glen Canyon was largely unknown before the construction of Glen Canyon Dam. This is the story of the building of the Glen Canyon Dam.

Availability: Schools, libraries, homeschoolers, nursing homes, and others in the United States and Canada.
Suggested Grade: 4-12
Order Number: order by title
Format: VHS videotape
Special Notes: May be copied for permanent retention. Cleared for TV broadcast with advance permission.
Terms: Borrowers pay return postage. Return 30 days after scheduled showing, via U.S. Mail. Book 30 days in advance. Up to 2 videos will be sent out to one customer at a time. Your next order will be mailed as soon as you return previously borrowed tapes.
Source: Bureau of Reclamation
U.S. Department of the Interior
Attn: Kristi Thompson, Library, 84-21320
6th Avenue & Kipling Street, Building 67
Denver, CO 80225-0007
Phone: 1-303-445-2039
Fax: 1-303-445-6303
World Wide Web URL: http://www.usbr.gov/library
Email Address: library@do.usbr.gov

American Bald Eagle
Explains the symbols on the Great Seal of the United States.

Availability: Schools, libraries, and homeschoolers in the United States who serve the hearing impaired.
Suggested Grade: 3-8
Order Number: 13563
Production Date: 2002
Format: DVD
Special Notes: Also available as live streaming video over the Internet.
Terms: Sponsor pays all transportation costs. Return one week after receipt. Participation is limited to deaf or hard of hearing Americans, their parents, families, teachers, counselors, or others whose use would benefit a deaf or hard of hearing person. Only one person in the audience needs to be hearing impaired. You must register--which is free. These videos are all open-captioned--no special equipment is required for viewing.
Source: Described and Captioned Media Program
National Association of the Deaf
4211 Church Street Ext.
Roebuck, SC 29376
Phone: 1-800-237-6213
Fax: 1-800-538-5636
World Wide Web URL: http://www.dcmp.org

American Story with Richard Rodriguez, An
In Part I, Rodriguez talks of growing up in America as the son of immigrants. In Part II he continues discussion of differences between the Mexican and American cultures.

Availability: Schools, libraries, and nursing homes in the United States.
Suggested Grade: 6-12
Order Number: HISP46-video
Production Date: 1990
Format: VHS videotape
Terms: Borrowers must have a User's Agreement on file with this source--available by mail or via the Internet. Return postage is paid by borrower; return 12 days after showing. Book at least three weeks in advance. All borrowers are limited to a total of ten items per semester.
Source: Latin American Resource Center
Stone Center for Latin American Studies
Tulane University
100 Jones Hall
New Orleans, LA 70118
Phone: 1-504-862-3143
Fax: 1-504-865-6719
World Wide Web URL:
http://stonecenter.tulane.edu/pages/detail/48/
Lending-Library
Email Address: crcrts@tulane.edu

America: The New Immigrants
Story of Asians, Latins, and Africans, and the challenges they face in adapting to life in the U. S.

Availability: Schools, libraries, and nursing homes in the United States.
Suggested Grade: 8-Adult
Order Number: SIUS2-video
Production Date: 1991
Format: VHS videotape
Terms: Borrowers must have a User's Agreement on file with this source--available by mail or via the Internet. Return postage is paid by borrower; return 12 days after showing. Book at least three weeks in advance. All borrowers are limited to a total of ten items per semester.
Source: Latin American Resource Center
Stone Center for Latin American Studies
Tulane University
100 Jones Hall
New Orleans, LA 70118
Phone: 1-504-862-3143
Fax: 1-504-865-6719
World Wide Web URL:
http://stonecenter.tulane.edu/pages/detail/48/
Lending-Library
Email Address: crcrts@tulane.edu

Arts of the Eskimo, The: An Arctic Adventure
Presents examples of Eskimo housing, clothing materials, amulets, and much more. Gives insight into Eskimo culture and religion.

Availability: Schools, libraries, and homeschoolers in the United States who serve the hearing impaired.
Suggested Grade: 5-13
Order Number: 12887
Production Date: 1995
Format: DVD

*All materials listed in this 2011-2012 edition are **BRAND NEW!***

Special Notes: Also available as live streaming video over the Internet.

Terms: Sponsor pays all transportation costs. Return one week after receipt. Participation is limited to deaf or hard of hearing Americans, their parents, families, teachers, counselors, or others whose use would benefit a deaf or hard of hearing person. Only one person in the audience needs to be hearing impaired. You must register--which is free. These videos are all open-captioned--no special equipment is required for viewing.

Source: Described and Captioned Media Program
National Association of the Deaf
4211 Church Street Ext.
Roebuck, SC 29376
Phone: 1-800-237-6213
Fax: 1-800-538-5636
World Wide Web URL: http://www.dcmp.org

Birth of Oroville Dam, The

Oroville Dam is the tallest dam in the United States. This video shows historic highlights of the dam's construction from ground breaking through its dedication by Ronald Reagan.

Availability: Schools, libraries, homeschoolers, and nursing homes in the United States.
Suggested Grade: 6-Adult
Order Number: order by title
Format: DVD
Special Notes: A number of titles from this organization are included on this DVD.
Terms: Borrower pays return postage. Return within 14 days after scheduled use, via UPS or Federal Express. Book at least 14 days in advance and include alternate date. Requests should include title(s), format, name of responsible person, organizational affiliation, phone, and complete delivery address. No part of any program can be used or duplicated without prior written permission. All programs are available for purchase at a nominal fee. May be available in other formats; inquire if interested. Online video previews are available.

Source: California Department of Water Resources
Attn: Video Library, Room 204-22
P. O. Box 942836
Sacramento, CA 94236-0001
Phone: 1-916-653-4893
Fax: 1-916-653-3310
World Wide Web URL: http://www.water.ca.gov/
Email Address: www.publicawillm@water.ca.gov

Birth of Oroville Dam, The

Oroville Dam is the tallest dam in the United States. This video shows historic highlights of the dam's construction from ground breaking through its dedication by Ronald Reagan.

Availability: Schools, libraries, homeschoolers, and nursing homes in the United States.
Suggested Grade: 6-Adult
Order Number: order by title

Format: VHS videotape
Special Notes: Closed captioned.
Terms: Borrower pays return postage. Return within 14 days after scheduled use, via UPS or Federal Express. Book at least 14 days in advance and include alternate date. Requests should include title(s), format, name of responsible person, organizational affiliation, phone, and complete delivery address. No part of any program can be used or duplicated without prior written permission. All programs are available for purchase at a nominal fee. May be available in other formats; inquire if interested. Online video previews are available.

Source: California Department of Water Resources
Attn: Video Library, Room 204-22
P. O. Box 942836
Sacramento, CA 94236-0001
Phone: 1-916-653-4893
Fax: 1-916-653-3310
World Wide Web URL: http://www.water.ca.gov/
Email Address: www.publicawillm@water.ca.gov

California's State Water Project: Meeting the Challenge

California has one of the most sophisticated water delivery systems in the world, the State Water Project (SWP). This program presents a concise overview of the SWP including its history, location and operation.

Availability: Schools, libraries, homeschoolers, and nursing homes in the United States.
Suggested Grade: 6-Adult
Order Number: order by title
Production Date: 1997
Format: VHS videotape
Special Notes: Closed captioned.
Terms: Borrower pays return postage. Return within 14 days after scheduled use, via UPS or Federal Express. Book at least 14 days in advance and include alternate date. Requests should include title(s), format, name of responsible person, organizational affiliation, phone, and complete delivery address. No part of any program can be used or duplicated without prior written permission. All programs are available for purchase at a nominal fee. May be available in other formats; inquire if interested. Online video previews are available.

Source: California Department of Water Resources
Attn: Video Library, Room 204-22
P. O. Box 942836
Sacramento, CA 94236-0001
Phone: 1-916-653-4893
Fax: 1-916-653-3310
World Wide Web URL: http://www.water.ca.gov/
Email Address: www.publicawillm@water.ca.gov

California's State Water Project: Meeting the Challenge

California has one of the most sophisticated water delivery systems in the world, the State Water Project (SWP). This program presents a concise overview of the SWP including its history, location and operation.

Availability: Schools, libraries, homeschoolers, and nursing homes in the United States.
Suggested Grade: 6-Adult
Order Number: order by title
Production Date: 1997
Format: DVD
Special Notes: Closed captioned.
Terms: Borrower pays return postage. Return within 14 days after scheduled use, via UPS or Federal Express. Book at least 14 days in advance and include alternate date. Requests should include title(s), format, name of responsible person, organizational affiliation, phone, and complete delivery address. No part of any program can be used or duplicated without prior written permission. All programs are available for purchase at a nominal fee. May be available in other formats; inquire if interested. Online video previews are available.

Source: California Department of Water Resources
Attn: Video Library, Room 204-22
P. O. Box 942836
Sacramento, CA 94236-0001
Phone: 1-916-653-4893
Fax: 1-916-653-3310
World Wide Web URL: http://www.water.ca.gov/
Email Address: www.publicawillm@water.ca.gov

Central Arizona Project--Lifeline to the Future

This program explains the history of the entire water project that covers large areas of Arizona and New Mexico. Fly-overs of the entire system are featured.

Availability: Schools, libraries, homeschoolers, nursing homes, and others in the United States and Canada.
Suggested Grade: 6-12
Order Number: order by title
Production Date: 1985
Format: VHS videotape
Special Notes: May be copied for permanent retention. Cleared for TV broadcast with advance permission.
Terms: Borrowers pay return postage. Return 30 days after scheduled showing, via U.S. Mail. Book 30 days in advance. Up to 2 videos will be sent out to one customer at a time. Your next order will be mailed as soon as you return previously borrowed tapes.

Source: Bureau of Reclamation
U.S. Department of the Interior
Attn: Kristi Thompson, Library, 84-21320
6th Avenue & Kipling Street, Building 67
Denver, CO 80225-0007
Phone: 1-303-445-2039
Fax: 1-303-445-6303
World Wide Web URL: http://www.usbr.gov/library
Email Address: library@do.usbr.gov

Choctaw Dances

Illustrates some of the traditional activities that connect the Mississippi Band of Choctaw Indians to their past. Activities include traditional dances, the use of traditional instruments.

Availability: All requesters
Suggested Grade: All ages
Order Number: not applicable
Format: Streaming Video

Source: Mississippi Band of Choctaw Indians
World Wide Web URL:
http://www.teachersdomain.org/resource/
echo07.lan.stories.choctaw/

Colorado, The

This program is a scenic tour of the Colorado River. It offers fly-overs of the most spectacular sections of the river.

Availability: Schools, libraries, homeschoolers, nursing homes, and others in the United States and Canada.
Suggested Grade: 6-12
Order Number: order by title
Format: VHS videotape
Special Notes: May be copied for permanent retention. Cleared for TV broadcast with advance permission.
Terms: Borrowers pay return postage. Return 30 days after scheduled showing, via U.S. Mail. Book 30 days in advance. Up to 2 videos will be sent out to one customer at a time. Your next order will be mailed as soon as you return previously borrowed tapes.

Source: Bureau of Reclamation
U.S. Department of the Interior
Attn: Kristi Thompson, Library, 84-21320
6th Avenue & Kipling Street, Building 67
Denver, CO 80225-0007
Phone: 1-303-445-2039
Fax: 1-303-445-6303
World Wide Web URL: http://www.usbr.gov/library
Email Address: library@do.usbr.gov

Drought Survival in California

This program shows how California survived the worst drought of the country by coordinating the efforts of all parties involved.

Availability: Schools, libraries, homeschoolers, and nursing homes in the United States.
Suggested Grade: 6-12
English; Spanish in VHS only
Order Number: order by title
Format: DVD
Special Notes: A number of titles from this organization are included on this DVD.
Terms: Borrower pays return postage. Return within 14 days after scheduled use, via UPS or Federal Express. Book at least 14 days in advance and include alternate date. Requests should include title(s), format, name of responsible person, organizational affiliation, phone, and complete delivery address. No part of any program

All materials listed in this 2011-2012 edition are **BRAND NEW!**

can be used or duplicated without prior written permission. All programs are available for purchase at a nominal fee. May be available in other formats; inquire if interested. Online video previews are available.

> **Source: California Department of Water Resources**
> **Attn: Video Library, Room 204-22**
> **P. O. Box 942836**
> **Sacramento, CA 94236-0001**
> **Phone: 1-916-653-4893**
> **Fax: 1-916-653-3310**
> **World Wide Web URL: http://www.water.ca.gov/**
> **Email Address: www.publicawillm@water.ca.gov**

Drought Survival in California

This program shows how California survived the worst drought of the country by coordinating the efforts of all parties involved.

Availability:	Schools, libraries, homeschoolers, and nursing homes in the United States.
Suggested Grade:	6-12
Languages:	English; Spanish in VHS only
Order Number:	order by title
Format:	VHS videotape
Special Notes:	Closed captioned.
Terms:	Borrower pays return postage. Return within 14 days after scheduled use, via UPS or Federal Express. Book at least 14 days in advance and include alternate date. Requests should include title(s), format, name of responsible person, organizational affiliation, phone, and complete delivery address. No part of any program can be used or duplicated without prior written permission. All programs are available for purchase at a nominal fee. May be available in other formats; inquire if interested. Online video previews are available.

> **Source: California Department of Water Resources**
> **Attn: Video Library, Room 204-22**
> **P. O. Box 942836**
> **Sacramento, CA 94236-0001**
> **Phone: 1-916-653-4893**
> **Fax: 1-916-653-3310**
> **World Wide Web URL: http://www.water.ca.gov/**
> **Email Address: www.publicawillm@water.ca.gov**

Eruption at the Sea

Depicts the eruption of a volcano at sea.

Availability:	All requesters through interlibrary loan.
Suggested Grade:	7-Adult
Order Number:	220 (950) E676 1990 VIDEOC
Format:	VHS videotape
Terms:	These videotapes are available through interlibrary loan only. Simply request the specific video by name and number at your local public library, university library, or company library. The librarian will submit your request using an ALA interlibrary loan form, and the videos will be mailed to your library for your use. Interlibrary loans are limited to two videos at a time. The address listed below is for the ALA loan form only--your librarian must submit requests to this address.

> **Source: U. S. Geological Survey Library**
> **345 Middlefield Road, MS 955**
> **Menlo Park, CA 94025**
> **World Wide Web URL:**

Florida Geography, History, and Culture

Presents an overview of Florida's history, climate, ecosystems, and economy. Also points out its cultural diversity and primary geographic features.

Availability:	Schools, libraries, and homeschoolers in the United States who serve the hearing impaired.
Suggested Grade:	7-10
Order Number:	11789
Production Date:	2002
Format:	DVD
Terms:	Sponsor pays all transportation costs. Return one week after receipt. Participation is limited to deaf or hard of hearing Americans, their parents, families, teachers, counselors, or others whose use would benefit a deaf or hard of hearing person. Only one person in the audience needs to be hearing impaired. You must register--which is free. These videos are all open-captioned--no special equipment is required for viewing.

> **Source: Described and Captioned Media Program**
> **National Association of the Deaf**
> **4211 Church Street Ext.**
> **Roebuck, SC 29376**
> **Phone: 1-800-237-6213**
> **Fax: 1-800-538-5636**
> **World Wide Web URL: http://www.dcmp.org**

Future Quakes

Shows how UGS scientists are imaging the deepest parts of Bay Area faults, trenching across faults, probing the upper sections of sediments, and deploying a rapid response network of instruments, all to better prepare the Bay Area for the next big quake.

Availability:	All requesters through interlibrary loan.
Suggested Grade:	5-12
Order Number:	(200) R29o no.99-519 VIDEOC
Production Date:	1999
Format:	VHS videotape
Terms:	These videotapes are available through interlibrary loan only. Simply request the specific video by name and number at your local public library, university library, or company library. The librarian will submit your request using an ALA interlibrary loan form, and the videos will be mailed to your library for your use. Interlibrary loans are limited to two videos at a time. The address listed below is for the ALA loan form only--your librarian must submit requests to this address.

> **Source: U. S. Geological Survey Library**
> **345 Middlefield Road, MS 955**
> **Menlo Park, CA 94025**

Hydropower

This video describes the Bureau of Reclamation's hydropower facilities.

Availability: Schools, libraries, homeschoolers, nursing homes, and others in the United States and Canada.
Suggested Grade: 6-12
Order Number: order by title
Format: VHS videotape
Special Notes: May be copied for permanent retention. Cleared for TV broadcast with advance permission.
Terms: Borrowers pay return postage. Return 30 days after scheduled showing, via U.S. Mail. Book 30 days in advance. Up to 2 videos will be sent out to one customer at a time. Your next order will be mailed as soon as you return previously borrowed tapes.

Source: Bureau of Reclamation
U.S. Department of the Interior
Attn: Kristi Thompson, Library, 84-21320
6th Avenue & Kipling Street, Building 67
Denver, CO 80225-0007
Phone: 1-303-445-2039
Fax: 1-303-445-6303
World Wide Web URL: http://www.usbr.gov/library
Email Address: library@do.usbr.gov

Lake Powell--Jewel of the Colorado

This program describes the historical background for building Glen Canyon Dam, Arizona. It takes you on a hike to see the beautiful scenery and on a boat ride to show you the recreational opportunities that were created with Lake Powell. It takes you into the dam, and you see Glen Canyon Dam in operation.

Availability: Schools, libraries, homeschoolers, nursing homes, and others in the United States and Canada.
Suggested Grade: 4-12
Order Number: order by title
Format: VHS videotape
Special Notes: May be copied for permanent retention. Cleared for TV broadcast with advance permission.
Terms: Borrowers pay return postage. Return 30 days after scheduled showing, via U.S. Mail. Book 30 days in advance. Up to 2 videos will be sent out to one customer at a time. Your next order will be mailed as soon as you return previously borrowed tapes.

Source: Bureau of Reclamation
U.S. Department of the Interior
Attn: Kristi Thompson, Library, 84-21320
6th Avenue & Kipling Street, Building 67
Denver, CO 80225-0007
Phone: 1-303-445-2039
Fax: 1-303-445-6303
World Wide Web URL: http://www.usbr.gov/library
Email Address: library@do.usbr.gov

Lassen Volcanic National Park: Land of Renewal

Features information about the human and physical geography of the Lassen area.

Availability: One copy to schools, libraries, and homeschoolers in the United States and Canada.
Suggested Grade: All ages
Order Number: order by title
Format: VHS videotape

Source: Lassen Volcanic National Park
Division of Interpretation & Education
P. O. Box 100
Mineral, CA 96063-0100
Phone: 1-530-595-6133
Fax: 1-530-595-6139
World Wide Web URL: http://www.nps.gov/lavo
Email Address: lavo_information@nps.gov

Lassen Volcanic National Park: Volcanoes, Glaciers, and Fumaroles

Highlights the fascinating geological story of this National Park.

Availability: One copy to schools, libraries, and homeschoolers in the United States and Canada.
Suggested Grade: All ages
Order Number: order by title
Format: VHS videotape

Source: Lassen Volcanic National Park
Division of Interpretation & Education
P. O. Box 100
Mineral, CA 96063-0100
Phone: 1-530-595-6133
Fax: 1-530-595-6139
World Wide Web URL: http://www.nps.gov/lavo
Email Address: lavo_information@nps.gov

Living Marsh, The

Hundreds of species of plants and animals depend upon the Suisun Marsh's brackish water environment. This is the story of the quest to preserve one of California's largest living marshes.

Availability: Schools, libraries, homeschoolers, and nursing homes in the United States.
Suggested Grade: 6-Adult
Order Number: order by title
Format: DVD
Special Notes: A number of titles from this organization are included on this DVD.
Terms: Borrower pays return postage. Return within 14 days after scheduled use, via UPS or Federal Express. Book at least 14 days in advance and include alternate date. Requests should include title(s), format, name of responsible person, organizational affiliation, phone, and complete delivery address. No part of any program can be used or duplicated without prior written permission. All programs are available for purchase at a nominal fee. May be available in other formats; inquire if interested. Online video previews are available.

Source: California Department of Water Resources
Attn: Video Library, Room 204-22
P. O. Box 942836
Sacramento, CA 94236-0001
Phone: 1-916-653-4893
Fax: 1-916-653-3310
World Wide Web URL: http://www.water.ca.gov/
Email Address: www.publicawillm@water.ca.gov

Living Marsh, The

Hundreds of species of plants and animals depend upon the Suisun Marsh's brackish water environment. This is the story of the quest to preserve one of California's largest living marshes.

Availability: Schools, libraries, homeschoolers, and nursing homes in the United States.
Suggested Grade: 6-Adult
Order Number: order by title
Format: VHS videotape
Special Notes: Closed captioned.
Terms: Borrower pays return postage. Return within 14 days after scheduled use, via UPS or Federal Express. Book at least 14 days in advance and include alternate date. Requests should include title(s), format, name of responsible person, organizational affiliation, phone, and complete delivery address. No part of any program can be used or duplicated without prior written permission. All programs are available for purchase at a nominal fee. May be available in other formats; inquire if interested. Online video previews are available.
Source: California Department of Water Resources
Attn: Video Library, Room 204-22
P. O. Box 942836
Sacramento, CA 94236-0001
Phone: 1-916-653-4893
Fax: 1-916-653-3310
World Wide Web URL: http://www.water.ca.gov/
Email Address: www.publicawillm@water.ca.gov

Living Waters of the Colorado

This program starts the viewer in Colorado's San Juan Mountains, and takes you down the Colorado River. It provides an overview of the Colorado River Storage Project for Arizona, Colorado, New Mexico, Utah, and Wyoming.

Availability: Schools, libraries, homeschoolers, nursing homes, and others in the United States and Canada.
Suggested Grade: 6-12
Order Number: order by title
Format: VHS videotape
Special Notes: May be copied for permanent retention. Cleared for TV broadcast with advance permission.
Terms: Borrowers pay return postage. Return 30 days after scheduled showing, via U.S. Mail. Book 30 days in advance. Up to 2 videos will be sent out to one customer at a time. Your next order will be mailed as soon as you return previously borrowed tapes.

Source: Bureau of Reclamation
U.S. Department of the Interior
Attn: Kristi Thompson, Library, 84-21320
6th Avenue & Kipling Street, Building 67
Denver, CO 80225-0007
Phone: 1-303-445-2039
Fax: 1-303-445-6303
World Wide Web URL: http://www.usbr.gov/library
Email Address: library@do.usbr.gov

Miracle of Water

This video tells about the heritage of the Bureau, and explains the evolving and changing program that is required for a well-watered prosperous land. This program also shows why the Bureau built multi-purpose projects such as Central Valley Project in California.

Availability: Schools, libraries, homeschoolers, nursing homes, and others in the United States and Canada.
Suggested Grade: 5-Adult
Order Number: order by title
Format: VHS videotape
Special Notes: May be copied for permanent retention. Cleared for TV broadcast with advance permission.
Terms: Borrowers pay return postage. Return 30 days after scheduled showing, via U.S. Mail. Book 30 days in advance. Up to 2 videos will be sent out to one customer at a time. Your next order will be mailed as soon as you return previously borrowed tapes.
Source: Bureau of Reclamation
U.S. Department of the Interior
Attn: Kristi Thompson, Library, 84-21320
6th Avenue & Kipling Street, Building 67
Denver, CO 80225-0007
Phone: 1-303-445-2039
Fax: 1-303-445-6303
World Wide Web URL: http://www.usbr.gov/library
Email Address: library@do.usbr.gov

Mountain Skywater

The Story of the Colorado River Basin Pilot Project in the San Juan Mountains, Colorado, is presented in this program. An overview of the cloud seeding program is included.

Availability: Schools, libraries, homeschoolers, nursing homes, and others in the United States and Canada.
Suggested Grade: 5-Adult
Order Number: order by title
Format: VHS videotape
Special Notes: May be copied for permanent retention. Cleared for TV broadcast with advance permission.
Terms: Borrowers pay return postage. Return 30 days after scheduled showing, via U.S. Mail. Book 30 days in advance. Up to 2 videos will be sent out to one customer at a time. Your next order will be mailed as soon as you return previously borrowed tapes.

Source: Bureau of Reclamation
U.S. Department of the Interior
Attn: Kristi Thompson, Library, 84-21320
6th Avenue & Kipling Street, Building 67
Denver, CO 80225-0007
Phone: 1-303-445-2039
Fax: 1-303-445-6303
World Wide Web URL: http://www.usbr.gov/library
Email Address: library@do.usbr.gov

One River, One Country

The border, as a place where the Mexican and American cultures, economies, communities, and destinies are merging.

Availability:	Schools, libraries, and nursing homes in the United States.
Suggested Grade:	6-12
Order Number:	SIMEX3-video
Format:	VHS videotape
Terms:	Borrowers must have a User's Agreement on file with this source--available by mail or via the Internet. Return postage is paid by borrower; return 12 days after showing. Book at least three weeks in advance. All borrowers are limited to a total of ten items per semester.

Source: Latin American Resource Center
Stone Center for Latin American Studies
Tulane University,
100 Jones Hall
New Orleans, LA 70118
Phone: 1-504-862-3143
Fax: 1-504-865-6719
World Wide Web URL:
http://stonecenter.tulane.edu/pages/detail/48/
Lending-Library
Email Address: crcrts@tulane.edu

Operation Glen Canyon

On the Colorado River you will see the first blast, the building of the world's highest steel bridge, and the construction of Glen Canyon Dam. The magnificent beauty of Glen Canyon is the backdrop for an achievement that serves a large community.

Availability:	Schools, libraries, homeschoolers, nursing homes, and others in the United States and Canada.
Suggested Grade:	All ages
Order Number:	order by title
Format:	VHS videotape
Special Notes:	May be copied for permanent retention. Cleared for TV broadcast with advance permission.
Terms:	Borrowers pay return postage. Return 30 days after scheduled showing, via U.S. Mail. Book 30 days in advance. Up to 2 videos will be sent out to one customer at a time. Your next order will be mailed as soon as you return previously borrowed tapes.

Source: Bureau of Reclamation
U.S. Department of the Interior
Attn: Kristi Thompson, Library, 84-21320
6th Avenue & Kipling Street, Building 67
Denver, CO 80225-0007
Phone: 1-303-445-2039
Fax: 1-303-445-6303
World Wide Web URL: http://www.usbr.gov/library
Email Address: library@do.usbr.gov

Performing "The Walrus Hunt"

Shows how students in Anchorage, Alaska, develop a song and dance to tell about a walrus hunt in order to connect with their ancestral culture.

Availability:	All requesters
Suggested Grade:	All ages
Order Number:	not applicable
Format:	Streaming Video

Source: Alaska Native Heritage Center
World Wide Web URL:
http://www.teachersdomain.org/resource/
echo07.lan.stories.walrus/

Portrait of America: Puerto Rico

Historical overview and possible options for the future.

Availability:	Schools, libraries, and nursing homes in the United States.
Suggested Grade:	6-12
Order Number:	IPUE3-video
Production Date:	1983
Format:	VHS videotape
Terms:	Borrowers must have a User's Agreement on file with this source--available by mail or via the Internet. Return postage is paid by borrower; return 12 days after showing. Book at least three weeks in advance. All borrowers are limited to a total of ten items per semester.

Source: Latin American Resource Center
Stone Center for Latin American Studies
Tulane University
100 Jones Hall
New Orleans, LA 70118
Phone: 1-504-862-3143
Fax: 1-504-865-6719
World Wide Web URL:
http://stonecenter.tulane.edu/pages/detail/48/
Lending-Library
Email Address: crcrts@tulane.edu

Quake, Bake and Shake

A study of the active earth.

Availability:	All requesters through interlibrary loan.
Suggested Grade:	4-Adult
Order Number:	210 Q343 1998 VIDEOC
Production Date:	1998
Format:	VHS videotape
Special Notes:	Includes a teacher's guide.
Terms:	These videotapes are available through interlibrary loan only. Simply request the specific video by name and number at your local public library, university library, or

*All materials listed in this 2011-2012 edition are **BRAND NEW!***

company library. The librarian will submit your request using an ALA interlibrary loan form, and the videos will be mailed to your library for your use. Interlibrary loans are limited to two videos at a time. The address listed below is for the ALA loan form only--your librarian must submit requests to this address.

Source: U. S. Geological Survey Library
345 Middlefield Road, MS 955
Menlo Park, CA 94025

Snowfall to Sandstone

Presents the history and development of the Colorado River Basin.

Availability:	Schools, libraries, homeschoolers, nursing homes, and others in the United States and Canada.
Suggested Grade:	4-12
Order Number:	order by title
Format:	VHS videotape
Special Notes:	May be copied for permanent retention. Cleared for TV broadcast with advance permission.
Terms:	Borrowers pay return postage. Return 30 days after scheduled showing, via U.S. Mail. Book 30 days in advance. Up to 2 videos will be sent out to one customer at a time. Your next order will be mailed as soon as you return previously borrowed tapes.

Source: Bureau of Reclamation
U.S. Department of the Interior
Attn: Kristi Thompson, Library, 84-21320
6th Avenue & Kipling Street, Building 67
Denver, CO 80225-0007
Phone: 1-303-445-2039
Fax: 1-303-445-6303
World Wide Web URL: http://www.usbr.gov/library
Email Address: library@do.usbr.gov

Southwest Region

Old photos, maps, graphics and more highlight the history, geography, capital, and more of four states--Arizona, New Mexico, Oklahoma, and Texas.

Availability:	Schools, libraries, and homeschoolers in the United States who serve the hearing impaired.
Suggested Grade:	3-9
Order Number:	13556
Production Date:	1998
Format:	DVD
Special Notes:	Also available as live streaming video over the Internet.
Terms:	Sponsor pays all transportation costs. Return one week after receipt. Participation is limited to deaf or hard of hearing Americans, their parents, families, teachers, counselors, or others whose use would benefit a deaf or hard of hearing person. Only one person in the audience needs to be hearing impaired. You must register--which is free. These videos are all open-captioned--no special equipment is required for viewing.

Source: Described and Captioned Media Program
National Association of the Deaf
4211 Church Street Ext.
Roebuck, SC 29376
Phone: 1-800-237-6213
Fax: 1-800-538-5636
World Wide Web URL: http://www.dcmp.org

Storm That Drowned a City

Experts and eyewitnesses reconstruct the devastating floods that Hurricane Katrina unleashed on New Orleans.

Availability:	All requesters
Suggested Grade:	7-Adult
Order Number:	not applicable
Production Date:	2005
Format:	Streaming Video

Source: NOVA
World Wide Web URL:
http://www.pbs.org/wgbh/nova/programs/index.html

Story of America's Great Volcanoes

Discusses the many volcanoes in our country.

Availability:	All requesters through interlibrary loan.
Suggested Grade:	7-Adult
Order Number:	220 (200) S867 1992 VIDEOC
Format:	VHS videotape
Terms:	These videotapes are available through interlibrary loan only. Simply request the specific video by name and number at your local public library, university library, or company library. The librarian will submit your request using an ALA interlibrary loan form, and the videos will be mailed to your library for your use. Interlibrary loans are limited to two videos at a time. The address listed below is for the ALA loan form only--your librarian must submit requests to this address.

Source: U. S. Geological Survey Library
345 Middlefield Road, MS 955
Menlo Park, CA 94025

Story of Hoover Dam, The

This program includes actual footage of the construction of Hoover Dam when it was being built in the 1930's.

Availability:	Schools, libraries, homeschoolers, nursing homes, and others in the United States and Canada.
Suggested Grade:	4-12
Order Number:	order by title
Format:	VHS videotape
Special Notes:	May be copied for permanent retention. Cleared for TV broadcast with advance permission.
Terms:	Borrowers pay return postage. Return 30 days after scheduled showing, via U.S. Mail. Book 30 days in advance. Up to 2 videos will be sent out to one customer at a time. Your next order will be mailed as soon as you return previously borrowed tapes.

Source: Bureau of Reclamation
U.S. Department of the Interior
Attn: Kristi Thompson, Library, 84-21320
6th Avenue & Kipling Street, Building 67
Denver, CO 80225-0007
Phone: 1-303-445-2039
Fax: 1-303-445-6303
World Wide Web URL: http://www.usbr.gov/library
Email Address: library@do.usbr.gov

Teton--Decision and Disaster

The Teton Range of the Rocky Mountains stretches from southeastern Idaho to northwestern Wyoming. It is truly the Grand Tetons. This videotape presentation details the background and reasons for the decision to build, and the disaster of Teton Dam, Idaho.

Availability:	Schools, libraries, homeschoolers, nursing homes, and others in the United States and Canada.
Suggested Grade:	4-12
Order Number:	order by title
Format:	VHS videotape
Special Notes:	May be copied for permanent retention. Cleared for TV broadcast with advance permission.
Terms:	Borrowers pay return postage. Return 30 days after scheduled showing, via U.S. Mail. Book 30 days in advance. Up to 2 videos will be sent out to one customer at a time. Your next order will be mailed as soon as you return previously borrowed tapes.

Source: Bureau of Reclamation
U.S. Department of the Interior
Attn: Kristi Thompson, Library, 84-21320
6th Avenue & Kipling Street, Building 67
Denver, CO 80225-0007
Phone: 1-303-445-2039
Fax: 1-303-445-6303
World Wide Web URL: http://www.usbr.gov/library
Email Address: library@do.usbr.gov

United States: Geography of a Nation (2nd Edition)

Presents an overview of the nine regions of the United States: New England, Mid-Atlantic, Southeast, South Central, North Central, Mountain West, Pacific West, and the unique states of Alaska and Hawaii. Describes each region's physical features, climate, natural resources, industries, and major occupations. Illustrates that the United States is a country with a wide range of physical characteristics which influence its citizens' lives.

Availability:	Schools, libraries, and homeschoolers in the United States who serve the hearing impaired.
Suggested Grade:	4-8
Order Number:	12928
Production Date:	1987
Format:	DVD
Special Notes:	Also available as live streaming video over the Internet.
Terms:	Sponsor pays all transportation costs. Return one week

after receipt. Participation is limited to deaf or hard of hearing Americans, their parents, families, teachers, counselors, or others whose use would benefit a deaf or hard of hearing person. Only one person in the audience needs to be hearing impaired. You must register--which is free. These videos are all open-captioned--no special equipment is required for viewing.

Source: Described and Captioned Media Program
National Association of the Deaf
4211 Church Street Ext.
Roebuck, SC 29376
Phone: 1-800-237-6213
Fax: 1-800-538-5636
World Wide Web URL: http://www.dcmp.org

Wings Over Water

Through stunning aerial cinematography this program introduces the largest state-built, multipurpose water project in the United States, the California State Water Project, a system of reservoirs, aqueducts, power and pumping plants spanning two-thirds of California, from the mountainous regions of the Feather River in Northern California, south over the 600 miles to Lake Perris.

Availability:	Schools, libraries, homeschoolers, and nursing homes in the United States.
Suggested Grade:	6-Adult
Order Number:	order by title
Format:	DVD
Special Notes:	A number of titles from this organization are included on this DVD.
Terms:	Borrower pays return postage. Return within 14 days after scheduled use, via UPS or Federal Express. Book at least 14 days in advance and include alternate date. Requests should include title(s), format, name of responsible person, organizational affiliation, phone, and complete delivery address. No part of any program can be used or duplicated without prior written permission. All programs are available for purchase at a nominal fee. May be available in other formats; inquire if interested. Online video previews are available.

Source: California Department of Water Resources
Attn: Video Library, Room 204-22
P. O. Box 942836
Sacramento, CA 94236-0001
Phone: 1-916-653-4893
Fax: 1-916-653-3310
World Wide Web URL: http://www.water.ca.gov/
Email Address: www.publicawillm@water.ca.gov

Wings Over Water

Through stunning aerial cinematography this program introduces the largest state-built, multipurpose water project in the United States, the California State Water Project, a system of reservoirs, aqueducts, power and pumping plants spanning two-thirds of California, from the mountainous regions of the Feather River in Northern California, south over the 600 miles to Lake Perris.

*All materials listed in this 2011-2012 edition are **BRAND NEW!***

Availability: Schools, libraries, homeschoolers, and nursing homes in the United States.

Suggested Grade: 6-Adult

Order Number: order by title

Production Date: 1997

Format: VHS videotape

Terms: Borrower pays return postage. Return within 14 days after scheduled use, via UPS or Federal Express. Book at least 14 days in advance and include alternate date. Requests should include title(s), format, name of responsible person, organizational affiliation, phone, and complete delivery address. No part of any program can be used or duplicated without prior written permission. All programs are available for purchase at a nominal fee. May be available in other formats; inquire if interested. Online video previews are available.

Source: California Department of Water Resources
Attn: Video Library, Room 204-22
P. O. Box 942836
Sacramento, CA 94236-0001
Phone: 1-916-653-4893
Fax: 1-916-653-3310
World Wide Web URL: http://www.water.ca.gov/
Email Address: www.publicawillm@water.ca.gov

SOCIAL STUDIES--GEOGRAPHY--WORLD

Africans, The: In Search of Stability

Ali Mazuri, from an African perspective, depicts several means of governing, asking which efforts have succeeded, which have failed, and why. Current unrest and new social orders are examined. The program explores Islamic and Westernized military regimes and examples of the one-party state.

Availability: Schools, libraries, homeschoolers, and nursing homes in the United States.
Suggested Grade: 7-Adult
Order Number: order by title
Production Date: 1986
Format: VHS videotape
Terms: Borrower pays return postage. Return the day after scheduled showing, via UPS or Priority Mail, insured for $100.00. Book 4 weeks in advance and include an alternate date. Order should include name of person responsible for handling the video, and complete mailing address. Please mention this Guide when ordering. Tapes may not be duplicated, edited or exhibited for a fee.

Source: Church World Service
Film & Video Library
28606 Phillips Street, P. O. Box 968
Elkhart, IN 46515
Phone: 1-800-297-1516, ext. 338
Fax: 1-574-262-0966
World Wide Web URL: http://www.churchworldservice.org
Email Address: videos@churchworldservice.org

Africans, The: Tools of Exploitation

Ali Mazuri examines how Africa's human and natural resources have been exploited before, during, and after the colonial period.

Availability: Schools, libraries, homeschoolers, and nursing homes in the United States.
Suggested Grade: 7-Adult
Order Number: order by title
Format: VHS videotape
Terms: Borrower pays return postage. Return the day after scheduled showing, via UPS or Priority Mail, insured for $100.00. Book 4 weeks in advance and include an alternate date. Order should include name of person responsible for handling the video, and complete mailing address. Please mention this Guide when ordering. Tapes may not be duplicated, edited or exhibited for a fee.

Source: Church World Service
Film & Video Library
28606 Phillips Street, P. O. Box 968
Elkhart, IN 46515
Phone: 1-800-297-1516, ext. 338
Fax: 1-574-262-0966
World Wide Web URL: http://www.churchworldservice.org
Email Address: videos@churchworldservice.org

Africa: South of the Sahara

Gives a broad overview of the countries of Africa that lie south of the Sahara desert.

Availability: Schools, libraries, and homeschoolers in the United States who serve the hearing impaired.
Suggested Grade: 7-10
Order Number: 12885
Production Date: 1999
Format: DVD
Special Notes: Also available as live streaming video over the Internet.
Terms: Sponsor pays all transportation costs. Return one week after receipt. Participation is limited to deaf or hard of hearing Americans, their parents, families, teachers, counselors, or others whose use would benefit a deaf or hard of hearing person. Only one person in the audience needs to be hearing impaired. You must register--which is free. These videos are all open-captioned--no special equipment is required for viewing.

Source: Described and Captioned Media Program
National Association of the Deaf
4211 Church Street Ext.
Roebuck, SC 29376
Phone: 1-800-237-6213
Fax: 1-800-538-5636
World Wide Web URL: http://www.dcmp.org

Alla Lejos y Hace Tiempo

Moving story of growing up in the pampas of Argentina.

Availability: Schools, libraries, and nursing homes in the United States.
Suggested Grade: 6-12
Languages: Spanish with English subtitles
Order Number: FFARG24-video
Production Date: 1974
Format: VHS videotape
Terms: Borrowers must have a User's Agreement on file with this source--available by mail or via the Internet. Return postage is paid by borrower; return 12 days after showing. Book at least three weeks in advance. All borrowers are limited to a total of ten items per semester.

Source: Latin American Resource Center
Stone Center for Latin American Studies
Tulane University
100 Jones Hall
New Orleans, LA 70118
Phone: 1-504-862-3143
Fax: 1-504-865-6719
World Wide Web URL:
http://stonecenter.tulane.edu/pages/detail/48/
Lending-Library
Email Address: crcrts@tulane.edu

Almost a Woman

A young woman, her mother and six siblings move from Puerto Rico to New York. The young woman is determined to overcome all the new challenges in her life including her new identity as an immigrant.

Availability: Schools and libraries in Iowa, Illinois, Michigan, Minnesota, and Wisconsin.
Suggested Grade: 7-12
Languages: Portuguese with subtitles

Order Number: FFPRAL6VHS
Production Date: 2002
Format: VHS videotape
Terms: Borrower pays return postage. Return 8 days after showing. Book 2 weeks in advance. Order may also be picked up for those near the Center.
Source: Center for Latin American and Caribbean Studies
UW-Milwaukee
P. O. Box 413
Milwaukee, WI 53201
Phone: 1-414-229-5987
World Wide Web URL: http://www.uwm.edu/Dept/CLACS
Email Address: audvis@usm.edu

Alpacas: An Andean Gamble

Focuses on the Inter-American Foundation and the Peruvian village of Aquia and its choice to raise alpaca herds.
Availability: Schools and libraries in the United States and Canada.
Suggested Grade: 6-12
Order Number: order by title
Production Date: 1988
Format: DVD
Terms: Videos will typically be lent for seven days if mailed out--due date will be indicated. Films not returned within the time limit will be subject to overdue fines of $2 per video, per day. All borrowed must have a lending agreement on file. Form can be downloaded from http://isa.unc.edu/film/borrow.asplaform. Borrowers are responsible for the cost of return shipping. Materials must be returned via a shipping method that has tracking information.
Source: Latin American Film Collection
3219 Fed Ex Global Education Center
301 Pittsboro Street, CB 3205
Chapel Hill, NC 27599-3205
Email Address: LA_Films@email.unc.edu

Alternatives Uncovered: "Moringa"

Discusses how the Moringa tree is proving to be an excellent, affordable, and locally accessible cure for malnutrition in parts of Senegal and beyond.
Availability: Schools, libraries, homeschoolers, and nursing homes in the United States.
Suggested Grade: 5-Adult
Order Number: order by title
Format: VHS videotape
Terms: Borrower pays return postage. Return the day after scheduled showing, via UPS or Priority Mail, insured for $100.00. Book 4 weeks in advance and include an alternate date. Order should include name of person responsible for handling the video, and complete mailing address. Please mention this Guide when ordering. Tapes may not be duplicated, edited or exhibited for a fee.
Source: Church World Service
Film & Video Library
28606 Phillips Street, P. O. Box 968
Elkhart, IN 46515

Phone: 1-800-297-1516, ext. 338
Fax: 1-574-262-0966
World Wide Web URL: http://www.churchworldservice.org
Email Address: videos@churchworldservice.org

Amazon

Four segments show development of the jungle rain forests and the industries that have developed in the forests.
Availability: Schools, libraries, and nursing homes in the United States.
Suggested Grade: 6-12
Order Number: GESA1-video
Production Date: 1985
Format: VHS videotape
Terms: Borrowers must have a User's Agreement on file with this source--available by mail or via the Internet. Return postage is paid by borrower; return 12 days after showing. Book at least three weeks in advance. All borrowers are limited to a total of ten items per semester.
Source: Latin American Resource Center
Stone Center for Latin American Studies
Tulane University
100 Jones Hall
New Orleans, LA 70118
Phone: 1-504-862-3143
Fax: 1-504-865-6719
World Wide Web URL:
http://stonecenter.tulane.edu/pages/detail/48/
Lending-Library
Email Address: crcrts@tulane.edu

Amazonia: Voices from the Rainforest

First person accounts, cinematography and an animation sequence give voice to the native peoples, as well as riverine dwellers, rubber tappers and small farmers, in their struggle to defend their homeland from extinction.
Availability: Schools and libraries in Iowa, Illinois, Michigan, Minnesota, and Wisconsin.
Suggested Grade: 6-12
Order Number: ENVAMZAM1.4VHS
Production Date: 1990
Format: VHS videotape
Terms: Borrower pays return postage. Return 8 days after showing. Book 2 weeks in advance. Order may also be picked up for those near the Center.
Source: Center for Latin American and Caribbean Studies
UW-Milwaukee
P. O. Box 413
Milwaukee, WI 53201
Phone: 1-414-229-5987
World Wide Web URL: http://www.uwm.edu/Dept/CLACS
Email Address: audvis@usm.edu

Amazon: Paradise Lost?

Efforts to balance economic development with the preservation of the Amazon region and its strategic contribution to the global ecosystem.
Availability: Schools, libraries, and nursing homes in the United States.

Suggested Grade: 6-12
Order Number: GESA6-video
Production Date: 1991
Format: VHS videotape
Terms: Borrowers must have a User's Agreement on file with this source--available by mail or via the Internet. Return postage is paid by borrower; return 12 days after showing. Book at least three weeks in advance. All borrowers are limited to a total of ten items per semester.
Source: Latin American Resource Center
Stone Center for Latin American Studies
Tulane University
100 Jones Hall
New Orleans, LA 70118
Phone: 1-504-862-3143
Fax: 1-504-865-6719
World Wide Web URL:
http://stonecenter.tulane.edu/pages/detail/48/
Lending-Library
Email Address: crcrts@tulane.edu

Amazon River Predators

Provides a general view of the Amazon Region with a focus on man and his role as a hunter.
Availability: Schools and libraries in Iowa, Illinois, Michigan, Minnesota, and Wisconsin.
Suggested Grade: 6-12
Order Number: ENVAMZAM1.3VHS
Format: VHS videotape
Special Notes: Produced by the Discovery Channel.
Terms: Borrower pays return postage. Return 8 days after showing. Book 2 weeks in advance. Order may also be picked up for those near the Center.
Source: Center for Latin American and Caribbean Studies
UW-Milwaukee
P. O. Box 413
Milwaukee, WI 53201
Phone: 1-414-229-5987
World Wide Web URL: http://www.uwm.edu/Dept/CLACS
Email Address: audvis@usm.edu

Amazon Sister

The human inhabitants of endangered rain forests, who are at times overlooked, are trying to preserve their homes in the face of inappropriate development.
Availability: Schools, libraries, and nursing homes in the United States.
Suggested Grade: 8-Adult
Languages: Spanish with English subtitles
Order Number: SISA1-video
Production Date: 1992
Format: VHS videotape
Terms: Borrowers must have a User's Agreement on file with this source--available by mail or via the Internet. Return postage is paid by borrower; return 12 days after showing. Book at least three weeks in advance. All borrowers are limited to a total of ten items per semester.

Source: Latin American Resource Center
Stone Center for Latin American Studies
Tulane University
100 Jones Hall
New Orleans, LA 70118
Phone: 1-504-862-3143
Fax: 1-504-865-6719
World Wide Web URL:
http://stonecenter.tulane.edu/pages/detail/48/
Lending-Library
Email Address: crcrts@tulane.edu

Amazon Steamboat

Travel through Brazil's Mato Grosso forests along the Rio Araguaia on a steam-powered raft.
Availability: Schools, libraries, and nursing homes in the United States.
Suggested Grade: 6-12
Order Number: GEBRA9-video
Production Date: 1989
Format: VHS videotape
Terms: Borrowers must have a User's Agreement on file with this source--available by mail or via the Internet. Return postage is paid by borrower; return 12 days after showing. Book at least three weeks in advance. All borrowers are limited to a total of ten items per semester.
Source: Latin American Resource Center
Stone Center for Latin American Studies
Tulane University
100 Jones Hall
New Orleans, LA 70118
Phone: 1-504-862-3143
Fax: 1-504-865-6719
World Wide Web URL:
http://stonecenter.tulane.edu/pages/detail/48/
Lending-Library
Email Address: crcrts@tulane.edu

Amazon, The

History of the Amazon River from its discovery in 1637 to modern times, as well as effects of industry and development.
Availability: Schools, libraries, and nursing homes in the United States.
Suggested Grade: 6-12
Order Number: GESA7-video
Production Date: 1991
Format: VHS videotape
Terms: Borrowers must have a User's Agreement on file with this source--available by mail or via the Internet. Return postage is paid by borrower; return 12 days after showing. Book at least three weeks in advance. All borrowers are limited to a total of ten items per semester.
Source: Latin American Resource Center
Stone Center for Latin American Studies
Tulane University
100 Jones Hall
New Orleans, LA 70118
Phone: 1-504-862-3143

Fax: 1-504-865-6719
World Wide Web URL:
http://stonecenter.tulane.edu/pages/detail/48/
Lending-Library
Email Address: crcrts@tulane.edu

Amazon, The: Heaven, Hell, and El Dorado--South American Journey 4

Plight of Indians, the failed rubber industry, and deforestation from Peru to Manaus, Brazil.

Availability: Schools, libraries, and nursing homes in the United States.
Suggested Grade: 6-12
Order Number: GESA4-video
Production Date: 1987
Format: VHS videotape
Terms: Borrowers must have a User's Agreement on file with this source--available by mail or via the Internet. Return postage is paid by borrower; return 12 days after showing. Book at least three weeks in advance. All borrowers are limited to a total of ten items per semester.
Source: Latin American Resource Center
Stone Center for Latin American Studies
Tulane University
100 Jones Hall
New Orleans, LA 70118
Phone: 1-504-862-3143
Fax: 1-504-865-6719
World Wide Web URL:
http://stonecenter.tulane.edu/pages/detail/48/
Lending-Library
Email Address: crcrts@tulane.edu

Ancient Futures: Learning from Ladakh

Ladakh, or "Little Tibet" is a wildly beautiful desert land, high in the western Himalayas. It is a place of few resources and an extreme climate. For more than a thousand years it has been home to a thriving culture. Then came "development" and with it pollution and devisiveness, inflation and unemployment, intolerance and greed. Centuries of ecological balance and social harmony are under threat from modernization.

Availability: Schools, libraries, homeschoolers, and nursing homes in the United States.
Suggested Grade: 6-12
Order Number: order by title
Format: VHS videotape
Terms: Borrower pays return postage. Return the day after scheduled showing, via UPS or Priority Mail, insured for $100.00. Book 4 weeks in advance and include an alternate date. Order should include name of person responsible for handling the video, and complete mailing address. Please mention this Guide when ordering. Tapes may not be duplicated, edited or exhibited for a fee.
Source: Church World Service
Film & Video Library
28606 Phillips Street, P. O. Box 968
Elkhart, IN 46515

Phone: 1-800-297-1516, ext. 338
Fax: 1-574-262-0966
World Wide Web URL: http://www.churchworldservice.org
Email Address: videos@churchworldservice.org

Archaeological Yucatan: Land of the Maya

Tourist guide to the Mayan ruins, followed by the travel, hotel, and restaurant segment.

Availability: Schools, libraries, and nursing homes in the United States.
Suggested Grade: 6-12
Order Number: MY25-video
Production Date: 1987
Format: VHS videotape
Terms: Borrowers must have a User's Agreement on file with this source--available by mail or via the Internet. Return postage is paid by borrower; return 12 days after showing. Book at least three weeks in advance. All borrowers are limited to a total of ten items per semester.
Source: Latin American Resource Center
Stone Center for Latin American Studies
Tulane University
100 Jones Hall
New Orleans, LA 70118
Phone: 1-504-862-3143
Fax: 1-504-865-6719
World Wide Web URL:
http://stonecenter.tulane.edu/pages/detail/48/
Lending-Library
Email Address: crcrts@tulane.edu

Arctic to Amazonia

Native activists from North and South America present information on impact of industrial development on their land and cultures.

Availability: Schools, libraries, and nursing homes in the United States.
Suggested Grade: 6-12
Order Number: IND5-video
Production Date: 1993
Format: VHS videotape
Terms: Borrowers must have a User's Agreement on file with this source--available by mail or via the Internet. Return postage is paid by borrower; return 12 days after showing. Book at least three weeks in advance. All borrowers are limited to a total of ten items per semester.
Source: Latin American Resource Center
Stone Center for Latin American Studies
Tulane University
100 Jones Hall
New Orleans, LA 70118
Phone: 1-504-862-3143
Fax: 1-504-865-6719
World Wide Web URL:
http://stonecenter.tulane.edu/pages/detail/48/
Lending-Library
Email Address: crcrts@tulane.edu

Argentina

Images of Argentina without narration, includes Buenos Aires, Patagonia, the coast, the highlands, Cuyo and Cordoba and the northeastern segment of Argentina.

Availability: Schools in the United States.
Suggested Grade: 7-12
Order Number: order by title
Production Date: 1988
Format: VHS videotape
Terms: Borrower pays return postage. Return 14 days after receipt, via USPS including insurance. All borrowers must have a current lending agreement on file with the Outreach program. This agreement is available via the web site or may be requested via phone or fax.
Source: Center for Latin American Studies
University of Florida
319 Grinter Hall
P. O. Box 115530
Gainesville, FL 32611-5530
Phone: 1-352-392-0375
Fax: 1-352-392-7682
World Wide Web URL: http://www.latam.ufl.edu/outreach
Email Address: maryr@ufl.edu

Argentina: Land of Natural Wonders

Journey through Argentina's deserts, rainforests, and rocky shores of Pategonia.

Availability: Schools, libraries, and nursing homes in the United States.
Suggested Grade: 6-12
Order Number: GEARG1-video
Production Date: 1990
Format: VHS videotape
Terms: Borrowers must have a User's Agreement on file with this source--available by mail or via the Internet. Return postage is paid by borrower; return 12 days after showing. Book at least three weeks in advance. All borrowers are limited to a total of ten items per semester.
Source: Latin American Resource Center
Stone Center for Latin American Studies
Tulane University
100 Jones Hall
New Orleans, LA 70118
Phone: 1-504-862-3143
Fax: 1-504-865-6719
World Wide Web URL:
http://stonecenter.tulane.edu/pages/detail/48/
Lending-Library
Email Address: crcrts@tulane.edu

Argentine Journey, An

Series features musical and cultural heritage of three regions in Argentina. A. Songs of the Gauchos. B. Songs of the Argentine provinces. C. Songs of the Poor.

Availability: Schools, libraries, and nursing homes in the United States.
Suggested Grade: 6-12
Order Number: MUARG8-video
Production Date: 1998

Format: VHS videotape
Special Notes: Specify program when ordering.
Terms: Borrowers must have a User's Agreement on file with this source--available by mail or via the Internet. Return postage is paid by borrower; return 12 days after showing. Book at least three weeks in advance. All borrowers are limited to a total of ten items per semester.
Source: Latin American Resource Center
Stone Center for Latin American Studies
Tulane University
100 Jones Hall
New Orleans, LA 70118
Phone: 1-504-862-3143
Fax: 1-504-865-6719
World Wide Web URL:
http://stonecenter.tulane.edu/pages/detail/48/
Lending-Library
Email Address: crcrts@tulane.edu

Around South America

Takes you on a journey around this continent to show culture and geography of different regions.

Availability: Schools in the United States.
Suggested Grade: 7-12
Order Number: order by title
Production Date: 1987
Format: VHS videotape
Terms: Borrower pays return postage. Return 14 days after receipt, via USPS including insurance. All borrowers must have a current lending agreement on file with the Outreach program. This agreement is available via the web site or may be requested via phone or fax.
Source: Center for Latin American Studies
University of Florida
319 Grinter Hall
P. O. Box 115530
Gainesville, FL 32611-5530
Phone: 1-352-392-0375
Fax: 1-352-392-7682
World Wide Web URL: http://www.latam.ufl.edu/outreach
Email Address: maryr@ufl.edu

Arranged Marriages

A Westerner explores the institution of arranged marriages with her married Indian friends. She finds that there are many variations in the way these marriages are arranged, but in all cases, the marriage is a family matter, often used to reinforce the social standing of the family, and to preserve values from generation to generation.

Availability: Schools, libraries, homeschoolers, and nursing homes in the southeastern United States.
Suggested Grade: 7-12
Order Number: order by title
Production Date: 2003
Format: VHS videotape
Terms: Borrower pays return postage. Return 2 days after showing via United Parcel Service, insured. Book 2 weeks in advance.

Source: Center for South Asian Studies
University of Virginia
Video Library Coordinator
P. O. Box 400169, 110 Minor Hall
Charlottesville, VA 22904-4169
Phone: 1-434-924-8815
Email Address: southasia@virginia.edu

Awaji, Japan Trip

Trip made by Professor Jane Marie Law to Awaji, a small island of Japan.

Availability: Schools, libraries, and nursing homes in the United States and Canada.
Suggested Grade: 6-Adult
Order Number: JV055
Format: VHS videotape
Terms: Borrower pays return postage. Return with 14 days after scheduled showing, via UPS or U. S. Mail. All requests must included an educational institution affiliation, a current address, and phone number. Order through web site only.

Source: Cornell University East Asia Program
World Wide Web URL:
http://www.einaudi.cornell.edu/eastasia/outreach/video.asp
Email Address: east_asia1@cornell.edu

Azucar Amarga (Bitter Sugar)

Contemporary look at Cuba depicts the relationship between Gustavo, an idealistic young Communist, and Yolanda, a disenchanted dancer who longs to escape to Miami.

Availability: Schools, libraries, and nursing homes in the United States.
Suggested Grade: 6-12
Languages: Spanish with English subtitles
Order Number: FFCUB24-video
Production Date: 1996
Format: VHS videotape
Terms: Borrowers must have a User's Agreement on file with this source--available by mail or via the Internet. Return postage is paid by borrower; return 12 days after showing. Book at least three weeks in advance. All borrowers are limited to a total of ten items per semester.

Source: Latin American Resource Center
Stone Center for Latin American Studies
Tulane University
100 Jones Hall
New Orleans, LA 70118
Phone: 1-504-862-3143
Fax: 1-504-865-6719
World Wide Web URL:
http://stonecenter.tulane.edu/pages/detail/48/
Lending-Library
Email Address: crcrts@tulane.edu

Banana Company, The

Exploration of Nicaragua's banana plantations.

Availability: Schools and libraries in Iowa, Illinois, Michigan, Minnesota, and Wisconsin.
Suggested Grade: 6-12

Languages: Spanish with English subtitles
Order Number: DEV/ECB22.2VHS
Production Date: 1982
Format: VHS videotape
Terms: Borrower pays return postage. Return 8 days after showing. Book 2 weeks in advance. Order may also be picked up for those near the Center.

Source: Center for Latin American and Caribbean Studies
UW-Milwaukee
P. O. Box 413
Milwaukee, WI 53201
Phone: 1-414-229-5987
World Wide Web URL: http://www.uwm.edu/Dept/CLACS
Email Address: audvis@usm.edu

Beauty Reborn

Construction of the Katsura Villa, one of Japan's most precious cultural relics, took place over a 50-year period during the seventeenth century. From 1976-1982, the villa was completely dismantled and repaired. This is a documentary of those six years

Availability: Schools, libraries and homeschoolers in Alabama, Georgia, North Carolina, South Carolina, and Virginia.
Suggested Grade: 4-12
Order Number: 707
Production Date: 1991
Format: VHS videotape
Special Notes: Part of the "Nippon Life II" series.
Terms: Borrower pays return postage. Two tapes may be borrowed at a time. Return within 7 days after receipt. Reservations may be made by filling the application found on the web site.

Source: Consulate General of Japan, Atlanta
Japan Information Center
One Alliance Center
3500 Lenox Road, Suite 1600
Atlanta, GA 30326
Phone: 1-404-365-9240
Fax: 1-404-240-4311
World Wide Web URL:
http://www.atlanta.us.emb-japan.go.jp
Email Address: info@cgjapanatlanta.org

Beauty Reborn

Construction of the Katsura Villa, one of Japan's most precious cultural relics, took place over a 50-year period during the seventeenth century. From 1976-1982, the villa was completely dismantled and repaired. This is a documentary of those six years

Availability: Schools, libraries, and nursing homes in Hawaii.
Suggested Grade: 4-12
Order Number: CU-32
Format: VHS videotape
Special Notes: Part of the "Nippon Life II" series.
Terms: Borrower pays return postage. A maximum of 3 videos may be borrowed per person. Return within one week of date borrowed.

Source: Consulate General of Japan, Honolulu
1742 Nuuanu Avenue
Honolulu, HI 96817-3294
Phone: 1-808-543-3111
Fax: 1-808-543-3170
World Wide Web URL:
http://www.honolulu.us.emb-japan.go.jp

Beauty Reborn

Construction of the Katsura Villa, one of Japan's most precious cultural relics, took place over a 50-year period during the seventeenth century. From 1976-1982, the villa was completely dismantled and repaired. This is a documentary of those six years

Availability: Schools, libraries, homeschoolers, and nursing homes in OREGON AND SOUTHERN IDAHO ONLY. Please make requests via the web site.
Suggested Grade: 4-12
Order Number: 177
Production Date: 1991
Format: VHS videotape
Special Notes: Part of the "Nippon Life II" series.
Terms: Borrower pays return postage. Return within three weeks after scheduled showing date. Book one month in advance if possible. Rewind the video and wrap securely for return. Be certain to indicate video number, date needed, name of your organization, and address to which video should be sent, along with phone number. Audience report enclosed with the video must be completed and returned.
Source: Consulate General of Japan, Oregon
Attn: Tamara, Video Library
1300 S. W. Fifth Avenue, Suite 2700
Portland, OR 97201
Phone: 1-503-221-1811, ext. 17
World Wide Web URL:
http://www.portland.us.emb-japan.go.jp/en/index.html
Email Address: tamara@cgjpdx.org

Belize, British Honduras

Shows general patterns of culture.
Availability: Schools, libraries, and nursing homes in the United States.
Suggested Grade: 6-12
Order Number: IBEL1-video
Production Date: 1970
Format: VHS videotape
Terms: Borrowers must have a User's Agreement on file with this source--available by mail or via the Internet. Return postage is paid by borrower; return 12 days after showing. Book at least three weeks in advance. All borrowers are limited to a total of ten items per semester.
Source: Latin American Resource Center
Stone Center for Latin American Studies
Tulane University
100 Jones Hall
New Orleans, LA 70118
Phone: 1-504-862-3143

Fax: 1-504-865-6719
World Wide Web URL:
http://stonecenter.tulane.edu/pages/detail/48/
Lending-Library
Email Address: crcrts@tulane.edu

Belize: Towards Independence

Discusses British colonization of Belize, political considerations and economic development.
Availability: Schools, libraries, and nursing homes in the United States.
Suggested Grade: 6-12
Order Number: HCBEL1-video
Production Date: 1975
Format: VHS videotape
Terms: Borrowers must have a User's Agreement on file with this source--available by mail or via the Internet. Return postage is paid by borrower; return 12 days after showing. Book at least three weeks in advance. All borrowers are limited to a total of ten items per semester.
Source: Latin American Resource Center
Stone Center for Latin American Studies
Tulane University
100 Jones Hall
New Orleans, LA 70118
Phone: 1-504-862-3143
Fax: 1-504-865-6719
World Wide Web URL:
http://stonecenter.tulane.edu/pages/detail/48/
Lending-Library
Email Address: crcrts@tulane.edu

Big Bird in China

Big Bird and Barkley follow clues to find the Phoenix in the tree. They search Beijing, along the Great Wall, aboard a boat on the Li River and many other sites until they discover the secret.
Availability: Schools, libraries, homeschoolers, and nursing homes in the United States and Canada.
Suggested Grade: K-4
Order Number: order by title
Format: VHS videotape
Special Notes: Follows the book by the same name.
Terms: Postage is paid by borrower both ways--send $3.00 per tape to cover initial shipping to you--MONEY MUST BE SENT WITH REQUEST. Return 10 days after showing via U. S. Postal Service, library rate. Shipping is $5.00 to Canadian addresses.
Source: Center for Teaching About China
Kathleen Trescott
1214 West Schwartz
Carbondale, IL 62901
Phone: 1-618-549-1555
Email Address: trescott@midwest.net

Bosque Eterno de los Ninos

Experience the rich green world of the international children's rain forest in Costa Rica.

Availability: Schools and libraries in Iowa, Illinois, Michigan, Minnesota, and Wisconsin.
Suggested Grade: 6-12
Order Number: ENVCRB65.1VHS
Format: VHS videotape
Terms: Borrower pays return postage. Return 8 days after showing. Book 2 weeks in advance. Order may also be picked up for those near the Center.

Source: Center for Latin American and Caribbean Studies
UW-Milwaukee
P. O. Box 413
Milwaukee, WI 53201
Phone: 1-414-229-5987
World Wide Web URL: http://www.uwm.edu/Dept/CLACS
Email Address: audvis@usm.edu

Bosque Tropical

The lush tropical rainforest is the home of almost one-half of all animal species in the world, approximately 5 million different forms of life. In this video you will travel to the rainforests of Costa Rica, and learn about the life that lies within.

Availability: Schools and libraries in Iowa, Illinois, Michigan, Minnesota, and Wisconsin.
Suggested Grade: 6-12
Language: Spanish
Order Number: ENVCRB65.2VHS
Production Date: 1983
Format: VHS videotape
Terms: Borrower pays return postage. Return 8 days after showing. Book 2 weeks in advance. Order may also be picked up for those near the Center.

Source: Center for Latin American and Caribbean Studies
UW-Milwaukee
P. O. Box 413
Milwaukee, WI 53201
Phone: 1-414-229-5987
World Wide Web URL: http://www.uwm.edu/Dept/CLACS
Email Address: audvis@usm.edu

Brazil: An Inconvenient History

Using contemporary accounts, the video reconstructs the world as seen by slaves in Brazil over 300 years.

Availability: Schools and libraries in Iowa, Illinois, Michigan, Minnesota, and Wisconsin.
Suggested Grade: 6-12
Order Number: AFRICABRAB73VHS
Production Date: 2000
Format: VHS videotape
Terms: Borrower pays return postage. Return 8 days after showing. Book 2 weeks in advance. Order may also be picked up for those near the Center.

Source: Center for Latin American and Caribbean Studies
UW-Milwaukee
P. O. Box 413
Milwaukee, WI 53201
Phone: 1-414-229-5987
World Wide Web URL: http://www.uwm.edu/Dept/CLACS
Email Address: audvis@usm.edu

Brazil's Independence Day Celebration

Shows the Brazil Independence Day celebration at Alterra at the Lakefront in 2004.

Availability: Schools and libraries in Iowa, Illinois, Michigan, Minnesota, and Wisconsin.
Suggested Grade: All ages
Order Number: DANUSABRAE73DVD
Production Date: 2004
Format: DVD
Terms: Borrower pays return postage. Return 8 days after showing. Book 2 weeks in advance. Order may also be picked up for those near the Center.

Source: Center for Latin American and Caribbean Studies
UW-Milwaukee
P. O. Box 413
Milwaukee, WI 53201
Phone: 1-414-229-5987
World Wide Web URL: http://www.uwm.edu/Dept/CLACS
Email Address: audvis@usm.edu

Bushido: Way of the Warrior

Bushido was the moral code that regulated the behavior and relationships between the samurai and their feudal lords, including concepts of loyalty, duty, and self-sacrifice.

Availability: Schools, libraries and homeschoolers in Alabama, Georgia, North Carolina, South Carolina, and Virginia.
Suggested Grade: 4-12
Order Number: 533
Production Date: 1995
Format: VHS videotape
Special Notes: No. 3 of the "Nihon No Kokoro" series.
Terms: Borrower pays return postage. Two tapes may be borrowed at a time. Return within 7 days after receipt. Reservations may be made by filling the application found on the web site.

Source: Consulate General of Japan, Atlanta
Japan Information Center
One Alliance Center
3500 Lenox Road, Suite 1600
Atlanta, GA 30326
Phone: 1-404-365-9240
Fax: 1-404-240-4311
World Wide Web URL:
http://www.atlanta.us.emb-japan.go.jp
Email Address: info@cgjapanatlanta.org

Bushido: Way of the Warrior

Bushido was the moral code that regulated the behavior and relationships between the samurai and their feudal lords, including concepts of loyalty, duty, and self-sacrifice.

Availability: Schools, libraries, and nursing homes in Hawaii.
Suggested Grade: 4-12
Order Number: CU-113
Production Date: 1995
Format: VHS videotape
Special Notes: No. 3 of the "Nihon No Kokoro" series.

Terms: Borrower pays return postage. A maximum of 3 videos may be borrowed per person. Return within one week of date borrowed.

Source: Consulate General of Japan, Honolulu
1742 Nuuanu Avenue
Honolulu, HI 96817-3294
Phone: 1-808-543-3111
Fax: 1-808-543-3170
World Wide Web URL:
http://www.honolulu.us.emb-japan.go.jp

Bushido: Way of the Warrior

Bushido was the moral code that regulated the behavior and relationships between the samurai and their feudal lords, including concepts of loyalty, duty, and self-sacrifice.

Availability: Schools, libraries, homeschoolers, and nursing homes in OREGON AND SOUTHERN IDAHO ONLY. Please make requests via the web site.
Suggested Grade: 4-12
Order Number: 352
Production Date: 1995
Format: VHS videotape
Special Notes: No. 3 of the "Nihon No Kokoro" series.
Terms: Borrower pays return postage. Return within three weeks after scheduled showing date. Book one month in advance if possible. Rewind the video and wrap securely for return. Be certain to indicate video number, date needed, name of your organization, and address to which video should be sent, along with phone number. Audience report enclosed with the video must be completed and returned.

Source: Consulate General of Japan, Oregon
Attn: Tamara, Video Library
1300 S. W. Fifth Avenue, Suite 2700
Portland, OR 97201
Phone: 1-503-221-1811, ext. 17
World Wide Web URL:
http://www.portland.us.emb-japan.go.jp/en/index.html
Email Address: tamara@cgjpdx.org

Bye Bye Brazil

Swallow, the muscle king; Salome, queen of the Rhumba; Lord Gypsy himself, and a country about to come to an end to make way for another about to begin.

Availability: Schools and libraries in Iowa, Illinois, Michigan, Minnesota, and Wisconsin.
Suggested Grade: 6-12
Languages: Portuguese with English subtitles
Order Number: FFBRAB99.1VHS
Production Date: 1980
Format: VHS videotape
Terms: Borrower pays return postage. Return 8 days after showing. Book 2 weeks in advance. Order may also be picked up for those near the Center.

Source: Center for Latin American and Caribbean Studies
UW-Milwaukee
P. O. Box 413
Milwaukee, WI 53201

Phone: 1-414-229-5987
World Wide Web URL: http://www.uwm.edu/Dept/CLACS
Email Address: audvis@usm.edu

Cartas del Parque

Questions the compatibility of Latin American culture with the values of the "modern" world.

Availability: Schools, libraries, and nursing homes in the United States.
Suggested Grade: 6-12
Languages: Spanish with English subtitles
Order Number: FFSPA8-video
Production Date: 1988
Format: VHS videotape
Terms: Borrowers must have a User's Agreement on file with this source--available by mail or via the Internet. Return postage is paid by borrower; return 12 days after showing. Book at least three weeks in advance. All borrowers are limited to a total of ten items per semester.

Source: Latin American Resource Center
Stone Center for Latin American Studies
Tulane University
100 Jones Hall
New Orleans, LA 70118
Phone: 1-504-862-3143
Fax: 1-504-865-6719
World Wide Web URL:
http://stonecenter.tulane.edu/pages/detail/48/
Lending-Library
Email Address: crcrts@tulane.edu

Cathedral at Puebla, Mexico

Plans were drawn up by architect Juan de Hererra and approved in 1562 by Philip II.

Availability: Schools, libraries, and nursing homes in the United States.
Suggested Grade: 6-12
Order Number: ACMEX12-video
Production Date: 1989
Format: VHS videotape
Terms: Borrowers must have a User's Agreement on file with this source--available by mail or via the Internet. Return postage is paid by borrower; return 12 days after showing. Book at least three weeks in advance. All borrowers are limited to a total of ten items per semester.

Source: Latin American Resource Center
Stone Center for Latin American Studies
Tulane University
100 Jones Hall
New Orleans, LA 70118
Phone: 1-504-862-3143
Fax: 1-504-865-6719
World Wide Web URL:
http://stonecenter.tulane.edu/pages/detail/48/
Lending-Library
Email Address: crcrts@tulane.edu

Celebration: A Caribbean Festival

Residents of the largest Caribbean community in the U.S.

prepare and celebrate Carnival to continue cultural traditions.

Availability: Schools and libraries in Iowa, Illinois, Michigan, Minnesota, and Wisconsin.
Suggested Grade: 6-12
Order Number: FESTUSC33VHS
Production Date: 1988
Format: VHS videotape
Terms: Borrower pays return postage. Return 8 days after showing. Book 2 weeks in advance. Order may also be picked up for those near the Center.
Source: **Center for Latin American and Caribbean Studies**
UW-Milwaukee
P. O. Box 413
Milwaukee, WI 53201
Phone: 1-414-229-5987
World Wide Web URL: http://www.uwm.edu/Dept/CLACS
Email Address: audvis@usm.edu

Celebration: A Caribbean Festival

Residents of the largest Caribbean community in the U.S. prepare and celebrate Carnival to continue cultural traditions.

Availability: Schools, libraries, and nursing homes in the United States.
Suggested Grade: 6-12
Order Number: DFUS1-video
Production Date: 1988
Format: VHS videotape
Terms: Borrowers must have a User's Agreement on file with this source--available by mail or via the Internet. Return postage is paid by borrower; return 12 days after showing. Book at least three weeks in advance. All borrowers are limited to a total of ten items per semester.
Source: **Latin American Resource Center**
Stone Center for Latin American Studies
Tulane University
100 Jones Hall
New Orleans, LA 70118
Phone: 1-504-862-3143
Fax: 1-504-865-6719
World Wide Web URL:
http://stonecenter.tulane.edu/pages/detail/48/
Lending-Library
Email Address: crcrts@tulane.edu

Central African Republic

The Central African Republic lies in the heart of Africa, remote and isolated. Briefly explores its geography, trade and transportation, and history. Shows the pygmy culture and the importance of the rain forest. Reviews government, religion, climate, exports, rulers, and population. Though rich in natural resources, the country's recent leadership has laid no plans for its brighter potential future. NOTE: some nudity.

Availability: Schools, libraries, and homeschoolers in the United States who serve the hearing impaired.
Suggested Grade: 7-12

Order Number: 12337
Production Date: 1994
Format: DVD
Special Notes: Produced by ACG/United Learning.
Terms: Sponsor pays all transportation costs. Return one week after receipt. Participation is limited to deaf or hard of hearing Americans, their parents, families, teachers, counselors, or others whose use would benefit a deaf or hard of hearing person. Only one person in the audience needs to be hearing impaired. You must register--which is free. These videos are all open-captioned--no special equipment is required for viewing.
Source: **Described and Captioned Media Program**
National Association of the Deaf
4211 Church Street Ext.
Roebuck, SC 29376
Phone: 1-800-237-6213
Fax: 1-800-538-5636
World Wide Web URL: http://www.dcmp.org

Central America Close-Up 1

Two portraits of contemporary youth in nations in conflict. Jeramias, a Guatemalan teen, and Flor, an El Salvadoran teen, both flee war in this video focusing on youth.

Availability: Schools in the United States.
Suggested Grade: 7-Adult
Order Number: order by title
Format: VHS videotape
Terms: Borrower pays return postage. Return 14 days after receipt, via USPS including insurance. All borrowers must have a current lending agreement on file with the Outreach program. This agreement is available via the web site or may be requested via phone or fax.
Source: **Center for Latin American Studies**
University of Florida
319 Grinter Hall
P. O. Box 115530
Gainesville, FL 32611-5530
Phone: 1-352-392-0375
Fax: 1-352-392-7682
World Wide Web URL: http://www.latam.ufl.edu/outreach
Email Address: maryr@ufl.edu

Central America Close-Up 1

Two portraits of contemporary youth in nations in conflict. Jeramias, a Guatemalan teen, and Flor, an El Salvadoran teen, both flee war in this video focusing on youth.

Availability: Schools and libraries in the United States and Canada.
Suggested Grade: 7-Adult
Order Number: order by title
Format: VHS videotape
Terms: Videos will typically be lent for seven days if mailed out--due date will be indicated. Films not returned within the time limit will be subject to overdue fines of $2 per video, per day. All borrowed must have a lending agreement on file. Form can be downloaded from http://isa.unc.edu/film/borrow.asplaform. Borrowers are responsible for the cost of return

shipping. Materials must be returned via a shipping method that has tracking information.

Source: Latin American Film Collection
3219 Fed Ex Global Education Center
301 Pittsboro Street, CB 3205
Chapel Hill, NC 27599-3205
Email Address: LA_Films@email.unc.edu

Central American Children Speak: Our Lives and Our Dreams

Questions by fourth graders who have been studying Central America guide the video. Viewers then travel to Central America, where they are introduced to children in Guatemala and Nicaragua, who share their dreams, fears, and hopes for peace. The children discover that despite the differences in their lives, all children have similar hopes and dreams.

Availability: Schools and libraries in Iowa, Illinois, Michigan, Minnesota, and Wisconsin.
Suggested Grade: 1-8
Languages: English; Spanish
Order Number: CHIGUA/NICC32.1VHS
Production Date: 1993
Format: VHS videotape
Terms: Borrower pays return postage. Return 8 days after showing. Book 2 weeks in advance. Order may also be picked up for those near the Center.

Source: Center for Latin American and Caribbean Studies
UW-Milwaukee
P. O. Box 413
Milwaukee, WI 53201
Phone: 1-414-229-5987
World Wide Web URL: http://www.uwm.edu/Dept/CLACS
Email Address: audvis@usm.edu

Central America Today: Nations in Transition

Four-part program introduces issues, economics, and cultures of seven Central American countries.

Availability: Schools, libraries, and nursing homes in the United States.
Suggested Grade: 6-12
Order Number: HCCA11-video
Production Date: 1987
Format: VHS videotape
Special Notes: Includes guide with discussion questions.
Terms: Borrowers must have a User's Agreement on file with this source--available by mail or via the Internet. Return postage is paid by borrower; return 12 days after showing. Book at least three weeks in advance. All borrowers are limited to a total of ten items per semester.

Source: Latin American Resource Center
Stone Center for Latin American Studies
Tulane University
100 Jones Hall
New Orleans, LA 70118
Phone: 1-504-862-3143
Fax: 1-504-865-6719

World Wide Web URL:

http://stonecenter.tulane.edu/pages/detail/48/
Lending-Library
Email Address: crcrts@tulane.edu

Children Creating Peace

Features a Global Peace Village where school children from Calcutta, India portray people from 15 countries through songs, dances and displays.

Availability: Schools, libraries, homeschoolers, and nursing homes in the United States.
Suggested Grade: 1-6
Order Number: order by title
Production Date: 1991
Format: VHS videotape
Terms: Borrower pays return postage. Return the day after scheduled showing, via UPS or Priority Mail, insured for $100.00. Book 4 weeks in advance and include an alternate date. Order should include name of person responsible for handling the video, and complete mailing address. Please mention this Guide when ordering. Tapes may not be duplicated, edited or exhibited for a fee.

Source: Church World Service
Film & Video Library
28606 Phillips Street, P. O. Box 968
Elkhart, IN 46515
Phone: 1-800-297-1516, ext. 338
Fax: 1-574-262-0966
World Wide Web URL: http://www.churchworldservice.org
Email Address: videos@churchworldservice.org

Children of the Mountains

The Negrito children of the Zambales Mountains are so different from us in what they have, but very much like us in what they need: to eat, sleep, play and learn. This emphasizes the religious learning provided by the Columban Fathers to the Negritos.

Availability: Schools, libraries, homeschoolers, church groups, nursing homes, and service clubs in the United States.
Suggested Grade: K-6
Order Number: order by title
Format: VHS videotape
Special Notes: A study guide is provided.
Terms: Borrower pays return postage. Return within 21 days after receipt. Book at least 3 weeks in advance. You will be notified as soon as possible, if your order cannot be filled. All videos are cleared for television broadcast use.

Source: Columban Fathers Mission Society
Mission Education Department
Attn: Connie Wacha
P. O. Box 10
St. Columbans, NE 68056
Phone: 1-402-291-1920
Fax: 1-402-715-5575
World Wide Web URL: http://columban.org/missioned

*All materials listed in this 2011-2012 edition are **BRAND NEW!***

China and the Forbidden City

Spell-binding tale captures life within China as it was in 1963 and had been for hundreds of years. Walk the streets and lanes of Beijing. Feel the excitement.

Availability:	Schools, libraries, homeschoolers, and nursing homes in the United States and Canada.
Suggested Grade:	6-Adult
Order Number:	order by title
Production Date:	1983
Format:	VHS videotape
Terms:	Postage is paid by borrower both ways--send $3.00 per tape to cover initial shipping to you--MONEY MUST BE SENT WITH REQUEST. Return 10 days after showing via U. S. Postal Service, library rate. Shipping is $5.00 to Canadian addresses.

Source: Center for Teaching About China
Kathleen Trescott
1214 West Schwartz
Carbondale, IL 62901
Phone: 1-618-549-1555
Email Address: trescott@midwest.net

China and the Forbidden City: The Great Within

Cameras roam the Forbidden City in Beijing, the Emperor's Palace for hundreds of years.

Availability:	Schools, libraries, homeschoolers, and nursing homes in the United States and Canada.
Suggested Grade:	6-Adult
Order Number:	order by title
Production Date:	1995
Format:	VHS videotape
Terms:	Postage is paid by borrower both ways--send $3.00 per tape to cover initial shipping to you--MONEY MUST BE SENT WITH REQUEST. Return 10 days after showing via U. S. Postal Service, library rate. Shipping is $5.00 to Canadian addresses.

Source: Center for Teaching About China
Kathleen Trescott
1214 West Schwartz
Carbondale, IL 62901
Phone: 1-618-549-1555
Email Address: trescott@midwest.net

Christmas in Mexico

Describes specific customs of the Christmas season in Mexico.

Availability:	Schools and libraries in the United States and Canada.
Suggested Grade:	6-8
Order Number:	order by title
Production Date:	1992
Format:	DVD
Terms:	Videos will typically be lent for seven days if mailed out--due date will be indicated. Films not returned within the time limit will be subject to overdue fines of $2 per video, per day. All borrowed must have a lending agreement on file. Form can be downloaded

from http://isa.unc.edu/film/borrow.asplaform. Borrowers are responsible for the cost of return shipping. Materials must be returned via a shipping method that has tracking information.

Source: Latin American Film Collection
3219 Fed Ex Global Education Center
301 Pittsboro Street, CB 3205
Chapel Hill, NC 27599-3205
Email Address: LA_Films@email.unc.edu

Common Experiences, Different Visions

Introduces shadow puppetry, silk embroidery, paper cutting, kite making and flying, lanterns, hand puppetry, and dragon and lion dances.

Availability:	Schools, libraries, and nursing homes in the United States and Canada.
Suggested Grade:	6-Adult
Order Number:	JV033
Format:	VHS videotape
Terms:	Borrower pays return postage. Return with 14 days after scheduled showing, via UPS or U. S. Mail. All requests must included an educational institution affiliation, a current address, and phone number. Order through web site only.

Source: Cornell University East Asia Program
World Wide Web URL:
http://www.einaudi.cornell.edu/eastasia/outreach/video.asp
Email Address: east_asia1@cornell.edu

Coronel Delimiro Gouveia

Depicts heroic fight against political persecutors from city and the sertao.

Availability:	Schools, libraries, and nursing homes in the United States.
Suggested Grade:	6-12
Language:	Portuguese
Order Number:	FFBRA16-video
Production Date:	1976
Format:	VHS videotape
Terms:	Borrowers must have a User's Agreement on file with this source--available by mail or via the Internet. Return postage is paid by borrower; return 12 days after showing. Book at least three weeks in advance. All borrowers are limited to a total of ten items per semester.

Source: Latin American Resource Center
Stone Center for Latin American Studies
Tulane University, 100 Jones Hall
New Orleans, LA 70118
Phone: 1-504-862-3143
Fax: 1-504-865-6719
World Wide Web URL:
http://stonecenter.tulane.edu/pages/detail/48/
Lending-Library
Email Address: crcrts@tulane.edu

Cosquin, City of Folklore

Folklore festival celebrated annually in Cosquin, Argentina.

Availability:	Schools, libraries, and nursing homes in the United States.

All materials listed in this 2011-2012 edition are BRAND NEW!

Suggested Grade: 6-12
Language: Spanish
Order Number: DFARG1-video
Production Date: 1970
Format: VHS videotape
Terms: Borrowers must have a User's Agreement on file with this source--available by mail or via the Internet. Return postage is paid by borrower; return 12 days after showing. Book at least three weeks in advance. All borrowers are limited to a total of ten items per semester.
Source: Latin American Resource Center
Stone Center for Latin American Studies
Tulane University
100 Jones Hall
New Orleans, LA 70118
Phone: 1-504-862-3143
Fax: 1-504-865-6719
World Wide Web URL:
http://stonecenter.tulane.edu/pages/detail/48/
Lending-Library
Email Address: crcrts@tulane.edu

Costa Rica

Development of Costa Rica in the twentieth century, and its international position as a neighbor to Nicaragua.
Availability: Schools, libraries, and nursing homes in the United States.
Suggested Grade: 6-12
Order Number: HCCOS1-video
Production Date: 1987
Format: VHS videotape
Terms: Borrowers must have a User's Agreement on file with this source--available by mail or via the Internet. Return postage is paid by borrower; return 12 days after showing. Book at least three weeks in advance. All borrowers are limited to a total of ten items per semester.
Source: Latin American Resource Center
Stone Center for Latin American Studies
Tulane University, 100 Jones Hall
New Orleans, LA 70118
Phone: 1-504-862-3143
Fax: 1-504-865-6719
World Wide Web URL:
http://stonecenter.tulane.edu/pages/detail/48/
Lending-Library
Email Address: crcrts@tulane.edu

Cuba, Guatemala, and El Salvador Perspectives

This video focuses on the current human rights conditions in Cuba, Guatemala and El Salvador.
Availability: Schools in the United States.
Suggested Grade: 7-Adult
Order Number: order by title
Production Date: 1996
Format: VHS videotape
Terms: Borrower pays return postage. Return 14 days after receipt, via USPS including insurance. All borrowers must have a current lending agreement on file with the Outreach program. This agreement is available via the web site or may be requested via phone or fax.

Source: Center for Latin American Studies
University of Florida
319 Grinter Hall
P. O. Box 115530
Gainesville, FL 32611-5530
Phone: 1-352-392-0375
Fax: 1-352-392-7682
World Wide Web URL: http://www.latam.ufl.edu/outreach
Email Address: maryr@ufl.edu

Cuba: The Children of Fidel

Examines the life of women under Castro's regime in Cuba. Features interviews with Cuba exiles living in Miami and with women still living on the island.
Availability: Schools in the United States.
Suggested Grade: 7-Adult
Order Number: order by title
Production Date: 1997
Format: VHS videotape
Terms: Borrower pays return postage. Return 14 days after receipt, via USPS including insurance. All borrowers must have a current lending agreement on file with the Outreach program. This agreement is available via the web site or may be requested via phone or fax.
Source: Center for Latin American Studies
University of Florida
319 Grinter Hall, P. O. Box 115530
Gainesville, FL 32611-5530
Phone: 1-352-392-0375
Fax: 1-352-392-7682
World Wide Web URL: http://www.latam.ufl.edu/outreach
Email Address: maryr@ufl.edu

Cultural Journey Into Japan, A

A journey through Japan that touches upon the cultural aspects of this country. Depicts beautiful crafts such as gold leaf painting, obi making, and kimono silk painting as well as showing the beauty of classic rock gardens.
Availability: Schools, libraries, and nursing homes in Hawaii.
Suggested Grade: 4-12
Order Number: TR-1
Production Date: 1984
Format: VHS videotape
Terms: Borrower pays return postage. A maximum of 3 videos may be borrowed per person. Return within one week of date borrowed.
Source: Consulate General of Japan, Honolulu
1742 Nuuanu Avenue
Honolulu, HI 96817-3294
Phone: 1-808-543-3111
Fax: 1-808-543-3170
World Wide Web URL:
http://www.honolulu.us.emb-japan.go.jp

Cuzco, la Ciudad y su Gente

Focuses on present day Cuzco whose character is derived from intercultural contact between Andeans, Spanish, and tourists.

*All materials listed in this 2011-2012 edition are **BRAND NEW!***

Availability: Schools and libraries in Iowa, Illinois, Michigan, Minnesota, and Wisconsin.
Suggested Grade: 6-12
Language: Spanish
Order Number: CI/URSPACU99VHS
Production Date: 1987
Format: VHS videotape
Terms: Borrower pays return postage. Return 8 days after showing. Book 2 weeks in advance. Order may also be picked up for those near the Center.

Source: Center for Latin American and Caribbean Studies
UW-Milwaukee
P. O. Box 413
Milwaukee, WI 53201
Phone: 1-414-229-5987
World Wide Web URL: http://www.uwm.edu/Dept/CLACS
Email Address: audvis@usm.edu

Dadi and Her Family

Dadi is the grandmother who manages an extended family. The women in this film discuss family tensions, women's labor in the fields and at home, and the loneliness of being a stranger in the husband's family.
Availability: Schools and libraries in the United States.
Suggested Grade: 7-12
Order Number: 2
Production Date: 1979
Format: VHS videotape
Terms: Borrower pays return postage. Return 3 days after showing via UPS. Book at least 2 weeks in advance.

Source: Syracuse University, South Asia Center
Video Library and Teaching Resources
346F Eggers Hall
The Maxwell School
Syracuse, NY 13244

Decade of Destruction

Five-part series looking at the changes in the Brazilian Amazon in a decade of increased contact with the civilized world.
Availability: Schools, libraries, and nursing homes in the United States.
Suggested Grade: 6-12
Order Number: GEBRA3-video
Production Date: 1985
Format: VHS videotape
Special Notes: Includes guide.
Terms: Borrowers must have a User's Agreement on file with this source--available by mail or via the Internet. Return postage is paid by borrower; return 12 days after showing. Book at least three weeks in advance. All borrowers are limited to a total of ten items per semester.

Source: Latin American Resource Center
Stone Center for Latin American Studies
Tulane University
100 Jones Hall
New Orleans, LA 70118
Phone: 1-504-862-3143
Fax: 1-504-865-6719

World Wide Web URL:
http://stonecenter.tulane.edu/pages/detail/48/
Lending-Library
Email Address: crcrts@tulane.edu

Discover Korea: Family and Home

Follows a day in the life of a 6th-grade boy in south Korea from school to home life and a visit to relatives in the country.
Availability: Schools, libraries, and nursing homes in the United States and Canada.
Suggested Grade: All ages
Order Number: KV001
Format: VHS videotape
Terms: Borrower pays return postage. Return with 14 days after scheduled showing, via UPS or U. S. Mail. All requests must included an educational institution affiliation, a current address, and phone number. Order through web site only.

Source: Cornell University East Asia Program
World Wide Web URL:
http://www.einaudi.cornell.edu/eastasia/outreach/video.asp
Email Address: east_asia1@cornell.edu

Discover Korea: School and Community

A 6th-grade girl and friend narrate a day at school in South Korea, highlighting social customs and scenes of local community life.
Availability: Schools, libraries, and nursing homes in the United States and Canada.
Suggested Grade: All ages
Order Number: KV003
Format: VHS videotape
Terms: Borrower pays return postage. Return with 14 days after scheduled showing, via UPS or U. S. Mail. All requests must included an educational institution affiliation, a current address, and phone number. Order through web site only.

Source: Cornell University East Asia Program
World Wide Web URL:
http://www.einaudi.cornell.edu/eastasia/outreach/video.asp
Email Address: east_asia1@cornell.edu

Dreams Ensnared

Contemporary economic issues facing emigrants from the Dominican Republic and other Caribbean nations.
Availability: Schools, libraries, and nursing homes in the United States.
Suggested Grade: 6-12
Order Number: HISP63-video
Production Date: 1994
Format: VHS videotape
Terms: Borrowers must have a User's Agreement on file with this source--available by mail or via the Internet. Return postage is paid by borrower; return 12 days after showing. Book at least three weeks in advance. All borrowers are limited to a total of ten items per semester.

Source: Latin American Resource Center
Stone Center for Latin American Studies
Tulane University
100 Jones Hall
New Orleans, LA 70118
Phone: 1-504-862-3143
Fax: 1-504-865-6719
World Wide Web URL:
http://stonecenter.tulane.edu/pages/detail/48/
Lending-Library
Email Address: crcrts@tulane.edu

Earth Is Our Mother, The

Study of two Indian tribes in Colombia and Venezuela in the face of encroaching white civilization.

Availability: Schools, libraries, and nursing homes in the United States.
Suggested Grade: 6-12
Order Number: INDSA1-video
Production Date: 1988
Format: VHS videotape
Terms: Borrowers must have a User's Agreement on file with this source--available by mail or via the Internet. Return postage is paid by borrower; return 12 days after showing. Book at least three weeks in advance. All borrowers are limited to a total of ten items per semester.

Source: Latin American Resource Center
Stone Center for Latin American Studies
Tulane University
100 Jones Hall
New Orleans, LA 70118
Phone: 1-504-862-3143
Fax: 1-504-865-6719
World Wide Web URL:
http://stonecenter.tulane.edu/pages/detail/48/
Lending-Library
Email Address: crcrts@tulane.edu

Education in Japan

Two urban households with school-age children give insight into Japanese education, which relies heavily on test scores to rank students and their aptitude.

Availability: Schools, libraries, and nursing homes in Illinois, Indiana, Iowa, Kansas, Minnesota, Missouri, Nebraska, North Dakota, South Dakota, and Wisconsin.
Suggested Grade: 4-Adult
Order Number: 12002
Production Date: 1991
Format: VHS videotape
Special Notes: No. 10 of the "Nippon the Land and Its People" series.
Terms: Borrower pays return postage by U. S. Mail, UPS, or Federal Express, including insurance for "original" videos. Write, call, fax, or e-mail to request an application. An application form MUST be sent in one month in advance but not more than six months in advance. Include alternate titles and dates if provider can substitute titles. Send a SASE with request if you

require confirmation. Return immediately after scheduled showing date. Videos may not be copied or broadcast without permission from the producer of the video. Borrower is responsible if video is lost or damaged.

Source: Consulate General of Japan at Chicago
Japan Information Center
Library
737 North Michigan Avenue, Suite 1000
Chicago, IL 60611
Phone: 1-312-280-0430
Fax: 1-312-280-6883
World Wide Web URL:
http://www.chicago.us.emb-japan.go.jp/jic.html
Email Address: jicchicago@webkddi.com

Education in Japan--Children and Their Dreams

Two urban households with school-age children give insight into Japanese education, which relies heavily on test scores to rank students and their aptitude.

Availability: Schools, libraries and homeschoolers in Alabama, Georgia, North Carolina, South Carolina, and Virginia.
Suggested Grade: 4-12
Order Number: 812
Production Date: 1991
Format: VHS videotape
Special Notes: No. 10 of the "Nippon the Land and Its People" series.
Terms: Borrower pays return postage. Two tapes may be borrowed at a time. Return within 7 days after receipt. Reservations may be made by filling the application found on the web site.

Source: Consulate General of Japan, Atlanta
Japan Information Center
One Alliance Center
3500 Lenox Road, Suite 1600
Atlanta, GA 30326
Phone: 1-404-365-9240
Fax: 1-404-240-4311
World Wide Web URL:
http://www.atlanta.us.emb-japan.go.jp
Email Address: info@cgjapanatlanta.org

Education in Japan--Children and Their Dreams

Two urban households with school-age children give insight into Japanese education, which relies heavily on test scores to rank students and their aptitude.

Availability: Schools, libraries, and nursing homes in Hawaii.
Suggested Grade: 4-12
Order Number: CU-25
Production Date: 1991
Format: VHS videotape
Special Notes: No. 10 of the "Nippon the Land and Its People" series.
Terms: Borrower pays return postage. A maximum of 3 videos may be borrowed per person. Return within one week of date borrowed.

*All materials listed in this 2011-2012 edition are **BRAND NEW!***

Source: Consulate General of Japan, Honolulu
1742 Nuuanu Avenue
Honolulu, HI 96817-3294
Phone: 1-808-543-3111
Fax: 1-808-543-3170
World Wide Web URL:
http://www.honolulu.us.emb-japan.go.jp

Education in Japan--Children and Their Dreams

Two urban households with school-age children give insight into Japanese education, which relies heavily on test scores to rank students and their aptitude.

Availability:	Schools, libraries, homeschoolers, and nursing homes in OREGON AND SOUTHERN IDAHO ONLY. Please make requests via the web site.
Suggested Grade:	4-12
Order Number:	302
Production Date:	1991
Format:	VHS videotape
Special Notes:	No. 10 of the "Nippon the Land and Its People" series.
Terms:	Borrower pays return postage. Return within three weeks after scheduled showing date. Book one month in advance if possible. Rewind the video and wrap securely for return. Be certain to indicate video number, date needed, name of your organization, and address to which video should be sent, along with phone number. Audience report enclosed with the video must be completed and returned.

Source: Consulate General of Japan, Oregon
Attn: Tamara, Video Library
1300 S. W. Fifth Avenue, Suite 2700
Portland, OR 97201
Phone: 1-503-221-1811, ext. 17
World Wide Web URL:
http://www.portland.us.emb-japan.go.jp/en/index.html
Email Address: tamara@cgjpdx.org

El Futuro Maya: Voces del Presente

Students, housewives, academics, community leaders, educators--provide perspectives on the meaning of the Maya Movement.

Availability:	Schools, libraries, and nursing homes in the United States.
Suggested Grade:	6-12
Languages:	Spanish or Spanish with English subtitles
Order Number:	INDGUA5-video
Production Date:	1998
Format:	VHS videotape
Terms:	Borrowers must have a User's Agreement on file with this source--available by mail or via the Internet. Return postage is paid by borrower; return 12 days after showing. Book at least three weeks in advance. All borrowers are limited to a total of ten items per semester.

Source: Latin American Resource Center
Stone Center for Latin American Studies
Tulane University, 100 Jones Hall
New Orleans, LA 70118

Phone: 1-504-862-3143
Fax: 1-504-865-6719
World Wide Web URL:
http://stonecenter.tulane.edu/pages/detail/48/
Lending-Library
Email Address: crcrts@tulane.edu

El Hombre y Su Medio: La Selva

Focuses on small farmers, and the gold, oil, and tourist industry around Iquitos, Peru.

Availability:	Schools, libraries, and nursing homes in the United States.
Suggested Grade:	6-12
Language:	Spanish
Order Number:	DEVPER4-video
Format:	VHS videotape
Terms:	Borrowers must have a User's Agreement on file with this source--available by mail or via the Internet. Return postage is paid by borrower; return 12 days after showing. Book at least three weeks in advance. All borrowers are limited to a total of ten items per semester.

Source: Latin American Resource Center
Stone Center for Latin American Studies
Tulane University
100 Jones Hall
New Orleans, LA 70118
Phone: 1-504-862-3143
Fax: 1-504-865-6719
World Wide Web URL:
http://stonecenter.tulane.edu/pages/detail/48/
Lending-Library
Email Address: crcrts@tulane.edu

El Hombre y Su Medio: La Sierra Central

Documentary with breathtaking shots of the Andes, shows rugged life of those living in the mountains.

Availability:	Schools, libraries, and nursing homes in the United States.
Suggested Grade:	6-12
Language:	Spanish
Order Number:	IPER7-video
Production Date:	1995
Format:	VHS videotape
Terms:	Borrowers must have a User's Agreement on file with this source--available by mail or via the Internet. Return postage is paid by borrower; return 12 days after showing. Book at least three weeks in advance. All borrowers are limited to a total of ten items per semester.

Source: Latin American Resource Center
Stone Center for Latin American Studies
Tulane University
100 Jones Hall
New Orleans, LA 70118
Phone: 1-504-862-3143
Fax: 1-504-865-6719
World Wide Web URL:
http://stonecenter.tulane.edu/pages/detail/48/
Lending-Library
Email Address: crcrts@tulane.edu

Ernesto Zedillo: Un Hombre de Palabra

Shows candidate Zedillo at work and home, as he expresses main campaign issues.

Availability: Schools, libraries, and nursing homes in the United States.
Suggested Grade: 6-12
Language: Spanish
Order Number: HCMEX9-video
Production Date: 1994
Format: VHS videotape
Terms: Borrowers must have a User's Agreement on file with this source--available by mail or via the Internet. Return postage is paid by borrower; return 12 days after showing. Book at least three weeks in advance. All borrowers are limited to a total of ten items per semester.

Source: Latin American Resource Center
Stone Center for Latin American Studies
Tulane University
100 Jones Hall
New Orleans, LA 70118
Phone: 1-504-862-3143
Fax: 1-504-865-6719
World Wide Web URL:
http://stonecenter.tulane.edu/pages/detail/48/
Lending-Library
Email Address: crcrts@tulane.edu

Escuela

A view into the lives of contemporary Mexican American migrants and their struggles to educate their children while obtaining employment. The focus is on a young Mexican girl who is beginning her first year of high school.

Availability: Schools and libraries in Iowa, Illinois, Michigan, Minnesota, and Wisconsin.
Suggested Grade: 7-12
Languages: Spanish with subtitles
Order Number: LAT/USUSES1VHS
Production Date: 2002
Format: VHS videotape
Terms: Borrower pays return postage. Return 8 days after showing. Book 2 weeks in advance. Order may also be picked up for those near the Center.

Source: Center for Latin American and Caribbean Studies
UW-Milwaukee
P. O. Box 413
Milwaukee, WI 53201
Phone: 1-414-229-5987
World Wide Web URL: http://www.uwm.edu/Dept/CLACS
Email Address: audvis@usm.edu

Ethiopia: The Land Beyond the Rivers

Presents an historical overview of Ethiopia, including the role of the church. Church World Service is a partner in these efforts.

Availability: Schools, libraries, homeschoolers, and nursing homes in the United States.
Suggested Grade: 5-Adult
Order Number: order by title
Production Date: 1989

Format: VHS or 3/4" U-matic videotape
Special Notes: Cleared for TV broadcast.
Terms: Borrower pays return postage. Return the day after scheduled showing, via UPS or Priority Mail, insured for $100.00. Book 4 weeks in advance and include an alternate date. Order should include name of person responsible for handling the video, and complete mailing address. Please mention this Guide when ordering. Tapes may not be duplicated, edited or exhibited for a fee.

Source: Church World Service
Film & Video Library
28606 Phillips Street, P. O. Box 968
Elkhart, IN 46515
Phone: 1-800-297-1516, ext. 338
Fax: 1-574-262-0966
World Wide Web URL: http://www.churchworldservice.org
Email Address: videos@churchworldservice.org

Face-to-Face: Teenagers Tour Nicaragua

United States teens meet their counterparts in Nicaragua and see first-hand the effects of war.

Availability: Schools in the United States.
Suggested Grade: 7-12
Order Number: order by title
Production Date: 1986
Format: VHS videotape
Terms: Borrower pays return postage. Return 14 days after receipt, via USPS including insurance. All borrowers must have a current lending agreement on file with the Outreach program. This agreement is available via the web site or may be requested via phone or fax.

Source: Center for Latin American Studies
University of Florida
319 Grinter Hall
P. O. Box 115530
Gainesville, FL 32611-5530
Phone: 1-352-392-0375
Fax: 1-352-392-7682
World Wide Web URL: http://www.latam.ufl.edu/outreach
Email Address: maryr@ufl.edu

Families of Sweden

Learn some of the customs, culture, history, and politics of Sweden as two young children share their typical days.

Availability: Schools, libraries, and homeschoolers in the United States who serve the hearing impaired.
Suggested Grade: 2-5
Order Number: 11818
Format: DVD
Special Notes: Also available as live streaming video over the Internet.
Terms: Sponsor pays all transportation costs. Return one week after receipt. Participation is limited to deaf or hard of hearing Americans, their parents, families, teachers, counselors, or others whose use would benefit a deaf or hard of hearing person. Only one person in the audience needs to be hearing impaired. You must register--which is free. These videos are all open-captioned--no special equipment is required for viewing.

Source: Described and Captioned Media Program
National Association of the Deaf
4211 Church Street Ext.
Roebuck, SC 29376
Phone: 1-800-237-6213
Fax: 1-800-538-5636
World Wide Web URL: http://www.dcmp.org

Gerbert Is Marco Polo

Cartoon character, Ferbert, imagines himself to be the famous world traveler, Marco Polo. Learn geography as he journeys to the east and stays a while in China.

Availability: Schools, libraries, homeschoolers, and nursing homes in the United States and Canada.
Suggested Grade: K-3
Order Number: order by title
Production Date: 1993
Format: VHS videotape
Terms: Postage is paid by borrower both ways--send $3.00 per tape to cover initial shipping to you--MONEY MUST BE SENT WITH REQUEST. Return 10 days after showing via U. S. Postal Service, library rate. Shipping is $5.00 to Canadian addresses.

> Source: Center for Teaching About China
> Kathleen Trescott
> 1214 West Schwartz
> Carbondale, IL 62901
> Phone: 1-618-549-1555
> Email Address: trescott@midwest.net

Hidden Korea

Focuses on the special foods of Korea.

Availability: Schools, libraries, and nursing homes in the United States and Canada.
Suggested Grade: 6-Adult
Order Number: KV005
Format: VHS videotape
Terms: Borrower pays return postage. Return with 14 days after scheduled showing, via UPS or U. S. Mail. All requests must included an educational institution affiliation, a current address, and phone number. Order through web site only.

> Source: Cornell University East Asia Program
> World Wide Web URL:
> http://www.einaudi.cornell.edu/eastasia/outreach/video.asp
> Email Address: east_asia1@cornell.edu

High Technology in Japan

Focuses on the latest technological advances in Japan including new ceramics for automobiles, knives, and computer parts.

Availability: Schools, libraries and homeschoolers in Alabama, Georgia, North Carolina, South Carolina, and Virginia.
Suggested Grade: 6-Adult
Order Number: 015
Production Date: 1990
Format: VHS videotape

Terms: Borrower pays return postage. Two tapes may be borrowed at a time. Return within 7 days after receipt. Reservations may be made by filling the application found on the web site.

> Source: Consulate General of Japan, Atlanta
> Japan Information Center
> One Alliance Center, 3500 Lenox Road, Suite 1600
> Atlanta, GA 30326
> Phone: 1-404-365-9240
> Fax: 1-404-240-4311
> World Wide Web URL:
> http://www.atlanta.us.emb-japan.go.jp
> Email Address: info@cgjapanatlanta.org

High Technology in Japan

Focuses on the latest technological advances in Japan including new ceramics for automobiles, knives, and computer parts.

Availability: Schools, libraries, and nursing homes in Hawaii.
Suggested Grade: 6-Adult
Order Number: BU-6
Production Date: 1990
Format: VHS videotape
Terms: Borrower pays return postage. A maximum of 3 videos may be borrowed per person. Return within one week of date borrowed.

> Source: Consulate General of Japan, Honolulu
> 1742 Nuuanu Avenue
> Honolulu, HI 96817-3294
> Phone: 1-808-543-3111
> Fax: 1-808-543-3170
> World Wide Web URL:
> http://www.honolulu.us.emb-japan.go.jp

High Technology in Japan

Focuses on the latest technological advances in Japan including new ceramics for automobiles, knives, and computer parts.

Availability: Schools, libraries, homeschoolers, and nursing homes in OREGON AND SOUTHERN IDAHO ONLY. Please make requests via the web site.
Suggested Grade: 6-Adult
Order Number: 165
Production Date: 1990
Format: VHS videotape
Terms: Borrower pays return postage. Return within three weeks after scheduled showing date. Book one month in advance if possible. Rewind the video and wrap securely for return. Be certain to indicate video number, date needed, name of your organization, and address to which video should be sent, along with phone number. Audience report enclosed with the video must be completed and returned.

> Source: Consulate General of Japan, Oregon
> Attn: Tamara, Video Library
> 1300 S. W. Fifth Avenue, Suite 2700
> Portland, OR 97201

*All materials listed in this 2011-2012 edition are **BRAND NEW!***

Phone: 1-503-221-1811, ext. 17
World Wide Web URL:
http://www.portland.us.emb-japan.go.jp/en/index.html
Email Address: tamara@cgjpdx.org

Hills of the Seasons

A beautiful scenic tour of Hokkaido with soft piano music.

Availability:	Schools, libraries and homeschoolers in Alabama, Georgia, North Carolina, South Carolina, and Virginia.
Suggested Grade:	All ages
Order Number:	208
Production Date:	1993
Format:	VHS videotape
Special Notes:	No narration.
Terms:	Borrower pays return postage. Two tapes may be borrowed at a time. Return within 7 days after receipt. Reservations may be made by filling the application found on the web site.

Source: Consulate General of Japan, Atlanta
Japan Information Center
One Alliance Center
3500 Lenox Road, Suite 1600
Atlanta, GA 30326
Phone: 1-404-365-9240
Fax: 1-404-240-4311
World Wide Web URL:
http://www.atlanta.us.emb-japan.go.jp
Email Address: info@cgjapanatlanta.org

Hills of the Seasons

A beautiful scenic tour of Hokkaido with soft piano music.

Availability:	Schools, libraries, and nursing homes in Hawaii.
Suggested Grade:	All ages
Order Number:	TR-8
Production Date:	1993
Format:	VHS videotape
Special Notes:	No narration.
Terms:	Borrower pays return postage. A maximum of 3 videos may be borrowed per person. Return within one week of date borrowed.

Source: Consulate General of Japan, Honolulu
1742 Nuuanu Avenue
Honolulu, HI 96817-3294
Phone: 1-808-543-3111
Fax: 1-808-543-3170
World Wide Web URL:
http://www.honolulu.us.emb-japan.go.jp

Holiday in Japan

Highlights of some popular tourist attractions in Japan are shown.

Availability:	Schools, libraries, and nursing homes in Hawaii.
Suggested Grade:	4-12
Order Number:	TR-6
Format:	VHS videotape

Terms:	Borrower pays return postage. A maximum of 3 videos may be borrowed per person. Return within one week of date borrowed.

Source: Consulate General of Japan, Honolulu
1742 Nuuanu Avenue
Honolulu, HI 96817-3294
Phone: 1-808-543-3111
Fax: 1-808-543-3170
World Wide Web URL:
http://www.honolulu.us.emb-japan.go.jp

Hong Kong: A Family Portrait

In July 1997, this bustling city was returned to the government of China. A boat family, caught on tape, made their home there for more than 100 years.

Availability:	Schools, libraries, homeschoolers, and nursing homes in the United States and Canada.
Suggested Grade:	6-12
Order Number:	order by title
Production Date:	1995
Format:	VHS videotape
Terms:	Postage is paid by borrower both ways--send $3.00 per tape to cover initial shipping to you--MONEY MUST BE SENT WITH REQUEST. Return 10 days after showing via U. S. Postal Service, library rate. Shipping is $5.00 to Canadian addresses.

Source: Center for Teaching About China
Kathleen Trescott
1214 West Schwartz
Carbondale, IL 62901
Phone: 1-618-549-1555
Email Address: trescott@midwest.net

India: Land of the Monsoon

A glimpse of how the people of India have learned to live with monsoons, which bring both needed rain and disastrous floods; includes a study of the different kinds of monsoons.

Availability:	Schools and libraries in the United States.
Suggested Grade:	7-12
Order Number:	36
Production Date:	1991
Format:	VHS videotape
Terms:	Borrower pays return postage. Return 3 days after showing via UPS. Book at least 2 weeks in advance.

Source: Syracuse University, South Asia Center
Video Library and Teaching Resources
346F Eggers Hall
The Maxwell School
Syracuse, NY 13244

Indian Pilgrimage, An: Kashi

Two Telugu-speaking brahmans and their wives have come from South India to Kashi (Banaras or Varanasi) to perform classical ancestor rites. They also shop in bazaars and visit tourist attractions.

Availability: Schools, libraries, homeschoolers, and nursing homes in the southeastern United States.
Suggested Grade: 7-12
Order Number: order by title
Production Date: 1976
Format: VHS videotape
Terms: Borrower pays return postage. Return 2 days after showing via United Parcel Service, insured. Book 2 weeks in advance.
> **Source: Center for South Asian Studies**
> **University of Virginia**
> **Video Library Coordinator**
> **P. O. Box 400169, 110 Minor Hall**
> **Charlottesville, VA 22904-4169**
> **Phone: 1-434-924-8815**
> **Email Address: southasia@virginia.edu**

Iron and Silk

True story of an English teacher in China who learns far more than he dreamed possible in two years.
Availability: Schools, libraries, homeschoolers, and nursing homes in the United States and Canada.
Suggested Grade: 7-Adult
Order Number: order by title
Production Date: 1991
Format: DVD
Terms: Postage is paid by borrower both ways--send $3.00 per tape to cover initial shipping to you--MONEY MUST BE SENT WITH REQUEST. Return 10 days after showing via U. S. Postal Service, library rate. Shipping is $5.00 to Canadian addresses.
> **Source: Center for Teaching About China**
> **Kathleen Trescott**
> **1214 West Schwartz**
> **Carbondale, IL 62901**
> **Phone: 1-618-549-1555**
> **Email Address: trescott@midwest.net**

Jagriti (The Awakening)

Interviews with local politicians and administrators of international aid organizations--and students' satirical sketches of the same people--provide a record of the first year of a school for children in the poorest district of Delhi.
Availability: Schools, libraries, homeschoolers, and nursing homes in the southeastern United States.
Suggested Grade: 7-12
Order Number: order by title
Format: VHS videotape
Terms: Borrower pays return postage. Return 2 days after showing via United Parcel Service, insured. Book 2 weeks in advance.
> **Source: Center for South Asian Studies**
> **University of Virginia**
> **Video Library Coordinator**
> **P. O. Box 400169, 110 Minor Hall**
> **Charlottesville, VA 22904-4169**

Phone: 1-434-924-8815
Email Address: southasia@virginia.edu

Journey Into India

Three travelogues on the west Indian city of Jaipur, the Hindi movie industry in Bombay, and the Indian army--the largest voluntary armed force in the world.
Availability: Schools and libraries in the United States.
Suggested Grade: 7-Adult
Order Number: SA13
Format: VHS videotape
Terms: Borrower pays return postage. Return 3 days after showing via UPS. Book at least 2 weeks in advance.
> **Source: Syracuse University, South Asia Center**
> **Video Library and Teaching Resources**
> **346F Eggers Hall**
> **The Maxwell School**
> **Syracuse, NY 13244**

Journey to Understanding: Facing the Future

Zimbabwean teenage actress Eldinah Tshatedi uses dramatic scenes from her "African Journey" TV series to introduce us to parts of modern-day Africa. She shows us that conflicts often exist between the traditional and modern ways and it's important to find a balance between the two.
Availability: Schools, libraries, homeschoolers, and nursing homes in the United States.
Suggested Grade: 7-12
Order Number: order by title
Production Date: 1990
Format: VHS videotape
Terms: Borrower pays return postage. Return the day after scheduled showing, via UPS or Priority Mail, insured for $100.00. Book 4 weeks in advance and include an alternate date. Order should include name of person responsible for handling the video, and complete mailing address. Please mention this Guide when ordering. Tapes may not be duplicated, edited or exhibited for a fee.
> **Source: Church World Service**
> **Film & Video Library**
> **28606 Phillips Street, P. O. Box 968**
> **Elkhart, IN 46515**
> **Phone: 1-800-297-1516, ext. 338**
> **Fax: 1-574-262-0966**
> **World Wide Web URL: http://www.churchworldservice.org**
> **Email Address: videos@churchworldservice.org**

Journey to Understanding: Women Changing Our Role

Zimbabwean teenage actress Eldinah Tshatedi shows us that although parts of Africa are rapidly modernizing, women's roles are changing more slowly. Women continue to grow 60-80% of their families' food, leaving little time for education--while many men migrate to find work, which leaves women shouldering even more of the burden at home.
Availability: Schools, libraries, homeschoolers, and nursing homes in the United States.

Suggested Grade: 7-Adult
Order Number: order by title
Production Date: 1990
Format: VHS videotape
Terms: Borrower pays return postage. Return the day after scheduled showing, via UPS or Priority Mail, insured for $100.00. Book 4 weeks in advance and include an alternate date. Order should include name of person responsible for handling the video, and complete mailing address. Please mention this Guide when ordering. Tapes may not be duplicated, edited or exhibited for a fee.

Source: Church World Service
Film & Video Library
28606 Phillips Street, P. O. Box 968
Elkhart, IN 46515
Phone: 1-800-297-1516, ext. 338
Fax: 1-574-262-0966
World Wide Web URL: http://www.churchworldservice.org
Email Address: videos@churchworldservice.org

Jungle Pharmacy: Protecting the Global Environment

Focuses on physicians, scientists and environmentalists who strive to heighten awareness of the ongoing destruction of the Amazon rainforest. Working with shamans, they are examining how the rain forest can also be a source of new drugs for the world.
Availability: Schools and libraries in Iowa, Illinois, Michigan, Minnesota, and Wisconsin.
Suggested Grade: 6-12
Order Number: ENVAMZJ95VHS
Production Date: 1989
Format: VHS videotape
Terms: Borrower pays return postage. Return 8 days after showing. Book 2 weeks in advance. Order may also be picked up for those near the Center.

Source: Center for Latin American and Caribbean Studies
UW-Milwaukee
P. O. Box 413
Milwaukee, WI 53201
Phone: 1-414-229-5987
World Wide Web URL: http://www.uwm.edu/Dept/CLACS
Email Address: audvis@usm.edu

Kaise Jeebo Re!

An enquiry into the effects of the Narmada dam project on the lives of the people it has uprooted and displaced.
Availability: Schools and libraries in the United States.
Suggested Grade: 7-Adult
Order Number: SA66
Production Date: 1997
Format: VHS videotape
Terms: Borrower pays return postage. Return 3 days after showing via UPS. Book at least 2 weeks in advance.

Source: Syracuse University, South Asia Center
Video Library and Teaching Resources
346F Eggers Hall
The Maxwell School
Syracuse, NY 13244

Kalasha, The: Rites of Spring

A view of the threatened way of life of the Kalasha people, of the valleys of the Hindu Kush Mountains in northwest Pakistan.
Availability: Schools, libraries, homeschoolers, and nursing homes in the southeastern United States.
Suggested Grade: 7-12
Order Number: order by title
Production Date: 1990
Format: VHS videotape
Terms: Borrower pays return postage. Return 2 days after showing via United Parcel Service, insured. Book 2 weeks in advance.

Source: Center for South Asian Studies
University of Virginia
Video Library Coordinator
P. O. Box 400169, 110 Minor Hall
Charlottesville, VA 22904-4169
Phone: 1-434-924-8815
Email Address: southasia@virginia.edu

Kasthuri

A 21-year-old Tamil film star named Kasthuri discusses her life and views on movies in India. The film aims to show another side of India than what is usually shown in United States media.
Availability: Schools and libraries in the United States.
Suggested Grade: 7-Adult
Order Number: SA24
Production Date: 1993
Format: VHS videotape
Terms: Borrower pays return postage. Return 3 days after showing via UPS. Book at least 2 weeks in advance.

Source: Syracuse University, South Asia Center
Video Library and Teaching Resources
346F Eggers Hall
The Maxwell School
Syracuse, NY 13244

Kimono, The

The beautiful and traditional Japanese robe, which is worn by both men and women.
Availability: Schools, libraries, and nursing homes in Hawaii.
Suggested Grade: All ages
Order Number: CU-37
Production Date: 1985
Format: VHS videotape
Terms: Borrower pays return postage. A maximum of 3 videos may be borrowed per person. Return within one week of date borrowed.

Source: Consulate General of Japan, Honolulu
1742 Nuuanu Avenue
Honolulu, HI 96817-3294
Phone: 1-808-543-3111
Fax: 1-808-543-3170
World Wide Web URL:
http://www.honolulu.us.emb-japan.go.jp

Kimono, The

The beautiful and traditional Japanese robe, which is worn by both men and women.

Availability: Schools, libraries, homeschoolers, and nursing homes in OREGON AND SOUTHERN IDAHO ONLY. Please make requests via the web site.

Suggested Grade: All ages
Order Number: 212
Production Date: 1985
Format: VHS videotape
Terms: Borrower pays return postage. Return within three weeks after scheduled showing date. Book one month in advance if possible. Rewind the video and wrap securely for return. Be certain to indicate video number, date needed, name of your organization, and address to which video should be sent, along with phone number. Audience report enclosed with the video must be completed and returned.

Source: Consulate General of Japan, Oregon
Attn: Tamara, Video Library
1300 S. W. Fifth Avenue, Suite 2700
Portland, OR 97201
Phone: 1-503-221-1811, ext. 17
World Wide Web URL:
http://www.portland.us.emb-japan.go.jp/en/index.html
Email Address: tamara@cgjpdx.org

Laughing Club of India, The

India is the birth place of laughing clubs--places where people gather to laugh and thus improve their health. Here is the history of this phenomenon which has spread to Europe and the United States.

Availability: Schools, libraries, homeschoolers, and nursing homes in the southeastern United States.

Suggested Grade: 7-12
Order Number: order by title
Production Date: 2003
Format: VHS videotape
Terms: Borrower pays return postage. Return 2 days after showing via United Parcel Service, insured. Book 2 weeks in advance.

Source: Center for South Asian Studies
University of Virginia
Video Library Coordinator
P. O. Box 400169, 110 Minor Hall
Charlottesville, VA 22904-4169
Phone: 1-434-924-8815
Email Address: southasia@virginia.edu

Life in Venezuela: Children of the Street

Alberto is a 12-year-old newspaper vendor in Caracas and an important source of income for his mother. This video shows what his daily life is like.

Availability: Schools and libraries in Iowa, Illinois, Michigan, Minnesota, and Wisconsin.

Suggested Grade: 5-8
Order Number: CHIVENL62VHS

Format: VHS videotape
Terms: Borrower pays return postage. Return 8 days after showing. Book 2 weeks in advance. Order may also be picked up for those near the Center.

Source: Center for Latin American and Caribbean Studies
UW-Milwaukee, P. O. Box 413
Milwaukee, WI 53201
Phone: 1-414-229-5987
World Wide Web URL: http://www.uwm.edu/Dept/CLACS
Email Address: audvis@usm.edu

Los Ninos

Follow Victor and Samuel, brothers in Santa Cruz, Bolivia, through a typical day of study, work and play. After breakfast, the whole family goes to school.

Availability: Schools, libraries, homeschoolers, and nursing homes in the United States.

Suggested Grade: 5-Adult
Order Number: order by title
Production Date: 1996
Format: VHS videotape
Terms: Borrower pays return postage. Return the day after scheduled showing, via UPS or Priority Mail, insured for $100.00. Book 4 weeks in advance and include an alternate date. Order should include name of person responsible for handling the video, and complete mailing address. Please mention this Guide when ordering. Tapes may not be duplicated, edited or exhibited for a fee.

Source: Church World Service
Film & Video Library
28606 Phillips Street, P. O. Box 968
Elkhart, IN 46515
Phone: 1-800-297-1516, ext. 338
Fax: 1-574-262-0966
World Wide Web URL: http://www.churchworldservice.org
Email Address: videos@churchworldservice.org

Madoka

A beautiful scenic video with soft background music. Shows the view from the eyes of a Buddha statue during the different seasons.

Availability: Schools, libraries, and nursing homes in Hawaii.

Suggested Grade: 4-12
Order Number: CU-99
Production Date: 1993
Format: VHS videotape
Special Notes: No narration.
Terms: Borrower pays return postage. A maximum of 3 videos may be borrowed per person. Return within one week of date borrowed.

Source: Consulate General of Japan, Honolulu
1742 Nuuanu Avenue
Honolulu, HI 96817-3294
Phone: 1-808-543-3111
Fax: 1-808-543-3170
World Wide Web URL:
http://www.honolulu.us.emb-japan.go.jp

Magical Coqui, The--Puerto Rico--Mi Tierra

Presents a story about a boy and his pet coqui (tree frog).
Includes music and scenes of life in Puerto Rico.

Availability:	Schools and libraries in Iowa, Illinois, Michigan, Minnesota, and Wisconsin.
Suggested Grade:	1-8
Order Number:	CHIPRM27VHS
Production Date:	1989
Format:	VHS videotape
Terms:	Borrower pays return postage. Return 8 days after showing. Book 2 weeks in advance. Order may also be picked up for those near the Center.

Source: Center for Latin American and Caribbean Studies
UW-Milwaukee
P. O. Box 413
Milwaukee, WI 53201
Phone: 1-414-229-5987
World Wide Web URL: http://www.uwm.edu/Dept/CLACS
Email Address: audvis@usm.edu

Man of Leather

Life of the vaqueiro, the Brazilian cowboy of the northeast where cattle raising is an important economic activity since colonial times.

Availability:	Schools, libraries, and nursing homes in the United States.
Suggested Grade:	6-12
Languages:	Portuguese with English subtitles
Order Number:	DEVBRA7-video
Format:	VHS videotape
Terms:	Borrowers must have a User's Agreement on file with this source--available by mail or via the Internet. Return postage is paid by borrower; return 12 days after showing. Book at least three weeks in advance. All borrowers are limited to a total of ten items per semester.

Source: Latin American Resource Center
Stone Center for Latin American Studies
Tulane University
100 Jones Hall
New Orleans, LA 70118
Phone: 1-504-862-3143
Fax: 1-504-865-6719
World Wide Web URL:
http://stonecenter.tulane.edu/pages/detail/48/
Lending-Library
Email Address: crcrts@tulane.edu

Marriages in Heaven

This illuminating documentary explores the ways in which globalization and modernization are affecting young people and changing the traditions of arranged marriages among Indians living both in India and in America.

Availability:	Schools, libraries, homeschoolers, and nursing homes in the southeastern United States.
Suggested Grade:	7-12
Order Number:	order by title
Production Date:	2001
Format:	VHS videotape
Terms:	Borrower pays return postage. Return 2 days after showing via United Parcel Service, insured. Book 2 weeks in advance.

Source: Center for South Asian Studies
University of Virginia
Video Library Coordinator
P. O. Box 400169, 110 Minor Hall
Charlottesville, VA 22904-4169
Phone: 1-434-924-8815
Email Address: southasia@virginia.edu

Mercado, El

An introduction to the markets of Latin America--the hub of life in villages.

Availability:	Schools in the United States.
Suggested Grade:	All ages
Language:	Spanish
Order Number:	order by title
Production Date:	1990
Format:	VHS videotape
Terms:	Borrower pays return postage. Return 14 days after receipt, via USPS including insurance. All borrowers must have a current lending agreement on file with the Outreach program. This agreement is available via the web site or may be requested via phone or fax.

Source: Center for Latin American Studies
University of Florida
319 Grinter Hall
P. O. Box 115530
Gainesville, FL 32611-5530
Phone: 1-352-392-0375
Fax: 1-352-392-7682
World Wide Web URL: http://www.latam.ufl.edu/outreach
Email Address: maryr@ufl.edu

Middle America: Mexico to Venezuela and the Caribbean Islands

Provides a glance at the geography, food production, cultures and economies of Mexico, Central America and the Caribbean. Maps are intermittently superimposed over scenes that link "where" with "what" is being seen.

Availability:	Schools in the United States.
Suggested Grade:	6-12
Order Number:	order by title
Production Date:	1995
Format:	VHS videotape
Terms:	Borrower pays return postage. Return 14 days after receipt, via USPS including insurance. All borrowers must have a current lending agreement on file with the Outreach program. This agreement is available via the web site or may be requested via phone or fax.

Source: Center for Latin American Studies
University of Florida
319 Grinter Hall, P. O. Box 115530
Gainesville, FL 32611-5530
Phone: 1-352-392-0375
Fax: 1-352-392-7682
World Wide Web URL: http://www.latam.ufl.edu/outreach
Email Address: maryr@ufl.edu

Modern Brides: Arranged Marriage in South India

Describes two marriages that occur in Mysore, South India in 1983. One marriage is an arranged marriage and the other is a "love" marriage.

Availability: Schools and libraries in the United States.
Suggested Grade: 7-Adult
Order Number: SA9
Production Date: 1985
Format: VHS videotape
Terms: Borrower pays return postage. Return 3 days after showing via UPS. Book at least 2 weeks in advance.
Source: Syracuse University, South Asia Center
Video Library and Teaching Resources
346F Eggers Hall
The Maxwell School
Syracuse, NY 13244

Mothers of Malappuram

Examines the changes in the attitudes of women's groups as well as the Indian government towards population issues.

Availability: Schools and libraries in the United States.
Suggested Grade: 7-Adult
Order Number: SA48
Format: VHS videotape
Terms: Borrower pays return postage. Return 3 days after showing via UPS. Book at least 2 weeks in advance.
Source: Syracuse University, South Asia Center
Video Library and Teaching Resources
346F Eggers Hall
The Maxwell School
Syracuse, NY 13244

My Gift Is Peace of Mind

Dr. Yoko went to medical school while raising her children, and successfully became a doctor at 42 years old. She comes to the northernmost island of Japan in Hokkaido, where there had been no doctors in the past.

Availability: Schools, libraries and homeschoolers in Alabama, Georgia, North Carolina, South Carolina, and Virginia.
Suggested Grade: 6-12
Order Number: 701
Production Date: 1991
Format: VHS videotape
Special Notes: No. 1 of the "Nippon Life II" series.
Terms: Borrower pays return postage. Two tapes may be borrowed at a time. Return within 7 days after receipt. Reservations may be made by filling the application found on the web site.
Source: Consulate General of Japan, Atlanta
Japan Information Center
One Alliance Center
3500 Lenox Road, Suite 1600
Atlanta, GA 30326
Phone: 1-404-365-9240
Fax: 1-404-240-4311
World Wide Web URL:
http://www.atlanta.us.emb-japan.go.jp
Email Address: info@cgjapanatlanta.org

My Gift Is Peace of Mind

Dr. Yoko went to medical school while raising her children, and successfully became a doctor at 42 years old. She comes to the northernmost island of Japan in Hokkaido, where there had been no doctors in the past.

Availability: Schools, libraries, and nursing homes in Hawaii.
Suggested Grade: 6-12
Order Number: CU-68
Production Date: 1991
Format: VHS videotape
Special Notes: No. 1 of the "Nippon Life II" series.
Terms: Borrower pays return postage. A maximum of 3 videos may be borrowed per person. Return within one week of date borrowed.
Source: Consulate General of Japan, Honolulu
1742 Nuuanu Avenue
Honolulu, HI 96817-3294
Phone: 1-808-543-3111
Fax: 1-808-543-3170
World Wide Web URL:
http://www.honolulu.us.emb-japan.go.jp

My Gift Is Peace of Mind

Dr. Yoko went to medical school while raising her children, and successfully became a doctor at 42 years old. She comes to the northernmost island of Japan in Hokkaido, where there had been no doctors in the past.

Availability: Schools, libraries, homeschoolers, and nursing homes in OREGON AND SOUTHERN IDAHO ONLY. Please make requests via the web site.
Suggested Grade: 6-12
Order Number: 171
Production Date: 1991
Format: VHS videotape
Special Notes: No. 1 of the "Nippon Life II" series.
Terms: Borrower pays return postage. Return within three weeks after scheduled showing date. Book one month in advance if possible. Rewind the video and wrap securely for return. Be certain to indicate video number, date needed, name of your organization, and address to which video should be sent, along with phone number. Audience report enclosed with the video must be completed and returned.
Source: Consulate General of Japan, Oregon
Attn: Tamara, Video Library
1300 S. W. Fifth Avenue, Suite 2700
Portland, OR 97201
Phone: 1-503-221-1811, ext. 17
World Wide Web URL:
http://www.portland.us.emb-japan.go.jp/en/index.html
Email Address: tamara@cgjpdx.org

Nati: A Mayan Teenager

Most of this video is devoted to the activities of daily life as practiced by people living in the rural Mexican community of Chiapas.

Availability: Schools in the United States.
Suggested Grade: 7-12
Order Number: order by title
Production Date: 1991
Format: VHS videotape
Terms: Borrower pays return postage. Return 14 days after receipt, via USPS including insurance. All borrowers must have a current lending agreement on file with the Outreach program. This agreement is available via the web site or may be requested via phone or fax.

Source: Center for Latin American Studies
University of Florida
319 Grinter Hall
P. O. Box 115530
Gainesville, FL 32611-5530
Phone: 1-352-392-0375
Fax: 1-352-392-7682
World Wide Web URL: http://www.latam.ufl.edu/outreach
Email Address: maryr@ufl.edu

Navidad en Mexico, La

Christmas in Mexico reveals Spanish, Native American, and North American influences as shown in this video.

Availability: Schools and libraries in Iowa, Illinois, Michigan, Minnesota, and Wisconsin.
Suggested Grade: All ages
Language: Spanish
Order Number: FESTMEXN22.1VHS
Format: VHS videotape
Terms: Borrower pays return postage. Return 8 days after showing. Book 2 weeks in advance. Order may also be picked up for those near the Center.

Source: Center for Latin American and Caribbean Studies
UW-Milwaukee
P. O. Box 413
Milwaukee, WI 53201
Phone: 1-414-229-5987
World Wide Web URL: http://www.uwm.edu/Dept/CLACS
Email Address: audvis@usm.edu

Neighbors

Presents a typical residential complex in China. Six families share one apartment.

Availability: Schools, libraries, homeschoolers, and nursing homes in the United States and Canada.
Suggested Grade: 6-12
Languages: English; Chinese
Order Number: order by title
Production Date: 1982
Format: VHS videotape
Terms: Postage is paid by borrower both ways--send $3.00 per tape to cover initial shipping to you--MONEY MUST BE SENT WITH REQUEST. Return 10 days after showing via U. S. Postal Service, library rate. Shipping is $5.00 to Canadian addresses.

Source: Center for Teaching About China
Kathleen Trescott
1214 West Schwartz
Carbondale, IL 62901

Phone: 1-618-549-1555
Email Address: trescott@midwest.net

NHK Special "Fujisan:" The Greatest Mountain of Japan

The Eiheiji is one of the best known Japanese temples of the Zen school, or more strictly of one of its branches the Soto Sect. Detail of the daily lives of the 150 novices, 90% of them college graduates, are covered.

Availability: Schools, libraries, and nursing homes in Hawaii.
Suggested Grade: 4-12
Order Number: CU-31
Production Date: 1991
Format: VHS videotape
Special Notes: Part of the "Nippon Life II" series. No narration.
Terms: Borrower pays return postage. A maximum of 3 videos may be borrowed per person. Return within one week of date borrowed.

Source: Consulate General of Japan, Honolulu
1742 Nuuanu Avenue
Honolulu, HI 96817-3294
Phone: 1-808-543-3111
Fax: 1-808-543-3170
World Wide Web URL:
http://www.honolulu.us.emb-japan.go.jp

Night of Nine Tribes, The

Recommended for those with a particular interest in state-sponsored revivals of indigenous ritual ceremonies. This video chronicles the International Year of the Indigenous People, featuring the Tayal people of Wu Lai, and hosted by the Taiwan Cultural Ministry in cooperation with other government ministries and bureaus.

Availability: Schools, libraries, and nursing homes in the United States and Canada.
Suggested Grade: All ages
Languages: Chinese; subtitled in English
Order Number: TV007
Format: VHS videotape
Terms: Borrower pays return postage. Return with 14 days after scheduled showing, via UPS or U. S. Mail. All requests must included an educational institution affiliation, a current address, and phone number. Order through web site only.

Source: Cornell University East Asia Program
World Wide Web URL:
http://www.einaudi.cornell.edu/eastasia/outreach/video.asp
Email Address: east_asia1@cornell.edu

No Longer Colonies: Hong Kong, 1997; Macau, 1999

Traces the history and prospects of the last European colonies in Chinese territory.

Availability: Schools, libraries, homeschoolers, and nursing homes in the United States and Canada.
Suggested Grade: 7-Adult

Order Number: order by title
Production Date: 1993
Format: VHS videotape
Terms: Postage is paid by borrower both ways--send $3.00 per tape to cover initial shipping to you--MONEY MUST BE SENT WITH REQUEST. Return 10 days after showing via U. S. Postal Service, library rate. Shipping is $5.00 to Canadian addresses.
      Source: Center for Teaching About China
          Kathleen Trescott
          1214 West Schwartz
          Carbondale, IL 62901
          Phone: 1-618-549-1555
      Email Address: trescott@midwest.net

Pakistan: Between the Chitralis and Pathans

This program looks at Pakistan's complex relations with Iran, India, and the United States and the contributions of its multicultural population.

Availability: Schools, libraries, homeschoolers, and nursing homes in the southeastern United States.
Suggested Grade: 7-12
Order Number: order by title
Production Date: 1999
Format: VHS videotape
Terms: Borrower pays return postage. Return 2 days after showing via United Parcel Service, insured. Book 2 weeks in advance.
      Source: Center for South Asian Studies
          University of Virginia
          Video Library Coordinator
          P. O. Box 400169, 110 Minor Hall
          Charlottesville, VA 22904-4169
          Phone: 1-434-924-8815
      Email Address: southasia@virginia.edu

Pakistan: Between the Chitralis and Pathans

Looks at Pakistan's complex relations with Iran, India, and the United States, and the contributions of its multicultural population.

Availability: Schools and libraries in the United States.
Suggested Grade: 7-Adult
Order Number: SA111
Format: VHS videotape
Terms: Borrower pays return postage. Return 3 days after showing via UPS. Book at least 2 weeks in advance.
      Source: Syracuse University, South Asia Center
          Video Library and Teaching Resources
          346F Eggers Hall
          The Maxwell School
          Syracuse, NY 13244

Panama: Crossroads of the World

History, culture, and geography of Panama from the Spanish conquest to present day.

Availability: Schools, libraries, and nursing homes in the United States.
Suggested Grade: 6-12

Order Number: HPAN1-video
Production Date: 1988
Format: VHS videotape
Terms: Borrowers must have a User's Agreement on file with this source--available by mail or via the Internet. Return postage is paid by borrower; return 12 days after showing. Book at least three weeks in advance. All borrowers are limited to a total of ten items per semester.
      Source: Latin American Resource Center
      Stone Center for Latin American Studies
          Tulane University
          100 Jones Hall
          New Orleans, LA 70118
          Phone: 1-504-862-3143
          Fax: 1-504-865-6719
          World Wide Web URL:
    http://stonecenter.tulane.edu/pages/detail/48/
          Lending-Library
      Email Address: crcrts@tulane.edu

Parties, Pinatas and Plays: Mexican Christmas Traditions

Discusses and depicts the origins of the celebration of Christmas in Mexico.

Availability: Schools in the United States.
Suggested Grade: 6-12
Order Number: order by title
Format: VHS videotape
Terms: Borrower pays return postage. Return 14 days after receipt, via USPS including insurance. All borrowers must have a current lending agreement on file with the Outreach program. This agreement is available via the web site or may be requested via phone or fax.
      Source: Center for Latin American Studies
          University of Florida
          319 Grinter Hall
          P. O. Box 115530
          Gainesville, FL 32611-5530
          Phone: 1-352-392-0375
          Fax: 1-352-392-7682
  World Wide Web URL: http://www.latam.ufl.edu/outreach
      Email Address: maryr@ufl.edu

Partition of India

Examines the role of Pakistan's founder, Mohammed Ali Jinnah, in Pakistan's fight to be recognized as a separate nation.

Availability: Schools and libraries in the United States.
Suggested Grade: 7-Adult
Order Number: SA121
Production Date: 1998
Format: VHS videotape
Terms: Borrower pays return postage. Return 3 days after showing via UPS. Book at least 2 weeks in advance.
      Source: Syracuse University, South Asia Center
          Video Library and Teaching Resources
          346F Eggers Hall
          The Maxwell School
          Syracuse, NY 13244

All materials listed in this 2011-2012 edition are BRAND NEW!

Passion for Whales, A: Tomohisa Nagaoka's Story

Tells the story of a former whaler and how the international moratorium on whaling affected his life and his work as well as the city of Muroto.

Availability: Schools, libraries, and nursing homes in Hawaii.
Suggested Grade: 6-12
Order Number: NA-3
Production Date: 1992
Format: VHS videotape
Terms: Borrower pays return postage. A maximum of 3 videos may be borrowed per person. Return within one week of date borrowed.

Source: Consulate General of Japan, Honolulu
1742 Nuuanu Avenue
Honolulu, HI 96817-3294
Phone: 1-808-543-3111
Fax: 1-808-543-3170
World Wide Web URL:
http://www.honolulu.us.emb-japan.go.jp

Pilot

An overview of the series of ten programs, "Nihon No Kokoro" to help the viewer understand the unique perspective of the Japanese; what is important to them, why they respond and believe the way they do.

Availability: Schools, libraries and homeschoolers in Alabama, Georgia, North Carolina, South Carolina, and Virginia.
Suggested Grade: 6-Adult
Order Number: 531
Format: VHS videotape
Special Notes: No. 1 of the "Nihon No Kokoro" series.
Terms: Borrower pays return postage. Two tapes may be borrowed at a time. Return within 7 days after receipt. Reservations may be made by filling the application found on the web site.

Source: Consulate General of Japan, Atlanta
Japan Information Center
One Alliance Center
3500 Lenox Road, Suite 1600
Atlanta, GA 30326
Phone: 1-404-365-9240
Fax: 1-404-240-4311
World Wide Web URL:
http://www.atlanta.us.emb-japan.go.jp
Email Address: info@cgjapanatlanta.org

Pinata, The

Shows a festive look at the holiday season in Mexico, focusing on the making of pinatas.

Availability: Schools and libraries in Iowa, Illinois, Michigan, Minnesota, and Wisconsin.
Suggested Grade: All ages
Order Number: ART/FOIMEXP65VHS
Format: VHS videotape
Terms: Borrower pays return postage. Return 8 days after showing. Book 2 weeks in advance. Order may also be picked up for those near the Center.

Source: Center for Latin American and Caribbean Studies
UW-Milwaukee, P. O. Box 413
Milwaukee, WI 53201
Phone: 1-414-229-5987
World Wide Web URL: http://www.uwm.edu/Dept/CLACS
Email Address: audvis@usm.edu

Rajiv's India

Interviews with various Indians show the country's early response to Rajiv Gandhi's "politics of conciliation," and show how the people are trying to keep their 5,000-year-old heritage while modernizing rapidly.

Availability: Schools, libraries, homeschoolers, and nursing homes in the southeastern United States.
Suggested Grade: 7-12
Order Number: order by title
Production Date: 1985
Format: VHS videotape
Terms: Borrower pays return postage. Return 2 days after showing via United Parcel Service, insured. Book 2 weeks in advance.

Source: Center for South Asian Studies
University of Virginia
Video Library Coordinator
P. O. Box 400169, 110 Minor Hall
Charlottesville, VA 22904-4169
Phone: 1-434-924-8815
Email Address: southasia@virginia.edu

Ricardo Montalban's South America

This tour of South American countries captures dozens of attractive images with special emphasis on music and dance.

Availability: Schools in the United States.
Suggested Grade: 7-12
Order Number: order by title
Format: VHS videotape
Terms: Borrower pays return postage. Return 14 days after receipt, via USPS including insurance. All borrowers must have a current lending agreement on file with the Outreach program. This agreement is available via the web site or may be requested via phone or fax.

Source: Center for Latin American Studies
University of Florida
319 Grinter Hall
P. O. Box 115530
Gainesville, FL 32611-5530
Phone: 1-352-392-0375
Fax: 1-352-392-7682
World Wide Web URL: http://www.latam.ufl.edu/outreach
Email Address: maryr@ufl.edu

Running and Running for Mayor

Takes a look at the role local government plays in the lives of Japanese people and the special relationship politicians must develop with their constituents.

Availability: Schools, libraries and homeschoolers in Alabama, Georgia, North Carolina, South Carolina, and Virginia.

Suggested Grade: 6-12
Order Number: 412
Production Date: 1988
Format: VHS videotape
Special Notes: Part of the "Faces of Japan" series.
Terms: Borrower pays return postage. Two tapes may be borrowed at a time. Return within 7 days after receipt. Reservations may be made by filling the application found on the web site.
Source: **Consulate General of Japan, Atlanta**
Japan Information Center
One Alliance Center
3500 Lenox Road, Suite 1600
Atlanta, GA 30326
Phone: 1-404-365-9240
Fax: 1-404-240-4311
World Wide Web URL:
http://www.atlanta.us.emb-japan.go.jp
Email Address: info@cgjapanatlanta.org

Running and Running for Mayor

Takes a look at the role local government plays in the lives of Japanese people and the special relationship politicians must develop with their constituents.
Availability: Schools, libraries, homeschoolers, and nursing homes in OREGON AND SOUTHERN IDAHO ONLY. Please make requests via the web site.
Suggested Grade: 6-12
Order Number: 525
Production Date: 1988
Format: VHS videotape
Special Notes: Part of the "Faces of Japan" series.
Terms: Borrower pays return postage. Return within three weeks after scheduled showing date. Book one month in advance if possible. Rewind the video and wrap securely for return. Be certain to indicate video number, date needed, name of your organization, and address to which video should be sent, along with phone number. Audience report enclosed with the video must be completed and returned.
Source: **Consulate General of Japan, Oregon**
Attn: Tamara, Video Library
1300 S. W. Fifth Avenue, Suite 2700
Portland, OR 97201
Phone: 1-503-221-1811, ext. 17
World Wide Web URL:
http://www.portland.us.emb-japan.go.jp/en/index.html
Email Address: tamara@cgjpdx.org

Salaam Bombay

Presents the tribulations of life on the streets of Bombay, India through the eyes of a young, homeless boy.
Availability: Schools and libraries in the United States.
Suggested Grade: 7-Adult
Order Number: SA127
Production Date: 1988
Format: VHS videotape

Terms: Borrower pays return postage. Return 3 days after showing via UPS. Book at least 2 weeks in advance.
Source: **Syracuse University, South Asia Center**
Video Library and Teaching Resources
346F Eggers Hall
The Maxwell School
Syracuse, NY 13244

Saudade do Futuro

Tells the story of the poor Nordestinos who travel south to try to find fame and fortune in Sao Paulo, Brazil.
Availability: Schools and libraries in Iowa, Illinois, Michigan, Minnesota, and Wisconsin.
Suggested Grade: 6-12
Portuguese with English subtitles
Order Number: FFBRASAT8DVD
Production Date: 2004
Format: DVD
Terms: Borrower pays return postage. Return 8 days after showing. Book 2 weeks in advance. Order may also be picked up for those near the Center.
Source: **Center for Latin American and Caribbean Studies**
UW-Milwaukee
P. O. Box 413
Milwaukee, WI 53201
Phone: 1-414-229-5987
World Wide Web URL: http://www.uwm.edu/Dept/CLACS
Email Address: audvis@usm.edu

Seeds of Plenty, Seeds of Sorrow; Developing Stories 1

A documentary from India about the effects of the Green Revolution, from India's point of view.
Availability: Schools and libraries in the United States.
Suggested Grade: 7-Adult
Order Number: SA95
Production Date: 1992
Format: VHS videotape
Terms: Borrower pays return postage. Return 3 days after showing via UPS. Book at least 2 weeks in advance.
Source: **Syracuse University, South Asia Center**
Video Library and Teaching Resources
346F Eggers Hall
The Maxwell School
Syracuse, NY 13244

Serial for Breakfast (Part I & II)

Explores the impact of global satellite television broadcasts on the Indian electronic mediascape.
Availability: Schools and libraries in the United States.
Suggested Grade: 7-Adult
Order Number: SA77
Production Date: 1998
Format: VHS videotape
Terms: Borrower pays return postage. Return 3 days after showing via UPS. Book at least 2 weeks in advance.
Source: **Syracuse University, South Asia Center**
Video Library and Teaching Resources
346F Eggers Hall, The Maxwell School
Syracuse, NY 13244

Sixteen Decisions

Refers to a 16-point social charter developed by poor Bangladeshi women and instituted by the Grameen Bank to encourage fundamental community and personal change. This focuses on the everyday life of 18-year-old Selina, one of the 2.5 million impoverished women who are building a stronger rural economy through small businesses they start with loans from the Grameen Bank.

Availability:	Schools, libraries, homeschoolers, and nursing homes in the southeastern United States.
Suggested Grade:	7-12
Order Number:	order by title
Production Date:	2000
Format:	VHS videotape
Terms:	Borrower pays return postage. Return 2 days after showing via United Parcel Service, insured. Book 2 weeks in advance.

Source: Center for South Asian Studies
University of Virginia
Video Library Coordinator
P. O. Box 400169, 110 Minor Hall
Charlottesville, VA 22904-4169
Phone: 1-434-924-8815
Email Address: southasia@virginia.edu

Sixteen Decisions

Refers to a 16-point social charter developed by poor Bangladeshi women and instituted by the Grameen Bank to encourage fundamental community and personal change. This focuses on the everyday life of 18-year-old Selina, one of the 2.5 million impoverished women who are building a stronger rural economy through small businesses they start with loans from the Grameen Bank.

Availability:	Schools and libraries in the United States.
Suggested Grade:	7-12
Order Number:	97
Production Date:	2000
Format:	VHS videotape
Terms:	Borrower pays return postage. Return 3 days after showing via UPS. Book at least 2 weeks in advance.

Source: Syracuse University, South Asia Center
Video Library and Teaching Resources
346F Eggers Hall
The Maxwell School
Syracuse, NY 13244

Suburban Tokyo High School Students: Video Letter from Japan II

Designed to show how Japanese high-school students can be modern and at the same time not be Western.

Availability:	Schools, libraries, and nursing homes in the United States and Canada.
Suggested Grade:	6-Adult
Order Number:	JV015
Format:	VHS videotape
Special Notes:	Teacher's manual included

Terms:	Borrower pays return postage. Return with 14 days after scheduled showing, via UPS or U. S. Mail. All requests must included an educational institution affiliation, a current address, and phone number. Order through web site only.

Source: Cornell University East Asia Program
World Wide Web URL:
http://www.einaudi.cornell.edu/eastasia/outreach/video.asp
Email Address: east_asia1@cornell.edu

Taj Mahal: The Story of Muslim India

Identifies key influence of the Muslim culture upon the India sub-continent including this famous building.

Availability:	Schools and libraries in the United States.
Suggested Grade:	7-Adult
Order Number:	SA40
Production Date:	1991
Format:	VHS videotape
Terms:	Borrower pays return postage. Return 3 days after showing via UPS. Book at least 2 weeks in advance.

Source: Syracuse University, South Asia Center
Video Library and Teaching Resources
346F Eggers Hall
The Maxwell School
Syracuse, NY 13244

Tea Drinking in Taipei

For thousands of years, tea drinking has been appreciated by Chinese people as a means to promote health and friendship. This video describes the art of drinking tea, growing and processing tea, and tea's history in China.

Availability:	Schools, libraries, and nursing homes in the United States and Canada.
Suggested Grade:	6-Adult
Order Number:	TV010
Format:	VHS videotape
Terms:	Borrower pays return postage. Return with 14 days after scheduled showing, via UPS or U. S. Mail. All requests must included an educational institution affiliation, a current address, and phone number. Order through web site only.

Source: Cornell University East Asia Program
World Wide Web URL:
http://www.einaudi.cornell.edu/eastasia/outreach/video.asp
Email Address: east_asia1@cornell.edu

Tea in Taiwan

Taiwan has always been among the world's top tea producers and exporters, and Taiwan tea has been called the "champagne" of teas. This video describes the history of tea in China and other parts of the world, growing, harvesting, preparation of leaves, refining, taste-testing, exporting, and current research.

Availability:	Schools, libraries, and nursing homes in the United States and Canada.
Suggested Grade:	6-Adult
Order Number:	TV011
Format:	VHS videotape

*All materials listed in this 2011-2012 edition are **BRAND NEW!***

Terms: Borrower pays return postage. Return with 14 days after scheduled showing, via UPS or U. S. Mail. All requests must included an educational institution affiliation, a current address, and phone number. Order through web site only.

Source: Cornell University East Asia Program
World Wide Web URL:
http://www.einaudi.cornell.edu/eastasia/outreach/video.asp
Email Address: east_asia1@cornell.edu

Tibet

A visual guide to Tibet's history, religion, culture, society and geography. Includes films, pictures, maps, music and everything you need to know about Tibet.

Availability: Schools, libraries, and nursing homes in the United States and Canada.
Suggested Grade: 6-Adult
Order Number: TBD005
Format: DVD
Terms: Borrower pays return postage. Return with 14 days after scheduled showing, via UPS or U. S. Mail. All requests must included an educational institution affiliation, a current address, and phone number. Order through web site only.

Source: Cornell University East Asia Program
World Wide Web URL:
http://www.einaudi.cornell.edu/eastasia/outreach/video.asp
Email Address: east_asia1@cornell.edu

Tokyo: The Changing Metropolis

Tokyo is world renowned as a city of modern architectural design employing much that is experimental as well as new, therefore in a continuous state of demolishing and rebuilding. This is in direct contrast to many great cities of the West.

Availability: Schools, libraries and homeschoolers in Alabama, Georgia, North Carolina, South Carolina, and Virginia.
Suggested Grade: 4-12
Order Number: 522
Production Date: 1989
Format: VHS videotape
Special Notes: No. 9 in the "Japan: Spirit and Form" series.
Terms: Borrower pays return postage. Two tapes may be borrowed at a time. Return within 7 days after receipt. Reservations may be made by filling the application found on the web site.

Source: Consulate General of Japan, Atlanta
Japan Information Center
One Alliance Center
3500 Lenox Road, Suite 1600
Atlanta, GA 30326
Phone: 1-404-365-9240
Fax: 1-404-240-4311
World Wide Web URL:
http://www.atlanta.us.emb-japan.go.jp
Email Address: info@cgjapanatlanta.org

Trans-Tokyo Road, The

Focuses on the enormous project of constructing the Trans-Tokyo Bay road between Kawasaki and Kisarazu, and its influence on the people.

Availability: Schools, libraries, and nursing homes in Hawaii.
Suggested Grade: 4-12
Order Number: BU-31
Production Date: 1990
Format: VHS videotape
Special Notes: No. 2 of the "Nippon Life" series.
Terms: Borrower pays return postage. A maximum of 3 videos may be borrowed per person. Return within one week of date borrowed.

Source: Consulate General of Japan, Honolulu
1742 Nuuanu Avenue
Honolulu, HI 96817-3294
Phone: 1-808-543-3111
Fax: 1-808-543-3170
World Wide Web URL:
http://www.honolulu.us.emb-japan.go.jp

Travel & Cultures Videos

Videos about a lot of different places and cultures.

Availability: All requesters
Suggested Grade: All ages
Order Number: not applicable
Format: Streaming Video

Source: National Geographic
World Wide Web URL:
http://video.nationalgeographic.com/video/

Travel Wise in Japan

Presents beautiful small towns and villages not often visited by tourists to Japan.

Availability: Schools, libraries and homeschoolers in Alabama, Georgia, North Carolina, South Carolina, and Virginia.
Suggested Grade: 4-12
Order Number: 322
Format: VHS videotape
Terms: Borrower pays return postage. Two tapes may be borrowed at a time. Return within 7 days after receipt. Reservations may be made by filling the application found on the web site.

Source: Consulate General of Japan, Atlanta
Japan Information Center
One Alliance Center
3500 Lenox Road, Suite 1600
Atlanta, GA 30326
Phone: 1-404-365-9240
Fax: 1-404-240-4311
World Wide Web URL:
http://www.atlanta.us.emb-japan.go.jp
Email Address: info@cgjapanatlanta.org

Travel Wise in Japan

Presents beautiful small towns and villages not often visited by tourists to Japan.

Availability: Schools, libraries, and nursing homes in Hawaii.

Suggested Grade: 4-12
Order Number: TR-21
Production Date: 1997
Format: VHS videotape
Terms: Borrower pays return postage. A maximum of 3 videos may be borrowed per person. Return within one week of date borrowed.

Source: Consulate General of Japan, Honolulu
1742 Nuuanu Avenue
Honolulu, HI 96817-3294
Phone: 1-808-543-3111
Fax: 1-808-543-3170
World Wide Web URL:
http://www.honolulu.us.emb-japan.go.jp

Travel Wise in Japan

Presents beautiful small towns and villages not often visited by tourists to Japan.

Availability: Schools, libraries, homeschoolers, and nursing homes in OREGON AND SOUTHERN IDAHO ONLY. Please make requests via the web site.

Suggested Grade: 4-12
Order Number: 423
Production Date: 1997
Format: VHS videotape
Terms: Borrower pays return postage. Return within three weeks after scheduled showing date. Book one month in advance if possible. Rewind the video and wrap securely for return. Be certain to indicate video number, date needed, name of your organization, and address to which video should be sent, along with phone number. Audience report enclosed with the video must be completed and returned.

Source: Consulate General of Japan, Oregon
Attn: Tamara, Video Library
1300 S. W. Fifth Avenue, Suite 2700
Portland, OR 97201
Phone: 1-503-221-1811, ext. 17
World Wide Web URL:
http://www.portland.us.emb-japan.go.jp/en/index.html
Email Address: tamara@cgjpdx.org

Tropical Kingdom of Belize

From mountaintop to barrier reef, the tiny Central American country of Belize features one of the most diverse natural environments in the world.

Availability: Schools in the United States.
Suggested Grade: All ages
Order Number: order by title
Production Date: 1986
Format: VHS videotape
Terms: Borrower pays return postage. Return 14 days after receipt, via USPS including insurance. All borrowers must have a current lending agreement on file with the Outreach program. This agreement is available via the web site or may be requested via phone or fax.

Source: Center for Latin American Studies
University of Florida
319 Grinter Hall
P. O. Box 115530
Gainesville, FL 32611-5530
Phone: 1-352-392-0375
Fax: 1-352-392-7682
World Wide Web URL: http://www.latam.ufl.edu/outreach
Email Address: maryr@ufl.edu

Tune in Japan: Global Connections

Looks at the world from a Japanese perspective. It offers a fascinating exploration of Japan's lively and exciting youth culture, examines the strong Japanese belief in community, and addresses the increasing environmental challenges and global communication issues that will shape Japan's (as well as the rest of the world's) political policies and future interpersonal relationships.

Availability: Schools, libraries, and nursing homes in the United States and Canada.

Suggested Grade: 6-12
Order Number: JV053
Format: VHS videotape
Special Notes: Includes a teacher's guide, lesson plans, and more.
Terms: Borrower pays return postage. Return with 14 days after scheduled showing, via UPS or U. S. Mail. All requests must included an educational institution affiliation, a current address, and phone number. Order through web site only.

Source: Cornell University East Asia Program
World Wide Web URL:
http://www.einaudi.cornell.edu/eastasia/outreach/video.asp
Email Address: east_asia1@cornell.edu

Tune in Korea: Legacy and Transformation

Explores the many facets of South Korea's history and culture by investigating such questions as: What is South Korea's place in the world today? Which world events led to the division of the Korean peninsula? How are North and South Korea poised for the future together?

Availability: Schools, libraries, and nursing homes in the United States and Canada.

Suggested Grade: 6-Adult
Order Number: KV067
Format: VHS videotape
Special Notes: Accompanied by a teacher's guide.
Terms: Borrower pays return postage. Return with 14 days after scheduled showing, via UPS or U. S. Mail. All requests must included an educational institution affiliation, a current address, and phone number. Order through web site only.

Source: Cornell University East Asia Program
World Wide Web URL:
http://www.einaudi.cornell.edu/eastasia/outreach/video.asp
Email Address: east_asia1@cornell.edu

Tuvans of Mongolia, The: Herders of Mongun-Taiga

Captures the lifestyle of the people of an inhospitable landscape, who number among their customs a storytelling tradition which requires a whole day to tell just one story and the remarkable musical phenomenon of "throat singing".

Availability: Schools, libraries, and nursing homes in the United States and Canada.
Suggested Grade: 6-Adult
Order Number: MV006
Format: VHS videotape
Terms: Borrower pays return postage. Return with 14 days after scheduled showing, via UPS or U. S. Mail. All requests must included an educational institution affiliation, a current address, and phone number. Order through web site only.

Source: Cornell University East Asia Program
World Wide Web URL:
http://www.einaudi.cornell.edu/eastasia/outreach/video.asp
Email Address: east_asia1@cornell.edu

Twilight for a Coal Mining Town: The Tale of Takashima

Looks at the crisis this Japanese town faces and it's flourishing coal mine closed.

Availability: Schools, libraries and homeschoolers in Alabama, Georgia, North Carolina, South Carolina, and Virginia.
Suggested Grade: 6-12
Order Number: 509
Format: VHS videotape
Special Notes: Tape 9 of the "Document Japan" series.
Terms: Borrower pays return postage. Two tapes may be borrowed at a time. Return within 7 days after receipt. Reservations may be made by filling the application found on the web site.

Source: Consulate General of Japan, Atlanta
Japan Information Center
One Alliance Center, 3500 Lenox Road, Suite 1600
Atlanta, GA 30326
Phone: 1-404-365-9240
Fax: 1-404-240-4311
World Wide Web URL:
http://www.atlanta.us.emb-japan.go.jp
Email Address: info@cgjapanatlanta.org

Twilight for a Coal Mining Town: The Tale of Takashima

Looks at the crisis this Japanese town faces and it's flourishing coal mine closed.

Availability: Schools, libraries, and nursing homes in Hawaii.
Suggested Grade: 6-12
Order Number: BU-27
Format: VHS videotape
Special Notes: Tape 9 of the "Document Japan" series.
Terms: Borrower pays return postage. A maximum of 3 videos may be borrowed per person. Return within one week of date borrowed.

Source: Consulate General of Japan, Honolulu
1742 Nuuanu Avenue
Honolulu, HI 96817-3294
Phone: 1-808-543-3111
Fax: 1-808-543-3170
World Wide Web URL:
http://www.honolulu.us.emb-japan.go.jp

We Are Guatemalans

Talks to the people of Guatemala who left refugee camps in Mexico to return to their homeland in the Ixcan jungle.

Availability: Schools in the United States.
Suggested Grade: 7-Adult
Order Number: order by title
Format: VHS videotape
Terms: Borrower pays return postage. Return 14 days after receipt, via USPS including insurance. All borrowers must have a current lending agreement on file with the Outreach program. This agreement is available via the web site or may be requested via phone or fax.

Source: Center for Latin American Studies
University of Florida
319 Grinter Hall
P. O. Box 115530
Gainesville, FL 32611-5530
Phone: 1-352-392-0375
Fax: 1-352-392-7682
World Wide Web URL: http://www.latam.ufl.edu/outreach
Email Address: maryr@ufl.edu

Wedding of the Goddess

Part 1 gives the historical background of the Chittirai festival of the city of Madurai, South India, in which the marriage of the goddess Minakshi to the god Sundaresshvara (the "beautiful Lord," Shiva), is re-enacted yearly. Part II follows the events of the nineteen-day festival, including the re-enactment of the goddess's coronation and marriage. There are scenes of public and private worship as well as interviews.

Availability: Schools, libraries, homeschoolers, and nursing homes in the southeastern United States.
Suggested Grade: 7-12
Order Number: order by title
Production Date: 1976
Format: VHS videotape
Terms: Borrower pays return postage. Return 2 days after showing via United Parcel Service, insured. Book 2 weeks in advance.

Source: Center for South Asian Studies
University of Virginia
Video Library Coordinator
P. O. Box 400169, 110 Minor Hall
Charlottesville, VA 22904-4169
Phone: 1-434-924-8815
Email Address: southasia@virginia.edu

All materials listed in this 2011-2012 edition are BRAND NEW!

Women in the Third World

Explores the condition of women throughout the developing world, emphasizing their central economic role as well as their ability to effect change in their societies. Women in Africa, Latin America, and Asia are portrayed.

Availability: Schools in the United States.
Suggested Grade: 7-Adult
Order Number: order by title
Production Date: 1987
Format: VHS videotape
Terms: Borrower pays return postage. Return 14 days after receipt, via USPS including insurance. All borrowers must have a current lending agreement on file with the Outreach program. This agreement is available via the web site or may be requested via phone or fax.

Source: Center for Latin American Studies
University of Florida
319 Grinter Hall
P. O. Box 115530
Gainesville, FL   32611-5530
Phone: 1-352-392-0375
Fax: 1-352-392-7682
World Wide Web URL: http://www.latam.ufl.edu/outreach
Email Address: maryr@ufl.edu

Working Women--Personal and Social Goals

Japanese women who have sought employment in remarkable numbers since the end of World War II now account for half of the work force. This video shows their roles both at home and at work.

Availability: Schools, libraries and homeschoolers in Alabama, Georgia, North Carolina, South Carolina, and Virginia.
Suggested Grade: 6-Adult
Order Number: 810
Production Date: 1991
Format: VHS videotape
Special Notes: No. 12 of the "Nippon the Land and Its People" series.
Terms: Borrower pays return postage. Two tapes may be borrowed at a time. Return within 7 days after receipt. Reservations may be made by filling the application found on the web site.

Source: Consulate General of Japan, Atlanta
Japan Information Center
One Alliance Center
3500 Lenox Road, Suite 1600
Atlanta, GA   30326
Phone: 1-404-365-9240
Fax: 1-404-240-4311
World Wide Web URL:
http://www.atlanta.us.emb-japan.go.jp
Email Address: info@cgjapanatlanta.org

Working Women--Personal and Social Goals

Japanese women who have sought employment in remarkable numbers since the end of World War II now account for half of the work force. This shows their roles both at home and at work.

Availability: Schools, libraries, and nursing homes in Hawaii.
Suggested Grade: 4-12
Order Number: CU-79
Production Date: 1991
Format: VHS videotape
Special Notes: No. 12 of the "Nippon the Land and Its People" series.
Terms: Borrower pays return postage. A maximum of 3 videos may be borrowed per person. Return within one week of date borrowed.

Source: Consulate General of Japan, Honolulu
1742 Nuuanu Avenue
Honolulu, HI   96817-3294
Phone: 1-808-543-3111
Fax: 1-808-543-3170
World Wide Web URL:
http://www.honolulu.us.emb-japan.go.jp

Yasawa, My Island Home

Life on the remote Yasawa Islands in Fiji without roads, vehicles, telephones, or television is traditional. But, what do kids do?

Availability: Schools, libraries, homeschoolers, church groups, nursing homes, and service clubs in the United States
Suggested Grade: K-4
Languages: English; Spanish
Order Number: order by title
Format: VHS videotape
Special Notes: Accompanied by a study guide.
Terms: Borrower pays return postage. Return within 21 days after receipt. Book at least 3 weeks in advance. You will be notified as soon as possible, if your order cannot be filled. All videos are cleared for television broadcast use.

Source: Columban Fathers Mission Society
Mission Education Department
Attn: Connie Wacha
P. O. Box 10
St. Columbans, NE   68056
Phone: 1-402-291-1920
Fax: 1-402-715-5575
World Wide Web URL: http://columban.org/missioned

America in the 20th Century: America Becomes a World Power

After the American Civil War, America's industrialization continued to grow, and the country entered a period of expansion. Covers events between 1854-1917.

Availability: Schools, libraries, and homeschoolers in the United States who serve the hearing impaired.
Suggested Grade: 7-12
Order Number: 11455
Production Date: 2003
Format: DVD
Special Notes: Also available as live streaming video over the Internet.
Terms: Sponsor pays all transportation costs. Return one week after receipt. Participation is limited to deaf or hard of hearing Americans, their parents, families, teachers, counselors, or others whose use would benefit a deaf or hard of hearing person. Only one person in the audience needs to be hearing impaired. You must register--which is free. These videos are all open-captioned--no special equipment is required for viewing.
Source: Described and Captioned Media Program
National Association of the Deaf
4211 Church Street Ext.
Roebuck, SC 29376
Phone: 1-800-237-6213
Fax: 1-800-538-5636
World Wide Web URL: http://www.dcmp.org

America's History in the Making

Uses video, online text, classroom activities, and Web-based activities to explore American history from the Pre-Columbian era through Reconstruction. Produced by Oregon Public Broadcasting.

Availability: All requesters
Suggested Grade: 6-12
Order Number: not applicable
Production Date: 2007
Format: Streaming Video
Special Notes: Also available for purchase for $450.00.
Terms: A simple FREE registration is required to view videos.
Source: Annenberg Media
World Wide Web URL:
http://www.learner.org/resources/browse.html

America's Transcontinental Railroad

America was once considered so vast that it could never be crossed. But on May 10, 1869, that idea vanished when the last spike in the transcontinental railroad was driven at Promontory, Utah. Uses old photos and reenactments to tell the story of Congressional debates, the planners and builders, and the problems overcome. Its impact changed the face of America and the west.

Availability: Schools, libraries, and homeschoolers in the United States who serve the hearing impaired.
Suggested Grade: 7-12
Order Number: 12978
Production Date: 1994

Format: DVD
Special Notes: Produced by Barr Media Group.
Terms: Sponsor pays all transportation costs. Return one week after receipt. Participation is limited to deaf or hard of hearing Americans, their parents, families, teachers, counselors, or others whose use would benefit a deaf or hard of hearing person. Only one person in the audience needs to be hearing impaired. You must register--which is free. These videos are all open-captioned--no special equipment is required for viewing.
Source: Described and Captioned Media Program
National Association of the Deaf
4211 Church Street Ext.
Roebuck, SC 29376
Phone: 1-800-237-6213
Fax: 1-800-538-5636
World Wide Web URL: http://www.dcmp.org

Appomattox Campaign, The

Covers the retreat of Lee's army and the surrender meeting.

Availability: Schools, libraries, and homeschoolers in the United States and Canada.
Suggested Grade: 6-Adult
Order Number: order by title
Format: DVD
Terms: Borrower pays return postage.
Source: Appomattox Court House National Historical Park
Education Coordinator
P. O. Box 218
Appomattox, VA 24522
Phone: 1-434-352-8987, ext. 31
Fax: 1-434-352-8568
World Wide Web URL:
http://www.nps.gov/apco/forteachers/index.htm
Email Address: www.nps.gov/apco

Aztecs, The

Explores Aztec culture and history, from the role of human sacrifice in the Aztec religion to their agricultural advances.

Availability: Schools in the United States.
Suggested Grade: 7-12
Order Number: order by title
Production Date: 1999
Format: VHS videotape
Terms: Borrower pays return postage. Return 14 days after receipt, via USPS including insurance. All borrowers must have a current lending agreement on file with the Outreach program. This agreement is available via the web site or may be requested via phone or fax.
Source: Center for Latin American Studies
University of Florida
319 Grinter Hall
P. O. Box 115530
Gainesville, FL 32611-5530
Phone: 1-352-392-0375
Fax: 1-352-392-7682
World Wide Web URL: http://www.latam.ufl.edu/outreach
Email Address: maryr@ufl.edu

Battle of Pointe du Hoc, The
Learn the story of the Rangers who fought the D-Day battle of Pointe du Hoc.

Availability: All requesters
Suggested Grade: 6-Adult
Order Number: not applicable
Format: Streaming Video
Source: American Battle Monuments Commission
World Wide Web URL: http://abmc.gov

Battle of the Gods
Tracks the brutal two-year Spanish campaign led by Hernán Cortés to conquer the land of central Mexico.

Availability: Schools in the United States.
Suggested Grade: 7-Adult
Order Number: order by title
Production Date: 2001
Format: VHS videotape
Terms: Borrower pays return postage. Return 14 days after receipt, via USPS including insurance. All borrowers must have a current lending agreement on file with the Outreach program. This agreement is available via the web site or may be requested via phone or fax.
Source: Center for Latin American Studies
University of Florida
319 Grinter Hall
P. O. Box 115530
Gainesville, FL 32611-5530
Phone: 1-352-392-0375
Fax: 1-352-392-7682
World Wide Web URL: http://www.latam.ufl.edu/outreach
Email Address: maryr@ufl.edu

Before Columbus Series
Native peoples of America tell their own story of the destruction of their culture and lands. A. Invasion, B. Rebellion, C. Temples into Churches, D. The Indian Experience in the 20th Century.

Availability: Schools, libraries, and nursing homes in the United States.
Suggested Grade: 6-12
Order Number: IND4-video
Production Date: 1993
Format: VHS videotape
Special Notes: Specify which program when ordering.
Terms: Borrowers must have a User's Agreement on file with this source--available by mail or via the Internet. Return postage is paid by borrower; return 12 days after showing. Book at least three weeks in advance. All borrowers are limited to a total of ten items per semester.
Source: Latin American Resource Center
Stone Center for Latin American Studies
Tulane University
100 Jones Hall
New Orleans, LA 70118
Phone: 1-504-862-3143
Fax: 1-504-865-6719

World Wide Web URL:
http://stonecenter.tulane.edu/pages/detail/48/
Lending-Library
Email Address: crcrts@tulane.edu

Behind the Scenes Tour of a Museum
What are museums? What are some kinds of museums? What do they do? There are art, history, and science and industry museums, made of collections of things that link us to the past and offer a glance into the future. Discusses acquisition, care and restoration, exhibits, and the importance of museums both in history and in life-long education.

Availability: Schools, libraries, and homeschoolers in the United States who serve the hearing impaired.
Suggested Grade: 6-10
Order Number: 12335
Production Date: 1994
Format: DVD
Special Notes: Produced by United Learning, Inc.
Terms: Sponsor pays all transportation costs. Return one week after receipt. Participation is limited to deaf or hard of hearing Americans, their parents, families, teachers, counselors, or others whose use would benefit a deaf or hard of hearing person. Only one person in the audience needs to be hearing impaired. You must register--which is free. These videos are all open-captioned--no special equipment is required for viewing.
Source: Described and Captioned Media Program
National Association of the Deaf
4211 Church Street Ext.
Roebuck, SC 29376
Phone: 1-800-237-6213
Fax: 1-800-538-5636
World Wide Web URL: http://www.dcmp.org

Birth of Pakistan, The
A survey of the history of Pakistan, from the religious unrest that led to Pakistan's separation from India at the time of independence to the election of Benazir Bhutto.

Availability: Schools, libraries, homeschoolers, and nursing homes in the southeastern United States.
Suggested Grade: 7-12
Order Number: order by title
Production Date: 1990
Format: VHS videotape
Terms: Borrower pays return postage. Return 2 days after showing via United Parcel Service, insured. Book 2 weeks in advance.
Source: Center for South Asian Studies
University of Virginia
Video Library Coordinator
P. O. Box 400169, 110 Minor Hall
Charlottesville, VA 22904-4169
Phone: 1-434-924-8815
Email Address: southasia@virginia.edu

Boom or Bust: Mining and the Opening of the American West

The lure of instant wealth attracted settlers to California, Colorado, Arizona, and Alaska. While only a few became rich, the discovery of gold, silver, and copper spurred the frontier economy, creating settlements, bringing merchants, and helping to expand the railroad system. Discusses placer and underground mining. Uses old photos and reenactments.

Availability: Schools, libraries, and homeschoolers in the United States who serve the hearing impaired.
Suggested Grade: 7-10
Order Number: 13041
Production Date: 1994
Format: DVD
Special Notes: Produced by United Learning, Inc.
Terms: Sponsor pays all transportation costs. Return one week after receipt. Participation is limited to deaf or hard of hearing Americans, their parents, families, teachers, counselors, or others whose use would benefit a deaf or hard of hearing person. Only one person in the audience needs to be hearing impaired. You must register--which is free. These videos are all open-captioned--no special equipment is required for viewing.
Source: Described and Captioned Media Program
National Association of the Deaf
4211 Church Street Ext.
Roebuck, SC 29376
Phone: 1-800-237-6213
Fax: 1-800-538-5636
World Wide Web URL: http://www.dcmp.org

Buried Mirror, The: Reflections on Spain and the New World

Five part series: A. The Virgin and the Bull; Spain's multicultural society. B. Conflict of the Gods; lives of peoples of America before 1492. C. The Age of Gold; Interaction between Spain and Latin America during the colonial era. D. The Price of

Availability: Schools and libraries in the United States and Canada.
Suggested Grade: 6-12
Order Number: order by title
Format: VHS videotape
Terms: Videos will typically be lent for seven days if mailed out--due date will be indicated. Films not returned within the time limit will be subject to overdue fines of $2 per video, per day. All borrowed must have a lending agreement on file. Form can be downloaded from http://isa.unc.edu/film/borrow.asp|aform. Borrowers are responsible for the cost of return shipping. Materials must be returned via a shipping method that has tracking information.
Source: Latin American Film Collection
3219 Fed Ex Global Education Center
301 Pittsboro Street, CB 3205
Chapel Hill, NC 27599-3205
Email Address: LA_Films@email.unc.edu

Caracol, the Lost Maya City

Recently-discovered Maya site in Belize illustrates features of Maya culture.

Availability: Schools, libraries, and nursing homes in the United States.
Suggested Grade: 6-12
Order Number: MY32-video
Production Date: 1987
Format: VHS videotape
Terms: Borrowers must have a User's Agreement on file with this source--available by mail or via the Internet. Return postage is paid by borrower; return 12 days after showing. Book at least three weeks in advance. All borrowers are limited to a total of ten items per semester.
Source: Latin American Resource Center
Stone Center for Latin American Studies
Tulane University
100 Jones Hall
New Orleans, LA 70118
Phone: 1-504-862-3143
Fax: 1-504-865-6719
World Wide Web URL:
http://stonecenter.tulane.edu/pages/detail/48/
Lending-Library
Email Address: crcrts@tulane.edu

Chaco Legacy, The

Road network, water control systems and huge architectural structures made by the Chaco Canyon civilization.

Availability: Schools, libraries, and nursing homes in the United States.
Suggested Grade: 6-12
Order Number: APUS3-video
Production Date: 1988
Format: VHS videotape
Terms: Borrowers must have a User's Agreement on file with this source--available by mail or via the Internet. Return postage is paid by borrower; return 12 days after showing. Book at least three weeks in advance. All borrowers are limited to a total of ten items per semester.
Source: Latin American Resource Center
Stone Center for Latin American Studies
Tulane University
100 Jones Hall
New Orleans, LA 70118
Phone: 1-504-862-3143
Fax: 1-504-865-6719
World Wide Web URL:
http://stonecenter.tulane.edu/pages/detail/48/
Lending-Library
Email Address: crcrts@tulane.edu

Chavez: Venezuela and the New Latin America

Explores Venezuela's explosive revolutionary terrain post-April 2002.

Availability: Schools and libraries in Iowa, Illinois, Michigan, Minnesota, and Wisconsin.

Suggested Grade: 6-12
Languages: Spanish with English subtitles
Order Number: POL/SOCVENCHAT39DD
Production Date: 2004
Format: DVD
Terms: Borrower pays return postage. Return 8 days after showing. Book 2 weeks in advance. Order may also be picked up for those near the Center.
Source: Center for Latin American and Caribbean Studies
UW-Milwaukee
P. O. Box 413
Milwaukee, WI 53201
Phone: 1-414-229-5987
World Wide Web URL: http://www.uwm.edu/Dept/CLACS
Email Address: audvis@usm.edu

Chavez: Venezuela and the New Latin America

Explores Venezuela's explosive revolutionary terrain post-April 2002.
Availability: Schools and libraries in the United States and Canada.
Suggested Grade: 6-12
Order Number: order by title
Production Date: 2004
Format: DVD
Terms: Videos will typically be lent for seven days if mailed out--due date will be indicated. Films not returned within the time limit will be subject to overdue fines of $2 per video, per day. All borrowed must have a lending agreement on file. Form can be downloaded from http://isa.unc.edu/film/borrow.asplaform. Borrowers are responsible for the cost of return shipping. Materials must be returned via a shipping method that has tracking information.
Source: Latin American Film Collection
3219 Fed Ex Global Education Center
301 Pittsboro Street, CB 3205
Chapel Hill, NC 27599-3205
Email Address: LA_Films@email.unc.edu

Chiapas: A Shot Heard Around the World

Filmed in January 1994, just days after the uprising in Chiapas began. This film analyzes the deeper causes of the rebellion.
Availability: Schools, libraries, and nursing homes in the United States.
Suggested Grade: 8-Adult
Languages: English with Spanish subtitles
Order Number: SIMEX7-video
Format: VHS videotape
Terms: Borrowers must have a User's Agreement on file with this source--available by mail or via the Internet. Return postage is paid by borrower; return 12 days after showing. Book at least three weeks in advance. All borrowers are limited to a total of ten items per semester.
Source: Latin American Resource Center
Stone Center for Latin American Studies
Tulane University, 100 Jones Hall
New Orleans, LA 70118

Phone: 1-504-862-3143
Fax: 1-504-865-6719
World Wide Web URL:
http://stonecenter.tulane.edu/pages/detail/48/
Lending-Library
Email Address: crcrts@tulane.edu

Chiapas: The Fight for Land and Liberty

Behind-the-scenes video portrays life of the indigenous in Chiapas to whom revolution makes sense.
Availability: Schools and libraries in the United States and Canada.
Suggested Grade: 8-Adult
Order Number: order by title
Production Date: 1994
Format: VHS videotape
Terms: Videos will typically be lent for seven days if mailed out--due date will be indicated. Films not returned within the time limit will be subject to overdue fines of $2 per video, per day. All borrowed must have a lending agreement on file. Form can be downloaded from http://isa.unc.edu/film/borrow.asplaform. Borrowers are responsible for the cost of return shipping. Materials must be returned via a shipping method that has tracking information.
Source: Latin American Film Collection
3219 Fed Ex Global Education Center
301 Pittsboro Street, CB 3205
Chapel Hill, NC 27599-3205
Email Address: LA_Films@email.unc.edu

Chiapas: The Fight for Land and Liberty

Behind-the-scenes video portrays life of the indigenous in Chiapas to whom revolution makes sense.
Availability: Schools, libraries, and nursing homes in the United States.
Suggested Grade: 8-Adult
Order Number: SIMEX5-video
Production Date: 1994
Format: VHS videotape
Terms: Borrowers must have a User's Agreement on file with this source--available by mail or via the Internet. Return postage is paid by borrower; return 12 days after showing. Book at least three weeks in advance. All borrowers are limited to a total of ten items per semester.
Source: Latin American Resource Center
Stone Center for Latin American Studies
Tulane University
100 Jones Hall
New Orleans, LA 70118
Phone: 1-504-862-3143
Fax: 1-504-865-6719
World Wide Web URL:
http://stonecenter.tulane.edu/pages/detail/48/
Lending-Library
Email Address: crcrts@tulane.edu

Chiapas: The Inside Story

History of the 30-year conflict between the Mexican

government and the indigenous population in Chiapas.

Availability: Schools, libraries, and nursing homes in the United States.
Suggested Grade: 8-Adult
Languages: Spanish with English subtitles
Order Number: SIMEX9-video
Production Date: 1999
Format: VHS videotape
Terms: Borrowers must have a User's Agreement on file with this source--available by mail or via the Internet. Return postage is paid by borrower; return 12 days after showing. Book at least three weeks in advance. All borrowers are limited to a total of ten items per semester.
Source: Latin American Resource Center
Stone Center for Latin American Studies
Tulane University
100 Jones Hall
New Orleans, LA 70118
Phone: 1-504-862-3143
Fax: 1-504-865-6719
World Wide Web URL:
http://stonecenter.tulane.edu/pages/detail/48/
Lending-Library
Email Address: crcrts@tulane.edu

China in Transition

Examines Chinese civilization after Tan Chien unified the country in 581. Covering the T'ang and Sung dynasties, it discusses the period's achievements, including Confucian scholarship and the building of the grand canals.

Availability: Schools, libraries, and nursing homes in the United States and Canada.
Suggested Grade: 6-Adult
Order Number: CV014
Format: VHS videotape
Terms: Borrower pays return postage. Return with 14 days after scheduled showing, via UPS or U. S. Mail. All requests must included an educational institution affiliation, a current address, and phone number. Order through web site only.
Source: Cornell University East Asia Program
World Wide Web URL:
http://www.einaudi.cornell.edu/eastasia/outreach/video.asp
Email Address: east_asia1@cornell.edu

Christians, The: The Conquest of Souls

Spanish missionary activity in the New World in the 16th century.

Availability: Schools, libraries, and nursing homes in the United States.
Suggested Grade: 6-12
Order Number: RLA2-video
Production Date: 1979
Format: VHS videotape
Terms: Borrowers must have a User's Agreement on file with this source--available by mail or via the Internet. Return postage is paid by borrower; return 12 days after showing. Book at least three weeks in advance. All borrowers are limited to a total of ten items per semester.

Source: Latin American Resource Center
Stone Center for Latin American Studies
Tulane University
100 Jones Hall
New Orleans, LA 70118
Phone: 1-504-862-3143
Fax: 1-504-865-6719
World Wide Web URL:
http://stonecenter.tulane.edu/pages/detail/48/
Lending-Library
Email Address: crcrts@tulane.edu

Classical Japan and the Tale of Genji (552-1185)

This series provides an overview of Japanese history from 552 to 1868 A.D., integrating key historical themes with the literature of the time. This program focuses on the Japanese genius for deliberate cultural borrowing.

Availability: Schools, libraries, and nursing homes in the United States and Canada.
Suggested Grade: 6-12
Order Number: JV042
Format: VHS videotape
Terms: Borrower pays return postage. Return with 14 days after scheduled showing, via UPS or U. S. Mail. All requests must included an educational institution affiliation, a current address, and phone number. Order through web site only.
Source: Cornell University East Asia Program
World Wide Web URL:
http://www.einaudi.cornell.edu/eastasia/outreach/video.asp
Email Address: east_asia1@cornell.edu

Columbus Didn't Discover Us

Indigenous activists from North, South, and Central America speak about issues important to them.

Availability: Schools and libraries in the United States and Canada.
Suggested Grade: 6-12
Order Number: order by title
Production Date: 1992
Format: DVD
Terms: Videos will typically be lent for seven days if mailed out--due date will be indicated. Films not returned within the time limit will be subject to overdue fines of $2 per video, per day. All borrowed must have a lending agreement on file. Form can be downloaded from http://isa.unc.edu/film/borrow.asplaform. Borrowers are responsible for the cost of return shipping. Materials must be returned via a shipping method that has tracking information.
Source: Latin American Film Collection
3219 Fed Ex Global Education Center
301 Pittsboro Street, CB 3205
Chapel Hill, NC 27599-3205
Fax: 919-962-0398 (ls)
World Wide Web URL:
Email Address: LA_Films@email.unc.edu

*All materials listed in this 2011-2012 edition are **BRAND NEW!***

SOCIAL STUDIES--HISTORY

Columbus Didn't Discover Us

Indigenous activists from North, South, and Central America speak about issues important to them.

Availability: Schools, libraries, and nursing homes in the United States.
Suggested Grade: 6-12
Languages: Spanish, several native languages, with English voice-over
Order Number: IND1-video
Production Date: 1992
Format: VHS videotape
Terms: Borrowers must have a User's Agreement on file with this source--available by mail or via the Internet. Return postage is paid by borrower; return 12 days after showing. Book at least three weeks in advance. All borrowers are limited to a total of ten items per semester.

Source: Latin American Resource Center
Stone Center for Latin American Studies
Tulane University
100 Jones Hall
New Orleans, LA 70118
Phone: 1-504-862-3143
Fax: 1-504-865-6719
World Wide Web URL:
http://stonecenter.tulane.edu/pages/detail/48/
Lending-Library
Email Address: crcrts@tulane.edu

Confesion a Laura

Gut-wrenching drama set in Colombia after the assassination of liberal leader Jorge Elieser Gaitan in 1948, an event which touched off civil war.

Availability: Schools and libraries in Iowa, Illinois, Michigan, Minnesota, and Wisconsin.
Suggested Grade: 6-12
Languages: Spanish with English subtitles
Order Number: FFCOLC76.1VHS
Production Date: 1990
Format: VHS videotape
Terms: Borrower pays return postage. Return 8 days after showing. Book 2 weeks in advance. Order may also be picked up for those near the Center.

Source: Center for Latin American and Caribbean Studies
UW-Milwaukee
P. O. Box 413
Milwaukee, WI 53201
Phone: 1-414-229-5987
World Wide Web URL: http://www.uwm.edu/Dept/CLACS
Email Address: audvis@usm.edu

Cracking the Maya Code

The story behind the centuries-long decipherment of ancient Maya hieroglyphs.

Availability: Schools and libraries in the United States and Canada.
Suggested Grade: 7-Adult
Order Number: order by title
Production Date: 2008
Format: DVD

Terms: Videos will typically be lent for seven days if mailed out--due date will be indicated. Films not returned within the time limit will be subject to overdue fines of $2 per video, per day. All borrowed must have a lending agreement on file. Form can be downloaded from http://isa.unc.edu/film/borrow.asplaform. Borrowers are responsible for the cost of return shipping. Materials must be returned via a shipping method that has tracking information.

Source: Latin American Film Collection
3219 Fed Ex Global Education Center
301 Pittsboro Street, CB 3205
Chapel Hill, NC 27599-3205
Email Address: LA_Films@email.unc.edu

Czar Nicholas II & the Romanovs

Archival footage, photos, and reenactments tell the story of the assassination of Russia's last czar.

Availability: Schools, libraries, and homeschoolers in the United States who serve the hearing impaired.
Suggested Grade: 5-12
Order Number: 10991
Production Date: 2003
Format: DVD
Special Notes: Also available as live streaming video over the Internet.
Terms: Sponsor pays all transportation costs. Return one week after receipt. Participation is limited to deaf or hard of hearing Americans, their parents, families, teachers, counselors, or others whose use would benefit a deaf or hard of hearing person. Only one person in the audience needs to be hearing impaired. You must register--which is free. These videos are all open-captioned--no special equipment is required for viewing.

Source: Described and Captioned Media Program
National Association of the Deaf
4211 Church Street Ext.
Roebuck, SC 29376
Phone: 1-800-237-6213
Fax: 1-800-538-5636
World Wide Web URL: http://www.dcmp.org

Empire!

The fourth program of the PBS series "The Shape of the World," this video recounts British efforts to map India, including the Lambton expedition of 1802, the Everest expedition of 1833 and the secret survey of India's borders with Russia and China.

Availability: Schools, libraries, homeschoolers, and nursing homes in the southeastern United States.
Suggested Grade: 7-12
Order Number: order by title
Production Date: 1991
Format: VHS videotape
Terms: Borrower pays return postage. Return 2 days after showing via United Parcel Service, insured. Book 2 weeks in advance.

*All materials listed in this 2011-2012 edition are **BRAND NEW!***

Source: Center for South Asian Studies
University of Virginia
Video Library Coordinator
P. O. Box 400169, 110 Minor Hall
Charlottesville, VA 22904-4169
Phone: 1-434-924-8815
Email Address: southasia@virginia.edu

Fashion Frenzy 100 Years of Clothing History

One hundred years of clothing history is reviewed.

Availability:	Schools, libraries, and homeschoolers in the United States who serve the hearing impaired.
Suggested Grade:	8-Adult
Order Number:	11429
Production Date:	2002
Format:	DVD
Special Notes:	Also available as live streaming video over the Internet.
Terms:	Sponsor pays all transportation costs. Return one week after receipt. Participation is limited to deaf or hard of hearing Americans, their parents, families, teachers, counselors, or others whose use would benefit a deaf or hard of hearing person. Only one person in the audience needs to be hearing impaired. You must register--which is free. These videos are all open-captioned--no special equipment is required for viewing.

Source: Described and Captioned Media Program
National Association of the Deaf
4211 Church Street Ext.
Roebuck, SC 29376
Phone: 1-800-237-6213
Fax: 1-800-538-5636
World Wide Web URL: http://www.dcmp.org

Fields of Honor

Take a video tour of America's overseas burial spots for servicemen.

Availability:	All requesters
Suggested Grade:	4-Adult
Order Number:	not applicable
Format:	Streaming Video

Source: American Battle Monuments Commission
World Wide Web URL: http://abmc.gov

Forgotten Roots, The

Details the history of Mexico's often overlooked African populations.

Availability:	Schools and libraries in Iowa, Illinois, Michigan, Minnesota, and Wisconsin.
Suggested Grade:	6-12
Order Number:	AFRICAMEXF76VHS
Production Date:	2001
Format:	VHS videotape
Terms:	Borrower pays return postage. Return 8 days after showing. Book 2 weeks in advance. Order may also be picked up for those near the Center.

Source: Center for Latin American and Caribbean Studies
UW-Milwaukee
P. O. Box 413
Milwaukee, WI 53201
Phone: 1-414-229-5987
World Wide Web URL: http://www.uwm.edu/Dept/CLACS
Email Address: audvis@usm.edu

Gandhi's India

Explores the British role in India, the struggle for independence, and the birth of modern India and Pakistan. Uses old news footage, with less emphasis on Gandhi than the title suggests.

Availability:	Schools, libraries, homeschoolers, and nursing homes in the southeastern United States.
Suggested Grade:	7-12
Order Number:	order by title
Production Date:	1970
Format:	VHS videotape
Special Notes:	Black and white.
Terms:	Borrower pays return postage. Return 2 days after showing via United Parcel Service, insured. Book 2 weeks in advance.

Source: Center for South Asian Studies
University of Virginia
Video Library Coordinator
P. O. Box 400169, 110 Minor Hall
Charlottesville, VA 22904-4169
Phone: 1-434-924-8815
Email Address: southasia@virginia.edu

Heritage of the Black West

African Americans played a significant role in shaping the American west as frontiersmen and women, buffalo soldiers, cowboys, lawmakers, lawbreakers, farmers, and entrepreneurs. Historical roots are reflected through present-day cowboys on the rodeo circuit, a ranch family, and a veterinarian. Uses vintage photos.

Availability:	Schools, libraries, and homeschoolers in the United States who serve the hearing impaired.
Suggested Grade:	7-10
Order Number:	12340
Production Date:	1995
Format:	DVD
Special Notes:	Produced by National Geographic Society.
Terms:	Sponsor pays all transportation costs. Return one week after receipt. Participation is limited to deaf or hard of hearing Americans, their parents, families, teachers, counselors, or others whose use would benefit a deaf or hard of hearing person. Only one person in the audience needs to be hearing impaired. You must register--which is free. These videos are all open-captioned--no special equipment is required for viewing.

Source: Described and Captioned Media Program
National Association of the Deaf
4211 Church Street Ext.
Roebuck, SC 29376
Phone: 1-800-237-6213

Fax: 1-800-538-5636
World Wide Web URL: http://www.dcmp.org

Hong Kong Handover Celebrations, The

The reunification of Hong Kong with China on 1st July 1997 attracted global attention. Here are highlights of the many ceremonies and celebrations.

Availability:	Schools, libraries, and nursing homes in the United States and Canada.
Suggested Grade:	6-Adult
Languages:	Chinese; subtitled in English
Order Number:	CV039
Format:	VHS videotape
Special Notes:	Accompanied by a booklet in both English and Chinese.
Terms:	Borrower pays return postage. Return with 14 days after scheduled showing, via UPS or U. S. Mail. All requests must included an educational institution affiliation, a current address, and phone number. Order through web site only.

Source: Cornell University East Asia Program
World Wide Web URL:
http://www.einaudi.cornell.edu/eastasia/outreach/video.asp
Email Address: east_asia1@cornell.edu

Honor Answers Honor

Inlcudes the reactions of soldiers to the surrender of Appomattox.

Availability:	Schools, libraries, and homeschoolers in the United States and Canada.
Suggested Grade:	6-Adult
Order Number:	order by title
Format:	DVD
Terms:	Borrower pays return postage.

Source: Appomattox Court House National Historical Park
Education Coordinator
P. O. Box 218
Appomattox, VA 24522
Phone: 1-434-352-8987, ext. 31
Fax: 1-434-352-8568
World Wide Web URL:
http://www.nps.gov/apco/forteachers/index.htm
Email Address: www.nps.gov/apco

Hunt for Pancho Villa, The

Pancho Villa led a deadly raid across the border into New Mexico, and President Wilson ordered General Pershing to catch Villa.

Availability:	Schools and libraries in Iowa, Illinois, Michigan, Minnesota, and Wisconsin.
Suggested Grade:	6-12
Order Number:	order by title
Production Date:	1993
Format:	VHS videotape
Terms:	Borrower pays return postage. Return 8 days after showing. Book 2 weeks in advance. Order may also be picked up for those near the Center.

Source: Center for Latin American and Caribbean Studies
UW-Milwaukee
P. O. Box 413
Milwaukee, WI 53201
Phone: 1-414-229-5987
World Wide Web URL: http://www.uwm.edu/Dept/CLACS
Email Address: audvis@usm.edu

I Am Cuba

Soviet-Cuban co-production with five parts, each of which illustrates a different aspect of the revolution.

Availability:	Schools and libraries in Iowa, Illinois, Michigan, Minnesota, and Wisconsin.
Suggested Grade:	6-12
Languages:	Spanish with English subtitles
Order Number:	FFCUB
Production Date:	1964
Format:	VHS videotape
Terms:	Borrower pays return postage. Return 8 days after showing. Book 2 weeks in advance. Order may also be picked up for those near the Center.

Source: Center for Latin American and Caribbean Studies
UW-Milwaukee
P. O. Box 413
Milwaukee, WI 53201
Phone: 1-414-229-5987
World Wide Web URL: http://www.uwm.edu/Dept/CLACS
Email Address: audvis@usm.edu

Iquitos

Explores history and mythology of Iquitos, Peru, located at the headwaters of the Amazon River.

Availability:	Schools, libraries, and nursing homes in the United States.
Suggested Grade:	6-12
Order Number:	IPER4-video
Format:	VHS videotape
Terms:	Borrowers must have a User's Agreement on file with this source--available by mail or via the Internet. Return postage is paid by borrower; return 12 days after showing. Book at least three weeks in advance. All borrowers are limited to a total of ten items per semester.

Source: Latin American Resource Center
Stone Center for Latin American Studies
Tulane University
100 Jones Hall
New Orleans, LA 70118
Phone: 1-504-862-3143
Fax: 1-504-865-6719
World Wide Web URL:
http://stonecenter.tulane.edu/pages/detail/48/
Lending-Library
Email Address: crcrts@tulane.edu

Japanese Tea Ceremony, The

The tea ceremony originated in China but was transformed in Japan into an art of infinite resonance. This program is devoted to the Omote Sen-ke school. It shows the way in which its traditions are handed down from generation to generation, and demonstrates that suspension of time by which Japanese paying obeisance to a 400-year-old tradition live in the past and present simultaneously.

Availability: Schools, libraries, and nursing homes in the United States and Canada.
Suggested Grade: 6-Adult
Order Number: JV073
Format: VHS videotape
Terms: Borrower pays return postage. Return with 14 days after scheduled showing, via UPS or U. S. Mail. All requests must included an educational institution affiliation, a current address, and phone number. Order through web site only.

Source: Cornell University East Asia Program
World Wide Web URL:
http://www.einaudi.cornell.edu/eastasia/outreach/video.asp
Email Address: east_asia1@cornell.edu

Kaya: The Ancient Kingdom and Korea '92

Inspired by an exhibition at the National Museum in Seoul, "Kaya: the Ancient Kingdom" explores the Kaya Kingdom of the fourth and fifth centuries through recent archeological findings and preserved relics.

Availability: Schools, libraries, and nursing homes in the United States and Canada.
Suggested Grade: 6-Adult
Order Number: KV006
Format: VHS videotape
Terms: Borrower pays return postage. Return with 14 days after scheduled showing, via UPS or U. S. Mail. All requests must included an educational institution affiliation, a current address, and phone number. Order through web site only.

Source: Cornell University East Asia Program
World Wide Web URL:
http://www.einaudi.cornell.edu/eastasia/outreach/video.asp
Email Address: east_asia1@cornell.edu

Kirghiz of Afghanistan, The

A last look at the tribal culture of the Kirghiz people of Afghanistan, unchanged since the Middle Ages; the Kirghiz have since been driven to Pakistan and then airlifted from there to Turkey. By the anthropologist Nazif Shahrani.

Availability: Schools, libraries, homeschoolers, and nursing homes in the southeastern United States.
Suggested Grade: 7-12
Order Number: order by title
Format: VHS videotape
Terms: Borrower pays return postage. Return 2 days after showing via United Parcel Service, insured. Book 2 weeks in advance.

Source: Center for South Asian Studies
University of Virginia, Video Library Coordinator
P. O. Box 400169, 110 Minor Hall
Charlottesville, VA 22904-4169
Phone: 1-434-924-8815
Email Address: southasia@virginia.edu

Korea: Ancient Treasure, Modern Wonder

Examines the combination of centuries old tradition and modern technology that have turned a small war-torn agrarian country into a major industrial power. It shows the effects of modernization on traditional values, covers the roles of education and religion, and relates Korean history, language, and culture to those of neighboring China.

Availability: Schools, libraries, and nursing homes in the United States and Canada.
Suggested Grade: 6-Adult
Order Number: KV004
Format: VHS videotape
Terms: Borrower pays return postage. Return with 14 days after scheduled showing, via UPS or U. S. Mail. All requests must included an educational institution affiliation, a current address, and phone number. Order through web site only.

Source: Cornell University East Asia Program
World Wide Web URL:
http://www.einaudi.cornell.edu/eastasia/outreach/video.asp
Email Address: east_asia1@cornell.edu

Korean History

Professor Mark Peterson of Brigham Young University presents an overview of the Korean people and their land, aimed at clearing up popular misconceptions of both the ancient culture and its modern state

Availability: Schools, libraries, and nursing homes in the United States and Canada.
Suggested Grade: 6-Adult
Order Number: KV009
Format: VHS videotape
Terms: Borrower pays return postage. Return with 14 days after scheduled showing, via UPS or U. S. Mail. All requests must included an educational institution affiliation, a current address, and phone number. Order through web site only.

Source: Cornell University East Asia Program
World Wide Web URL:
http://www.einaudi.cornell.edu/eastasia/outreach/video.asp
Email Address: east_asia1@cornell.edu

Korean War, The

Documents the partitioning of Korea, the battles for Seoul, Inchon, and Pusan, the entry of Chinese troops into the war, the armistice at Panmunjom, and the establishment of the demilitarized zone. Shows the post-war developments in both North and South Korea--warts and all.

Availability: Schools, libraries, and nursing homes in the United States and Canada.
Suggested Grade: 6-Adult
Order Number: KV010
Format: VHS videotape
Terms: Borrower pays return postage. Return with 14 days after scheduled showing, via UPS or U. S. Mail. All requests must included an educational institution affiliation, a current address, and phone number. Order through web site only.

*All materials listed in this 2011-2012 edition are **BRAND NEW!***

Source: Cornell University East Asia Program
World Wide Web URL:
http://www.einaudi.cornell.edu/eastasia/outreach/video.asp
Email Address: east_asia1@cornell.edu

La Boca del Lobo

A disturbed lieutenant in the Peruvian army declares entire village guilty of treason.

Availability:	Schools and libraries in Iowa, Illinois, Michigan, Minnesota, and Wisconsin.
Suggested Grade:	6-12
Languages:	Spanish with English subtitles
Order Number:	FFPERB63VHS
Production Date:	1988
Format:	VHS videotape
Terms:	Borrower pays return postage. Return 8 days after showing. Book 2 weeks in advance. Order may also be picked up for those near the Center.

Source: **Center for Latin American and Caribbean Studies**
UW-Milwaukee
P. O. Box 413
Milwaukee, WI 53201
Phone: 1-414-229-5987
World Wide Web URL: http://www.uwm.edu/Dept/CLACS
Email Address: audvis@usm.edu

Last Emperor, The

Traces the life of Pu Yi, the last emperor of China.

Availability:	Schools, libraries, homeschoolers, and nursing homes in the United States and Canada.
Suggested Grade:	6-12
Order Number:	order by title
Production Date:	1987
Format:	VHS videotape
Terms:	Postage is paid by borrower both ways--send $3.00 per tape to cover initial shipping to you--MONEY MUST BE SENT WITH REQUEST. Return 10 days after showing via U. S. Postal Service, library rate. Shipping is $5.00 to Canadian addresses.

Source: **Center for Teaching About China**
Kathleen Trescott
1214 West Schwartz
Carbondale, IL 62901
Phone: 1-618-549-1555
Email Address: trescott@midwest.net

Last Zapatista, The

Features the last living man who actually fought along side Emiliano Zapata in conflict between peasant farming population and Mexican government.

Availability:	Schools and libraries in Iowa, Illinois, Michigan, Minnesota, and Wisconsin.
Suggested Grade:	6-12
Order Number:	order by title
Production Date:	1995
Format:	VHS videotape
Terms:	Borrower pays return postage. Return 8 days after showing. Book 2 weeks in advance. Order may also be picked up for those near the Center.

Source: **Center for Latin American and Caribbean Studies**
UW-Milwaukee
P. O. Box 413
Milwaukee, WI 53201
Phone: 1-414-229-5987
World Wide Web URL: http://www.uwm.edu/Dept/CLACS
Email Address: audvis@usm.edu

Mayans, The

Cultural historian Iain Grain delves into Mayan history, investigating topics such as the Mayans' mastery of mathematics, their extremely hierarchical society, their use of human sacrifice to induce rain, and Mayan art.

Availability:	Schools in the United States.
Suggested Grade:	7-12
Order Number:	order by title
Production Date:	1999
Format:	VHS videotape
Terms:	Borrower pays return postage. Return 14 days after receipt, via USPS including insurance. All borrowers must have a current lending agreement on file with the Outreach program. This agreement is available via the web site or may be requested via phone or fax.

Source: **Center for Latin American Studies**
University of Florida
319 Grinter Hall
P. O. Box 115530
Gainesville, FL 32611-5530
Phone: 1-352-392-0375
Fax: 1-352-392-7682
World Wide Web URL: http://www.latam.ufl.edu/outreach
Email Address: maryr@ufl.edu

Memoria en la Piedra (Memory in Stone)

Tour of pre-Hispanic Mexican cities focusing on varying architectural styles.

Availability:	Schools, libraries, and nursing homes in the United States.
Suggested Grade:	6-12
Order Number:	APMEX42-video
Production Date:	1993
Format:	VHS videotape
Terms:	Borrowers must have a User's Agreement on file with this source--available by mail or via the Internet. Return postage is paid by borrower; return 12 days after showing. Book at least three weeks in advance. All borrowers are limited to a total of ten items per semester.

Source: **Latin American Resource Center**
Stone Center for Latin American Studies
Tulane University
100 Jones Hall
New Orleans, LA 70118
Phone: 1-504-862-3143
Fax: 1-504-865-6719
World Wide Web URL:
http://stonecenter.tulane.edu/pages/detail/48/
Lending-Library
Email Address: crcrts@tulane.edu

All materials listed in this 2011-2012 edition are **BRAND NEW!**

Memorias de un Mexicano

Key events of the Mexican Revolution from 1904 to 1924.

Availability:	Schools and libraries in Iowa, Illinois, Michigan, Minnesota, and Wisconsin.
Suggested Grade:	6-12
Order Number:	order by title
Production Date:	1985
Format:	VHS videotape
Terms:	Borrower pays return postage. Return 8 days after showing. Book 2 weeks in advance. Order may also be picked up for those near the Center.

Source: Center for Latin American and Caribbean Studies
UW-Milwaukee
P. O. Box 413
Milwaukee, WI 53201
Phone: 1-414-229-5987
World Wide Web URL: http://www.uwm.edu/Dept/CLACS
Email Address: audvis@usm.edu

Mexico's Colonial Towns

A journey back in time through some of Mexico's oldest and most unique colonial towns including Guanajuato, Oaxaca and San Miguel de Allende. An exploration of the historic old churches and cobblestone streets and views of how the art of creating beautiful handicrafts has survived over the years.

Availability:	Schools in the United States.
Suggested Grade:	8-12
Order Number:	order by title
Production Date:	1992
Format:	VHS videotape
Terms:	Borrower pays return postage. Return 14 days after receipt, via USPS including insurance. All borrowers must have a current lending agreement on file with the Outreach program. This agreement is available via the web site or may be requested via phone or fax.

Source: Center for Latin American Studies
University of Florida
319 Grinter Hall
P. O. Box 115530
Gainesville, FL 32611-5530
Phone: 1-352-392-0375
Fax: 1-352-392-7682
World Wide Web URL: http://www.latam.ufl.edu/outreach
Email Address: maryr@ufl.edu

Missing in MiG Alley

What happened to American pilots shot down over Korea half a century ago?

Availability:	All requesters
Suggested Grade:	7-Adult
Order Number:	not applicable
Production Date:	2007
Format:	Streaming Video

Source: NOVA
World Wide Web URL:
http://www.pbs.org/wgbh/nova/programs/index.html

Native Land

History and culture of Native Americans who civilized North and South America tens of thousands of years ago.

Availability:	Schools, libraries, and nursing homes in the United States.
Suggested Grade:	6-12
Order Number:	ILA20-video
Production Date:	1986
Format:	VHS videotape
Terms:	Borrowers must have a User's Agreement on file with this source--available by mail or via the Internet. Return postage is paid by borrower; return 12 days after showing. Book at least three weeks in advance. All borrowers are limited to a total of ten items per semester.

Source: Latin American Resource Center
Stone Center for Latin American Studies
Tulane University
100 Jones Hall
New Orleans, LA 70118
Phone: 1-504-862-3143
Fax: 1-504-865-6719
World Wide Web URL:
http://stonecenter.tulane.edu/pages/detail/48/
Lending-Library
Email Address: crcrts@tulane.edu

New World Colonized, The

Who were the colonists to the New World? What hardships did they face? Why did they come? Examines four different colonies and their reasons for success or failure. Discusses the French Huguenots, Sir Walter Raleigh's Lost Colony, and the establishment of Jamestown and Plymouth. Also includes the colonists' treatment of the native people. Reviews the reasons for colonizing.

Availability:	Schools, libraries, and homeschoolers in the United States who serve the hearing impaired.
Suggested Grade:	6-10
Order Number:	12837
Production Date:	1998
Format:	DVD
Special Notes:	Produced by Rainbow Educational Media.
Terms:	Sponsor pays all transportation costs. Return one week after receipt. Participation is limited to deaf or hard of hearing Americans, their parents, families, teachers, counselors, or others whose use would benefit a deaf or hard of hearing person. Only one person in the audience needs to be hearing impaired. You must register--which is free. These videos are all open-captioned--no special equipment is required for viewing.

Source: Described and Captioned Media Program
National Association of the Deaf
4211 Church Street Ext.
Roebuck, SC 29376
Phone: 1-800-237-6213
Fax: 1-800-538-5636
World Wide Web URL: http://www.dcmp.org

New World Encountered, The

During the early 1500s, Spanish, Portuguese, and English

explorers, looking for passage to the Far East, made many voyages to the New World discovered by Columbus in 1492. Presents an overview of the initial European contacts with the Americas and the conquests of the Mayan and Aztec civilizations. Reviews at the end.

Availability: Schools, libraries, and homeschoolers in the United States who serve the hearing impaired.
Suggested Grade: 6-10
Order Number: 12838
Production Date: 1998
Format: DVD
Special Notes: Produced by Rainbow Educational Media.
Terms: Sponsor pays all transportation costs. Return one week after receipt. Participation is limited to deaf or hard of hearing Americans, their parents, families, teachers, counselors, or others whose use would benefit a deaf or hard of hearing person. Only one person in the audience needs to be hearing impaired. You must register--which is free. These videos are all open-captioned--no special equipment is required for viewing.

Source: Described and Captioned Media Program
National Association of the Deaf
4211 Church Street Ext.
Roebuck, SC 29376
Phone: 1-800-237-6213
Fax: 1-800-538-5636
World Wide Web URL: http://www.dcmp.org

New World Explored, The

From 1520-1620, Europeans encountered and explored North America. Spanish explorers Coronado and De Soto, looking for gold, exploited native people as they mapped the southern portion of the United States. Cartier and Champlain, Frenchmen, explored the St. Lawrence River and set up profitable trading posts. Hudson also founded trade centers for the Netherlands. These explorers and others established Europe's control of the New World.

Availability: Schools, libraries, and homeschoolers in the United States who serve the hearing impaired.
Suggested Grade: 6-10
Order Number: 13086
Production Date: 1998
Format: DVD
Special Notes: Produced by Rainbow Educational Media.
Terms: Sponsor pays all transportation costs. Return one week after receipt. Participation is limited to deaf or hard of hearing Americans, their parents, families, teachers, counselors, or others whose use would benefit a deaf or hard of hearing person. Only one person in the audience needs to be hearing impaired. You must register--which is free. These videos are all open-captioned--no special equipment is required for viewing.

Source: Described and Captioned Media Program
National Association of the Deaf
4211 Church Street Ext.
Roebuck, SC 29376
Phone: 1-800-237-6213
Fax: 1-800-538-5636
World Wide Web URL: http://www.dcmp.org

Panama Canal

Here is the history of the conception and construction of the Panama Canal.

Availability: Schools in the United States.
Suggested Grade: 7-Adult
Order Number: order by title
Production Date: 1994
Format: VHS videotape
Special Notes: A History Channel video.
Terms: Borrower pays return postage. Return 14 days after receipt, via USPS including insurance. All borrowers must have a current lending agreement on file with the Outreach program. This agreement is available via the web site or may be requested via phone or fax.

Source: Center for Latin American Studies
University of Florida
319 Grinter Hall
P. O. Box 115530
Gainesville, FL 32611-5530
Phone: 1-352-392-0375
Fax: 1-352-392-7682
World Wide Web URL: http://www.latam.ufl.edu/outreach
Email Address: maryr@ufl.edu

Power of Unification: Lim Sukyung

This documentary tells part of the story of Sukyung Lim, a South Korean student leader who was charged with violating the National Security Act in 1989 for traveling to North Korea and imprisoned for three and a half years.

Availability: Schools, libraries, and nursing homes in the United States and Canada.
Suggested Grade: 6-Adult
Order Number: KV065
Format: VHS videotape
Terms: Borrower pays return postage. Return with 14 days after scheduled showing, via UPS or U. S. Mail. All requests must included an educational institution affiliation, a current address, and phone number. Order through web site only.

Source: Cornell University East Asia Program
World Wide Web URL:
http://www.einaudi.cornell.edu/eastasia/outreach/video.asp
Email Address: east_asia1@cornell.edu

Puerto Rico and the Statehood Question

Details the history of Puerto Rico since 1898. Discusses the ramifications of statehood.

Availability: Schools in the United States.
Suggested Grade: 7-12
Order Number: order by title
Production Date: 1994
Format: VHS videotape
Terms: Borrower pays return postage. Return 14 days after receipt, via USPS including insurance. All borrowers must have a current lending agreement on file with the Outreach program. This agreement is available via the web site or may be requested via phone or fax.

*All materials listed in this 2011-2012 edition are **BRAND NEW!***

Source: Center for Latin American Studies
University of Florida
319 Grinter Hall
P. O. Box 115530
Gainesville, FL 32611-5530
Phone: 1-352-392-0375
Fax: 1-352-392-7682
World Wide Web URL: http://www.latam.ufl.edu/outreach
Email Address: maryr@ufl.edu

Puerto Rico: History and Culture

Available in English or Spanish versions and thus can be used in social studies or in Spanish language class. The material covers a broad review of the island's early history, its traditions and culture and its relations with the mainland. Especially useful when employed as part of an introductory overview unit.

Availability:	Schools in the United States.
Suggested Grade:	7-12
Languages:	English; Spanish
Order Number:	order by title
Format:	VHS videotape

Terms: Borrower pays return postage. Return 14 days after receipt, via USPS including insurance. All borrowers must have a current lending agreement on file with the Outreach program. This agreement is available via the web site or may be requested via phone or fax.

Source: Center for Latin American Studies
University of Florida
319 Grinter Hall
P. O. Box 115530
Gainesville, FL 32611-5530
Phone: 1-352-392-0375
Fax: 1-352-392-7682
World Wide Web URL: http://www.latam.ufl.edu/outreach
Email Address: maryr@ufl.edu

Reed: Mexico Insurgente

John Reed is a U. S. journalist who covers the Mexican Revolution of 1914. It poses the question of whether a journalist can be impartial when surrounded by suffering.

Availability:	Schools and libraries in Iowa, Illinois, Michigan, Minnesota, and Wisconsin.
Suggested Grade:	6-12
Languages:	Spanish
Order Number:	FFMEXR25VHS
Production Date:	1971
Format:	VHS videotape

Terms: Borrower pays return postage. Return 8 days after showing. Book 2 weeks in advance. Order may also be picked up for those near the Center.

Source: Center for Latin American and Caribbean Studies
UW-Milwaukee
P. O. Box 413
Milwaukee, WI 53201
Phone: 1-414-229-5987
World Wide Web URL: http://www.uwm.edu/Dept/CLACS
Email Address: audvis@usm.edu

Reincarnation of Khensur Rinpoche, The

An account of the discovery in Chinese-occupied Tibet, of the three-year-old boy recognized as the reincarnation of a revered Tibetan monk who died in 1985.

Availability:	Schools, libraries, homeschoolers, and nursing homes in the southeastern United States.
Suggested Grade:	7-12
Order Number:	order by title
Production Date:	1991
Format:	VHS videotape

Terms: Borrower pays return postage. Return 2 days after showing via United Parcel Service, insured. Book 2 weeks in advance.

Source: Center for South Asian Studies
University of Virginia
Video Library Coordinator
P. O. Box 400169, 110 Minor Hall
Charlottesville, VA 22904-4169
Phone: 1-434-924-8815
Email Address: southasia@virginia.edu

Romero

Oscar Romero, the archbishop of El Salvador who was murdered for his ability to stir the masses into thoughts of political reform.

Availability:	Schools and libraries in Iowa, Illinois, Michigan, Minnesota, and Wisconsin.
Suggested Grade:	6-12
Order Number:	FFUSAR66.1VHS
Production Date:	1984
Format:	VHS videotape

Terms: Borrower pays return postage. Return 8 days after showing. Book 2 weeks in advance. Order may also be picked up for those near the Center.

Source: Center for Latin American and Caribbean Studies
UW-Milwaukee
P. O. Box 413
Milwaukee, WI 53201
Phone: 1-414-229-5987
World Wide Web URL: http://www.uwm.edu/Dept/CLACS
Email Address: audvis@usm.edu

Sacagawea: Over the Rockies to the Pacific

A reenactment of Sacagawea's journey with Lewis and Clark.

Availability:	Schools, libraries, and homeschoolers in the United States who serve the hearing impaired.
Suggested Grade:	5-8
Order Number:	11434
Production Date:	2004
Format:	DVD
Special Notes:	Also available as live streaming video over the Internet.

Terms: Sponsor pays all transportation costs. Return one week after receipt. Participation is limited to deaf or hard of hearing Americans, their parents, families, teachers, counselors, or others whose use would benefit a deaf or hard of hearing person. Only one person in the audience

All materials listed in this 2011-2012 edition are BRAND NEW!

needs to be hearing impaired. You must register--which is free. These videos are all open-captioned--no special equipment is required for viewing.

Source: Described and Captioned Media Program
National Association of the Deaf
4211 Church Street Ext.
Roebuck, SC 29376
Phone: 1-800-237-6213
Fax: 1-800-538-5636
World Wide Web URL: http://www.dcmp.org

Sixteenth Century Perceptions of Latin America: Civil or Savage?

Examines how Europeans who arrived in Latin America viewed its inhabitants and how those perceptions were often biased.

Availability:	Schools, libraries, and nursing homes in the United States.
Suggested Grade:	6-12
Order Number:	HLA21-video
Production Date:	1988
Format:	VHS videotape
Terms:	Borrowers must have a User's Agreement on file with this source--available by mail or via the Internet. Return postage is paid by borrower; return 12 days after showing. Book at least three weeks in advance. All borrowers are limited to a total of ten items per semester.

Source: Latin American Resource Center
Stone Center for Latin American Studies
Tulane University
100 Jones Hall
New Orleans, LA 70118
Phone: 1-504-862-3143
Fax: 1-504-865-6719
World Wide Web URL:
http://stonecenter.tulane.edu/pages/detail/48/
Lending-Library
Email Address: crcrts@tulane.edu

Spanish Armada, The

In 1588, Phillip II of Spain, a devout Catholic, determined to invade the Protestant England of Elizabeth I. He launched the Spanish Armada, a fleet of 130 ships, but Sir Francis Drake and the smaller, lighter English navy defeated the Armada by using fire ships. The broken Armada lost ships and sailors on the return home, and Phillip lost his dream and Spain's domination of the world.

Availability:	Schools, libraries, and homeschoolers in the United States who serve the hearing impaired.
Suggested Grade:	8-12
Order Number:	13142
Production Date:	1997
Format:	DVD
Special Notes:	Produced by Ambrose Video Publishing, Inc..
Terms:	Sponsor pays all transportation costs. Return one week after receipt. Participation is limited to deaf or hard of hearing Americans, their parents, families, teachers, counselors, or others whose use would benefit a deaf or hard of hearing person. Only one person in the audience

needs to be hearing impaired. You must register--which is free. These videos are all open-captioned--no special equipment is required for viewing.

Source: Described and Captioned Media Program
National Association of the Deaf
4211 Church Street Ext.
Roebuck, SC 29376
Phone: 1-800-237-6213
Fax: 1-800-538-5636
World Wide Web URL: http://www.dcmp.org

Sputnik Declassified

Top-secret documents rewrite the history of the famous satellite and the early space race.

Availability:	All requesters
Suggested Grade:	7-Adult
Order Number:	not applicable
Production Date:	2007
Format:	Streaming Video

Source: NOVA
World Wide Web URL:
http://www.pbs.org/wgbh/nova/programs/index.html

Tibet: The Bamboo Curtain Falls

This riveting video, a companion to Tibet: The Lost Mystery, uses Chinese and Tibetan sources to document the history of Tibet from the Chinese invasion in the 1950's to the 1979 visit of the first delegation of the Tibetan government in exile.

Availability:	Schools, libraries, homeschoolers, and nursing homes in the southeastern United States.
Suggested Grade:	7-12
Order Number:	order by title
Production Date:	1981
Format:	VHS videotape
Terms:	Borrower pays return postage. Return 2 days after showing via United Parcel Service, insured. Book 2 weeks in advance.

Source: Center for South Asian Studies
University of Virginia
Video Library Coordinator
P. O. Box 400169, 110 Minor Hall
Charlottesville, VA 22904-4169
Phone: 1-434-924-8815
Email Address: southasia@virginia.edu

U. S. in Latin America, The: Yankee Go Home

Examines the state of America's past and present relations with Latin America.

Availability:	Schools in the United States.
Suggested Grade:	7-Adult
Order Number:	order by title
Production Date:	1996
Format:	VHS videotape
Special Notes:	From the History Channel. Hosted by Mike Wallace.
Terms:	Borrower pays return postage. Return 14 days after receipt, via USPS including insurance. All borrowers

must have a current lending agreement on file with the Outreach program. This agreement is available via the web site or may be requested via phone or fax.

Source: Center for Latin American Studies
University of Florida
319 Grinter Hall
P. O. Box 115530
Gainesville, FL 32611-5530
Phone: 1-352-392-0375
Fax: 1-352-392-7682
World Wide Web URL: http://www.latam.ufl.edu/outreach
Email Address: maryr@ufl.edu

Veronico Cruz

Follows life of an Indian boy from his birth in the hinterlands to his death during the Falklands/Malvinas war.

Availability: Schools and libraries in Iowa, Illinois, Michigan, Minnesota, and Wisconsin.
Suggested Grade: 6-12
Languages: Spanish with English subtitles
Order Number: order by title
Production Date: 1988
Format: VHS videotape
Terms: Borrower pays return postage. Return 8 days after showing. Book 2 weeks in advance. Order may also be picked up for those near the Center.

Source: Center for Latin American and Caribbean Studies
UW-Milwaukee
P. O. Box 413
Milwaukee, WI 53201
Phone: 1-414-229-5987
World Wide Web URL: http://www.uwm.edu/Dept/CLACS
Email Address: audvis@usm.edu

Yogis of Tibet, The

A yogi is an individual who has spent years in isolated retreat practicing secret self-transforming physical and mental exercises, and through these techniques has developed extraordinary control over both mind and body. The Yogis in this film took unprecedented risks. Once vowed to extreme secrecy to maintain the purity of their practices, they agreed to these unique interviews and rare demonstrations to help preserve for posterity their vanishing culture.

Availability: Schools, libraries, and nursing homes in the United States and Canada.
Suggested Grade: 6-Adult
Order Number: TBV025
Format: VHS videotape
Terms: Borrower pays return postage. Return with 14 days after scheduled showing, via UPS or U. S. Mail. All requests must included an educational institution affiliation, a current address, and phone number. Order through web site only.

Source: Cornell University East Asia Program
World Wide Web URL:
http://www.einaudi.cornell.edu/eastasia/outreach/video.asp
Email Address: east_asia1@cornell.edu

About the UN: Palestine

Young reporters talk with Palestinians and Israelis about the Intifada and life in the occupied territories, as well as their feelings towards each other. The history of Palestine is followed by archive footage of the Intifada.

Availability: Schools, libraries, homeschoolers, and nursing homes in the United States.
Suggested Grade: 7-Adult
Order Number: order by title
Production Date: 1990
Format: VHS videotape
Terms: Borrower pays return postage. Return the day after scheduled showing, via UPS or Priority Mail, insured for $100.00. Book 4 weeks in advance and include an alternate date. Order should include name of person responsible for handling the video, and complete mailing address. Please mention this Guide when ordering. Tapes may not be duplicated, edited or exhibited for a fee.
Source: Church World Service
Film & Video Library
28606 Phillips Street, P. O. Box 968
Elkhart, IN 46515
Phone: 1-800-297-1516, ext. 338
Fax: 1-574-262-0966
World Wide Web URL: http://www.churchworldservice.org
Email Address: videos@churchworldservice.org

Black Women of Brazil

Presents ways Black women in Brazil have coped with racism while validating their lives through their own music and religion.

Availability: Schools, libraries, and nursing homes in the United States.
Suggested Grade: 6-12
Language: English voice-over
Order Number: AFLABRA2-video
Production Date: 1986
Format: VHS videotape
Terms: Borrowers must have a User's Agreement on file with this source--available by mail or via the Internet. Return postage is paid by borrower; return 12 days after showing. Book at least three weeks in advance. All borrowers are limited to a total of ten items per semester.
Source: Latin American Resource Center
Stone Center for Latin American Studies
Tulane University
100 Jones Hall
New Orleans, LA 70118
Phone: 1-504-862-3143
Fax: 1-504-865-6719
World Wide Web URL:
http://stonecenter.tulane.edu/pages/detail/48/
Lending-Library
Email Address: crcrts@tulane.edu

Children in Debt

Discusses debt crisis and poverty in Bolivia, Argentina, and Peru from a Latin American viewpoint.

Availability: Schools and libraries in Iowa, Illinois, Michigan, Minnesota, and Wisconsin.
Suggested Grade: 6-12
Languages: Spanish with English subtitles
Order Number: CHISAC43VHS
Production Date: 1987
Format: VHS videotape
Terms: Borrower pays return postage. Return 8 days after showing. Book 2 weeks in advance. Order may also be picked up for those near the Center.
Source: Center for Latin American and Caribbean Studies
UW-Milwaukee
P. O. Box 413
Milwaukee, WI 53201
Phone: 1-414-229-5987
World Wide Web URL: http://www.uwm.edu/Dept/CLACS
Email Address: audvis@usm.edu

Circle of Plenty

Recognizing the failure of the Green Revolution for many of the world's hungry peoples, John Jeavons has developed bio-intensive agriculture producing the maximum amount of food on the smallest plot with minimum inputs. It is making a difference in the town of Tula, Mexico, and elsewhere.

Availability: Schools, libraries, homeschoolers, and nursing homes in the United States.
Suggested Grade: 5-Adult
Order Number: order by title
Format: VHS videotape
Terms: Borrower pays return postage. Return the day after scheduled showing, via UPS or Priority Mail, insured for $100.00. Book 4.weeks in advance and include an alternate date. Order should include name of person responsible for handling the video, and complete mailing address. Please mention this Guide when ordering. Tapes may not be duplicated, edited or exhibited for a fee.
Source: Church World Service
Film & Video Library
28606 Phillips Street, P. O. Box 968
Elkhart, IN 46515
Phone: 1-800-297-1516, ext. 338
Fax: 1-574-262-0966
World Wide Web URL: http://www.churchworldservice.org
Email Address: videos@churchworldservice.org

Cuba and Human Rights

Explores perceptions of human rights in Cuba by U.S. policymakers, Cuban policymakers, and Cubans. The video includes interviews with the U.S. Under Secretary of State and follows Emmy Award winning filmmaker Jon Alpert into Cuba to gauge popular sentiment.

Availability: Schools in the United States.
Suggested Grade: 7-Adult
Order Number: order by title
Production Date: 1997
Format: VHS videotape
Terms: Borrower pays return postage. Return 14 days after receipt, via USPS including insurance. All borrowers

All materials listed in this 2011-2012 edition are BRAND NEW!

must have a current lending agreement on file with the Outreach program. This agreement is available via the web site or may be requested via phone or fax.

Source: Center for Latin American Studies
University of Florida
319 Grinter Hall
P. O. Box 115530
Gainesville, FL 32611-5530
Phone: 1-352-392-0375
Fax: 1-352-392-7682
World Wide Web URL: http://www.latam.ufl.edu/outreach
Email Address: maryr@ufl.edu

Development Education: A World of Connections

This video makes the case for a universal course of education for everyone which raises one's awareness to that connectedness with people and events around the world.

Availability: Schools, libraries, homeschoolers, and nursing homes in the United States.
Suggested Grade: 5-Adult
Order Number: order by title
Production Date: 1989
Format: VHS videotape
Terms: Borrower pays return postage. Return the day after scheduled showing, via UPS or Priority Mail, insured for $100.00. Book 4 weeks in advance and include an alternate date. Order should include name of person responsible for handling the video, and complete mailing address. Please mention this Guide when ordering. Tapes may not be duplicated, edited or exhibited for a fee.
Source: Church World Service
Film & Video Library
28606 Phillips Street, P. O. Box 968
Elkhart, IN 46515
Phone: 1-800-297-1516, ext. 338
Fax: 1-574-262-0966
World Wide Web URL: http://www.churchworldservice.org
Email Address: videos@churchworldservice.org

Displaced in the New South

Explores cultural collision between Asian and Hispanic immigrants and the suburban communities near Atlanta, Georgia, where they have settled.

Availability: Schools, libraries, and nursing homes in the United States.
Suggested Grade: 6-12
Order Number: HISP68-video
Production Date: 1995
Format: VHS videotape
Terms: Borrowers must have a User's Agreement on file with this source--available by mail or via the Internet. Return postage is paid by borrower; return 12 days after showing. Book at least three weeks in advance. All borrowers are limited to a total of ten items per semester.
Source: Latin American Resource Center
Stone Center for Latin American Studies
Tulane University, 100 Jones Hall
New Orleans, LA 70118

Phone: 1-504-862-3143
Fax: 1-504-865-6719
World Wide Web URL:
http://stonecenter.tulane.edu/pages/detail/48/
Lending-Library
Email Address: crcrts@tulane.edu

Escape from Affluenza

With stories ranging from America's simplicity capital--Seattle--to the Netherlands, this video uses expert commentary, thought-provoking vignettes and humor to show people how they can reduce their consumption and simplify their lives.

Availability: Schools, libraries, homeschoolers, and nursing homes in the United States.
Suggested Grade: 6-Adult
Order Number: order by title
Production Date: 1998
Format: VHS videotape
Special Notes: A sequel to the PBS special "Affluenza."
Terms: Borrower pays return postage. Return the day after scheduled showing, via UPS or Priority Mail, insured for $100.00. Book 4 weeks in advance and include an alternate date. Order should include name of person responsible for handling the video, and complete mailing address. Please mention this Guide when ordering. Tapes may not be duplicated, edited or exhibited for a fee.
Source: Church World Service
Film & Video Library
28606 Phillips Street, P. O. Box 968
Elkhart, IN 46515
Phone: 1-800-297-1516, ext. 338
Fax: 1-574-262-0966
World Wide Web URL: http://www.churchworldservice.org
Email Address: videos@churchworldservice.org

Global Village, The

The planet is shrinking as telecommunications brings us all together. This video explores the positive and negative ramifications of India's use of satellite communications.

Availability: Schools, libraries, homeschoolers, and nursing homes in the United States.
Suggested Grade: 5-Adult
Order Number: order by title
Production Date: 1985
Format: VHS videotape
Terms: Borrower pays return postage. Return the day after scheduled showing, via UPS or Priority Mail, insured for $100.00. Book 4 weeks in advance and include an alternate date. Order should include name of person responsible for handling the video, and complete mailing address. Please mention this Guide when ordering. Tapes may not be duplicated, edited or exhibited for a fee.
Source: Church World Service
Film & Video Library
28606 Phillips Street, P. O. Box 968
Elkhart, IN 46515

Phone: 1-800-297-1516, ext. 338
Fax: 1-574-262-0966
World Wide Web URL: http://www.churchworldservice.org
Email Address: videos@churchworldservice.org

Hunger Hotline Revisited

Using a talk show format, this piece explores world hunger--its causes and what groups and individuals can do about it.

Availability: Schools, libraries, homeschoolers, and nursing homes in the United States.
Suggested Grade: 7-Adult
Order Number: order by title
Production Date: 1984
Format: VHS videotape
Terms: Borrower pays return postage. Return the day after scheduled showing, via UPS or Priority Mail, insured for $100.00. Book 4 weeks in advance and include an alternate date. Order should include name of person responsible for handling the video, and complete mailing address. Please mention this Guide when ordering. Tapes may not be duplicated, edited or exhibited for a fee.

Source: Church World Service
Film & Video Library
28606 Phillips Street, P. O. Box 968
Elkhart, IN 46515
Phone: 1-800-297-1516, ext. 338
Fax: 1-574-262-0966
World Wide Web URL: http://www.churchworldservice.org
Email Address: videos@churchworldservice.org

If the Mango Tree Could Speak

A documentary about children and war in Central America. Children talk about peace, justice, ethnic identity, friendship, and marriage.

Availability: Schools and libraries in Iowa, Illinois, Michigan, Minnesota, and Wisconsin.
Suggested Grade: 4-12
Order Number: CHLA1F1.1VHS
Production Date: 1993
Format: VHS videotape
Terms: Borrower pays return postage. Return 8 days after showing. Book 2 weeks in advance. Order may also be picked up for those near the Center.

Source: Center for Latin American and Caribbean Studies
UW-Milwaukee
P. O. Box 413
Milwaukee, WI 53201
Phone: 1-414-229-5987
World Wide Web URL: http://www.uwm.edu/Dept/CLACS
Email Address: audvis@usm.edu

Immigration Reform

Two immigration reform activists answer questions from an audience of high school students.

Availability: Schools, libraries, and nursing homes in the United States.
Suggested Grade: 6-12
Order Number: SILA6-video

Production Date: 1987
Format: VHS videotape
Terms: Borrowers must have a User's Agreement on file with this source--available by mail or via the Internet. Return postage is paid by borrower; return 12 days after showing. Book at least three weeks in advance. All borrowers are limited to a total of ten items per semester.

Source: Latin American Resource Center
Stone Center for Latin American Studies
Tulane University
100 Jones Hall
New Orleans, LA 70118
Phone: 1-504-862-3143
Fax: 1-504-865-6719
World Wide Web URL:
http://stonecenter.tulane.edu/pages/detail/48/
Lending-Library
Email Address: crcrts@tulane.edu

Increase and Multiply?

Consequences of withdrawing family planning support from the United States, to countries of the Third World. Filmed in Kenya, Zimbabwe, China, Guatemala, and Mexico.

Availability: Schools, libraries, and nursing homes in the United States.
Suggested Grade: 8-Adult
Order Number: SI8-video
Production Date: 1995
Format: VHS videotape
Terms: Borrowers must have a User's Agreement on file with this source--available by mail or via the Internet. Return postage is paid by borrower; return 12 days after showing. Book at least three weeks in advance. All borrowers are limited to a total of ten items per semester.

Source: Latin American Resource Center
Stone Center for Latin American Studies
Tulane University
100 Jones Hall
New Orleans, LA 70118
Phone: 1-504-862-3143
Fax: 1-504-865-6719
World Wide Web URL:
http://stonecenter.tulane.edu/pages/detail/48/
Lending-Library
Email Address: crcrts@tulane.edu

Interview with Daniel Ortega

Discusses U. S. defiance of international law, repression, Soviet support and Nicaraguan desire for better relations with the U. S.

Availability: Schools, libraries, and nursing homes in the United States.
Suggested Grade: 6-12
Order Number: HCNIC11-video
Production Date: 1986
Format: VHS videotape
Special Notes: From the TV show, Nightline.
Terms: Borrowers must have a User's Agreement on file with this source--available by mail or via the Internet. Return

postage is paid by borrower; return 12 days after showing. Book at least three weeks in advance. All borrowers are limited to a total of ten items per semester.
Source: Latin American Resource Center
Stone Center for Latin American Studies
Tulane University
100 Jones Hall
New Orleans, LA 70118
Phone: 1-504-862-3143
Fax: 1-504-865-6719
World Wide Web URL:
http://stonecenter.tulane.edu/pages/detail/48/
Lending-Library
Email Address: crcrts@tulane.edu

Interview with Guatemalan President Cerezo

Problems running a democracy when military coups are a threat.

Availability: Schools, libraries, and nursing homes in the United States.
Suggested Grade: 6-12
Order Number: HCGUA4-video
Production Date: 1986
Format: VHS videotape
Special Notes: A CBS Sixty Minuts episode.
Terms: Borrowers must have a User's Agreement on file with this source--available by mail or via the Internet. Return postage is paid by borrower; return 12 days after showing. Book at least three weeks in advance. All borrowers are limited to a total of ten items per semester.
Source: Latin American Resource Center
Stone Center for Latin American Studies
Tulane University
100 Jones Hall
New Orleans, LA 70118
Phone: 1-504-862-3143
Fax: 1-504-865-6719
World Wide Web URL:
http://stonecenter.tulane.edu/pages/detail/48/
Lending-Library
Email Address: crcrts@tulane.edu

Isle of Flowers

Darkly comic look at the eating hierarchy of a Brazilian island where pigs are fed first.

Availability: Schools, libraries, and nursing homes in the United States.
Suggested Grade: 6-12
Order Number: GEBRA11-video
Production Date: 1990
Format: VHS videotape
Terms: Borrowers must have a User's Agreement on file with this source--available by mail or via the Internet. Return postage is paid by borrower; return 12 days after showing. Book at least three weeks in advance. All borrowers are limited to a total of ten items per semester.
Source: Latin American Resource Center
Stone Center for Latin American Studies
Tulane University
100 Jones Hall, New Orleans, LA 70118

Phone: 1-504-862-3143
Fax: 1-504-865-6719
World Wide Web URL:
http://stonecenter.tulane.edu/pages/detail/48/
Lending-Library
Email Address: crcrts@tulane.edu

Journey for Survival

Life without water means death. But life with contaminated water is life without health. This video examines water problems around the world and shows how they are being solved, not by technological advances, but by local people digging wells, laying pipelines, and installing latrines.

Availability: Schools, libraries, homeschoolers, and nursing homes in the United States.
Suggested Grade: 7-Adult
Order Number: order by title
Format: VHS videotape
Terms: Borrower pays return postage. Return the day after scheduled showing, via UPS or Priority Mail, insured for $100.00. Book 4 weeks in advance and include an alternate date. Order should include name of person responsible for handling the video, and complete mailing address. Please mention this Guide when ordering. Tapes may not be duplicated, edited or exhibited for a fee.
Source: Church World Service
Film & Video Library
28606 Phillips Street, P. O. Box 968
Elkhart, IN 46515
Phone: 1-800-297-1516, ext. 338
Fax: 1-574-262-0966
World Wide Web URL: http://www.churchworldservice.org
Email Address: videos@churchworldservice.org

Kashmir: Valley of Despair

Provides a history and thorough analysis of the political, religious, and ethnic causes of the Kashmir conflict--as Kashmir struggles to seek independence, India and Pakistan deny it.

Availability: Schools and libraries in the United States.
Suggested Grade: 7-Adult
Order Number: SA112
Production Date: 1998
Format: VHS videotape
Terms: Borrower pays return postage. Return 3 days after showing via UPS. Book at least 2 weeks in advance.
Source: Syracuse University, South Asia Center
Video Library and Teaching Resources
346F Eggers Hall
The Maxwell School
Syracuse, NY 13244

Landmines: Overcoming a Lethal Legacy

In the next 20 minutes someone will be killed or injured by an anti-personnel landmine. What will you do to make a difference? Find out more about the deadly problem and ways you can help.

*All materials listed in this 2011-2012 edition are **BRAND NEW!***

Availability: Schools, libraries, homeschoolers, and nursing homes in the United States.
Suggested Grade: 5-Adult
Order Number: order by title
Production Date: 1997
Format: VHS videotape
Terms: Borrower pays return postage. Return the day after scheduled showing, via UPS or Priority Mail, insured for $100.00. Book 4 weeks in advance and include an alternate date. Order should include name of person responsible for handling the video, and complete mailing address. Please mention this Guide when ordering. Tapes may not be duplicated, edited or exhibited for a fee.

Source: Church World Service
Film & Video Library
28606 Phillips Street, P. O. Box 968
Elkhart, IN 46515
Phone: 1-800-297-1516, ext. 338
Fax: 1-574-262-0966
World Wide Web URL: http://www.churchworldservice.org
Email Address: videos@churchworldservice.org

Los Ninos Abandonados

Classically realistic story made in the streets of a small Colombian city, with a cast of abandoned children.
Availability: Schools and libraries in Iowa, Illinois, Michigan, Minnesota, and Wisconsin.
Suggested Grade: 8-Adult
Languages: Spanish with English subtitles
Order Number: CHICOLN62VHS
Format: VHS videotape
Terms: Borrower pays return postage. Return 8 days after showing. Book 2 weeks in advance. Order may also be picked up for those near the Center.

Source: Center for Latin American and Caribbean Studies
UW-Milwaukee
P. O. Box 413
Milwaukee, WI 53201
Phone: 1-414-229-5987
World Wide Web URL: http://www.uwm.edu/Dept/CLACS
Email Address: audvis@usm.edu

Los Olvidados

Some abandoned children live in the streets and rob and even commit murder in order to survive in a violent society.
Availability: Schools and libraries in Iowa, Illinois, Michigan, Minnesota, and Wisconsin.
Suggested Grade: 6-12
Languages: Spanish with English subtitles
Order Number: FFMEXOL9VHS
Production Date: 1950
Format: VHS videotape
Terms: Borrower pays return postage. Return 8 days after showing. Book 2 weeks in advance. Order may also be picked up for those near the Center.

Source: Center for Latin American and Caribbean Studies
UW-Milwaukee
P. O. Box 413
Milwaukee, WI 53201

Phone: 1-414-229-5987
World Wide Web URL: http://www.uwm.edu/Dept/CLACS
Email Address: audvis@usm.edu

Make a Little Difference

Through the cases, voices, and stories of uprooted children all over the world, this video introduces the harsh reality of refugees to North American children.
Availability: Schools, libraries, homeschoolers, and nursing homes in the United States.
Suggested Grade: 4-Adult
Order Number: order by title
Production Date: 1993
Format: VHS videotape
Terms: Borrower pays return postage. Return the day after scheduled showing, via UPS or Priority Mail, insured for $100.00. Book 4 weeks in advance and include an alternate date. Order should include name of person responsible for handling the video, and complete mailing address. Please mention this Guide when ordering. Tapes may not be duplicated, edited or exhibited for a fee.

Source: Church World Service
Film & Video Library
28606 Phillips Street, P. O. Box 968
Elkhart, IN 46515
Phone: 1-800-297-1516, ext. 338
Fax: 1-574-262-0966
World Wide Web URL: http://www.churchworldservice.org
Email Address: videos@churchworldservice.org

Mickey Mouse Goes to Haiti: Walt Disney and the Science of Exploitation

Discusses the use of Haitian labor--paid low wages in terrible conditions--to produce items for the Disney empire.
Availability: Schools in the United States.
Suggested Grade: 7-Adult
Order Number: order by title
Production Date: 1996
Format: VHS videotape
Terms: Borrower pays return postage. Return 14 days after receipt, via USPS including insurance. All borrowers must have a current lending agreement on file with the Outreach program. This agreement is available via the web site or may be requested via phone or fax.

Source: Center for Latin American Studies
University of Florida
319 Grinter Hall
P. O. Box 115530
Gainesville, FL 32611-5530
Phone: 1-352-392-0375
Fax: 1-352-392-7682
World Wide Web URL: http://www.latam.ufl.edu/outreach
Email Address: maryr@ufl.edu

Miss Universe in Peru

Juxtaposes the glamour of the pageant with the realities of Peruvian women's lives.

*All materials listed in this 2011-2012 edition are **BRAND NEW!***

Availability: Schools, libraries, and nursing homes in the United States.
Suggested Grade: 6-12
Languages: Spanish with English subtitles
Order Number: SIPER1-video
Production Date: 1986
Format: VHS videotape
Terms: Borrowers must have a User's Agreement on file with this source--available by mail or via the Internet. Return postage is paid by borrower; return 12 days after showing. Book at least three weeks in advance. All borrowers are limited to a total of ten items per semester.

Source: Latin American Resource Center
Stone Center for Latin American Studies
Tulane University
100 Jones Hall
New Orleans, LA   70118
Phone: 1-504-862-3143
Fax: 1-504-865-6719
World Wide Web URL:
http://stonecenter.tulane.edu/pages/detail/48/
Lending-Library
Email Address: crcrts@tulane.edu

New Generation, The
Born after the 1960's, this "new race" grew up in the midst of Japanese prosperity and never experienced war. Are they changing Japan's social and economic values?
Availability: Schools, libraries and homeschoolers in Alabama, Georgia, North Carolina, South Carolina, and Virginia.
Suggested Grade: 6-Adult
Order Number: 405
Production Date: 1988
Format: VHS videotape
Special Notes: Part of the "Faces of Japan" series.
Terms: Borrower pays return postage. Two tapes may be borrowed at a time. Return within 7 days after receipt. Reservations may be made by filling the application found on the web site.

Source: Consulate General of Japan, Atlanta
Japan Information Center
One Alliance Center
3500 Lenox Road, Suite 1600
Atlanta, GA   30326
Phone: 1-404-365-9240
Fax: 1-404-240-4311
World Wide Web URL:
http://www.atlanta.us.emb-japan.go.jp
Email Address: info@cgjapanatlanta.org

New Generation, The
Born after the 1960's, this "new race" grew up in the midst of Japanese prosperity and never experienced war. Are they changing Japan's social and economic values?
Availability: Schools, libraries, homeschoolers, and nursing homes in OREGON AND SOUTHERN IDAHO ONLY. Please make requests via the web site.

Suggested Grade: 6-Adult
Order Number: 518
Production Date: 1988
Format: VHS videotape
Special Notes: Part of the "Faces of Japan" series.
Terms: Borrower pays return postage. Return within three weeks after scheduled showing date. Book one month in advance if possible. Rewind the video and wrap securely for return. Be certain to indicate video number, date needed, name of your organization, and address to which video should be sent, along with phone number. Audience report enclosed with the video must be completed and returned.

Source: Consulate General of Japan, Oregon
Attn: Tamara, Video Library
1300 S. W. Fifth Avenue, Suite 2700
Portland, OR   97201
Phone: 1-503-221-1811, ext. 17
World Wide Web URL:
http://www.portland.us.emb-japan.go.jp/en/index.html
Email Address: tamara@cgjpdx.org

No More Separate Futures
An exploration of the nature of global education and of issues that demand a global perspective are discussed: peace, militarism, the farm crisis, global hunger, water and population. Factual data and provocative questions are presented.
Availability: Schools, libraries, homeschoolers, and nursing homes in the United States.
Suggested Grade: 5-Adult
Order Number: order by title
Production Date: 1986
Format: VHS videotape
Terms: Borrower pays return postage. Return the day after scheduled showing, via UPS or Priority Mail, insured for $100.00. Book 4 weeks in advance and include an alternate date. Order should include name of person responsible for handling the video, and complete mailing address. Please mention this Guide when ordering. Tapes may not be duplicated, edited or exhibited for a fee.

Source: Church World Service
Film & Video Library
28606 Phillips Street, P. O. Box 968
Elkhart, IN   46515
Phone: 1-800-297-1516, ext. 338
Fax: 1-574-262-0966
World Wide Web URL: http://www.churchworldservice.org
Email Address: videos@churchworldservice.org

Nowhere Else to Live
Depicts the plight of the urban poor in Mexico City.
Availability: Schools and libraries in Iowa, Illinois, Michigan, Minnesota, and Wisconsin.
Suggested Grade: 6-12
Order Number: CI/URMEXN86VHS
Production Date: 1998
Format: VHS videotape

*All materials listed in this 2011-2012 edition are **BRAND NEW!***

Terms: Borrower pays return postage. Return 8 days after showing. Book 2 weeks in advance. Order may also be picked up for those near the Center.
Source: **Center for Latin American and Caribbean Studies**
UW-Milwaukee
P. O. Box 413
Milwaukee, WI 53201
Phone: 1-414-229-5987
World Wide Web URL: http://www.uwm.edu/Dept/CLACS
Email Address: audvis@usm.edu

Politics of Food, The: The Avoidable Famine

Demonstrates that hunger, in most parts of the world, does not mean there is a shortage of food, but rather that people have lost the means to buy it. Changes in farming methods effect both the economy and the society.
Availability: Schools, libraries, homeschoolers, and nursing homes in the United States.
Suggested Grade: 5-Adult
Order Number: order by title
Production Date: 1988
Format: VHS videotape
Terms: Borrower pays return postage. Return the day after scheduled showing, via UPS or Priority Mail, insured for $100.00. Book 4 weeks in advance and include an alternate date. Order should include name of person responsible for handling the video, and complete mailing address. Please mention this Guide when ordering. Tapes may not be duplicated, edited or exhibited for a fee.
Source: **Church World Service**
Film & Video Library
28606 Phillips Street, P. O. Box 968
Elkhart, IN 46515
Phone: 1-800-297-1516, ext. 338
Fax: 1-574-262-0966
World Wide Web URL: http://www.churchworldservice.org
Email Address: videos@churchworldservice.org

Politics of Food, The: The Food Machine

Introduces viewers to the global effects of agribusiness and to the causes and effects of farm crises in the U. S. and Sudan.
Availability: Schools, libraries, homeschoolers, and nursing homes in the United States.
Suggested Grade: 5-Adult
Order Number: order by title
Production Date: 1988
Format: VHS videotape
Terms: Borrower pays return postage. Return the day after scheduled showing, via UPS or Priority Mail, insured for $100.00. Book 4 weeks in advance and include an alternate date. Order should include name of person responsible for handling the video, and complete mailing address. Please mention this Guide when ordering. Tapes may not be duplicated, edited or exhibited for a fee.

Source: **Church World Service**
Film & Video Library
28606 Phillips Street, P. O. Box 968
Elkhart, IN 46515
Phone: 1-800-297-1516, ext. 338
Fax: 1-574-262-0966
World Wide Web URL: http://www.churchworldservice.org
Email Address: videos@churchworldservice.org

Popular Little Planet, A

Explores overpopulation and rapid industrialization, threatening to destroy earth's non-renewable resources.
Availability: Schools, libraries, and homeschoolers in Connecticut, Maine, Massachusetts, New Hampshire, Rhode Island, and Vermont.
Suggested Grade: K-6
Order Number: VID 133
Format: VHS videotape
Terms: Borrower pays return postage. Return within three weeks of receipt. If the tape you request is available, it will be mailed within 5 business days. If not, you will be notified that this video is already out on loan. No more than three titles may be borrowed by one requestor at a time. No reservations for a specific date will be accepted. It is most efficient to order via the web site.
Source: **U. S. Environmental Protection Agency, Region 1**
Customer Service Center
One Congress Street, Suite 1100
Boston, MA 02214
World Wide Web URL:
http://yosemite.epa.gov/r1/videolen.nsf/

Remember Me

Filmed in the United States, the Middle East, and in Asia, this Academy Award-winning documentary contrasts children's youthful beauty with the squalor, hardship, and wasted potential of their daily lives. Students learn how many of their counterparts around the world really live, and are encouraged to think about what these children need to thrive.
Availability: Schools, libraries, homeschoolers, and nursing homes in the United States.
Suggested Grade: 4-Adult
Order Number: order by title
Format: VHS videotape
Terms: Borrower pays return postage. Return the day after scheduled showing, via UPS or Priority Mail, insured for $100.00. Book 4 weeks in advance and include an alternate date. Order should include name of person responsible for handling the video, and complete mailing address. Please mention this Guide when ordering. Tapes may not be duplicated, edited or exhibited for a fee.
Source: **Church World Service**
Film & Video Library
28606 Phillips Street, P. O. Box 968
Elkhart, IN 46515
Phone: 1-800-297-1516, ext. 338
Fax: 1-574-262-0966

*All materials listed in this 2011-2012 edition are **BRAND NEW!***

World Wide Web URL: http://www.churchworldservice.org
Email Address: videos@churchworldservice.org

Shepherds of Hallim

Shows the interaction among religious and lay volunteers and the Korean fishermen and farmers on this island in the Yellow Sea.

Availability:	Schools, libraries, homeschoolers, church groups, nursing homes, and service clubs in the United States.
Suggested Grade:	7-Adult
Order Number:	order by title
Format:	VHS videotape
Special Notes:	A study guide is provided.
Terms:	Borrower pays return postage. Return within 21 days after receipt. Book at least 3 weeks in advance. You will be notified as soon as possible, if your order cannot be filled. All videos are cleared for television broadcast use.

> **Source: Columban Fathers Mission Society**
> **Mission Education Department**
> **Attn: Connie Wacha**
> **P. O. Box 10**
> **St. Columbans, NE 68056**
> **Phone: 1-402-291-1920**
> **Fax: 1-402-715-5575**
> **World Wide Web URL: http://columban.org/missioned**

Street Where Prescilla Lives, The

Deals with Third World poverty and struggles in an honest, hopeful, and dignified manner. Issues faced by Prescilla in Manila and millions of other children in the developing world are presented.

Availability:	Schools, libraries, homeschoolers, and nursing homes in the United States.
Suggested Grade:	7-Adult
Order Number:	order by title
Production Date:	1991
Format:	VHS videotape
Terms:	Borrower pays return postage. Return the day after scheduled showing, via UPS or Priority Mail, insured for $100.00. Book 4 weeks in advance and include an alternate date. Order should include name of person responsible for handling the video, and complete mailing address. Please mention this Guide when ordering. Tapes may not be duplicated, edited or exhibited for a fee.

> **Source: Church World Service**
> **Film & Video Library**
> **28606 Phillips Street, P. O. Box 968**
> **Elkhart, IN 46515**
> **Phone: 1-800-297-1516, ext. 338**
> **Fax: 1-574-262-0966**
> **World Wide Web URL: http://www.churchworldservice.org**
> **Email Address: videos@churchworldservice.org**

Struggle and Success: The African American Experience in Japan

The first documentary to thoroughly examine the complex relationships of African Americans and Japanese people, produced by Reggie Life, the recipient of many awards. This is the culmination of two years of research, development and production in Japan and the United States.

Availability:	Schools, libraries and homeschoolers in Alabama, Georgia, North Carolina, South Carolina, and Virginia.
Suggested Grade:	6-Adult
Languages:	English; Japanese
Order Number:	213
Production Date:	1993
Format:	VHS videotape
Terms:	Borrower pays return postage. Two tapes may be borrowed at a time. Return within 7 days after receipt. Reservations may be made by filling the application found on the web site.

> **Source: Consulate General of Japan, Atlanta**
> **Japan Information Center**
> **One Alliance Center**
> **3500 Lenox Road, Suite 1600**
> **Atlanta, GA 30326**
> **Phone: 1-404-365-9240**
> **Fax: 1-404-240-4311**
> **World Wide Web URL:**
> **http://www.atlanta.us.emb-japan.go.jp**
> **Email Address: info@cgjapanatlanta.org**

Terror in the Mine Fields

Every twenty minutes, someone, somewhere in the world is killed or maimed by an antipersonnel land mine. This piece focuses on those in Cambodia and efforts to provide prosthetics to injured people.

Availability:	Schools, libraries, homeschoolers, and nursing homes in the United States.
Suggested Grade:	6-12
Order Number:	order by title
Production Date:	1996
Format:	VHS videotape
Terms:	Borrower pays return postage. Return the day after scheduled showing, via UPS or Priority Mail, insured for $100.00. Book 4 weeks in advance and include an alternate date. Order should include name of person responsible for handling the video, and complete mailing address. Please mention this Guide when ordering. Tapes may not be duplicated, edited or exhibited for a fee.

> **Source: Church World Service**
> **Film & Video Library**
> **28606 Phillips Street, P. O. Box 968**
> **Elkhart, IN 46515**
> **Phone: 1-800-297-1516, ext. 338**
> **Fax: 1-574-262-0966**
> **World Wide Web URL: http://www.churchworldservice.org**
> **Email Address: videos@churchworldservice.org**

They Shoot Children Don't They?

Documents the lives of street children in Guatemala City and those that try to help them survive. It gives a horrifying picture of the human rights violations committed against those children and how some agencies that are designed to protect actually hinder the process.

Availability: Schools and libraries in Iowa, Illinois, Michigan, Minnesota, and Wisconsin.
Suggested Grade: 6-12
Order Number: CHIGUAT34VHS
Format: VHS videotape
Terms: Borrower pays return postage. Return 8 days after showing. Book 2 weeks in advance. Order may also be picked up for those near the Center.
Source: Center for Latin American and Caribbean Studies
UW-Milwaukee
P. O. Box 413
Milwaukee, WI 53201
Phone: 1-414-229-5987
World Wide Web URL: http://www.uwm.edu/Dept/CLACS
Email Address: audvis@usm.edu

Time Out

Three students, perhaps for the first time, see beyond his or her own world. One sees children in Latin America. Another sees women and the need for clean water in west Africa. The last sees refugees in southern Asia.

Availability: Schools, libraries, homeschoolers, and nursing homes in the United States.
Suggested Grade: 5-Adult
Order Number: order by title
Production Date: 1990
Format: VHS or 3/4" U-matic videotape
Terms: Borrower pays return postage. Return the day after scheduled showing, via UPS or Priority Mail, insured for $100.00. Book 4 weeks in advance and include an alternate date. Order should include name of person responsible for handling the video, and complete mailing address. Please mention this Guide when ordering. Tapes may not be duplicated, edited or exhibited for a fee.
Source: Church World Service
Film & Video Library
28606 Phillips Street, P. O. Box 968
Elkhart, IN 46515
Phone: 1-800-297-1516, ext. 338
Fax: 1-574-262-0966
World Wide Web URL: http://www.churchworldservice.org
Email Address: videos@churchworldservice.org

Turning the Tide Part 5: The Great Gene Robbery

As plant species are lost, we lose the opportunity to find new food crops, medicines to fight disease, and compounds to fight pests. In the Andes, David Bellamy finds that the potato's wild relatives are threatened. Hundreds of potato varieties were grown by the Incas to ensure against crop failure in their highly viable climate. But, now only a few are grown. No amount of genetic engineering can protect crops without diverse genetic resources.

Availability: Schools, libraries, homeschoolers, and nursing homes in the United States.
Suggested Grade: 6-Adult

Order Number: order by title
Production Date: 1988
Format: VHS videotape
Terms: Borrower pays return postage. Return the day after scheduled showing, via UPS or Priority Mail, insured for $100.00. Book 4 weeks in advance and include an alternate date. Order should include name of person responsible for handling the video, and complete mailing address. Please mention this Guide when ordering. Tapes may not be duplicated, edited or exhibited for a fee.
Source: Church World Service
Film & Video Library
28606 Phillips Street, P. O. Box 968
Elkhart, IN 46515
Phone: 1-800-297-1516, ext. 338
Fax: 1-574-262-0966
World Wide Web URL: http://www.churchworldservice.org
Email Address: videos@churchworldservice.org

Turning the Tide Part 7: Bright Green

Environmentalists are challenging the view that current problems can be solved by more output and greater industrial growth. David Bellamy puts environmentalists on trial to see what solutions to hunger, unemployment and environmental destruction they have to offer future generations.

Availability: Schools, libraries, homeschoolers, and nursing homes in the United States.
Suggested Grade: 6-Adult
Order Number: order by title
Production Date: 1988
Format: VHS videotape
Terms: Borrower pays return postage. Return the day after scheduled showing, via UPS or Priority Mail, insured for $100.00. Book 4 weeks in advance and include an alternate date. Order should include name of person responsible for handling the video, and complete mailing address. Please mention this Guide when ordering. Tapes may not be duplicated, edited or exhibited for a fee.
Source: Church World Service
Film & Video Library
28606 Phillips Street, P. O. Box 968
Elkhart, IN 46515
Phone: 1-800-297-1516, ext. 338
Fax: 1-574-262-0966
World Wide Web URL: http://www.churchworldservice.org
Email Address: videos@churchworldservice.org

War and Peace

Filmed over three years in India, Pakistan, Japan and the United States, after the 1998 nuclear tests on the Indian subcontinent, this film documents the current, epic journey of peace activism in the face of global militarism and war.

Availability: Schools, libraries, homeschoolers, and nursing homes in the southeastern United States.
Suggested Grade: 7-12

*All materials listed in this 2011-2012 edition are **BRAND NEW!***

Order Number: order by title
Production Date: 2001
Format: VHS videotape
Terms: Borrower pays return postage. Return 2 days after showing via United Parcel Service, insured. Book 2 weeks in advance.

    Source: Center for South Asian Studies
          University of Virginia
        Video Library Coordinator
    P. O. Box 400169, 110 Minor Hall
    Charlottesville, VA   22904-4169
       Phone: 1-434-924-8815
   Email Address: southasia@virginia.edu

Dimensions in Food Textures, Preparation and Feeding Techniques for Special Needs Children

This program covers the laws which stipulate responsibility for special needs children; understanding the modified textures diets which are required for these children and how to prepare them; how to feed and prepare children with special needs; and current techniques used to control special needs children. Program designed for school administrators, food preparation staff and students.

Availability: Staff at schools with NET, WIC, CSFP, FDPIR, CACFP, UMD or Child Nutrition Program food programs in the United States. Those not having such an affiliation should contact their library to place an interlibrary loan request.

Suggested Grade: Teacher Reference
Order Number: NAL Video 2252
Production Date: 1995
Format: Set of 4 VHS videotapes
Terms: Borrower pays return postage. RETURN the day after scheduled use. Book at least 4 weeks in advance. Requests must include your name, phone, mail address, eligibility program, title, NAL number, show date, and a statement, "I have read the warning on copyright restrictions and accept full responsibility for compliance." One title per request.

Source: National Agricultural Library
Document Delivery Services Branch
4th Floor, Photo Lab, 10301 Baltimore Avenue
Beltsville, MD 20705-2351
Phone: 1-301-504-5994
Fax: 1-301-504-5675
World Wide Web URL: http://www.nal.usda.gov/fnic
Email Address: lending@nal.usda.gov

Dyslexia: A Different Kind of Mind

Explains how dyslexia has come to be understood to be a biologically based brain disorder which may be diagnosed and effectively treated.

Availability: Schools, libraries, and homeschoolers in the United States who serve the hearing impaired.
Suggested Grade: Teacher Reference
Order Number: 11070
Production Date: 1997
Format: DVD
Special Notes: Also available as live streaming video over the Internet.
Terms: Sponsor pays all transportation costs. Return one week after receipt. Participation is limited to deaf or hard of hearing Americans, their parents, families, teachers, counselors, or others whose use would benefit a deaf or hard of hearing person. Only one person in the audience needs to be hearing impaired. You must register--which is free. These videos are all open-captioned--no special equipment is required for viewing.

Source: Described and Captioned Media Program
National Association of the Deaf
4211 Church Street Ext.
Roebuck, SC 29376

Phone: 1-800-237-6213
Fax: 1-800-538-5636
World Wide Web URL: http://www.dcmp.org

Enable: People with Disabilities and Computers

Explains how people with disabilities can still join the computer age.

Availability: All requesters through interlibrary loan.
Suggested Grade: Teacher Reference
Order Number: 065.41 E52241999 VIDEOC
Production Date: 1999
Format: VHS videotape
Terms: These videotapes are available through interlibrary loan only. Simply request the specific video by name and number at your local public library, university library, or company library. The librarian will submit your request using an ALA interlibrary loan form, and the videos will be mailed to your library for your use. Interlibrary loans are limited to two videos at a time. The address listed below is for the ALA loan form only--your librarian must submit requests to this address.

Source: U. S. Geological Survey Library
345 Middlefield Road, MS 955
Menlo Park, CA 94025

Locked Out

J. J. is the leader of an exclusive, secret club. When Alex, a blind girl, is introduced to the group, J. J. doesn't want her to join. After learning that Alex is really no different from the others, J. J. realizes she was wrong. A surprise revelation at the end tests viewers' perceptions. Presentation encourages welcome and acceptance of one another.

Availability: Schools, libraries, and homeschoolers in the United States who serve the hearing impaired.
Suggested Grade: 4-8
Order Number: 12418
Production Date: 1998
Format: DVD
Special Notes: Produced by Aims Multimedia.
Terms: Sponsor pays all transportation costs. Return one week after receipt. Participation is limited to deaf or hard of hearing Americans, their parents, families, teachers, counselors, or others whose use would benefit a deaf or hard of hearing person. Only one person in the audience needs to be hearing impaired. You must register--which is free. These videos are all open-captioned--no special equipment is required for viewing.

Source: Described and Captioned Media Program
National Association of the Deaf
4211 Church Street Ext.
Roebuck, SC 29376
Phone: 1-800-237-6213
Fax: 1-800-538-5636
World Wide Web URL: http://www.dcmp.org

Mirrors and Windows: Shattering Stereotypes

Demonstrates that people with disabilities are basically no different from anyone else. When Catherine attends a friend's party, no one knows she's blind. As they discover the truth, some guests act differently around her. Catherine shows that she's not so unlike them after all. At the conclusion, the actresses who portray Catherine and her friend talk to the viewers.

Availability:	Schools, libraries, and homeschoolers in the United States who serve the hearing impaired.
Suggested Grade:	7-12
Order Number:	12392
Production Date:	1997
Format:	DVD
Special Notes:	Produced by Aims Multimedia.
Terms:	Sponsor pays all transportation costs. Return one week after receipt. Participation is limited to deaf or hard of hearing Americans, their parents, families, teachers, counselors, or others whose use would benefit a deaf or hard of hearing person. Only one person in the audience needs to be hearing impaired. You must register--which is free. These videos are all open-captioned--no special equipment is required for viewing.

Source: Described and Captioned Media Program
National Association of the Deaf
4211 Church Street Ext.
Roebuck, SC 29376
Phone: 1-800-237-6213
Fax: 1-800-538-5636
World Wide Web URL: http://www.dcmp.org

Misunderstood Minds

Investigates how students with learning differences and disabilities perceive reading, writing, and math concepts. Provides tips for success in helping these students.

Availability:	Schools, libraries, and homeschoolers in the United States who serve the hearing impaired.
Suggested Grade:	Adult
Order Number:	10844
Production Date:	2002
Format:	DVD
Special Notes:	Also available as live streaming video over the Internet.
Terms:	Sponsor pays all transportation costs. Return one week after receipt. Participation is limited to deaf or hard of hearing Americans, their parents, families, teachers, counselors, or others whose use would benefit a deaf or hard of hearing person. Only one person in the audience needs to be hearing impaired. You must register--which is free. These videos are all open-captioned--no special equipment is required for viewing.

Source: Described and Captioned Media Program
National Association of the Deaf
4211 Church Street Ext.
Roebuck, SC 29376
Phone: 1-800-237-6213
Fax: 1-800-538-5636
World Wide Web URL: http://www.dcmp.org

Reaching the Autistic Mind: An Educational Challenge

Follows six families with autistic children for two years. Features the Eden II School for Autistic Children in Staten

Island, New York. Interviews parents and teachers who advocate early intervention and applied behavioral analysis (ABA).

Availability:	Schools, libraries, and homeschoolers in the United States who serve the hearing impaired.
Suggested Grade:	Adult
Order Number:	11377
Production Date:	2002
Format:	DVD
Special Notes:	Also available as live streaming video over the Internet.
Terms:	Sponsor pays all transportation costs. Return one week after receipt. Participation is limited to deaf or hard of hearing Americans, their parents, families, teachers, counselors, or others whose use would benefit a deaf or hard of hearing person. Only one person in the audience needs to be hearing impaired. You must register--which is free. These videos are all open-captioned--no special equipment is required for viewing.

Source: Described and Captioned Media Program
National Association of the Deaf
4211 Church Street Ext.
Roebuck, SC 29376
Phone: 1-800-237-6213
Fax: 1-800-538-5636
World Wide Web URL: http://www.dcmp.org

Reaching the Autistic Mind: An Educational Challenge

Follows six families with autistic children for two years. Features the Eden II School for Autistic Children in Staten Island, New York. Interviews parents and teachers who advocate early intervention and applied behavioral analysis (ABA).

Availability:	Schools, libraries, and homeschoolers in the United States who serve the hearing impaired.
Suggested Grade:	Adult
Order Number:	11377
Production Date:	2002
Format:	DVD
Special Notes:	Also available as live streaming video over the Internet.
Terms:	Sponsor pays all transportation costs. Return one week after receipt. Participation is limited to deaf or hard of hearing Americans, their parents, families, teachers, counselors, or others whose use would benefit a deaf or hard of hearing person. Only one person in the audience needs to be hearing impaired. You must register--which is free. These videos are all open-captioned--no special equipment is required for viewing.

Source: Described and Captioned Media Program
National Association of the Deaf
4211 Church Street Ext.
Roebuck, SC 29376
Phone: 1-800-237-6213
Fax: 1-800-538-5636
World Wide Web URL: http://www.dcmp.org

Sound of Sunshine--Sound of Rain

This animated program gives rare insights into the life of a blind seven-year-old black boy and his intimate world of sounds and touch. The world of fantasy and imagination is sharply contrasted with the world of reality--a world which limits the horizon of the handicapped, the poor, and people of color.

Availability: Schools, libraries, homeschoolers, and nursing homes in the United States.
Suggested Grade: 1-4
Order Number: order by title
Format: VHS videotape
Terms: Borrower pays return postage. Return the day after scheduled showing, via UPS or Priority Mail, insured for $100.00. Book 4 weeks in advance and include an alternate date. Order should include name of person responsible for handling the video, and complete mailing address. Please mention this Guide when ordering. Tapes may not be duplicated, edited or exhibited for a fee.

Source: Church World Service
Film & Video Library
28606 Phillips Street, P. O. Box 968
Elkhart, IN 46515
Phone: 1-800-297-1516, ext. 338
Fax: 1-574-262-0966
World Wide Web URL: http://www.churchworldservice.org
Email Address: videos@churchworldservice.org

Special Foods for Special Kids
Explains how child care providers can plan, respond to, and provide for a child with special needs.

Availability: Staff at schools with NET, WIC, CSFP, FDPIR, CACFP, UMD or Child Nutrition Program food programs in the United States. Those not having such an affiliation should contact their library to place an interlibrary loan request.
Suggested Grade: Teacher Reference
Order Number: NAL Video 2547
Production Date: 1995
Format: VHS videotape
Terms: Borrower pays return postage. RETURN the day after scheduled use. Book at least 4 weeks in advance. Requests must include your name, phone, mail address, eligibility program, title, NAL number, show date, and a statement, "I have read the warning on copyright restrictions and accept full responsibility for compliance." One title per request.

Source: National Agricultural Library
Document Delivery Services Branch
4th Floor, Photo Lab
10301 Baltimore Avenue
Beltsville, MD 20705-2351
Phone: 1-301-504-5994
Fax: 1-301-504-5675
World Wide Web URL: http://www.nal.usda.gov/fnic
Email Address: lending@nal.usda.gov

Tragedy To Triumph
Felix harasses a blind girl in his high school. Through a series of mysterious events, he finds himself blind and sent back to 1935, where he meets Helen Keller and Annie Sullivan. Felix lives with them and learns about blindness, "seeing" with his heart, and kindness. Sight restored, he applies the lessons learned. Stars deaf actress Phyllis Frelich.

Availability: Schools, libraries, and homeschoolers in the United States who serve the hearing impaired.
Suggested Grade: 7-12
Order Number: 13063
Production Date: 1995
Format: DVD
Special Notes: Produced by Grace Products Corporation.
Terms: Sponsor pays all transportation costs. Return one week after receipt. Participation is limited to deaf or hard of hearing Americans, their parents, families, teachers, counselors, or others whose use would benefit a deaf or hard of hearing person. Only one person in the audience needs to be hearing impaired. You must register--which is free. These videos are all open-captioned--no special equipment is required for viewing.

Source: Described and Captioned Media Program
National Association of the Deaf
4211 Church Street Ext.
Roebuck, SC 29376
Phone: 1-800-237-6213
Fax: 1-800-538-5636
World Wide Web URL: http://www.dcmp.org

*All materials listed in this 2011-2012 edition are **BRAND NEW!***

Behavioral Problems in Children

Behavior specialists discuss attention deficit/hyperactivity disorder and childhood depression. They present a balanced view on the use of Ritalin and antidepressants with children and suggest other remedies.

Availability:	Schools, libraries, and homeschoolers in the United States who serve the hearing impaired.
Suggested Grade:	Adult
Order Number:	23982
Production Date:	2000
Format:	DVD
Special Notes:	Also available as live streaming video over the Internet.

Terms: Sponsor pays all transportation costs. Return one week after receipt. Participation is limited to deaf or hard of hearing Americans, their parents, families, teachers, counselors, or others whose use would benefit a deaf or hard of hearing person. Only one person in the audience needs to be hearing impaired. You must register--which is free. These videos are all open-captioned--no special equipment is required for viewing.

> **Source: Described and Captioned Media Program**
> **National Association of the Deaf**
> **4211 Church Street Ext.**
> **Roebuck, SC 29376**
> **Phone: 1-800-237-6213**
> **Fax: 1-800-538-5636**
> **World Wide Web URL: http://www.dcmp.org**

Breakfast Makes It Happen

Discusses how a school breakfast program can benefit the children who participate, their parents, and the community.

Availability:	Staff at schools with NET, WIC, CSFP, FDPIR, CACFP, UMD or Child Nutrition Program food programs in the United States. Those not having such an affiliation should contact their library to place an interlibrary loan request.
Suggested Grade:	Teacher Reference
Order Number:	NAL Video TX733.B73.B73
Production Date:	1995
Format:	VHS videotape
Special Notes:	Also available as NAL Video 2111, which is a National Dairy Council production with leader guide, 3 charts and a pamphlet.

Terms: Borrower pays return postage. RETURN the day after scheduled use. Book at least 4 weeks in advance. Requests must include your name, phone, mail address, eligibility program, title, NAL number, show date, and a statement, "I have read the warning on copyright restrictions and accept full responsibility for compliance." One title per request.

> **Source: National Agricultural Library**
> **Document Delivery Services Branch**
> **4th Floor, Photo Lab**
> **10301 Baltimore Avenue**
> **Beltsville, MD 20705-2351**
> **Phone: 1-301-504-5994**
> **Fax: 1-301-504-5675**

> **World Wide Web URL: http://www.nal.usda.gov/fnic**
> **Email Address: lending@nal.usda.gov**

Cold Is Cool--The Care and Handling of Milk in Schools

Written for a one hour inservice for school foodserve staff.

Availability:	Staff at schools with NET, WIC, CSFP, FDPIR, CACFP, UMD or Child Nutrition Program food programs in the United States. Those not having such an affiliation should contact their library to place an interlibrary loan request.
Suggested Grade:	Adult
Order Number:	NAL Video 2896
Production Date:	1999
Format:	VHS videotape
Special Notes:	Includes a leader's guide and poster.

Terms: Borrower pays return postage. RETURN the day after scheduled use. Book at least 4 weeks in advance. Requests must include your name, phone, mail address, eligibility program, title, NAL number, show date, and a statement, "I have read the warning on copyright restrictions and accept full responsibility for compliance." One title per request.

> **Source: National Agricultural Library**
> **Document Delivery Services Branch**
> **4th Floor, Photo Lab, 10301 Baltimore Avenue**
> **Beltsville, MD 20705-2351**
> **Phone: 1-301-504-5994**
> **Fax: 1-301-504-5675**
> **World Wide Web URL: http://www.nal.usda.gov/fnic**
> **Email Address: lending@nal.usda.gov**

Experience: The Dietary Guidelines

This program consists primarily of interviews with food service staff, principals, students, and educators explaining successful ways to implement the Dietary Guidelines for Americans in schools. Designed for school food preparation staff and students.

Availability:	Staff at schools with NET, WIC, CSFP, FDPIR, CACFP, UMD or Child Nutrition Program food programs in the United States. Those not having such an affiliation should contact their library to place an interlibrary loan request.
Suggested Grade:	Teacher Reference
Order Number:	NAL Video 2242
Production Date:	1995
Format:	VHS videotape

Terms: Borrower pays return postage. RETURN the day after scheduled use. Book at least 4 weeks in advance. Requests must include your name, phone, mail address, eligibility program, title, NAL number, show date, and a statement, "I have read the warning on copyright restrictions and accept full responsibility for compliance." One title per request.

> **Source: National Agricultural Library**
> **Document Delivery Services Branch**
> **4th Floor, Photo Lab, 10301 Baltimore Avenue**
> **Beltsville, MD 20705-2351**

All materials listed in this 2011-2012 edition are BRAND NEW!

TEACHER REFERENCE

Phone: 1-301-504-5994
Fax: 1-301-504-5675
World Wide Web URL: http://www.nal.usda.gov/fnic
Email Address: lending@nal.usda.gov

Feeding Children Well: A Pyramid for Preschoolers

Created to help care givers of exceptional children build self feeding skills and improve the nutritional health of these children. Designed for school administrators, food preparation staff and students.

Availability:	Staff at schools with NET, WIC, CSFP, FDPIR, CACFP, UMD or Child Nutrition Program food programs in the United States. Those not having such an affiliation should contact their library to place an interlibrary loan request.
Suggested Grade:	Teacher Reference
Order Number:	NAL Video 2193
Production Date:	1995
Format:	VHS videotape
Terms:	Borrower pays return postage. RETURN the day after scheduled use. Book at least 4 weeks in advance. Requests must include your name, phone, mail address, eligibility program, title, NAL number, show date, and a statement, "I have read the warning on copyright restrictions and accept full responsibility for compliance." One title per request.

Source: National Agricultural Library
Document Delivery Services Branch
4th Floor, Photo Lab, 10301 Baltimore Avenue
Beltsville, MD 20705-2351
Phone: 1-301-504-5994
Fax: 1-301-504-5675
World Wide Web URL: http://www.nal.usda.gov/fnic
Email Address: lending@nal.usda.gov

Feeding with Love and Good Sense

Shows the care giver how to feed young children.

Availability:	Staff at schools with NET, WIC, CSFP, FDPIR, CACFP, UMD or Child Nutrition Program food programs in the United States. Those not having such an affiliation should contact their library to place an interlibrary loan request.
Suggested Grade:	Teacher Reference
Order Number:	NAL Video 2545
Format:	VHS videotape
Special Notes:	Includes a teacher's guide.
Terms:	Borrower pays return postage. RETURN the day after scheduled use. Book at least 4 weeks in advance. Requests must include your name, phone, mail address, eligibility program, title, NAL number, show date, and a statement, "I have read the warning on copyright restrictions and accept full responsibility for compliance." One title per request.

Source: National Agricultural Library
Document Delivery Services Branch
4th Floor, Photo Lab, 10301 Baltimore Avenue
Beltsville, MD 20705-2351

Phone: 1-301-504-5994
Fax: 1-301-504-5675
World Wide Web URL: http://www.nal.usda.gov/fnic
Email Address: lending@nal.usda.gov

Geography: A Voyage of Discovery

A fictitious geographer sets out as a cartographer to chart the tiniest of islands and instead ends up developing a perspective on the whole earth, an island in a much larger sea. Geography helps us understand our world, its people, the environment, and global interdependence.

Availability:	Schools, libraries, homeschoolers, and nursing homes in the United States.
Suggested Grade:	5-Adult
Order Number:	order by title
Production Date:	1987
Format:	VHS videotape
Terms:	Borrower pays return postage. Return the day after scheduled showing, via UPS or Priority Mail, insured for $100.00. Book 4 weeks in advance and include an alternate date. Order should include name of person responsible for handling the video, and complete mailing address. Please mention this Guide when ordering. Tapes may not be duplicated, edited or exhibited for a fee.

Source: Church World Service
Film & Video Library
28606 Phillips Street, P. O. Box 968
Elkhart, IN 46515
Phone: 1-800-297-1516, ext. 338
Fax: 1-574-262-0966
World Wide Web URL: http://www.churchworldservice.org
Email Address: videos@churchworldservice.org

Make a Difference: Tips for Teaching Students Who Are Deaf or Hard of Hearing

Addresses the problems faced with teaching mainstreamed deaf or hard of hearing students and presents teaching tips.

Availability:	Schools, libraries, and homeschoolers in the United States who serve the hearing impaired.
Suggested Grade:	Teacher Reference
Order Number:	27748
Production Date:	2000
Format:	Streaming Video
Special Notes:	Also available as live streaming video over the Internet.
Terms:	Sponsor pays all transportation costs. Return one week after receipt. Participation is limited to deaf or hard of hearing Americans, their parents, families, teachers, counselors, or others whose use would benefit a deaf or hard of hearing person. Only one person in the audience needs to be hearing impaired. You must register--which is free. These videos are all open-captioned--no special equipment is required for viewing.

Source: Described and Captioned Media Program
National Association of the Deaf
4211 Church Street Ext.
Roebuck, SC 29376
Phone: 1-800-237-6213

*All materials listed in this 2011-2012 edition are **BRAND NEW!***

Fax: 1-800-538-5636
World Wide Web URL: http://www.dcmp.org

Make Nutrition Come Alive
This video contains ideas and information on how to teach nutrition and fitness to kids from ages 5 to 19, as well as to adults in a community group setting. It shows activities to be used in opening and closing a 4-H meeting, as well as a variety of main event activities.

Availability: Staff at schools with NET, WIC, CSFP, FDPIR, CACFP, UMD or Child Nutrition Program food programs in the United States. Those not having such an affiliation should contact their library to place an interlibrary loan request.
Suggested Grade: All ages
Order Number: NAL Video 1146
Production Date: 1990
Format: VHS videotape
Special Notes: Includes a teacher's guide.
Terms: Borrower pays return postage. RETURN the day after scheduled use. Book at least 4 weeks in advance. Requests must include your name, phone, mail address, eligibility program, title, NAL number, show date, and a statement, "I have read the warning on copyright restrictions and accept full responsibility for compliance." One title per request.
**Source: National Agricultural Library
Document Delivery Services Branch
4th Floor, Photo Lab, 10301 Baltimore Avenue
Beltsville, MD 20705-2351
Phone: 1-301-504-5994
Fax: 1-301-504-5675
World Wide Web URL: http://www.nal.usda.gov/fnic
Email Address: lending@nal.usda.gov**

Nutrition for Enhancing Children's Health
Covers the Dietary Guidelines and the Food Guide Pyramid and their applications to service involvement, and programs, resources and successful nutrition education methods. It also discusses the importance of variety in children's diets and methods to promote variety with children.

Availability: Staff at schools with NET, WIC, CSFP, FDPIR, CACFP, UMD or Child Nutrition Program food programs in the United States. Those not having such an affiliation should contact their library to place an interlibrary loan request.
Suggested Grade: K-6
Order Number: NAL Video 1688
Production Date: 1993
Format: Set of 2 VHS videotapes
Terms: Borrower pays return postage. RETURN the day after scheduled use. Book at least 4 weeks in advance. Requests must include your name, phone, mail address, eligibility program, title, NAL number, show date, and a statement, "I have read the warning on copyright restrictions and accept full responsibility for compliance." One title per request.

**Source: National Agricultural Library
Document Delivery Services Branch
4th Floor, Photo Lab, 10301 Baltimore Avenue
Beltsville, MD 20705-2351
Phone: 1-301-504-5994
Fax: 1-301-504-5675
World Wide Web URL: http://www.nal.usda.gov/fnic
Email Address: lending@nal.usda.gov**

Poison Schools Presentation
Matt Wilson, author of "Poisoned Schools Report," discusses the findings. He discusses toxic substances used in schools as cleaning products, pesticides, etc. that can poison students. Also addresses solutions.

Availability: Schools, libraries, and homeschoolers in Connecticut, Maine, Massachusetts, New Hampshire, Rhode Island, and Vermont.
Suggested Grade: Teacher Reference
Order Number: VID 336
Production Date: 2001
Format: VHS videotape
Terms: Borrower pays return postage. Return within three weeks of receipt. If the tape you request is available, it will be mailed within 5 business days. If not, you will be notified that this video is already out on loan. No more than three titles may be borrowed by one requestor at a time. No reservations for a specific date will be accepted. It is most efficient to order via the web site.
**Source: U. S. Environmental Protection Agency, Region 1
Customer Service Center
One Congress Street, Suite 1100
Boston, MA 02214
World Wide Web URL:
http://yosemite.epa.gov/r1/videolen.nsf/**

Project 2001: Nutrition for a New Century
Project 2001 is an invitation to schools to shape their food service around the concept of the Food Guide Pyramid.

Availability: Staff at schools with NET, WIC, CSFP, FDPIR, CACFP, UMD or Child Nutrition Program food programs in the United States. Those not having such an affiliation should contact their library to place an interlibrary loan request.
Suggested Grade: Teacher Reference
Order Number: NAL Video 2549
Production Date: 1997
Format: VHS videotape
Terms: Borrower pays return postage. RETURN the day after scheduled use. Book at least 4 weeks in advance. Requests must include your name, phone, mail address, eligibility program, title, NAL number, show date, and a statement, "I have read the warning on copyright restrictions and accept full responsibility for compliance." One title per request.
**Source: National Agricultural Library
Document Delivery Services Branch
4th Floor, Photo Lab, 10301 Baltimore Avenue
Beltsville, MD 20705-2351**

Phone: 1-301-504-5994
Fax: 1-301-504-5675
World Wide Web URL: http://www.nal.usda.gov/fnic
Email Address: lending@nal.usda.gov

Reactions in Chemistry

An eight-part workshop for the professional development of high school chemistry and physical science teachers

Availability: All requesters
Suggested Grade: 9-Adult
Order Number: not applicable
Production Date: 2003
Format: Streaming Video
Terms: A simple FREE registration is required to view videos.

Source: Annenberg Media
World Wide Web URL:
http://www.learner.org/resources/browse.html

Safety First

A panel of food safety experts provides information and answers to questions about irradiated beef.

Availability: Staff at schools with NET, WIC, CSFP, FDPIR, CACFP, UMD or Child Nutrition Program food programs in the United States. Those not having such an affiliation should contact their library to place an interlibrary loan request.
Suggested Grade: Teacher Reference
Order Number: NAL DVD No. 14
Production Date: 2003
Format: DVD
Terms: Borrower pays return postage. RETURN the day after scheduled use. Book at least 4 weeks in advance. Requests must include your name, phone, mail address, eligibility program, title, NAL number, show date, and a statement, "I have read the warning on copyright restrictions and accept full responsibility for compliance." One title per request.

Source: National Agricultural Library
Document Delivery Services Branch
4th Floor, Photo Lab
10301 Baltimore Avenue
Beltsville, MD   20705-2351
Phone: 1-301-504-5994
Fax: 1-301-504-5675
World Wide Web URL: http://www.nal.usda.gov/fnic
Email Address: lending@nal.usda.gov

Safety First

A panel of food safety experts provides information and answers to questions about irradiated beef.

Availability: Staff at schools with NET, WIC, CSFP, FDPIR, CACFP, UMD or Child Nutrition Program food programs in the United States. Those not having such an affiliation should contact their library to place an interlibrary loan request.
Suggested Grade: Teacher Reference
Order Number: NAL Video 3321

Production Date: 2003
Format: VHS videotape
Terms: Borrower pays return postage. RETURN the day after scheduled use. Book at least 4 weeks in advance. Requests must include your name, phone, mail address, eligibility program, title, NAL number, show date, and a statement, "I have read the warning on copyright restrictions and accept full responsibility for compliance." One title per request.

Source: National Agricultural Library
Document Delivery Services Branch
4th Floor, Photo Lab
10301 Baltimore Avenue
Beltsville, MD   20705-2351
Phone: 1-301-504-5994
Fax: 1-301-504-5675
World Wide Web URL: http://www.nal.usda.gov/fnic
Email Address: lending@nal.usda.gov

Shaping Healthy Choices into Action: Implementation Materials for the Child Nutrition, Shaping Healthy Choices Campaign

This program is designed to help schools and child development programs introduce children and youth to dietary practices that promote health, reduce the risk of chronic disease, and provide for optimal learning, growth, development, and physical activity.

Availability: Staff at schools with NET, WIC, CSFP, FDPIR, CACFP, UMD or Child Nutrition Program food programs in the United States. Those not having such an affiliation should contact their library to place an interlibrary loan request.
Suggested Grade: 5-8
Order Number: NAL Kit 155
Production Date: 1992
Format: Set of 2 VHS videotapes
Terms: Borrower pays return postage. RETURN the day after scheduled use. Book at least 4 weeks in advance. Requests must include your name, phone, mail address, eligibility program, title, NAL number, show date, and a statement, "I have read the warning on copyright restrictions and accept full responsibility for compliance." One title per request.

Source: National Agricultural Library
Document Delivery Services Branch
4th Floor, Photo Lab
10301 Baltimore Avenue
Beltsville, MD   20705-2351
Phone: 1-301-504-5994
Fax: 1-301-504-5675
World Wide Web URL: http://www.nal.usda.gov/fnic
Email Address: lending@nal.usda.gov

Standards & Inclusion: Can We Have Both?

Addresses many of the critical issues facing educators who are supporting students with disabilities in inclusive settings.

Availability: Schools, libraries, and homeschoolers in the United States who serve the hearing impaired.
Suggested Grade: Adult
Order Number: 13559
Production Date: 1988
Format: DVD
Special Notes: Also available as live streaming video over the Internet.
Terms: Sponsor pays all transportation costs. Return one week after receipt. Participation is limited to deaf or hard of hearing Americans, their parents, families, teachers, counselors, or others whose use would benefit a deaf or hard of hearing person. Only one person in the audience needs to be hearing impaired. You must register--which is free. These videos are all open-captioned--no special equipment is required for viewing.

Source: Described and Captioned Media Program
National Association of the Deaf
4211 Church Street Ext.
Roebuck, SC 29376
Phone: 1-800-237-6213
Fax: 1-800-538-5636
World Wide Web URL: http://www.dcmp.org

Starting Smarter

Surveys school breakfast programs in Illinois. The video discusses how a program is established, the importance of coordinating the arrival of children to school with the eating of their breakfast, supervision of the food preparation staff, and menu selection.
Availability: Staff at schools with NET, WIC, CSFP, FDPIR, CACFP, UMD or Child Nutrition Program food programs in the United States. Those not having such an affiliation should contact their library to place an interlibrary loan request.
Suggested Grade: Teacher Reference
Order Number: NAL Video 1588
Production Date: 1992
Format: VHS videotape
Terms: Borrower pays return postage. RETURN the day after scheduled use. Book at least 4 weeks in advance. Requests must include your name, phone, mail address, eligibility program, title, NAL number, show date, and a statement, "I have read the warning on copyright restrictions and accept full responsibility for compliance." One title per request.

Source: National Agricultural Library
Document Delivery Services Branch
4th Floor, Photo Lab
10301 Baltimore Avenue
Beltsville, MD 20705-2351
Phone: 1-301-504-5994
Fax: 1-301-504-5675
World Wide Web URL: http://www.nal.usda.gov/fnic
Email Address: lending@nal.usda.gov

Teaching Come and See! School Edition

Specially developed for Elementary Schools, grades K through 8, this program is an in-service video that affirms teachers in their ministry, challenges them to a new vision of mission, and explores the development of mission. Contains descriptive overviews, curriculum cross reference charts, ordering forms, and a four color poster.
Availability: Schools, libraries, homeschoolers, church groups, nursing homes, and service clubs in the United States
Suggested Grade: Teacher Reference
Order Number: order by title
Format: VHS videotape
Terms: Borrower pays return postage. Return within 21 days after receipt. Book at least 3 weeks in advance. You will be notified as soon as possible, if your order cannot be filled. All videos are cleared for television broadcast use.

Source: Columban Fathers Mission Society
Mission Education Department
Attn: Connie Wacha
P. O. Box 10
St. Columbans, NE 68056
Phone: 1-402-291-1920
Fax: 1-402-715-5575
World Wide Web URL: http://columban.org/missioned

Teaching Geography

A video workshop for grade 7-12 teachers; graduate credit available.
Availability: All requesters
Suggested Grade: Teacher Reference
Order Number: not applicable
Production Date: 2002
Format: Streaming Video
Special Notes: Available on DVD for purchase price of $220.
Terms: A simple FREE registration is required to view videos.

Source: Annenberg Media
World Wide Web URL:
http://www.learner.org/resources/browse.html

Things That Make You Go MMMMM

Discusses the advantages of offer vs. serve with regard to school meal programs.
Availability: Staff at schools with NET, WIC, CSFP, FDPIR, CACFP, UMD or Child Nutrition Program food programs in the United States. Those not having such an affiliation should contact their library to place an interlibrary loan request.
Suggested Grade: preK-6
Order Number: NAL Video 1434
Production Date: 1992
Format: VHS videotape
Special Notes: This Florida NET production includes a sheet of instructions and a questionnaire.
Terms: Borrower pays return postage. RETURN the day after scheduled use. Book at least 4 weeks in advance. Requests must include your name, phone, mail address, eligibility program, title, NAL number, show date, and a statement, "I have read the warning on copyright

restrictions and accept full responsibility for compliance." One title per request.

Source: National Agricultural Library
Document Delivery Services Branch
4th Floor, Photo Lab
10301 Baltimore Avenue
Beltsville, MD 20705-2351
Phone: 1-301-504-5994
Fax: 1-301-504-5675
World Wide Web URL: http://www.nal.usda.gov/fnic
Email Address: lending@nal.usda.gov

Top Priority Nutrition Friendly Schools

Provides a comprehensive overview of how to make schools "nutrition friendly" and why various stakeholders should be interested in improving the school nutrition environment.

Availability: Staff at schools with NET, WIC, CSFP, FDPIR, CACFP, UMD or Child Nutrition Program food programs in the United States. Those not having such an affiliation should contact their library to place an interlibrary loan request.

Suggested Grade: Adult
Order Number: NAL Video 3296
Format: VHS videotape
Terms: Borrower pays return postage. RETURN the day after scheduled use. Book at least 4 weeks in advance. Requests must include your name, phone, mail address, eligibility program, title, NAL number, show date, and a statement, "I have read the warning on copyright restrictions and accept full responsibility for compliance." One title per request.

Source: National Agricultural Library
Document Delivery Services Branch
4th Floor, Photo Lab
10301 Baltimore Avenue
Beltsville, MD 20705-2351
Phone: 1-301-504-5994
Fax: 1-301-504-5675
World Wide Web URL: http://www.nal.usda.gov/fnic
Email Address: lending@nal.usda.gov

*All materials listed in this 2011-2012 edition are **BRAND NEW!***

-T-

SUBJECT INDEX

SUBJECT INDEX

SUBJECT INDEX

SUBJECT INDEX

SUBJECT INDEX

SUBJECT INDEX

SUBJECT INDEX

SUBJECT INDEX

SUBJECT INDEX

The SOURCE INDEX is an alphabetical list of the organizations from which the materials listed in the EDUCATORS GUIDE TO FREE VIDEOS–ELEMENTARY/MIDDLE SCHOOL EDITION may be obtained. There are 43 sources listed in this Twelfth Edition of the GUIDE, **20 of which are new**. The numbers following each listing are the page numbers on which the materials from each source are annotated in the body of the GUIDE.

When requesting materials via mail or fax, please use a letter of request similar to the sample shown in the front part of the GUIDE. When requesting via telephone, please have the name of the material you desire in front of you (along with the order number if necessary). Please read each listing carefully to be certain that the material you are requesting is available via the method through which you choose to order.

Bold type indicates a source that is new in the 2011-2012 edition. Complete addresses for each source are found following the description of the material in the body of the GUIDE.